GENDER IN HI

Series editors:
Lynn Abrams, Cordelia Beattie, Pam Sharpe and Penny Summerfield

+⊱━━⊰+

The expansion of research into the history of women and gender since the 1970s has changed the face of history. Using the insights of feminist theory and of historians of women, gender historians have explored the configuration in the past of gender identities and relations between the sexes. They have also investigated the history of sexuality and family relations, and analysed ideas and ideals of masculinity and femininity. Yet gender history has not abandoned the original, inspirational project of women's history: to recover and reveal the lived experience of women in the past and the present.

The series Gender in History provides a forum for these developments. Its historical coverage extends from the medieval to the modern periods, and its geographical scope encompasses not only Europe and North America but all corners of the globe. The series aims to investigate the social and cultural constructions of gender in historical sources, as well as the gendering of historical discourse itself. It embraces both detailed case studies of specific regions or periods, and broader treatments of major themes. Gender in History titles are designed to meet the needs of both scholars and students working in this dynamic area of historical research.

Infidel feminism

Manchester University Press

ALSO AVAILABLE
IN THE SERIES

Myth and materiality in a woman's world: Shetland 1800–2000
Lynn Abrams

Destined for a life of service: Defining African-Jamaican womanhood, 1865–1938
Henrice Altink

Gender and housing in Soviet Russia: private life in a public space
Lynne Attwood

Love, intimacy and power: Marital relationships in Scotland, 1650–1850
Katie Barclay

History, patriarchy and the challenge of feminism (with University of Pennsylvania Press)
Judith Bennett

Gender and medical knowledge in early modern history
Susan Broomhall

'The truest form of patriotism': pacifist feminism in Britain, 1870–1902
Heloise Brown

Artisans of the body in early modern Italy: identities, families and masculinities
Sandra Cavallo

Women of the right spirit: paid organisers of the Women's Social and Political Union (WSPU) 1904–18
Krista Cowman

Modern motherhood: women and family in England, c. 1945–2000
Angela Davis

Masculinities in politics and war: gendering modern history
Stefan Dudink, Karen Hagemann and John Tosh (eds)

Victorians and the Virgin Mary: religion and gender in England 1830–1885
Carol Engelhardt Herringer

Living in sin: cohabiting as husband and wife in nineteenth-century England
Ginger S. Frost

Jewish women in Europe in the Middle Ages: a quiet revolution
Simha Goldin

Murder and morality in Victorian Britain: the story of Madeleine Smith
Eleanor Gordon and Gwyneth Nair

The military leadership of Matilda of Canossa, 1046–1115
David J. Hay

The shadow of marriage: singleness in England, 1914–60
Katherine Holden

Women police: gender, welfare and surveillance in the twentieth century
Louise Jackson

Noblewomen, aristocracy and power in the twelfth-century Anglo-Norman realm
Susan Johns

The business of everyday life: gender, practice and social politics in England, c.1600–1900
Beverly Lemire

Women and the shaping of British Methodism: persistent preachers, 1807–1907
Jennifer Lloyd

The independent man: citizenship and gender politics in Georgian England
Matthew McCormack

The feminine public sphere: middle-class women and civic life in Scotland, c.1870–1914
Megan Smitley

Being boys: working-class masculinities and leisure
Melanie Tebbutt

Elizabeth Wolstenholme Elmy and the Victorian feminist movement: the biography of an insurgent woman
Maureen Wright

INFIDEL FEMINISM

SECULARISM, RELIGION AND WOMEN'S EMANCIPATION, ENGLAND 1830–1914

⇥ Laura Schwartz ⇤

Manchester University Press

The right of Laura Schwartz to be identified as the author of this work has been asserted by her in accordance with the Copyright, Designs and Patents Act 1988.

Published by Manchester University Press
Altrincham Street, Manchester M1 7JA, UK
www.manchesteruniversitypress.co.uk

British Library Cataloguing-in-Publication Data is available

Library of Congress Cataloging-in-Publication Data is available

ISBN 978 0 7190 9728 7 *paperback*

First published by Manchester University Press in hardback 2013

This paperback edition first published 2015

The publisher has no responsibility for the persistence or accuracy of URLs for any external or third-party internet websites referred to in this book, and does not guarantee that any content on such websites is, or will remain, accurate or appropriate.

Printed by Lightning Source

Contents

LIST OF FIGURES   *page* vi
ACKNOWLEDGEMENTS   vii

Introduction   1

1 Freethinking feminists: women in the Freethought movement   41

2 Counter-conversion: Freethinking feminists and the
   renunciation of religion   73

3 Preachers of truth: women's activism in the
   Secularist movement   101

4 Infidel feminism: feminism in the Freethought movement   129

5 Freethinking feminists and the women's movement   154

6 Freethought and Free Love? Marriage, birth control and
   sexual morality   178

   Conclusion   217

SELECT BIBLIOGRAPHY   227
INDEX   251

Figures

1   Annie Besant   *page* 54
    [*Secular Chronicle*, 10 February 1878, Bishopsgate Library,
    George Jacob Holyoake Archive]

2   Leicester Secular Hall   112
    [Insert into *Secular Chronicle* vol. VIII (1877) bound volume,
    George Jacob Holyoake Archive, Bishopsgate Library]

3   Hyde Park during 1866 Reform Bill Agitation   169
    [Bishopsgate Library]

4   Mary Wollstonecraft as headline news   193
    [*Secular Chronicle*, 10 February 1878, p. 145, Bishopsgate
    Library, George Jacob Holyoake Archive]

5   Advertisement for contraception   206
    [A. Besant, *The Law of Population: Its Consequences and its
    Bearing upon Human Conduct and Morals* (London:
    Freethought Publishing Company, 1889), Bishopsgate Library]

Acknowledgements

I should like to thank the University of East London and the Arts and Humanities Research Council, for funding the PhD thesis upon which this book is based, and St Hugh's College, University of Oxford for the Career Development Fellowship which made it possible to transform it into a monograph. I am also very grateful to Kate Hodgkin and Maggie Humm, for reading and commenting on many early drafts; Anna Davin, Cath Fletcher and Jane Garnett, for their thoughts and encouragement; Kathryn Gleadle, Deborah Lavin, Phyllis Mack, Janette Martin, Helen Rogers, Marie Terrier, Will Van Reyk and Maureen Wright, for sharing their work in progress with me; and to Jane Miller, for kindly letting me to look at the Collet family papers. The History of Feminism Network provided a crucial intellectual forum throughout the research, so my special thanks to Madisson Brown, Marc Calvini Lefebvre, Esme Cleall, Erin Cullen, Daniel Grey, Angela Grainger and Naomi Hetherington for being such good friends and colleagues. One of my greatest debts is to my supervisor, Barbara Taylor, who was endlessly generous with her time, her advice, her support and her ideas. I was also lucky to have as examiners Lucy Bland and David Nash, whose insight and encouragement enabled my first venture into the twentieth century.

Infidel Feminism was originally conceived amidst protests against the Iraq war and the intense discussions on religion and gender that it generated. The book was finally completed in a moment of fundamental transformation in (and potential decimation of) Higher Education in Britain. Such events inevitably informed the questions this book asks about what it means to be a political actor, a feminist subject and a producer of knowledge. They also changed the kinds of relationships that could be expected to be forged during a period of research, so that staff at the Women's Library also became friends on a picket line, while the Bishopsgate Institute offered not only a wonderful archive but also much-needed space for collectives to meet and organise. A different kind of thanks should therefore go to Indy Bhullar, Gail Cameron and Dianne Shepherd at the WL and especially to Stefan Dickers at the BI. This book is dedicated with love to all those involved in Feminist Fightback, XTalk and *The Paper*, who taught me that reading and writing is best done together.

LAURA SCHWARTZ
London, 2011

Introduction

I n the spring of 1869 Mrs Harriet Law climbed onto a platform in Newcastle upon Tyne to defend Eve's rebellion against God. Law informed her audience that, instead of 'cursing' our Biblical mother for bringing about the Fall of Mankind, she in fact deserved our 'reverence'. For Eve's 'partaking of the forbidden fruit' had brought knowledge into the world against the will of an authoritarian God.[1] For Harriet Law, Eve's refusal to remain in ignorance was inspiration for a growing number of Victorian women, who, like Law herself, had rejected the authority of religion as part of their struggle for emancipation. Law's deliberately provocative speech was typical of a longstanding tradition of 'Freethinking feminists' who combined their campaigning for women's rights with a militant and antagonistic renunciation of Christianity. Such women often proudly referred themselves 'infidels' – reclaiming a title initially employed as a term of abuse by their Christian opponents. Such a name implied a refusal of faith and a betrayal of God's law – acts which Freethinking feminists believed to be essential to ending the subjugation of their sex.[2] For them, religion, particularly Christianity, was the primary cause of women's oppression.

The question of 'religion' versus 'secularism' and which offers a better guarantee of women's rights has a long history. As currently discussed by twenty-first-century feminists, religious leaders and world governments such concerns are, of course, the product of a post-9/11 world, but they are far from being new. In fact, the issue of women's rights was integral to the creation of modern definitions of 'religion' and 'secularism' in the nineteenth and early twentieth centuries, when feminists and anti-feminists, Christians and Freethinkers battled over who had women's best interests at heart. Such contests were fundamental to the development of feminist thought in England, but have been almost entirely passed over in the historiography of the women's movement. This book examines these

debates and offers the first ever in-depth study of 'Freethinking feminism' – a distinctive brand of women's rights discourse that emerged out
of the Secularist movement during this period.[3]

The Secularist or Freethought movement, as it was also known, was
dedicated to ridding society of false and repressive belief-systems through
the critique of orthodox religion. This book looks at the lives and work of
a number of female activists associated with organised Secularism, and
at how their rejection of religion encouraged and shaped their support
for women's rights. These self-proclaimed 'infidel' feminists championed moral autonomy, free speech, and the democratic dissemination
of knowledge. Alongside their rejection of God-given notions of sexual
difference and a critique of the Christian institution of marriage, such
Freethinking principles provided powerful intellectual tools with which
to challenge dominant and oppressive constructions of womanhood.

Infidel Feminism traces this current of Freethinking women's rights
advocacy from the 1830s through to the beginning of the First World
War; and in doing so raises a number of important questions for our
understanding of the chronology and intellectual trajectories of first wave
feminism. A fuller understanding of the important role played by infidel
feminists enables us to identify a more continuous women's rights tradition throughout the century, connecting the 'radical' Owenite feminists
of the 1830s and 1840s with the 'respectable' post-1850 women's movement. Freethinking feminists kept alive the Owenites' libertarian critique
of traditional sexual morality in the middle decades of the century,
when many in the women's movement were unwilling to countenance
any form of sexual expression outside marriage. They can therefore be
viewed as a 'missing link', connecting early nineteenth-century feminist
visions of greater sexual freedom with the re-emergence of discussions
of Free Love and sexuality at the *fin de siècle*.

An anti-religious intellectual culture was profoundly important to the
development of women's rights discourses during this period. Although
nineteenth and early twentieth-century feminism was predominantly
Christian, it was built around religious controversy and contestation
rather than a unified adherence to a particular set of religious values. This
study looks in detail at the extensive discussions that took place between
Freethinking feminists and their Christian sisters, and between Secularists
and conservative Christians. It reveals the extent to which their respective ideological stances developed not only in opposition to, but also in
dialogue with, each other. *Infidel Feminism* thus offers a re-thinking of the
'religious'/'secular' distinction, demonstrating the need for historians to
view these categories as interdependent rather than merely oppositional.

The Freethinking roots of first wave feminism

The last three decades have witnessed a 'religious turn' in gender history, whereby accounts of both femininity and feminism have begun to open up to the many ways in which religion shaped women's 'private selves and public roles'.[4] In the pioneering years of women's history, social and economic concerns often dominated over consideration of religious factors and Christianity tended to be analysed primarily in terms of its oppressive agenda.[5] Since the 1980s, however, there has been a slowly expanding body of research into women's activity in the churches and the influence of religion in the lives of female public figures in nineteenth- and early twentieth-century Britain.[6] Christianity also began to be recognised as a key factor in the emergence of an organised women's rights movement post-1850. Historians noted how Victorian women's involvement in parish work expanded their activities outside the home, preparing the ground for feminist campaigns to participate more fully in the public sphere. They also pointed to the ambiguities of evangelical doctrines, especially the belief that women were socially subordinate but spiritually equal to men, and identified the potential for female self-assertion deriving from apparently reactionary teachings.[7] Research has furthermore emphasised the importance of individual piety and inner faith in providing women with the sense of self-worth and moral justification necessary to challenging oppressive gender roles.[8] Historians have also begun to look beyond evangelical Christianity, to highlight, for example, the role of Unitarianism in shaping women's rights discourses during this period.[9] Recent edited collections spanning topics from female theological cultures to Christian sex manuals have nevertheless demonstrated that there is still some way to go in assessing the breadth and depth of encounters between gender and religion in modern British history.[10]

Infidel Feminism positions itself as part of this broader move in gender history towards taking religion seriously. Yet it also marks a departure from much existing work in that it points to the anti-religious or Freethinking roots of feminism. Freethought has never received more than a brief mention in histories of the post-1850 women's movement.[11] The freethinking views of prominent figures have sometimes been noted, though without positioning them as part of a wider trend among feminists during this period.[12] Likewise, histories of feminist debates on sexuality have noted the presence of Freethinkers in campaigns around marriage and prostitution, but the possibility of a broader and more sustained Freethinking feminist tradition has not yet been explored in the historiography of the post-1850 women's movement.[13]

The centrality of heterodox thought to the emergence of radical debates on women in the late eighteenth and early nineteenth century (the period prior to the emergence of a large scale and organised women's movement) has been more widely recognised. Mary Wollstonecraft, for example, was part of a critical freethinking tradition, ceasing at the age of twenty-eight to attend the Anglican Church in which she had been raised. Although she never adopted the atheism of her husband William Godwin she came to practise a form of religion that was, according to Godwin, 'almost entirely of her own creation'. Wollstonecraft drew on a powerful pro-woman dimension of the Christian tradition while at the same time rejecting what she believed to be overly emotional evangelical extremism in favour of 'rational religious impulses'. Her emphasis on the inner authority of the individual believer was celebrated by the Rational Dissenters of her radical London circle but was also at the heart of more explicitly Secularist forms of Freethought in the nineteenth century.[14]

Wollstonecraft and the other pro-women thinkers in her radical coterie were part of an English radical Enlightenment which celebrated, even if it did not fully endorse, the attacks on orthodox religion made by European *philosophes* and the French Revolutionaries.[15] They can be linked to a longer tradition of 'enlightened libertinage' that stretched back to seventeenth-century Freethinkers such as Pierre Bayle, and which combined a critique of religion with an equally 'free' approach to traditional sexual morality. Wollstonecraft herself notoriously entered into 'free unions' and bore her first child out of wedlock, while William Godwin and fellow atheist Percy Shelley were vocal critics of the institution of marriage.[16] Nineteenth-century Freethinkers strongly identified with these freethinking radicals and their combination of religious and sexual unorthodoxies. Wollstonecraft was anachronistically claimed as an out and out Freethinker[17], while Shelley's attitudes to marriage were discussed and championed in Freethought publications.[18]

The revolutionary enthusiasm of Mary Wollstonecraft's circle died out in the late 1790s, partly in response to the terror in France, partly as a result of government repression. Feminist ideas re-merged within British radicalism in the 1820s, again closely tied to Freethought, as part of Richard Carlile's anti-Christian Zetetic movement. In the 1830s and 1840s the Utopian Socialist Owenite movement provided a freethinking environment in which feminism was able to thrive.[19] Barbara Taylor's work on Owenism established it as one of the key forerunners of first wave feminism, yet posited a break between this more radical form of feminism and the respectable post-1850 women's movement. She argued that, with the collapse of Owenism from 1845 onwards, the link between class emancipation and women's freedom disintegrated so that the feminism of the second half of the nineteenth century emerged as a far more middle-class and reformist movement.[20] While it is true that the political location of feminism shifted around mid-century, in fact the Owenite feminists' more radical and unrespectable brand of women's rights advocacy did continue as a minority current (which this book terms Freethinking or 'infidel' feminism) based, after 1850, in the Secularist movement.

Organised Freethought, 1830–1914

If histories of feminism have tended to overlook the part played by anti-religious ideas, the role of women and feminism has also been neglected in Freethought historiography. In part, this reflects the very low numbers of women involved in the movement. Estimates suggest that, nationwide, women made up no more than a quarter of the total audience at Secularist public meetings.[21] An in-depth study of Leicester Secular Society revealed a similar pattern at a local level: women made up only 12 per cent of the membership between 1881 and 1891, and almost half of these were wives or daughters of male members.[22] The importance of feminism to Freethought was noted by its foremost historian Edward Royle, who simultaneously acknowledged the paucity of existing research in this area.[23] Women are also neglected in the extensive literature that exists on the Victorian 'crisis of faith', which has tended to focus on a handful of 'great men' – George Eliot being a rare exception.[24] For Freethinking women themselves, however, the emancipation of the female sex was at the heart of their Secularist worldview. When Harriet Law, for example, took over a national Freethought newspaper, she devoted a large section of her first editorial to arguing that social progress was impossible without the full emancipation of women.[25] Even if the number of women involved was small, feminism was a vibrant and important current within the Freethought movement.

The nineteenth century witnessed a significant rise in the number and outspokenness of Freethinkers – the term applied to those who questioned religious assumptions about the ordering of the world and who, as a result, tended to reject all forms of organised religion. During the latter half of the century such Freethought sentiment found organisational expression in the Secularist movement, which campaigned for the separation of political, cultural and moral life from religion. The term 'Secularist' will be used here to describe the self-identified local societies and national organisations after the formation of the first Central Secular

Society in 1851, while 'secular' implies the general concept of secularity. 'Freethinker' and 'Freethought' is used to refer to those who actively identified with an organised anti-religious movement both prior to and during the establishment of Secular societies. The term 'Freethinker', in lower case, will be applied to those individuals who held unorthodox religious beliefs but who did not identify with the organised movement. Secularism did not simply denote support for the separation of Church and State based upon a neutral disregard for religious faith. The Secularist movement had its roots in a far more partisan and embattled debate, which was concerned not only with the role of religion in politics, but also with whether religion – specifically Christianity – could be considered both true and morally just.

The crucial distinction between organised Freethinkers and the more affluent 'honest doubters' normally associated with the Victorian 'crisis of faith', was that Freethinkers 'were political as well as intellectual radicals, and their agitation was organised as a political movement'.[26] Popular irreligion had been an important part of the radical unrest that erupted in Britain in response to the French Revolution of 1789 and it continued to play a role in nineteenth-century radicalism. In the 1790s Thomas Paine gave birth to a more politicised form of Freethought by disseminating Enlightenment critiques of religion to a large and popular audience, and nineteenth-century Freethinkers continued in this mode.[27] In the 1820s and 1830s the notorious Freethinker Richard Carlile published Paine's *Age of Reason* along with other 'blasphemous' works from his own pen. He was imprisoned three times between 1817 and 1831 and on the second occasion his wife and sister (and his children with them) were sent to join him for continuing to distribute dangerous literature. Such persecution provoked nationwide agitation and for the rest of the century the Freethought movement was to take a leading role in campaigns for a free press. Carlile also found support for his Freethinking ideas among some British radicals, who in the 1820s formed themselves into infidel Zetetic societies dedicated to 'seeking after truth'.[28] Carlile also held feminist views, particularly on questions of marriage and sexuality, and women played a particularly important role in his successive campaigns against the religious establishment.[29]

The next wave of Freethought occurred within the Owenite movement.[30] As early as 1814, Robert Owen had argued that religion should be opposed for rational and moral reasons, but it was not until after 1828, against a backdrop of economic depression and mounting popular unrest, that his views came to be seen as pernicious 'infidelism'.[31] Between 1835 and 1845 the critique of orthodox religion became one of the most vocal, widely printed and publicly prominent aspects of Owenite doctrine.[32] Owenism did not preach a single uniform religious position but included millenarian, quasi-Christian and atheist viewpoints. These ranged from belief in a messianic 'man–woman power'[33] to the idea that Socialism was the embodiment of 'True' or 'Primitive Christianity' – the practical implementation on earth of Christ's original message of Christian brotherhood.[34] However, from the late 1830s onwards, the Owenite leadership began to disassociate the 'religious' critique of the Christian churches from the more extreme atheism of some members. In 1839, when the Owenite Universal Community Society of Rational Religionists was formed, the Central Board was at pains to stress that individuals did not have to relinquish their belief in God in order to join the Society or to support the Socialist project. Robert Owen's pre-conference *Address* declared that 'Provision must be made ... for all individuals to worship the Supreme Power of the Universe, according to their consciences.'[35] Religion was defined in broad and largely positive terms as 'whatever unites men, restrains their inordinate selfishness, or promotes their well-being ... [and] the practice of goodness'.[36] Condemnation of particular churches or clergy was discouraged. Robert Owen informed the Society that, because of the need to appear open to members of all religions, '[i]t consequently becomes necessary that your missionaries forbear all future public contests on mere localised religious subjects'.[37] In 1840 the leadership also began to permit, and even encourage, Owenite lecturers to take the dissenting preachers' oath in order to avoid prosecution for taking money at non-religious events on the Sabbath.[38]

Anyone who continued to champion an intransigent defence of outright atheism soon came into conflict with the Owenite leadership. Owen's advice to forego all public confrontation with the churches was greatly at odds with the lecturing style of Owenite 'social missionaries' (paid itinerant lecturers) such as Emma Martin and Charles Southwell, who frequently challenged their opponents to debate and sometimes invaded churches and Christian meetings to harangue the presiding clergymen.[39] Martin's continued commitment to public and deliberately controversial debate eventually jeopardised her career as a social missionary. In 1845 she was forced to defend herself to fellow members of the Owenite executive, who had criticised her for continuing to confront local clergy during her tour of Scotland. Martin's defence told of a powerful sense of betrayal:

> some of the branches had made use of her as a tool to help fill their purses – as she had suffered much, even imprisonment, in enabling her to do so, she thought it too bad that delegates from these branches

should turn round at the Congress table and say she had been the means of doing them no good.[40]

Later that year her career as a social missionary ended.

Charles Southwell, similarly frustrated with the Central Board's increasingly 'religious' tone, resigned his position as a social missionary in 1841 and began editing the hard-line atheist journal the *Oracle of Reason*. The journal's commitment to an outspoken championing of atheism led to the imprisonment of successive editors, including Southwell and George Jacob Holyoake, for blasphemous libel. The *New Moral World* failed to fully condemn these attacks on the free speech of their fellow Owenites. In 1841, an editorial commenting on Southwell's imprisonment hastened to add that 'We are no admirers of the spirit which prompts too violent attacks upon the opinions of our fellow-beings, for we know that they cannot avoid having these impressed upon their minds...'[41] In response to the leadership's inaction, the Anti-Persecution Union (APU) was established in 1842, by advocates of Southwell and Holyoake's position, to support those charged under the blasphemy laws.[42] Leading Freethinking feminists Emma Martin and Margaret Chappellsmith also supported the APU. The *Oracle of Reason* attacked 'the milk-and-water, namby pamby infidelity' of certain sections of the Owenite movement, claiming that 'Deists are only the more contemptible, because they affect the *language*, while they ruthlessly sacrifice the only admissible *principles*, of philosophy.' Its editors clearly positioned themselves as the enemies of more moderate Owenites: 'We say then to those reformers who seek to establish political justice, without striving or caring to destroy every vestige of superstition – *you must fail*.'[43] Martin also defied her Owenite critics, refusing to renounce the title of 'infidel'.[44]

The more militant Freethought commitment to cleansing society of religion survived the collapse of the Owenite movement after 1845. As editor of *The Movement* and then *The Reasoner*, Holyoake began to develop his idea of 'Secularism', which sought to abandon the old adversarial and negative connotations of the term 'infidel' and to argue instead for Secularism as a positive agenda and alternative value system, independent of religion.[45] Secularism was to teach 'the law of humanity, the conditions of human progress, and the nature of human duty': 'The term Secularism expresses this object ... The term freethinking expresses *how* we think – Secularism *why* we think. Our object is to promote personal morality.'[46] In 1851 Holyoake organised the first meeting of the Central Secular Society, which declared its commitment to science and reason and opposition to the arbitrary authority of religion. Over the next fifteen years, the Secularist movement took the form of a loose network of local societies (many of which had existed in a previous incarnation as local Owenite branches), sustained by branch activities and sporadic lecture tours by national Freethought figures.

This period also witnessed the rise of Charles Bradlaugh as a leading champion of Secularism. In 1866 he organised the first conference of the National Secular Society (NSS), which promptly elected him president. The founding statement of the NSS declared:

> That human improvement and happiness cannot be effectively promoted without civil and religious liberty; and that, therefore, it is the duty of every individual … to actively attack all barriers to equal freedom of thought and utterance for all, upon Political and Theological subjects.[47]

Over the next few years the majority of local Secular societies were incorporated into this national structure. For the rest of the century Secularism was dominated at a national level by the exploits of the charismatic Bradlaugh and, from 1874, the equally compelling Annie Besant, another Freethinking feminist. These included their trial for the publication of a birth control pamphlet in 1877 and Bradlaugh's bids to become the MP for Northampton from 1868 onwards. He was elected as the official Liberal candidate in 1880, after which he was forced to run a long campaign to win his right to take his seat in parliament against those who ruled that as an atheist he was permitted neither to take the Judeo-Christian oath, nor to swear a secular affirmation.[48]

Such events brought Secularism onto the national stage and attracted new members. Yet not everyone in the movement approved of Bradlaugh's ascendancy, nor of his tactics. The rivalry between the movement's two most prominent figures, Charles Bradlaugh and George Jacob Holyoake, was both personal and ideological. As mentioned, Holyoake wished to work towards a society independent of, though not necessarily in conflict with, religion. Although he did not personally believe in any form of divine being, he preferred Secularism to rest on the agnostic principle that, since it was impossible to know whether or not God existed, it was better simply to focus on 'this-worldism' and to avoid theological controversy.[49] Bradlaugh, in contrast, revived the more adversarial infidel spirit and argued that Secularism should actively proclaim a 'positive' atheism in opposition to the untruths spread by religion.[50] This difference in outlook informed tensions in Secularism throughout the century. Yet it should not be overstated as a fundamental division within the movement. Some individuals moved from one 'camp' to another; others remained loyal to Holyoake for historical reasons or because they resented Bradlaugh's authoritarian style of leadership. Most rank and file members engaged with both Holyoake's vision of positive Secularism at a local level and Bradlaugh's struggles on the national.[51]

The Secularist movement reached the height of its powers in the 1880s, by which time Charles Bradlaugh had come to figure as one of the heavyweights of Victorian politics.[52] In the early 1880s his name was virtually synonymous with radicalism, winning the NSS new members and placing it at the centre of popular politics. His journal, *The National Reformer*, became more focused on parliamentary political issues and more sober in its reportage, but the older iconoclastic and adversarial Freethought traditions were kept alive elsewhere in pages of *The Freethinker*. This journal was edited by G. W. Foote, who had opposed Bradlaugh's leadership in 1876, forming the British Secular Union with George Jacob Holyoake the following year, and only returning to the NSS in 1880 to fight the exclusion of atheists from the House of Commons.[53] In 1883 Foote was prosecuted for blasphemy and sentenced to one year in Holloway prison – a reminder of a more embattled period of persecution earlier in the century which rallied the movement and boosted NSS membership to its highest level yet.

Between 1883 and 1884 the NSS boasted 2,845 subscribers. From there in, however, it began to decline so that by 1889 there were only fifty-nine branches, half the peak total in 1883.[54] Foote became President in 1890 and many blamed the shrinking membership on his lack of charisma, though Secularism was also the victim of more general shifts within radical politics, particularly the rapidly growing interest in Socialism (to which Bradlaugh and Foote were adamantly opposed). Competition also came from the Ethical societies, freethinking organisations brought to the UK by Stanton Coit in 1888 which remained unaffiliated to existing Secularist organisations. Instead, they worked closely with the Labour churches and Positivist societies, tapping into a less aggressive, less overtly anti-Christian freethinking identity[55]. A range of freethinking views were, by this period, becoming more acceptable to and common within upper-middle-class educated society. Earlier in the century the Secular societies had provided a sense of kinship and solidarity among those whose rejection of religion had often entailed a break with their families and local communities. The incremental but nonetheless significant shift towards the intellectual and political mainstream decreased the need for such provision. In 1899 the NSS had under a thousand members, and it was further damaged by its opposition to the Anglo-Boer War (1903–6), which marked a more general turn towards conservatism in British popular culture. By the onset of the First World War Freethought had ceased to be a significant national movement.[56]

It is impossible to assess the general impact and significance of the Secularist movement based upon membership figures alone. Membership tended to be unstable: between half and a quarter paid-up members in any one year were new recruits, with older sympathisers perhaps remaining active without bothering to join formally. This meant that local societies had a much larger circle of adherents than membership figures suggest.[57] Leading Freethought journals such as *The Reasoner* and *The National Reformer* would have circulated beyond these networks in lending libraries and mechanics' institutes.[58] The controversial and entertaining style of Freethought public lecturers also drew in audiences who might otherwise have no connection with Secularism, and by 1871 Old Street Hall of Science, the central London Freethought venue, regularly filled its capacity of 1,200 on occasions when Bradlaugh spoke, leading to the decision to add further galleries to accommodate 400 more people.[59] Royle has concluded that in the period prior to the formation of the NSS there was a maximum of 20,000 people actively associated with Freethought, rising to 100,000 if sympathisers are included. But figures for a committed core should be estimated at only 2,000 or 3,000.[60] After 1866, the members of the 120 local branches of the NSS at its height, plus a generous estimate of the numbers of non-members each branch managed to draw in and influence on a regular basis, might have amounted to 60,000.[61]

Secularism was relatively small compared to contemporary radical organisations and cannot in any sense be considered a mass movement. Yet it wielded influence out of proportion to its size in the nineteenth-century radical milieu.[62] Secularists played an active role in most of the 'causes' of the period, including Owenism and Chartism in the earlier part of the century, Co-operation, the campaign for the repeal of the taxes on knowledge, republicanism, franchise reform, freedom of the press, and education. This was in addition to explicitly Secularist campaigns such as anti-Sabbatarianism, the abolition of compulsory church rates and the introduction of legal oaths that did not require pledging faith in God.[63]

Secularists tended to come from the lower-middle or upper-working classes.[64] Susan Budd's analysis of the obituaries of 263 Secularists between 1852 and 1965 found 40 per cent to be semi-skilled or unskilled workers, 20 per cent skilled or craft workers, 20 per cent white collar workers, and 15 per cent owners of small businesses, leaving 3 per cent rural workers and under 2 per cent from the professional classes.[65] Royle's study of local societies in the period 1866–1914 found a smaller proportion of semi-skilled and unskilled workers, and a larger number of men who ran their own businesses, noting that Freethought was overwhelmingly an urban movement.[66] The only in-depth analysis of local membership was produced by David Nash for the Leicester Secular Society, in which 39 per cent of the membership were unskilled or semi-skilled workers. Nash pointed out that using the national press as a source for such figures tends to exclude the more plebeian rank and file members who did not rise to local prominence.[67]

Secularism was by no means a rigidly defined ideology and although its tone and style were probably more appealing to confirmed atheists, it was also home to some deists and pantheists.[68] All Freethinkers, however, argued for a universe governed by natural laws and rejected belief in an interventionist, personal God. Freethinkers identified most enthusiastically with the intellectual heritage of Enlightenment scepticism,[69] but the ideas of the *philosophes* were filtered through an older artisanal radical tradition characterised by a defiant 'independence of thought and action often deliberately at variance with orthodox hierarchies and customs'.[70] Thomas Paine's irreverent attack on the lack of internal logic and historical accuracy in Scripture had a profound effect on Freethought critiques of the Bible, perhaps even more than the subsequent development of the German school of higher criticism and historicist approaches to Scripture of which Freethinkers were also aware.[71] The works of Peter Annet, David Hume, Baron d'Holbach, Thomas Paine, Volney and Voltaire were frequently referred to in Freethought publications, and Freethinkers drew on these eighteenth-century discussions of materialism, religious tyranny, anti-clericalism, comparative religion and anthropological interpretations of the Bible.[72] Enlightenment ideas often reached Freethinkers second-hand, through 'non-popular propaganda' such as Geoffrey Higgin's *Anacalypsis* (1836), which identified the pagan and mythical roots of Bible stories and characters, and Robert Cooper's *The Infidel Text Book* (1846).[73]

Freethinkers were self-proclaimed 'Rationalists', which they defined as 'the scientific quest for the knowable' or an empirical approach to understanding the world around them.[74] 'Science' (positioned in opposition to religion) was also a crucial aspect of the Freethinkers' intellectual identity. Early geological discoveries were keenly reported in the Freethought press, while William Chilton's writings on 'The Theory of Regular Gradation' in the *Oracle of Reason* popularised theories of evolution long before the publication of Darwin's *Origin of Species*.[75] In the latter half of the century, Freethinkers were to continually brandish the arguments of Charles Darwin, and professional scientists

T. H. Huxley and John Tyndall in the face of their opponents. Edward Aveling explained 'Darwin and his Views' in a series of articles in *The National Reformer* in 1879 and 1880.[76] In the late-nineteenth and early-twentieth century the language of social Darwinism was to creep into some Freethinkers' discussions of neo-Malthusianism, social progress and critiques of socialism.[77]

Materialism was a central component of the philosophy of Freethought. It was, to some extent, an ill-defined concept, since eighteenth-century thinkers had promoted many different theories of materialism and Freethinkers also used the term in a variety of ways.[78] Its primary importance to Freethinkers was as a means of refuting God's existence. Though many eighteenth-century materialists did not deny the existence of God *a priori*, their argument that all natural phenomena could be explained according to physical laws rather than with recourse to an immaterial prime mover or intelligent structuring principle, opened the way for an atheist explanation of the universe.[79] Freethinkers thus appropriated the arguments of the Enlightened *philosophes* on thought and experience as properties of matter to argue for a cruder, 'common sense' form of atheistic materialism.[80] Emma Martin, for example, began her 'conversations' on the 'Being of God' with a debate between a 'Querist' and a 'Theist' in which the former proved that 'vitality' or life spirit was not ordained by God but was simply a physical property of matter. The Querist built on these arguments about matter to refute a 'theist' conception of the universe, and, in the second conversation, to prove that if God did not exist as a physical being then it was impossible for Him to exist at all. Martin's discussions of materialism had a clear practical agenda, to promote a rigorous form of 'this-worldism', declaring: 'I cannot neglect the interests of this world because there may chance to be another. I cannot refuse my assistance to instruct and benefit man because there may be a God...'[81] Martin, like other Freethinkers, used materialism to argue for the primacy of life on earth over empty promises of happiness in the afterlife.

This generalised and common sense materialist world-view necessarily raised questions of free will and moral responsibility. Eighteenth-century materialists had already begun to ask whether the claim that thought was determined by material factors – whether structures of mind or external sensory experience – entailed denying free will. A few did refuse any notion of free will, suggesting that the individual could not be held responsible for her actions and that morality (in its traditional Christian form) was therefore redundant.[82] Secularists did not subscribe to such a libertine view, however, and instead followed the 'philosophical doctrine of necessity' promoted by Unitarian philosopher Joseph Priestley.[83] Priestley affirmed that materialism implied necessarianism, the belief that individual actions were always determined by environment or circumstances and were therefore necessary. This did not, however, conflict with *liberty* for although necessity was the recognition that the universe was governed by scientific laws (the same cause would always produce the same effect) the individual was also able to learn from experience, to understand cause and effect and to act on this knowledge, which in turn created a new set of circumstances.[84] Robert Owen subsequently developed his own 'doctrine of necessity', which also emphasised the influence of the environment on the individual, as did Charles Bray in *The Philosophy of Necessity* (1841).

These philosophical debates were important to Freethinkers in that they offered a new framework for understanding questions that had previously been answered with reference to religion. Throughout the century, Freethinkers took a positive view of necessarianism, emphasising the need to study and comprehend the laws of nature and the potential for human growth and improvement once this had been achieved.[85] With this, Freethinkers tended to emphasise individual moral autonomy, rejecting and condemning the determinism of the doctrine of Original Sin. They argued that Christians, whose moral choices were determined by fear of hell or desire for the rewards of heaven, were morally irresponsible, unlike Freethinkers, who were guided only by their own conscience and the laws of nature.[86] This was closely related to their belief that morality in the abstract was embedded in these natural laws and could exist independently of religion.[87] Freethinkers thus used contemporary philosophical debates to concrete ends, viewing them as potential ammunition in the war against religion.

It should be noted that Freethinkers defined their views against a stereotyped version of Christianity that did not necessarily reflect the positions of the majority of nineteenth-century and early twentieth-century believers. Freethinkers caricatured Christianity as superstitious, dogmatic, and vehemently opposed to science, reason and the values of the Enlightenment. Harriet Law denounced religion as 'the mental faculty which, independent of, nay, *in spite of sense and reason*, enables man to apprehend the Infinite'.[88] This was of course to ignore the developments of the last century, during which Christian theologians increasingly came to justify revealed religion in terms of the natural world (Paley's creation by design for example), to argue that Christianity was inherently reasonable and that use of reason would lead one to God.[89] Perhaps the Freethinkers' portrayal of Christianity simply reflected their own experiences in provincial evangelical and dissenting churches. Yet when Freethinkers did encounter more liberal Christians who welcomed scientific developments (such as Darwin's theory of evolution), they often refused to accept that Christianity was capable of incorporating such tolerant views.[90] Organised Freethought may have defined itself through its hostility to Christianity, yet the relationship between Secularism and Christianity was characterised not just by opposition but by shared preoccupations and mutual influence. This was also the case for the movement's brand of feminism, which developed not only as a reaction to but also in dialogue with Christian debates on women.

Women and changing religious landscapes

Freethinking feminists remained immersed in Christian culture long after they had renounced religion, and their infidel feminism was articulated as part of a dialogue with their religious opponents.[91] The debates between Freethinkers and Christians, and their views on womanhood more generally, must be understood in the context of religious transformations occurring over the course of the period. Throughout the Victorian era, 'serious Christianity' remained a defining force within moral, intellectual, social and political life.[92] There was widespread fear – whether real or imagined – that Christianity was in decline and that the Established Church was unable to cope with urban expansion, industrial society, and working-class unrest. This led to a series of reforms in the Anglican Church in the 1830s and 1840s and to new efforts to reach out to the working class through city missions and the building of churches in urban areas.[93] The Established Church was also concerned that where it had failed the Nonconformist churches had gained ground, so that by the mid-nineteenth century about half of churchgoers attended non-Establishment institutions. The nineteenth century was thus an age of religious pluralism, in which different churches proliferated and competed with each other in an open market. The Established Church was also home to number of different viewpoints or 'parties' – the Evangelicals, the more liberal Broad Churchmen and the Anglo-Catholic Oxford Movement.

The Nonconformist churches had flourished during what has become known as the first evangelical revival, which began with John Wesley's Methodist movement in the 1730s and lasted until about 1840. Evangelicalism also found a home in the Anglican Church, led by men such as William Wilberforce and Lord Shaftesbury, who typified the evangelical commitment to 'activism', encompassing both the promotion of faith amongst unbelievers at home and abroad, and humanitarian causes such as anti-slavery and factory reform. Although a broad and diverse movement, evangelicalism was also characterised by an emphasis on Biblicalism (the belief that the Bible was the word of God and contained all spiritual truths); by conversion and personal experience of God's grace; and by an emphasis on the doctrine of the Atonement (the belief that Christ's sacrifice on the cross had atoned for the sins of mankind). A second evangelical revival occurred in the 1860s, producing revivalist sects such as the Salvation Army, in which women played a prominent role. By contrast, Anglo-Catholics (those who remained within the Church of England in the second half of the nineteenth century after some of the Oxford Movement's leading figures had gone over to Rome) opposed the Evangelicals and defended instead 'High Church principles' (the Catholicity of the Church of England, the Apostolic Succession, the centrality of the Sacraments, the importance of prayer and the beauty of holiness). Anglo-Catholics also denounced the Broad Churchmen whose assertion (in the second half of the nineteenth century) that Scripture did not have to be interpreted literally, was perhaps more successful in adapting to the twin challenges of biblical criticism and professionalised science.[94]

Attitudes towards women were strongly shaped by Christian teachings. Religion thus formed the grounds upon which Freethinking feminists based their arguments and provided a common framework for debate with their Christian opponents. A key notion, with which all parties engaged, involved sentimentalised depictions of woman's 'higher nature'. 'Woman' was portrayed as physically and intellectually weaker than man yet also his moral superior, with a stronger tendency to care for others and place their needs before her own. This natural benevolence – which complemented man's natural assertiveness and stronger physical and mental capacities – made woman ideally suited to domestic life where her talents were exercised in caring for the home and family. Christian commentators of all denominations were central to promoting such an idealised and prescriptive view of womanhood. The Baptist Minister John Angell James, for example, wrote a guide for young women in which he taught that woman's mind was neither 'equal' nor 'unequal' to man's, but simply 'different'. Woman's strongest quality was her *gentleness*, and her role was not to act, but to influence, '[h]er influence, however, is a kind of passive power – it is the power that draws, rather than drives, and commands by obeying.'[95] Such teaching at once sought to elevate woman without challenging her subordinate social status.

Historians Leonore Davidoff and Catherine Hall termed this constellation of nineteenth-century ideas on womanhood 'domestic ideology'.[96] They emphasised in particular the popularity of a language of separate spheres, whereby man was destined for the public world of work, women for the home or 'domestic realm'. As a category of historical analysis, 'separate spheres' has been considerably nuanced and critiqued over the last two decades. Increasingly, historians have focused on the contradictions to be found within the language of domestic ideology and how women used this discourse to challenge the boundaries between the public and the private.[97] The concept of 'woman's mission', a central theme in nineteenth-century didactic literature, was a useful notion in enabling and justifying such transgression.[98] Sarah Lewis' 1839 best-seller *Woman's Mission*, for example, argued that although Christianity deemed women socially subordinate to men, it recognised that they possessed a superior moral power which gave them 'no less office than that of instruments (under God) for the regeneration of the world.'[99] Many commentators suggested that although women's primary responsibility was towards her husband and children, it was sometimes permissible for her to extend her influence beyond the home for the social and moral improvement of society at large.[100] 'Woman's mission' thus had at its heart a contradiction, for some women could, and did, use it to justify the expansion of their activities into the public sphere. Middle-class women embarked on a variety of philanthropic endeavours, ministering to the working class, while overseas missionary women argued that the 'heathen' nations were in need of the moral and civilising influence of British women.[101] Yet the idea of 'woman's mission' was not limited to Christianity. Owenite Socialists, for example, appropriated it to argue that women must be free to usher in the 'new moral world', believing that the struggle against capitalism depended upon the emancipation of women.[102] 'Woman's mission' rhetoric was also utilised by 'rationalist, liberal and republican exponents of women's rights'.[103] Although 'woman's mission' was not as important to the Secularist movement as it was to the Owenites, it nevertheless influenced Freethinkers' accounts of progress, civilisation and female emancipation.[104]

Theological disputes and resulting institutional developments had an important impact upon women's role in the churches as well as shaping attitudes towards women's demands for equality in society at large. A belief in women's subordination to man retained a powerful hold over attitudes in the Church of England throughout the nineteenth century.[105] The more literal interpretation of scripture favoured by both Evangelicals and Anglo-Catholics could reinforce the idea – set out in

Genesis – that God had created woman to exist only as man's helpmeet. The Anglo-Catholic novelist Charlotte Yonge wrote in (1876) that she had 'no hesitation in declaring my full belief in the inferiority of woman, nor that she brought it upon herself' since 'it was woman who was the first to fall, and to draw her husband into the same transgression.'[106] However, while Broad Churchmen were less concerned to interpret the texts upon which woman's subordination was justified as divine truth, this did not always lead them to argue for greater sexual equality. The liberal theologian F. D. Maurice, who was forced out of his position at King's College for questioning the doctrine of eternal punishment, held decidedly less radical views when it came to women, arguing that claims to female independence were wrong-headed and ignored the complementary relationship of the sexes.[107]

In the Nonconformist churches, the rejection of ecclesiastical hierarchy and the emphasis on the individual believer's relationship with God could sometimes lead to greater equality of status for women members. This had certainly been the case in some of the radical dissenting sects of the seventeenth century, from which the Baptist church had derived, though historians have argued that after this women's status declined as Baptism became more established.[108] The extent to which the radical potential of Baptist ecclesiology was used to grant women a greater degree of control over church governance varied from church to church, and some churches certainly used the doctrine of church government to justify women voting in elections for ministers and officers.[109] Among Unitarians, rejection of Original Sin in favour of the idea that the individual was shaped by her environment led to the belief that education was the key to virtue and intimacy with God, and that the intellectual capacity of women was no different from that of men. Yet Unitarians did not necessarily believe that women should have the same kind of education as men, and although Unitarian women ran schools, wrote on pedagogy, and took on the crucial task of educating children, they were excluded from the dissenting academies and the intellectual clubs and societies.[110]

Women's growing contribution to the churches – as district visitors, Sunday school teachers, hymn writers, missionary society workers, leaders of study circles, and rescuers of 'fallen women' did not go unacknowledged by male church leaders (though the ancillary nature of such work was frequently stressed).[111] Nineteenth-century commentators frequently argued that their great efforts on behalf of religion reflected women's more spiritual natures. Best-selling Christian author Sarah Stickney Ellis expressed a common view when she wrote in 1839 that:

> Women are said to be more easily brought under [the influence of religion] than men; and we consequently see, in places of public worship, and on all occasions in which a religious object is the motive for exertion, a greater proportion of women than men.[112]

Yet commentators also regarded this 'feminisation' of religion – as modern historians have described it – as a problem. Throughout the nineteenth century, writers, politicians and church officials connected women's dominance of church and chapel congregations with the declining influence of Christianity in an increasingly urbanised, industrialised and fragmented society. Historians have suggested various reasons for the relative predominance of women in the churches. James Obelkevich has argued that as the importance of church attendance as a public duty declined, men left it to their womenfolk.[113] Hugh McLeod posited more positive reasons for women's attraction to religion, suggesting that it provided them with a sphere for action and emotional and spiritual support.[114] Yet contemporaries often assumed that the increased presence of women in the churches was due to their greater *natural* piety.[115]

This was of course closely related to the idea of women's superior morality, but it also harked back to older seventeenth- and eighteenth-century debates about women's greater susceptibility to religious 'enthusiasm'.[116] The idea of 'enthusiasm' had a strongly gendered element. Enthusiastic religion tended to be the religion of 'experience', based on bodily encounters with the divine, such as fits, trances and visions, and with a focus on emotion over religious text or doctrine. Women, with their emotional natures, lack of critical faculties, over-active imaginations and dangerous sexuality were deemed especially susceptible.[117] The harshest critics of 'enthusiasm' were usually Christians who wished to promote a more 'reasonable' kind of religion, but Freethinkers also found it useful to brand all revealed religion as a form of 'enthusiasm'.[118] Although 'enthusiasm' was a predominantly seventeenth- and eighteenth-century preoccupation, it did continue to influence religious discourse in the nineteenth century.[119] Its legacy can certainly be traced in Freethinkers' pathologising of all forms of religious experience, and in their references to women as 'slaves' to the priesthood, resorting to religion to release repressed sexual desire.[120] Victorian discussions of women's greater piety were, therefore, double edged: celebrations of their greater spirituality might also imply a lack of reason or self-control. This questioning of women's capacity for rationality in light of their greater susceptibility to religion also influenced Freethinking attitudes, existing in tension with their professed feminism.

Towards the end of the nineteenth century and into the Edwardian period, Britain's religious cultures were again transformed with the rise of esoteric and occult religions which became particularly popular in intellectual and progressive circles.[121] Victorian Freethinkers often wished to portray society as divided into two camps – orthodox versus heterodox, Christian versus Secularist. Even in the earlier nineteenth century, however, such definitions were often hard to maintain. The line between orthodox and unorthodox faith was blurred by developments such as the growing popularity of spiritualism both within and outside the Christian churches; the increasing acceptance of a historical approach to biblical criticism; and high profile cases in which Established Churchmen publicly proclaimed heterodox positions. The picture was further complicated at the *fin de siècle* by the explosion of interest in unorthodox spiritualities, such as the Theosophical Society (which took off in England in the 1880s) and occult fellowships such as the Hermetic Order of the Golden Dawn (est. 1888). Without committing themselves to any particular dogma or even a clear position regarding the existence of the divine, they combined an interest in comparative religion and Eastern faiths, with a commitment to self-development and the evolutionary transformation of humanity.[122] While these were ridiculed by some Secularists as antithetical to science and rationalism, to their adherents they were a self-conscious attempt to incorporate advancements in evolutionary and physical sciences into a new religious outlook which could transcend the limits of materialism.[123] Freethinking feminist Annie Besant converted to Theosophy in 1889, insisting that the Theosophical Society agreed with Freethought in its rejection of the supernatural. Yet she maintained that the Secularists' materialist creed was inadequate to understanding certain scientific phenomena such as hypnotism and psychology, for which Theosophy could offer more convincing answers.[124]

The notion of woman as naturally religious or inherently more spiritual was both challenged and re-inscribed within these new spiritualities. Many feminist women joined the Theosophical Society in the early twentieth century, and in doing so struggled to carve out what came to be defined as a feminised form of spirituality emphasising emotion and the value of subjective, interior experiences.[125] The occult also offered women a spiritualised vision of social change, which was at once a radical rejection of 'domesticated' piety while also accessible in its appeal to prevailing ideas of women's role as moral leaders.[126] As the twentieth century progressed, the women's movement became more religiously heterogeneous, though Christian motifs of moral

transformation, self-sacrifice and spiritual conversion retained a prominent role – particularly in the suffrage movement.[127] Between 1911 and 1912,
the feminist periodical *The Freewoman* published correspondence from
Theosophists, radically heterodox Christians, atheists, and Freethinkers,
who continued to debate women's innate 'religious sense' or natural aver-
sion to 'materialism'.[128] Uncovering a longstanding Freethinking feminist
tradition, operating within a symbiotic and antiphonal relationship with
Christianity, thus highlights the extent to which first wave feminism
developed out of a battle of ideas over religion. These emerging notions
of women's rights were likewise central to the formation of modern definitions of faith and secularisation.

Defining the religious and the secular

The extent to which Freethought was shaped by Christianity was
recognised even in the movement's own lifetime. One contemporary
'continental' Freethinker commented of English Freethought in 1877 that
'it shares with all other isms the principles, attributes, and paraphernalia
of a sect'.

> Like every other sectarian organisation, the English Secularists have
> their chief (President of the National Secular Society for the time
> being) … they have their sacred code (the "Freethinkers' Text-Book"
> … their missionaries (probational or accredited lecturers) … [and]
> their rituals (the Burial Service and the Naming of Infants)….[129]

The editor of the *Secular Review*, in which this comment appeared,
fiercely refuted the opinions of 'the foreigner', though twentieth-century
historians have tended to concur with it – noting the Christian backgrounds of the vast majority of Freethinkers and also that the movement
as a whole tended to recruit from the same socio-economic milieu as the
Protestant Dissenting sects. Secularism's organisation and propaganda
tactics closely resembled those of the evangelical revival: reading groups,
Sunday schools, tract circulation and itinerant preaching.[130] Nor was this
only a matter of similar activities and structures, for it has been argued
that the influence of religion extended beyond the personnel and organisational structures of organised Freethought, to shape its categories of
thought.[131]

> The [Secularist] insistence on an intimate knowledge of the Bible and
> of little else, on the supremacy of individual judgement, and the abso-
> lute certainty that there was only one right, one truth, and one morality
> did not strike many of its listeners as strange: the nonconformist

chapels in which religion had taken its *shape* for them had stressed the
same things.[132]

Secularism was a manifestation of a highly religious age, it is argued,
and the decline of religion ultimately heralded the movement's demise.[133]
Certainly, at its height, Secularism was engaged in an 'antiphonal relationship' with the churches, thriving on their attacks and gaining
publicity through their opposition.[134] In 1994, Edward Royle suggested
that 'Radical freethought can, indeed, best be understood as an
anti-religious sect, an extreme form of Nonconformity within which
many of the emotional and social satisfactions of the religious life were
met without the burden of a dogma based on revealed religion.'[135] I argue,
however, that Secularism was not just another form of evangelicalism.
Nor is it enough to simply trace the influence of religion upon the
Freethought movement. This study aims instead to illuminate the relationship between the two categories of 'the religious' and 'the secular', to
show how they were interdependent and mutually constitutive.

This question of the relationship between Christianity and the
Secularist movement needs to be considered in the context of wider
debates about religion and secularisation. Although the orthodox secularisation thesis continues to be defended in some quarters,[136] in general it
has fallen from favour. Most people now agree that the idea that religion
automatically declines with modernisation, that is with industrialisation,
urbanisation and the other socio-economic phenomena associated with
Western capitalism, is neither true nor heuristically useful in advancing
our understanding of modern belief-systems.[137] The standard secularisation thesis does not explain why religion sometimes continues to thrive
in the West, nor does it illuminate secularity itself, that is irreligion and
loss of faith, since it tends to define secularism wholly negatively, merely
as an *absence of religion*, instead of examining it as an intellectual and
moral stance in its own right.

In recent years, the most fruitful critiques of the secularisation thesis
have been focused on re-defining and expanding the category of religion
to encompass personal beliefs, linguistic structures and modes of identity.[138] Religion is identified with a variety of phenomena beyond those
traditionally associated with ecclesiastical institutions and doctrinal
belief-systems, leading some historians to argue that 'transformation'
rather than 'decline' ought to be the key organising factor when thinking
about religion in modern society.[139] It has also been suggested that our
study of religion should not be restricted to believers, but that we also
ought to investigate how religion has shaped the lives and thinking of

non-believers.[140] As part of a related set of debates, historians have also revealed the extent to which modernity, far from being wholly secularised, has in fact continued to be permeated with 'enchantment', with religious and magical beliefs co-existing with and sometimes complementing the scientific and rational modes of thought that were previously thought to define modernity and, in the sociologist Max Weber's terms, signify the end of enchantment.[141]

However, useful as some of this more recent work has been for gaining greater insight into modern religion, it does not necessarily aid our understanding of the secular. Callum Brown, for example, has focused on *expanding* the concept of religious belief, claiming for it territory previously considered to belong to the secular realm. His concept of 'discursive Christianity' defined religion not as an institution, or even a set of beliefs, but as a 'dominant discourse' which 'infused public culture and was adopted by individuals, whether churchgoers or not, in forming their own identities'. One example he gives was the popular press in the 1830s which, though dealing with 'secular' subjects nevertheless absorbed the evangelical narrative structure so that, Brown argues, it is not possible to distinguish between a 'secular' or 'religious' press until the end of the nineteenth century.[142]

The effect of this has been to obscure the secular rather than to offer more meaningful understandings of it. If religion is conceived as discursive, as an all-encompassing intellectual and linguistic framework which structures the thoughts of believers and non-believers alike, the secular sphere effectively disappears and 'secularism' becomes meaningless as a descriptive term. Some might argue that this is because secularisation and secularism have become useless historical categories. Yet a study focusing on self-proclaimed Secularists actively engaged in constructing a secular public sphere, obviously does not allow for the category of the secular to be left unexamined. Freethinking feminists affirmed precisely that which critics of the secularisation thesis have sought to challenge: that religion would wither away in the face of science, reason and modernisation. Their desire to establish a clear opposition between the religious world and the secular world sits in tension with the historian's realisation that Secularist activities must be studied within the context of Christian thought and culture. And yet, if it is no longer possible to take at face value the Freethinkers' own analysis of their project, how can we find a way of taking seriously their loss of faith and the Secularist ideology that arose from it?

It is necessary then to begin to interrogate the category of secularism itself. In order to start this task, we need first to leave behind a definition that treats secularity as a mental stance that is free from or untainted by religion and look instead at what *positively* constitutes a stance of 'irreligion' or self-proclaimed Secularism. Useful here is Charles Taylor's recent criticism of what he terms the 'subtraction stories' used to account for secularisation, the idea that over the centuries society has sloughed off or liberated itself from supernatural forms of belief and that the modern, secular mode of being is the truly human and natural state. Instead, Taylor insists that secularity itself 'is the fruit of new inventions, newly constructed self-understandings and related practices'.[143] This seems to be a valuable starting point since it moves away from the assumption that the emergence of a secular society is a given, that a secular worldview is the default position and therefore does not require clear delineation or investigation. It is essential to find more compelling explanations of why individuals lost their faith and/or explicitly rejected the moral and cultural authority of religion; why 'secularism' emerged as a category at all; why self-proclaimed Secularists in the nineteenth and early-twentieth century wished to define it as such, and how this definition changed over time. Once secularism is approached as a substantive rather than a negative category – as something more than simply an absence of religion – it becomes possible to see how religion may indeed play a role within a secular worldview without simply collapsing secularism into the wider category of religion. Free from the need to declare whether a particular idea, stance or mode of thought is either fully religious or fully secular, the historian has greater space to consider in more detail how these two categories relate to each other.

One interesting way of approaching this relationship is to look at how, in Western Europe, some aspects of secularism can be seen to have emerged out of religion itself. In fact, the concept of the 'secular' was arguably created by the Christian distinction between the sacred and the social. Ever since Christ's command to render unto Caesar, Christian communities at different points in history have wrestled with the question of how far their faith should extend into the social (one version of the 'secular') realm. It has also been suggested that the Judeo-Christian tradition, by putting forward a 'rational', monolithic understanding of the universe, in fact provided the grounds for its own critical refutation.[144] Charles Taylor has examined some of the ways in which, in the context of eighteenth- and nineteenth-century Europe and America, secular movements for social reform could be viewed as emerging out of religion as well as in opposition to it. Such movements were motivated by a concept of benevolence that had its roots in the Christian idea of *Agape* but which, during the eighteenth and nineteenth century, came to be increasingly defined in purely humanist terms, whereby one could dedicate oneself to improving the human condition without necessarily dedicating one's life to God.

By the nineteenth century, Taylor argues, an exclusively humanist benevolence had come into direct competition with Christianity, to the point where religion itself came to be measured according to secularised standards of morality. For example, in religiously inspired movements for social reform such as the anti-slavery campaigns, some activists became frustrated by what they saw as a lack of commitment on the part of church leaders. A hyper-Augustinian emphasis on faith over works alienated activists dedicated to social improvement in this world rather than merely awaiting the next. Thus, some felt compelled to reject that faith which had motivated their reforming zeal in the first place. As Taylor notes: 'The paradox is that a religious impulse and vision may sometimes drive people out of religious belief.' This could also lead to a situation in which 'religion' and self-proclaimed 'secularism' came to co-exist in 'mutually supportive opposition', each strengthening the other's beliefs and suspicion of one another. What Taylor wants to emphasise, however, is that the moral framework and intensity of the religious and secular derived from basically the same source, even while its focus or centre had shifted. This is not to argue that the nineteenth-century shift towards secular reform movements, and the confident assertion of unbelief that sometimes accompanied this, was not significant, but that the emergence of what we might call a secular morality did not result from a 'smooth, continuing and unidirectional move towards "secularisation"' but was initially stimulated by a deeply religious impulse.[145]

Whether and how secularisation occurs (or rather 'the secular' emerges as a significant category) depends upon the particular character of religious beliefs and arguments to be found in a society at a particular time. Darwin's theories of evolution and natural selection, for example, had such devastating consequences for belief precisely because the Christian Church had previously invested so heavily in the argument of Creation by design as proof of the existence of a Divine Being. As well as this, the emphasis on biblical literalism in Protestant churches and the focus on Christ's miracles as the foremost sign of His deity made Christianity particularly vulnerable to the impact of biblical criticism. This can be taken further, to argue that the specific intellectual imperatives central to a faith could themselves ultimately propel their adherents towards atheism. The outlook of militantly rationalist unbelievers in the nineteenth century was based on the premise that 'One *ought* not to believe what one has insufficient evidence for…' At the heart of this stance was a concept of 'self-responsible rational freedom', which affirmed that the individual had a duty to make up her own mind based on the evidence without looking to any authority to lead the way: that is, a strong version of the Protestant notion of the right of private judgement and the emphasis on a personal, unmediated relationship with God. Moreover, the compulsion among those who had lost their faith to speak out about their doubts, honestly and publicly, clearly revealed their filiation to evangelical Christianity which insisted not only upon strict examination of one's soul but also upon a clear distinction between right and wrong, between what was true and what was not.[146]

The intellectual cast of nineteenth-century religion, particularly the emphasis on intellectual and moral autonomy and clear moral boundaries, also structured much Secularist thought. Throughout this book particular attention will be paid to the points at which the religious and the secular came together within the Secularists' worldview. In particular, Chapter 2 will use the idea that religion and secularism were symbiotic as well as oppositional as a way of understanding the process by which Freethinking feminists rejected religion. An approach which emphasises the degree to which Secularist ideology emerged out of a Christian faith, in much the same way as its individual members almost invariably hailed from pious religious backgrounds, will provide a way of demonstrating the importance of religion to Secularism while maintaining the notion of the secular as a distinct category.

Reading the Freethought archive in conjunction with Christian sources makes very apparent the extent to which both parties were interacting with each other – identifying themselves in opposition to a stereotyped characterisation of their enemy; inflating the strength and influence of their opponents in order to emphasise the necessity of each of their causes; and sometimes engaging with each other's arguments. Although the necessary concentration on textual sources makes it difficult to convey the rich oral culture of organised Freethought – in which Freethinkers and Christians debated with each other at public lectures, meetings and even on the street – placing these texts side by side ensures that some of the adversarial, polemical and dialogic nature of the world of Freethought is represented. In addition, Freethought sources have also been read here in relation to the key feminist events and campaigns of the period, such as women's successive attempts to participate in the public forums of religion and politics, the struggle to repeal the Contagious Diseases Acts, the beginnings of the suffrage campaigns, and the debates over prostitution, marriage and women's sexuality. By approaching

Freethinking feminism and 'mainstream' women's rights advocacy not as two separate entities, but as parts of the same diverse movement, it become possible to identify specifically Freethinking contributions to feminist thought.

The focus of this study is on the individual authors of Freethinking feminist texts, rather than on a detailed analysis of audience demographic or readership patterns. It does aim, however, to provide a rounded picture of an intellectual universe, in which Freethinkers, Christians and feminists read, critiqued, digested and responded to each other's contributions to the debate on women and religion. This book, therefore, is a history of popular thought and belief. It also asks how shifts in ideas and beliefs can shape social action, both in the lives of individuals and in social movements. The women who form the subject of this study were not especially innovative thinkers or first-rate intellectuals, talented though many of them were. They reiterated the ideas of Enlightenment *philosophes*, and radical thinkers such as Thomas Paine, Mary Wollstonecraft, Robert Owen and John Stuart Mill, but in doing so they reformulated them to make them relevant to their own lives. The focus, therefore, of this study is on ideas within a highly specific historical and intellectual context. It treats its subjects not simply as ideologues of infidel feminism but as activists within a movement, whose ideas emerged out of the messy reality of public meetings, arguments, encounters with the enemy and attempts to carve out a space for themselves in a male dominated world.

A prosopographical approach is used to provide a window into this world. Biographical information about a group of women – some of whom, such as Harriet Law, have been very little explored, while others, such as Annie Besant, have inspired numerous studies – is employed to create a collective portrait of the Freethinking feminist. The women chosen for this study rose to prominence within the Freethought movement and their varying outlooks represent a cross-section of Freethinking views. Their lives are viewed against a wider social and intellectual context, and common patterns are identified to find out what motivated women to renounce their religion in favour of Freethought, and what kind of a woman was able to become a Freethinking feminist. It is not, however, the aim of this book to present the women studied here as representative of women in their period, nor of feminists at the time, nor even of women involved in the Freethought movement – most of whom never achieved their degree of prominence. In fact, the unrepresentative nature of these women's lives is emphasised as testament to how immensely difficult it was for women in this period to break out of Christian-defined norms and lay claim to a language of science and reason, and individual autonomy.

Chapter 1 introduces the women who form the subject of this study – tracing their class and denominational backgrounds, examining their lives in the context of wider female involvement in the Secularist movement, and identifying areas of continuity and change in the role of 'Freethinking feminists' between 1830 and 1914. Chapter 2 goes on to examine in detail the 'counter-conversions' of these women from religion to Freethought. It uses their personal narratives to ask wider questions about the relationship between Christianity and the Secularist movement and how we might understand the religious and irreligious beliefs of women in the past from a feminist perspective. Chapter 3 follows the journeys of these women from Christianity into the organised Freethought movement and examines their attempts to carve out a 'public' role as prominent lecturers, journalists and authors. It positions the struggle of Freethinking feminists to access male-dominated intellectual and religious domains in relation to wider attempts by women to intervene in the public sphere, arguing that the Freethinking emphasis on freedom of discussion opened the way for women to participate in conversations on science and reason while simultaneously marginalizing the 'feminine' from this discourse. The tensions surrounding the place of 'woman' in Freethought ideology are returned to in Chapter 4, which discusses 'infidel feminism' and Freethought support for woman's rights alongside its more problematic definitions of 'woman' and her relationship to religion. Chapter 5 looks at the contributions of Freethinking feminists to the women's rights movement and how they negotiated its predominantly Christian culture. Chapter 6 expands this discussion of the influence of Freethought in the development of first wave feminism, focusing on debates over marriage, birth control and sexual morality. It examines the tensions between feminism, Free Love and Freethought, while showing that despite these tensions Freethought provided an intellectual framework in which it was possible to envisage a more radical transformation of heterosexual relations than the rest of the women's movement was willing to imagine.

The chronological scope of this book (1830 to 1914) covers the point from which the 'Freethinking feminist' first emerged as a public figure in England, through the heyday of Secularism and the emergence of a mass women's rights movement focused around the campaign for the suffrage in the early twentieth century, to the First World War, which effectively marked the end of organised Freethought as a national movement. Freethought ideas and individuals continued into the twentieth century, contributing in particular to later feminist campaigns for sexual freedom and birth control. It is hoped that this study, in uncovering a vibrant Freethinking feminist tradition and revealing the legacy of anti-religious ideas to feminist thought, can shed light on struggles that continued long after the deaths of the women discussed here. Today, especially, when religion and secularism have again become highly controversial and contested terms within feminist discourse, a fuller understanding of the history of such debates may assist us in unravelling some of their complexities.

Notes

1 *The National Reformer* (*NR*), 4 April 1869, p. 223.
2 For a positive 'reclaiming' of the title of 'infidel', see Harriet Teresa Law in the *Secular Chronicle*, 11 March 1877, p. 123, 16 December 1877, p. 293; E. Martin, *A Few Reasons for Renouncing Christianity and Professing and Disseminating Infidel Opinions* (London: Watson, 1840–50[?]).
3 The term 'feminism' was not used in England until the 1890s, and historians have debated its utility for describing the diverse activities of those advocating women's rights in the nineteenth century. This book, however, follows convention in referring to 'feminism' in the nineteenth century according to Levine's definition as women's recognition of their collective oppression and their positive identification with each other in the context of political struggle; P. Levine, *Victorian Feminism, 1850–1900* (London: Hutchinson, 1987), p. 14. For the complexities involved in using the term 'feminism', see N. F. Cott, *The Grounding of Modern Feminism* (New Haven & London: Yale University Press, 1987); K. Offen, 'Defining Feminism: A Comparative Historical Approach', *Signs* 14:1 (1988), 119–57; B. Caine, *English Feminism, 1780–1980* (Oxford: Oxford University Press, 1997); L. Delap, 'Feminist and Anti-Feminist Encounters in Edwardian Britain', *Historical Research* 78:201 (August 2005), 377–99.
4 S. Morgan & J. de Vries, 'Introduction', in S. Morgan & J. de Vries (eds.), *Women, Gender and Religious Cultures in Britain 1800–1940* (Abingdon: Routledge, 2010), pp. 1–10, 1–2.
5 For an extended discussion of the historiography of women, religion and feminism, see S. Morgan, *A Passion for Purity: Ellice Hopkins and the Politics of Gender in the Late-Victorian Church* (Bristol: Centre for Comparative Studies in Religion and Gender, University of Bristol, 1999), pp. 3–35. See also E. Jay, 'The Return of the Culturally Repressed – Religion and Women', *Nineteenth Century Studies* 17 (2003), 1–12.
6 Early examples of attention to religion in gender history include P. Holden (ed.), *Women's Religious Experience* (London: Croom Helm, 1983); G. Malmgreen (ed.), *Religion in the Lives of English Women 1760–1930* (London & Sydney: Croom Helm, 1986).
7 O. Banks, *Faces of Feminism. A Study of Feminism as a Social Movement* (Oxford: Basil Blackwell, 1993) (first published 1981); J. Rendall, *The Origins of Modern Feminism. Women in Britain, France and the United States, 1780–1860* (Basingstoke:

Macmillan Education, 1985). The ambiguities and tensions within evangelical doctrines were also noted in B. Taylor, *Eve and the New Jerusalem: Socialism and Feminism in the Nineteenth Century* (London: Virago, 1983), p. 124; and L. Davidoff & C. Hall, *Family Fortunes. Men and Women of the English Middle Class, 1780–1850* (London: Hutchinson, 1987), p. 329, though both works tended to focus on its ultimately conservative tendencies. The term 'Evangelical' is used here to denote the Evangelical Party within the Church of England, while 'evangelical' is used to imply the general revival that affected many different churches.

8 See, for example, H. Mathers, 'The Evangelical Spirituality of a Victorian Feminist: Josephine Butler, 1828–1906', *Journal of Ecclesiastical History*, 52:2 (April 2001), 282–312.

9 K. Gleadle, *The Early Feminists. Radical Unitarians and the Emergence of the Women's Rights Movement, 1831–51* (Basingstoke & London: Macmillan 1995). For Unitarianism, see also H. Plant, '"Ye Are All One in Christ Jesus": Aspects of Unitarianism and Feminism in Birmingham, c. 1869–1890', *Women's History Review* 9:4 (2000), 721–42; H. Plant, *Unitarianism, Philanthropy and Feminism in York, 1782–1821: The Career of Catherine Cappe* (York: Borthwick Institute of Historical Research, 2003); R. Watts, *Gender, Power and the Unitarians in England 1760–1860* (Harlow: Addison Wesley Longman Ltd, 1998); R. Watts, 'Rational Religion and Feminism: the Challenge of Unitarianism in the Nineteenth Century', in Morgan (2002), 39–52.

10 S. Morgan (ed.), *Women, Religion and Feminism in Britain, 1750–1900* (Basingstoke: Palgrave Macmillan, 2002); S. Morgan & J. de Vries (2010).

11 It is entirely absent from overviews such as R. Strachey, *The Cause. A Short History of the Women's Rights Movement in Great Britain* (London: G. Bell & Sons Ltd, 1928); Banks (1993); Rendall (1985); J. Rendall (ed.), *Equal or Different: Women's Politics 1800–1914* (Oxford: Basil Blackwell, 1987); Levine (1987); P. Levine *Feminist Lives in Victorian England: Private Roles and Public Commitment* (Oxford: Basil Blackwell, 1990); Caine (1997). Olive Banks, five years after her first study of the women's movement, surveyed biographical data for 98 women active in first wave feminism and found that 32 per cent were agnostics or Freethinkers. She noted this as 'significant', but although she suggested that 'religious scepticism and freethought represent an important tradition within feminism' it was not within the scope of her study to explore this further; O. Banks, *Becoming a Feminist: The Social Origins of 'First Wave' Feminism* (Brighton: Wheatsheaf, 1986), pp. 14–15.

12 S. J. Peacock, *The Theological and Ethical Writings of Frances Power Cobbe, 1822–1904* (Lampeter: The Edwin Mellen Press, 2002); B. Caine, *Victorian Feminists* (Oxford: Oxford University Press, 1992), pp. 115–19; see also B. Caine, 'Feminist History and Feminist Biography', *Women's History Review* 3:2 (1994), 247–61.

13 See J. Walkowitz, *Prostitution and Victorian Society: Women, Class and the State* (Cambridge: Cambridge University Press, 1980), pp. 101–2; L. Bland, *Banishing the Beast. English Feminism and Sexual Morality, 1885–1914* (London: Penguin Books, 1995), esp. Chapter 1.

14 While arguing for Wollstonecraft's feminism to be understood within a 'theistic framework', Barbara Taylor nevertheless positions her in relation to an older, critical freethinking tradition; B. Taylor, *Mary Wollstonecraft and the Feminist Imagination* (Cambridge: Cambridge University Press, 2003), esp. Chapter 3.

15 Wollstonecraft's friend and fellow feminist Mary Hays (1759–1843), for example, was strongly influenced by the French materialist Claude-Adrien Helvetius; see M. L. Brooks, 'Hays, Mary (1759–1843)' *Oxford Dictionary of National Biography* (online edn; Oxford: Oxford University Press, 2004).

16 Taylor (2003), pp. 198–201. Taylor notes that – at least in the case of Godwin – this form of progressive sex reform was, far from being hedonistic, extremely serious and somewhat 'puritan'.

17 *Secular Chronicle (SC)*, 31 March 1878, pp. 145–6.

18 *The Reasoner (Reasoner)*, 15 July 1846, pp. 99–101.

19 For Freethinking feminism in the first half of the nineteenth-century, see G. Malmgreen, *Neither Bread, Nor Roses: Utopian Feminists and the English Working Class, 1800–1850* (Brighton: Noyce, 1978); I. McCalman, 'Females, Feminism and Free Love in an Early Nineteenth-Century Radical Movement', *Labour History* 38 (1980), 1–25; H. Rogers, 'The Prayer, the Passion and Reason of Eliza Sharples: Freethought, Women's Rights and Republicanism', in E. Yeo (ed.), *Radical Femininity: Women's Self-Representation in the Public Sphere* (Manchester: Manchester University Press, 1998), 52–78; Taylor (1983).

20 Taylor (1983), pp. 263–76. The Freethinking feminism of the Secularist movement did not on the whole continue to promote the liberation of women as the key to the end of capitalist society.

21 S. Budd, *Varieties of Unbelief: Atheists and Agnostics in English Society 1850–1950* (London: Heinemann, 1977), pp. 50, 94.

22 D. Nash, 'The Leicester Secular Society: Unbelief, Freethought and Freedom in a Nineteenth-Century City' (unpublished doctoral thesis, University of York, 1990), p. 230; D. Nash, *Secularism, Art and Freedom* (Leicester, London & New York: Leicester University Press, 1992), pp. 76–7.

23 E. Royle, 'Freethought: The Religion of Irreligion', in D. G. Paz (ed.), *Nineteenth-Century English Religious Traditions. Retrospect and Prospect* (London: Greenwood, 1995), pp. 170–196, 192. For the most comprehensive discussion of feminism in the Secularist movement to date, see Chapter 13 'Women, Sex and Birth Control', in E. Royle, *Radicals, Secularists and Republicans. Popular Freethought in Britain, 1866–1915* (Manchester: Manchester University Press, 1980), pp. 246–62. For female Freethinkers, see A. L. Gaylor (ed.), *Women Without Superstition. 'No Gods – No Masters'. The Collected Writings of Women Freethinkers of the Nineteenth and Twentieth Centuries* (Madison, Wisconsin: Freedom from Religion Foundation, 1997).

24 The Victorian 'crisis of faith' is a term used to describe the experiences of a number of nineteenth-century authors and intellectuals, including George Eliot, Francis Newman and Charles Hennell, who stopped believing in orthodox Christianity and left a record of the often painful process by which this came about; see B. Willey, *Nineteenth Century Studies. Coleridge to Matthew Arnold* (London: Chatto & Windus, 1949); F. M. Turner, *Between Science and Religion: the Reaction to Scientific Naturalism in Late Victorian England* (London & New Haven: Yale University Press, 1974); R. Helmstadter & B. Lightman (eds.), *Victorian Faith in Crisis. Essays on Continuity and Change in Nineteenth-Century Religious Belief* (London & Basingstoke: Macmillan, 1990). For recent attempts to extend the focus of crisis of

faith studies from social elites to encompass popular movements, see J. Marsh, *Word Crimes: Blasphemy, Culture, and Literature in Nineteenth-Century England* (Chicago & London: University of Chicago Press,1998); T. Larsen, *Crisis of Doubt* (Oxford: Oxford University Press, 2006).

Elizabeth Jay's essay on 'Doubt and the Victorian Woman' did not examine the feminism of the Freethought movement, but looked at [mainly fictional] middle-class women who, she found, tended to hold conservative views on the Woman Question in contrast to their unorthodox religious position; E. Jay, 'Doubt and the Victorian Woman', in D. Jasper & T. Wright (eds.), *The Critical Spirit and the Will to Believe* (Basingstoke: Macmillan, 1989), pp. 88–103.

25 *SC*, 2 January 1876, pp. 1–2.

26 E. Royle, *Victorian Infidels. The Origins of the British Secularist Movement, 1791–1866* (Manchester: Manchester University Press, 1974), p. 4. Early histories of organised Freethought focused primarily on its intellectual content and motivation, for example, see J. M. Robertson, *A History of Freethought in the Nineteenth Century* (London: Watts and Co., 1929). H. R. Murphy was among the first to challenge such an approach and he argued that 'ethical' issues should be considered; see H. R. Murphy 'The Ethical Revolt Against Christian Orthodoxy in Early Victorian England', *American Historical Review* 60 (1955), 800–17. Susan Budd made a call to historians to examine the rank and file movement more closely; see S. Budd, 'The Loss of Faith: Reasons for Unbelief Among Members of the Secular Movement in England, 1850–1950', *Past and Present* 36 (1967), 106–25. Angus McLaren argued that organised Freethought represented 'working-class' antagonism to the social conservatism of the churches; see A. McLaren, 'George Jacob Holyoake and the Secular Society: British Popular Freethought, 1851–1858', *Canadian Journal of History* 7:3 (1972), 235–51. More recently, historians have stressed the desire for middle-class respectability found within the movement; see S. A. Mullen, *Organised Freethought: the Religion of Unbelief in Victorian England* (New York: Garland, 1987), p. 234. David Nash, however, maintains that Freethought commitment to self-education and free discussion should not be seen merely as an attempt to emulate the middle class but as aspects of the Secularists' efforts to develop a 'democratic epistemology', see Nash (1992), p. 139; Nash (2005), p. 116.

27 Royle (1974), pp. 1–2, 29.

28 J. Wiener, *Radicalism and Freethought in Nineteenth-Century Britain: The Life of Richard Carlile* (Westport, Connecticut: Greenwood Press, 1983).

29 For the role of women in Carlile's campaigns, see M. L. Bush, 'Richard Carlile and the Female Reformers of Manchester: A Study of Gender in the 1820s Viewed Through the Radical Filter of Republicanism, Freethought and a Philosophy of Sexual Satisfaction', *Manchester Region History Review* 16 (2002–3), 2–12; C. Parolin, '"The She-Champion of Impiety": A Case Study of Female Radicalism', in M. Davis & P. Pickering (eds.), *Unrespectable Radicals? Popular Politics in the Age of Reform* (Aldershot: Ashgate, 2008), pp. 185–99.

30 For a history of the Owenite movement, see J. F. C. Harrison, *Robert Owen and the Owenites in Britain and America. The Quest for the New Moral World* (London: Routledge & K. Paul, 1969).

31 Royle (1974), pp. 60–1. Owen set out his opposition to religion in his third *Essay on the Formation of Character* (1814), but it was not until his famous 'Address', delivered

at the City of London Tavern on 21 August 1817, that his views on religion became widely circulated.

32 By 1839, lectures on 'theological and ethical' issues formed up to one third of the menu in the national diet of Socialist propaganda; Taylor (1983), p. 136.

33 *New Moral World (NMW)*, 1 May 1841, pp. 268–9.

34 *NMW*, 18 May 1839, p. 477, 4 January 1840, pp. 996–1,000.

35 *NMW*, 4 May 1839, p. 441.

36 *NMW*, 6 April 1839, p. 381.

37 *NMW*, 4 May 1839, p. 441.

38 Royle (1974), pp. 66–8.

39 See, for example, E. Martin, *The Missionary Jubilee Panic and the Hypocrites' Prayer. Addressed to the Supporters of the Christian Mission* (London: Hetherington, 1844).

40 *NMW*, 26 July 1845, p. 65.

41 *NMW*, 11 December 1841, p. 191.

42 The impetus for the formation of the APU came from public meetings in the Birmingham Hall of Science and the London John Street Institute while Holyoake was on bail before serving a prison sentence for blasphemy; see Royle (1974), p. 82.

43 *Oracle of Reason* 1 (1842), pp. iv–vi.

44 E. Martin, *A Few Reasons for Renouncing Christianity and Professing and Disseminating Infidel Opinions* (London: Watson, 1840–1850?), p. 3.

45 Royle (1974), pp. 150–55. In April 1848 *The Reasoner* adopted the subtitle 'Secular and Eclectic Journal', the term 'secular' having been suggested to Holyoake by Robert Owen's lawyer W. H. Ashurst.

46 *Reasoner*, 10 September 1854, p. 161.

47 Quoted in Royle (1980), p. 6.

48 Royle (1980), pp.23–7.

49 The term agnosticism (to imply openness and indecision on the question of God's existence) was coined in 1869 by the scientist T. H. Huxley, though its meaning remained unstable throughout the 1870s and 1880s; B. Lightman, 'Huxley and Scientific Agnosticsm: The Strange History of a Failed Rhetorical Strategy', *The British Journal for the History of Science*, 35:3 (2002), 271–89. Prior to this, 'atheist' was often used to include 'negative atheists', those who did not think that there was enough evidence to 'positively' assert the non-existence of God.

50 For discussion of these divisions, see Budd (1977), pp. 45–49; Royle (1980), p. 114; D. Berman, *A History of Atheism in Britain. From Hobbes to Russell* (London: Croom Helm, 1988), pp. 213–14; Nash (1992), p. 18.

51 Royle suggests that Holyoake also drew support and loyalty from those who had been involved in the Owenite movement, see Royle (1980), p. 118.

52 Bradlaugh was, for example, far more of a household name during his own lifetime than his adversary Karl Marx; see D. Lavin, *Bradlaugh Contra Marx Radicalism versus Socialism in the First International* Socialist History Society Occasional Publication 28 (2011).

53 The British Secular Union was established in 1877 as an alternative to the NSS by those who either resented Bradlaugh's authoritarianism and/or supported less adversarial tactics.

54 Royle (1980), pp. 135, 36.

55 Royle (1980), p. 42. Labour churches were founded throughout the 1890s in many northern industrial towns. They offered an anti-dogmatic faith in social justice and God's work in the 'here and now'. Positivist Societies, established in England in the second half of the century, likewise rejected theology and dogma in favour of a broad 'religion of humanity'; K. S. Inglis, 'The Labour Church Movement', *International Review of Social History* (1958) 3:3, 445–460, pp. 447–8. 'Militant Freethinkers' continued to criticise the 'religious' nature of Ethical societies, preferring to continue more straightforward attacks on Christianity, *Reformer*, 15 October 1897, pp. 222–5.

56 Royle (1980), pp. 36–43.

57 *Ibid.*, pp. 135–6.

58 *Ibid.*, pp. 156–7; Royle (1974), pp. 234–5.

59 Royle (1980), pp. 45–6. The size and sympathy of lecture audiences varied considerably. In the period before the formation of the NSS maybe as little as a third of audiences in rural areas would have supported the Secularist cause, whereas in Manchester a Secularist lecturer might attract an audience of over a thousand, most of whom would have been favourable to her views; see Royle (1974), p. 235.

60 Royle (1974), p. 237.

61 Royle (1980), p. 133.

62 This was particularly the case for London, see D. Nash, 'Secularism in the City: Geographies of Dissidence and the Importance of Radical Culture in the Metropolis', in M. Cragoe & A. Taylor (eds.), *London Politics 1760–1914* (Basingstoke & New York: Palgrave Macmillan, 2005), pp. 97–120.

63 Royle (1974), pp. 257–67; Royle (1980), p. 221.

64 Royle (1980), p. 126.

65 Budd (1977), pp. 95–6.

66 Royle (1980), pp. 127–8.

67 Nash (1992), p. 76.

68 Local Secularist branches followed their Owenite predecessors in their eclectic intellectual tastes, including 'dabbling in Phrenology, Mesmerism and Spiritualism'; Nash (1992), p. 19.

69 Budd (1977), pp. 11–12.

70 Nash traces this tradition back to the 'mechanick' tradition of seventeenth-century radicalism; Nash (1992), p. 8.

71 Royle (1974), pp. 11–15; Robertson (1929), pp. 129–153.

72 Royle (1974), p. 107.

73 Robertson (1929), pp. 79, 83–91.

74 Royle (1974), p. 126.

75 *Ibid.*, p. 123. Timothy Larsen maintains that, what he terms 'plebeian' Freethinkers were far in advance of middle-class intellectuals during this period in grasping and endorsing new scientific developments; see Larsen (2006), p. 246.

76 Royle (1980), p. 171.

77 Royle (1980), p. 227.

78 'Materialism should therefore be seen as a much more diverse and multifaceted phenomenon … When its diverse manifestations are taken into account, it can be seen to represent not so much a body of doctrine as a complex of tendencies,

questions and attempted solutions put forward by thinkers who generally refused metaphysical systems', A. Thomson, 'Materialism', in A. C. Kors (ed.), *Encyclopaedia of the Enlightenment*, 4 vols (Oxford: Oxford University Press, 2003) pp. iii, 26–31. For a history of materialism see also J. Yolton, *Thinking Matter. Materialism in Eighteenth-Century Britain* (Oxford: Basil Blackwell, 1984).

79   In the eighteenth century materialism was compatible with a deist belief that God had imbued matter with its inherent force. Prior to this John Locke suggested that God might have enabled matter to think, while the Irish Freethinker John Toland's *Pantheisticon* (1720) combined materialism with a pantheistic conception of the soul of the world; see Thomson (2004), p. 27. For the atheistic implications of materialism, see Yolton (1984), pp. 3–4; Royle (1974), pp. 18–20.

80   The Freethinker Robert Cooper's collection of essays *The Immortality of the Soul, Religious and Philosophically Considered* (1853) was the most systematic attempt by a Freethinker to explain how matter could 'think' and humans could operate without a motivating 'essence', using arguments by Priestley and Locke; see Royle (1974), pp. 115–17. Nash has identified the continued importance of 'the seventeenth century … tradition of lower class materialism', Nash (1992), p. 8.

81   E. Martin, *A Conversation on the Being of God* (London: n.p. 1840–50[?]), p. 7; E. Martin, *Second Conversation on the Being of God* (London: for the author, 1840–50[?]). Royle has suggested that Bradlaugh promoted a more 'refined' understanding of materialism, though questioned the extent to which most Freethinker's understood his interpretation of Spinoza; Royle (1980), p. 172.

82   Thomson (2004), p. 30.

83   J. Priestley, *The Doctrine of Philosophical Necessity Illustrated* (1777).

84   Thomson (2004), p. 29; B. Willey, *The Eighteenth-Century Background. Studies in the Idea of Nature in the Thought of the Period* (London & New York: Arc Paperbacks, 1986) (first published 1940), pp. 178–9.

85   Royle (1974), p. 22.

86   For Eliza Macauley on the subject of moral responsibility, see *The Crisis*, 16 June 1832, p. 49; for Harriet Law, see *NR*, 14 June 1862, pp. 6–7.

87   See, for example, E. Martin, *Religion Superseded or the Moral Code of Nature Sufficient for the Guidance of Man* (London: n.p., 1840–50[?]); Sophia Dobson Collet believed 'That Moral Obligation is inherently sacred, and that the sense of obligation does not necessarily imply belief in a Person who claims our obedience … it is a truth which needs to be clearly recognised, and which *is* recognised by many of the most religious thinkers of the day'; S. D. Collet, *Phases of Atheism, Described, Examined and Answered* (Holyoake & Co., London, 1860), p. 6.

88   *SC*, 5 May 1878, p. 212.

89   Willey (1940), pp. 3–17. Moreover, in recent years historians have increasingly stressed the contributions of religious thinking to the Enlightenment, in contrast to the assertion of Freethinkers that they constituted two opposing belief systems. J. Sheehan, 'Enlightenment, Religion and the Enigma of Secularisation: A Review Essay', *The American Historical Review* 108:4 (October 2003), 1061–80, 1062; N. Aston, *Christianity and Revolutionary Europe, 1750–1830* (Cambridge: Cambridge University Press, 2002), p. 93.

90   *SC*, 20 August 1876, p. 85.

91 In making this argument, this study therefore departs from earlier work in this area, which tended to conceptualise the relationship between Freethinking feminism and Christianity as overwhelmingly oppositional; see McCalman (1980), pp. 9–10. Taylor acknowledged the contradictions regarding 'evangelical' views of woman's role but nevertheless focused on the antagonism between the two camps; Taylor (1983), pp. 123–4. For opposition to radical feminism from 'evangelical ladies', see also B. Taylor, 'The Woman Power: Religious Heresy and Feminism in Early English Socialism', in S. Lipshitz, *Tearing the Veil: Essays on Femininity* (London: Routledge & Kegan Paul, 1979), pp. 117–144, 134–9.

92 For an overview of religion in the nineteenth century and its accompanying historiography, see M. A. Smith, 'Religion', in C. Williams (ed.) *A Companion to Nineteenth-Century Britain* (Oxford: Blackwell Publishing, 2004), pp. 337–52.

93 For the argument that the established Church was in fact more successful in adapting to social change than many contemporaries and subsequent historians gave it credit for; see R. A. Burns, *The Diocesan Revival in the Church of England c.1800–1870* (Oxford: Clarendon Press, 1999). Historians have recently come to question whether urbanisation did in fact bring about a decline in Christianity, though they agree that this was a powerful perception among contemporaries; see for example J. Cox, *The English Churches in a Secular Society: Lambeth 1870–1930* (Oxford: Oxford University Press, 1982); J. N. Morris, *Religion and Urban Change: Croydon, 1840–1914* (Woodbridge, Suffolk: Boydell Press, 1992); C. Brown, 'Did Urbanisation Secularise Britain?', *Urban History Yearbook 1988*.

94 For the most comprehensive discussion of evangelicalism, see D. Bebbington, *Evangelicalism in Modern Britain* (London: Unwin Hyman, 1989). For the Oxford Movement, see P. B. Nockles, *The Oxford Movement in Context* (Cambridge: Cambridge University Press, 1994). For Broad Churchmen, see E. Jay, *Faith and Doubt in Victorian Britain* (Basingstoke & London: Macmillan Education, 1986), Chapter 3.

95 J. A. James, *Female Piety: or the Young Woman's Friend and Guide Through Life to Immortality* (London: Hamilton, Adams & Co., 1852), p. 66.

96 See Hall (1979); Davidoff & Hall (1987). Since the publication of these seminal works 'domestic ideology' has been referred to by almost all historians of nineteenth-century women, while some have explored and expanded this category; for example, see E. Langland, *Nobody's Angels: Middle-Class Women and Domestic Ideology in Victorian Culture* (Ithica & London: Cornell University Press, 1995).

97 For debates on 'separate spheres', see A. Vickery, 'From Golden Age to Separate Spheres? A Review of the Categories and Chronology of English Women's History', *Historical Journal* 36 (1993), 383–414; A. Summers, *Female Lives, Moral States: Women, Religion and Public Life in Britain 1800–1930* (Newbury: Threshold Press, 2000), esp. Chapter 1; L. Davidoff & C. Hall, 'Introduction', in *Family Fortunes. Men and Women of the English Middle Class* rev. edn. (London: Routledge, 2002), pp. xiii–l; L. Davidoff, 'Gender and the "Great Divide": Public and Private in British Gender History', *Journal of Women's History* 15:1 (2003), 11–27; K. Gleadle, 'Revisiting *Family Fortunes*: Reflections on the Twentieth Anniversary of the Publication of L. Davidoff & C. Hall (1987) Family Fortunes: Men and Women of the English Middle Class, 1780–1850', *Women's History Review* 16:5 (November 2007), 773–82.

98 C. Midgley, 'Can Women Be Missionaries? Envisioning Female Agency in the Early Nineteenth-Century British Empire', *Journal of British Studies* 45:2 (2006), pp. 335–58, 348–9; Taylor (1983), pp. 123–8.

99 S. Lewis, *Woman's Mission* 7th edn (London: John W. Parker, 1840) (first published 1839) pp. 50, 15.

100 See, for example, James (1852), pp. 49–66.

101 For overviews of the historiography, see S. Mumm, 'Women and Philanthropic Cultures', in Morgan & de Vries (2010), 54–71; R. A. Semple, 'Professionalising their Faith: Women, Religion and the Cultures of Mission and Empire', in Morgan & de Vries (2010), pp. 117–37.

102 Taylor (1983), pp. 28–30.

103 H. Rogers, 'Poetesses and Politicians: Gender, Knowledge and Power in Radical Culture, 1830–1870' (unpublished doctoral thesis, University of York, 1994), p. 18.

104 Sara Hennell was the only Freethinker in this study to develop a comprehensive Freethinking version of 'woman's mission'. She believed that women would play a key role in ushering in the new Freethinking religious order, see S. S. Hennell, *Present Religion as Faith Owning Fellowship with Thought* 3 vols (London: Trubnor and Co., 1865, 1873, 1887) iii (1887), p. 289; *The Women's Penny Paper (PP)*, 6 July 1889, p. 10, 20 July 1889, p. 5.

105 B. Heeney, *The Women's Movement in the Church of England 1850–1930* (Oxford: Clarendon, 1988), p. 7.

106 C. Yonge, *Womankind* (1876), quoted in Gill (1994), p. 80.

107 Gill (1994), p. 82.

108 For this argument, see R. Gouldbourne *Reinventing the Wheel. Women and Ministry in English Baptist Life* (Oxford: Whitley Publications, Regents Park College, 1997–98).

109 T. Larsen, '"How Many Sisters Make a Brotherhood?" A Case Study in Gender and Ecclesiology in Early Nineteenth-Century English Dissent', *Journal of Ecclesiastical History* 49:2 (1998), 282–92, 288–9.

110 Watts (1998), pp. 77–80. See also Gleadle (1995), p. 102.

111 Heeney (1988), pp. 5–6, 27–8. For Baptist women's church work, see M. Farningham, *A Working Woman's Life: An Autobiography* (London: James Clarke & Co., 1907). For other Non-conformist churches, see L. Wilson, *Constrained by Zeal: Female Spirituality Amongst Nonconformists, 1825–1875* (Carlile: Paternoster Biblical Monographs, 2000).

112 S. Stickney Ellis, *The Women of England, Their Social Duties and Domestic Habits* 9th edn (London: Fisher, Son & Co., 1839), p. 37.

113 J. Obelkevich, *Religion and Rural Society: South Lindsey 1825–75* (Oxford: Clarendon Press, 1976), p. 313.

114 H. McLeod, *Religion and the People of Western Europe, 1789–1970* (Oxford: Oxford University Press, 1981), esp. Chapter 2.

115 Historians have debated the reality of this supposed 'feminisation' of religion, though undoubtedly it was a powerful perception in the nineteenth century; see Davidoff & Hall (1987), pp. 107–8. Callum Brown has supported the idea that piety came to be gendered as overwhelmingly feminine during this period, but questioned the extent to which the urban male working class underwent mass secularisation; C. Brown,

The Death of Christian Britain. Understanding Secularisation, 1800-2000 (London: Routledge, 2001), pp. 9, 27-8.

116 Enthusiasm was defined by Ronald Knox as 'ultrasupernaturalism' or 'where an excess of piety threatens unity', whereby especially pious members of a particular faith seek to remake it in their own image, often causing schism; R. A. Knox, *Enthusiasm. A Chapter in the History of Religion: With Special Reference to the 17th and 18th Centuries* (London: Collins, 1987) (first published 1950), pp. 1-2. See also M. Heyd, '*Be Sober and Reasonable*', *The Critique of Enthusiasm in the Seventeenth and Early Eighteenth Centuries* (New York: E.J. Brill, 1995), pp. 3-4. Enthusiasm was also often associated with political radicalism; see L. Klein & A. La Volpa (eds.), *Enthusiasm and Enlightenment in Europe, 1650-1850* (San Marino, CA: Huntingdon Library, 1999), p. 1; J. Mee, 'Anxieties of Enthusiasm: Coleridge, Prophecy and Popular Politics in the 1790s', in Klein & La Volpa (1999), pp. 179-203; I. McCalman, 'Newgate in Revolution: Radical Enthusiasm and Romantic Counterculture', *Eighteenth-Century Life* 22:1 (1998), 95-110. Atheism and 'hyper-rationality' was also sometimes accused of enthusiasm; see Heyd (1995), p. 4; Klein & La Volpa (1999), p. 1.

117 For the gendered associations of enthusiasm, see Klein & La Volpa (1999), p. 5; S. Juster, 'Sinners and Saints: Women and Religion in Colonial America', in N. A. Hewitt (ed.), *A Companion to American Women's History* (Oxford: Blackwell Publishers, 2002), pp. 66-80; M. D. Sheriff, 'Passionate Spectators: On Enthusiasm, Nymphomania and the Imagined Tableau', in Klein & La Volpa (1999), pp. 51-83. To highlight the gendered element of enthusiasm is not to say that it was only applied to women: many of the earliest attacks on enthusiasm focused on men.

118 For the critique of enthusiasm, see Heyd (1995), p. 3.

119 Knox claimed that the word 'enthusiasm' was hardly used without inverted commas after 1823, though the Irvingites and Joanna Southcott both get a mention at later stages in his work; Knox (1950), p. 6. For post eighteenth-century discussions of enthusiasm, see C. Wilson, 'Enthusiasm and its Critics: Historical and Modern Perspectives', *History of European Ideas*, 17:4 (1993), 461-7.

120 See, for example, Eliza Sharples' descriptions of her early self as a 'slave' to Methodism, *Isis*, 11 February 1832, p. 7; Richard Carlile claimed that women's religiosity was a result of sexual frustration; see McCalman (1980), pp. 17-18. For Freethinking ridicule of the religious 'Old Maid' see *The National Reformer* (*NR*), 15 June 1861, p. 3.

121 D. Burfield, 'Theosophy and Feminism: Some Explorations in Nineteenth-Century Biography', in P. Holden (ed.), *Women's Religious Experience* (London: Croom Helm, 1983), pp. 27-56, 30-33. For *fin de siècle* esoteric religions, see also A. Owen, *The Place of Enchantment. British Occultism and the Culture of the Modern* (Chicago & London: University of Chicago Press, 2004); J. Dixon, *Divine Feminine: Theosophy and Feminism in England* (Baltimore: The Johns Hopkins University Press, 2001); J. Dixon, 'Modernity, Heterodoxy and the Transformation of Religious Cultures', in Morgan & de Vries (2010), pp. 211-30.

122 Dixon (2001), p. 4; Owen (2004), pp. 45-6.

123 Burfield (1983), p. 33; Dixon (2001), pp. 42-4; Owen (2004), pp. 8, 11.

124 A. Besant, *Why I Became a Theosophist* (London: Freethought Publishing Company, 1889), pp. 10–13, 17.

125 Dixon (2001), p. 68.

126 Owen (2004), p. 87.

127 For Christian motifs in the suffrage movement, see K. Hartman, '"What Made Me a Suffragette": the New Woman and the New (?) Conversion Narrative', *Women's History Review* 12:1 (2003), 35–50; B. Harrison, *Peaceable Kingdom: Stability and Change in Modern Britain* (Oxford: Clarendon Press, 1982), pp. 44–5; M. Vicinus, *Independent Women: Work and Community for Single Women, 1850–1920* (London: Virago, 1985), Chapter 7; J. de Vries, 'Transforming the Pulpit: Preaching and Prophecy in the British Women's Suffrage Movement', in B. Mayne Kienzle & P. J. Walker (eds.), *Women Preachers and Prophets Through Two Millennia of Christianity* (Los Angeles: University of California Press, 1998), pp. 318–34, 322.

128 *The Freewoman*, 7 December 1911, p. 52; 28 December 1911, pp. 101–2; 18 April 1912, p. 496; 23 May 1912, pp. 18–19; 8 August 1912, pp. 221–2.

129 *Secular Review (SR)*, 25 March 1877, pp. 59–60.

130 F. B. Smith, 'The Atheist Mission, 1840–1900', in R. Robson (ed.), *Ideas and Institutions of Victorian Britain. Essays in Honour of George Kitson Clark* (London: G. Bell & Son, 1967), pp. 205–35, 229, 207; H. McLeod, *Class and Religion in the Late Victorian City* (London: Croom Helm, 1974), p. 54; Royle (1995), pp. 172–3; Royle (1980), p. 136.

131 Mullen (1987).

132 Budd (1977), p. 45. Author's emphasis.

133 Mullen (1987), pp. 8, 13; Royle (1995), p. 196.

134 Royle (1980), p. 3.

135 E. Royle, 'Secularists and Rationalists, 1800–1940', in S. Gilley & W. J. Sheils (eds.), *A History of Religion in Britain: Practice and Belief from Pre-Roman Times to the Present* (Oxford: Blackwell, 1994), pp. 406–422, 407.

136 R. Wallis & S. Bruce, 'Secularisation: The Orthodox Model', in S. Bruce (ed.), *Religion and Modernisation. Sociologists and Historians Debate the Secularisation Thesis* (Oxford: Clarendon, 1992), pp. 8–30.

137 For a discussion of critiques of the secularisation thesis, see D. Nash, 'Reconnecting Religion with Social and Cultural History – Secularisation's Failure as a Master Narrative', *Cultural and Social History* 1:1 (2004), pp. 203–35.

138 Brown (1996); S. Williams, 'Religious Belief and Popular Culture: A Study of the South London Borough of Southwark c.1880–1939' (unpublished doctoral thesis, University of Oxford, 1993); S. Williams, 'The Language of Belief: An Alternative Agenda for the Study of Victorian Working-Class Religion', *Journal of Victorian Culture* 1:2 (Autumn 1996), 303–317.

139 J. Garnett, M. Grimley, A. Harris, W. Whyte & S. Williams (eds.), *Redefining Christian Britain: Post 1945 Perspectives* (London: SCM Press, 2007), pp. 1–2.

140 G. Davie, 'Sociology of Religion', in R. Segal (ed.), *The Blackwell Companion to the Sociology of Religion* (Oxford: Blackwell Publishing, 2006), pp. 171–91, 174–5; Morgan (1999), p. 26.

141 M. Saler, 'Modernity and Enchantment: A Historiographic Review', *The American Historical Review* 3:3 (June 2006), 692–716; Owen (2004).

142 Brown (2001), pp. 2, 79–80.

143 C. Taylor, *A Secular Age* (Cambridge, MA & London: The Belknap Press of Harvard University Press, 2007), p. 22.

144 Wallis & Bruce (1992), pp. 12–13.

145 C. Taylor, *Sources of the Self. The Making of the Modern Identity* (Cambridge: Cambridge University Press, 1989), pp. 396–401.

146 Taylor (1989), pp. 401–6; Taylor (2007), pp. 364–5.

1

Freethinking feminists:
women in the Freethought movement

H istorians have characterised Freethought as a largely masculine affair. The low levels of female involvement led David Nash to conclude that 'When looking at the role of women ... in secularism the historian is struck by their sheer absence.'[1] Yet organised Freethought did boast a small but active number of women who gained prominence as lecturers, journalists and authors, while research into local societies has suggested that there were some opportunities for women to participate in the movement at the rank and file level. Leading female Freethinkers were on the whole from the upper-working and lower-middle class (though a few came from wealthier backgrounds) and for them a commitment to Freethought often entailed financial insecurity. They combined their Freethinking views with adherence to a variety of radical causes, including, of course, women's rights. Their anti-religious beliefs reflected the cross-section of views found in the Freethought movement, ranging from militantly materialist atheism or 'this worldism', through pantheism or agnosticism which valued some notion of the 'spiritual', to different forms of theism. They were united, however, in their firm rejection of all forms of orthodox religion, especially Christianity.

The emblematic figure of the 'Freethinking feminist' was established early on by leading women in the Owenite movement, who continued to be looked up to by female Secularists later in the century when Freethought became more established and respectable. Although there is no evidence that it became harder for women to become involved in the movement as the century progressed (Freethinking women were always such a tiny minority that it is difficult to draw firm conclusions on this question), it does appear that feminists active in the later Secularist societies felt a greater pressure to conform to the ladylike stereotype of the domestic ideal. This study focuses on a core group of activist women who proselytised for Freethought in its organised and most militant forms. Yet such figures need to be situated within a wider spectrum of women who subscribed to a broad range of freethinking beliefs and who identified with organised Freethought to greater and lesser degrees. Freethinking ideas permeated the broader radical milieu and played a central role in the development of feminist thought during this period. A survey of Freethinking feminists also includes many leading figures from the early women's movement, highlighting the overlapping networks of Freethought and organised feminism.

Women's role in Freethought organisations

After the collapse of the Owenite movement in the mid-1840s, many of its branches were eventually absorbed into the structures of the new Secularism that George Jacob Holyoake was attempting to establish as a nationwide project. A number of these Secularist branches later signed up to the National Secular Society (NSS) or remained as independent local societies, some of which were loyal to the British Secular Union or Freethought League. The Secularist societies followed the Owenite branches in opening their meetings, lectures and membership of local societies to women, a practice relatively unusual among metropolitan radical clubs during this period.[2] Even more significantly, Secularism did not distinguish between male and female members in its committee structures.[3] Both men and women were permitted to run for executive positions in the NSS, the British Secular Union and the Freethought League. For example, Harriet Law became president of the Freethought League in 1869 and was repeatedly elected to (but declined) the position of vice president of the NSS.[4] Annie Besant was elected to this position in 1875, followed by Hypatia and Alice Bradlaugh in 1883. A similarly egalitarian approach to membership seems also to have existed at a local level. Leicester Secular Society, one of the only local societies for which extensive records survive, made sure to mention that 'persons of both sexes ... may join the Club, and shall ... be eligible to vote for the officers'. It was less clear whether women were permitted to stand for the position of the 'seven Committee-*men*'.[5] Although women were undoubtedly in the minority, it is also possible that the low figures for formal female membership reflect the fact that wives and daughters of fully paid male members could join for free (a practice common to may radical clubs of the period) and do not therefore appear on the registers.[6] On the other hand, male membership should not be taken to automatically indicate even passive support for Secularism from wives and daughters. At

Leicester, for example, the male members of the Gimson family played a prominent role in the local Secular society while their womenfolk continued to attend the Unitarian chapel.[7]

Freethought generated a dissident and often 'macho' intellectual culture, dominated by autodidacts and combative debaters. One possible reason for the low level of female membership in the Secularist societies was that women were put off by the emphasis on rationalist intellectualism and sharp ideological debate, which were at odds with Victorian and Edwardian constructions of femininity (though, as this study testifies, some women thrived in such an atmosphere).[8] Some Freethinkers also felt that women would respond more positively to their movement if it could offer a more emotive aspect, and they occasionally discussed introducing a greater element of ritual and feeling into their 'services'.[9] In the Secularist branches there was no lack of more traditionally 'feminine' activities on offer to female members. The more established Secular societies competed with local dissenting chapels and churches in offering their members a wide range of recreational and educational pastimes, opening up a whole new arena for female participation. Secularist women frequently taught in Secularist Sunday schools, where they might be responsible for the education of well over 100 students. This was the case for Rachael Clough, who, as a teacher at the Failsworth Secular Sunday School in the 1860s, was also in charge of the Christmas performance. Her pupils 'sang two hymns with credit to their tutor', while 'the female portion of the scholars took part in reciting and singing'.[10] Leicester Secular Society also put on a number of theatrical performances in which women took a leading role. The actress and Secularist Mrs Theodore Wright delivered the society's 'dedicatory' poem in 1879 and later performed a scene from *The Hunchback*.[11] Mrs Chadwick was also granted the platform in 1877 for 'the delivery of pieces of a secular character' and the collection of two pounds, four shillings and sevenpence was given to her as payment.[12] In London in 1856, a 'Ladies' Committee of the Bazaar' promoted the Christmas festivities as an activist opportunity for Secularist women. They published an 'Address' in *The Reasoner* in which they expressed the 'wish particularly to impress their lady friends with this opportunity of testifying their sympathy in the progress of Freethought'.[13]

It was common, in many nineteenth-century reform movements, for women to politicise ostensibly auxiliary roles such as fundraising and tea parties.[14] What distinguished the position of women in Freethought was that they were not compelled to subvert seemingly apolitical roles in order to acquire the influence denied them elsewhere since, in theory, the political leadership of the movement was open to them. Nevertheless, in November 1876 a group of Secularist women met in London and formed the Ladies' Secularist Association.[15] Their meeting resolved 'that an association should be formed, to enable ladies of liberal views to co-operate in promoting the mutual improvement of women in matters pertaining to the educational, social, and political advancement of their sex'. It is not clear whether it was intended to exist as a separate women's section within the NSS (comparable to the Ladies' National Association in the campaign for the repeal of the Contagious Diseases Acts or the National Reform League Ladies' Committee in the agitation leading up to the 1867 Reform Act) or as a Secularist association specifically devoted to women's rights.[16] The latter seems more likely, given that women could sit alongside men on the central executive committees. Nevertheless, the establishment of the Ladies' Secular Association does suggest that perhaps some women felt the need to organise separately within the movement with other members of their sex.[17]

However, it was also possible for some women active in the rank and file of the movement to take on roles indistinguishable from those of their male counterparts. Mrs Lipsham, for example, sat on the executive of Liverpool Secular Society and appeared frequently in reports of meetings in the northwest in the late 1860s. Lipsham seems to have been the most active of all the Liverpool members in promoting Freethought.[18] Public lecturing was not limited to the handful of women who became famous for it, but was also carried out in a more localised manner by less high-profile women. In the late 1840s *The Reasoner* printed verbatim the speeches of some of these lesser-known female speakers, and in 1846 launched a financial appeal for a Mrs Emery – a former lecturer now facing destitution.[19] In the later Secularist movement, Mrs Lipsham spoke on 'Female Education' and 'The Temperance Question', while a Louisa Wade cropped up repeatedly in reports in *The National Reformer*, lecturing on women's rights at various East End political clubs in 1869 and 1870.[20] Leicester Secular Society hosted local female speakers as well as the better-known Annie Besant and Harriet Law. In 1889, for example, a Mrs Mary Snowdon lectured on 'The Origin and Growth of Religions as Illustrated by the Ancient Babylonians'.[21] Women might also exert financial influence, particularly in societies struggling to raise funds to build an independent Secularist venue. Clara King ('spinster') and Mary Jane Bray ('school girl') both owned shares in Leicester Secular Society, though they were two of only four women enrolled as members for the period 1873–83.[22]

Early Freethinking and Owenite feminists c. 1830–50

Prominent female Freethinkers active in the first half of the nineteenth century laid the foundations for a continuous tradition of Freethinking feminism and became icons for subsequent generations of women. The Secularist lecturer Harriet Law, for example, was applauded in 1870 for 'filling the gap left in our ranks' by the death of Frances Wright, who had performed a similar role 40 years before.[23] Wright (1795–1852) was the first woman to gain notoriety as a Freethought lecturer. She was born in Scotland and travelled to America in her twenties where she met Robert Owen at New Harmony.[24] She was immediately converted to Owenism and was soon making plans to invest her entire personal fortune in a similar co-operative community in Tennessee. The Nashoba Community was established in 1825 by a colony of enslaved people bought by Wright, who intended that they should spend five years working out their freedom through communal labour. By this time, Wright had rejected the Established Church in which she had been brought up, and embraced Freethought. She described herself in 1828 as 'no Christian, in the sense usually attached to the word. I am neither Jew nor Gentile, Mahomedan nor Theist; I am a member of the human family.'[25] The Nashoba community was explicitly secular, and although religious individuals were not barred from it, they were advised 'to examine the extent of their liberality before entering the precincts of a society whose opinions might wound those feelings.'[26] The community also committed itself to sexual egalitarianism, including a rejection of the Christian institution of marriage. Wright set out to proclaim her Freethinking feminist views in her series of 'Popular Lectures', which she delivered in a number of US states. Her fearsome attacks on the religious revival which was at that time sweeping America, not to mention her penchant for wearing bloomers on stage, gained her notoriety in her adopted country and great admiration from Freethinking Owenites back in Britain.[27]

Frances Wright became a role model for another early female public advocate of Freethought, Eliza Sharples.[28] Sharples (1803–52) also saw her own work as contributing to a female Freethinking tradition, and she frequently expressed the hope that her example might encourage other 'ladies' to ascend the public platform as Reason's warriors in the battle against superstition.[29] The daughter of an affluent counterpane manufacturer from Bolton, Sharples had little experience of radical politics until her career as a public Freethought lecturer was launched in London in 1832. She had been a pious Methodist up until her early twenties, when the death of her beloved father invited the spectre of doubt.

Shortly after this bereavement, in December 1831, she encountered Richard Carlile's magazine the *Republican*, which caused her to lose her faith and strike up a correspondence with its editor. Carlile wrote from his gaol cell in Giltspur Street, where he was serving a two-year sentence for his Freethinking activities. Sharples felt herself to be in a similar position of confinement, as an unmarried woman obliged to spend all her time nursing her ailing mother and surrounded by 'strict religionists' with whom she now had nothing in common. In January 1832, she accepted Richard Carlile's offer to join him in London as his pupil and 'missionary' for Freethought. Carlile directed Sharples in her new career as 'Lady of the Rotunda', where, cast in the role of the Egyptian Goddess Isis, she performed a series of 'discourses' attacking established religion and expounding instead her own distinctive form of theism. She also argued in favour of the Reform Act, and, most vehemently, for women's rights. Her lectures were printed in the journal the *Isis*, which she edited for most of 1832.

During this period Sharples and Carlile were joined in a 'moral union'. Carlile was still legally married to his first wife, Jane, from whom he was separated. After the birth of the first of their three children in 1833, most of Sharples' time was taken up with raising her family, though she continued to take Carlile's place on the platform when his asthma prevented him from performing. In 1843 Carlile died intestate, leaving his family destitute. Sharples was reduced to pleading for support from the Freethought movement, and she was eventually set up as manageress of a Freethinking coffee house and discussion room in Hackney, London. It was here that she met the young Charles Bradlaugh, who had been recently disowned by his parents for adopting freethinking views. Sharples invited him to stay with her and her children, despite the fact that 'motives of economy' imposed a 'strict vegetarian' diet on the household.[30] Sharples, however, did not succeed at business and she died in 1852, exhausted by twenty years of poverty.[31]

The career of Eliza Macauley (1785[?]–1837) was also marked by the necessity to employ her literary and theatrical skills not only in the battle against superstition, but also in the struggle to make ends meet. Women such as Macauley and Sharples have been described as part of the 'uneasy' classes, those trying to earn a living in the cultural industries as journalists, booksellers or writers of political propaganda.[32] These 'sub-professions' played an important part in metropolitan radicalism during the early part of the century, alongside artisans and small tradespeople. Many Freethinking women active in the Owenite movement came from these kinds of upper-working and lower-middle class backgrounds, 'right on the edge of bourgeois gentility, at the point where gruelling work and poverty blurred the line between themselves and the lower orders'.[33] Eliza Macauley began life as the daughter of a poor man, who died when she was only two years old, leaving his family destitute. In her teens, she began to scratch a living as an actress performing in country barns and then moving to London in 1805. Her first appearance as a political preacher in a 'Jacobinical' chapel in Grub Street followed her failure as an actress in the more prestigious Covent Garden venues. She soon moved on to Owenite platforms, where she attacked the selfish doctrines of orthodox Christianity, condemned the oppression of women, and championed the Co-operative movement. Macauley and Sharples were known to each other, and in 1832, when Macauley was first wavering in her former faith and 'beginning to doubt the reality of the gospel dream', Sharples suggested that Macauley join her in the Rotunda.[34] Throughout the 1820s and 1830s Macauley continued to try her hand at a variety of literary pursuits, including a collection of essays on 'poetical effusions'. Like Sharples, however, she never achieved financial security and her 1835 memoirs were written from Marshalsea debtors' prison. She died two years later, while on lecture tour in York.[35]

Margaret Chappellsmith (1806–83) followed Sharples and Macauley in becoming a prominent Freethought propagandist. Chappellsmith was more closely allied with the Owenite movement, having been converted from the Baptism of her youth to Socialism by her first encounter with Robert Owen's ideas. In 1836 she began writing political articles for *The Dispatch* on communitarianism, women's position and political economy – themes that would become enduring interests throughout her long career. In 1839 she was employed as an Owenite social missionary, and she toured the country lecturing on the evils of Christianity. Chappellsmith was among the more hard-line anti-religionists in the Owenite movement, and she sided with George Jacob Holyoake and Charles Southwell in 1841–42, when the Owenite leadership attempted to repress the more militant Owenite attacks upon religion. Chappellsmith joined the Anti-Persecution Union (APU) and was active in supporting the *Oracle of Reason* martyrs. In 1850, she emigrated to Indiana, USA, along with her husband, and does not appear to have contributed to British radicalism after that date. She remained politically active, however, and continued to write articles for the *Boston Investigator*, some of which strongly condemned Robert Dale Owen for returning to what she believed to be superstitious religion.[36]

Chappellsmith was accompanied in her work as a social missionary by Emma Martin (1811/2–1851). Born in Bristol to a cooper and the daughter of prosperous yeoman stock, Martin received a 'conventional religious upbringing' in the Established Church, but joined the Particular Baptists at the age of seventeen.[37] In 1831 she began earning a living conducting a 'Ladies' Seminary', and she continued teaching after her marriage that same year to Isaac Martin, a grocer and fellow Particular Baptist.[38] In 1839 she lost her faith and became a Socialist following a series of debates with the Owenite Alexander Campbell. Martin then decided to leave her unhappy marriage and to take her three daughters to live in London. By 1840 she was employed as an Owenite social missionary and her lectures on feminism and religion soon earned her a reputation as one of the most intransigent and outspoken advocates of Freethought and women's rights. She also formed a 'moral union' with a fellow Owenite with whom she had another daughter, although she remained legally married to her former husband. Despite her fame and success as a lecturer and tract writer, Martin was edged out of the movement after she too lent her support to Holyoake and Southwell, and helped to establish the APU. In 1845 she resigned her position as social missionary and looked for other ways to support her four daughters. She trained to be a midwife, conducted lessons in 'female physiology', advertised the service of 'hot and cold baths' from her house, and, like Sharples, was also compelled to appeal to the public for funds. She died of consumption in 1851. A militant atheist until the end, she was reported to have been reading George Eliot's translation of Strauss' *Leben Jesu* on her deathbed.[39] Martin remained, however, famous within the Freethought movement long after her death and, like the other Owenites discussed here, posthumously inspired a subsequent generation of Freethinking feminists.

Freethinking feminists in the Secularist movement, c. 1850–1914

The 1820s, 1830s and 1840s were times of significant social and economic upheaval, generating an explosion of radical visions of a new moral world. Against this backdrop, we can see how a handful of women from undistinguished backgrounds might have felt inspired not only to reject their former religion, but also to publicly declare their newfound intellectual freedom and advocate that others should follow them. From the late 1840s, however, the Owenite and Chartist movements began to fall apart, making way for a period of relative political stability in the middle decades of the century.[40] Christian lady philanthropists and respectable, middle-class women's rights campaigners are more likely to occupy the pages of a historical study of the 1850s, 1860s and 1870s than

Freethinking militants in the style of Margaret Chappellsmith or Emma Martin.[41] Some historians have suggested that women were driven out of radical politics in the second half of the nineteenth century[42], yet within the Freethought movement it appears that there was still a place for the more outspoken, intransigent brand of female activism practised by the early Freethinking feminists. The Secularist propagandist Harriet Law certainly thought so. When Law embarked on her lecturing career in the 1860s she was applauded for following in the footsteps of the late Emma Martin, and in 1877, as chief editor of the *Secular Chronicle,* she printed a glowing eulogy to her famous predecessor.[43] We therefore see many themes of the earlier period – financial instability, unconventional family arrangements, and self-consciously militant public personas – re-emerging in the lives of feminists in the Secularist movement.

The early life of Harriet Law (1831–97) followed a similar pattern to her Owenite predecessors. Born in Ongar, Essex, to a farmer and refreshment manufacturer, her family was forced to move to London after losing most of their money through unfortunate investment. Law took a job teaching in a Sunday school in order to help support her family, and eventually she was able to start her own establishment.[44] In 1851 she was baptised into the Particular Baptist Church, the same church that Emma Martin had rejected a little over ten years earlier.[45] After a brief period of challenging East End Secularists with Christian arguments, she became convinced by the views of her opponents and joined their ranks. In 1855 she married Edward Law, a property dealer who was undergoing a similar loss of faith. They settled in South London and became active in Walworth Freethought Institute. Edward helped to care for their children while Harriet became a salaried Freethought lecturer, touring the local Secular societies that had begun to grow up around Britain.[46] Like her predecessors, Harriet was committed to the furthering of women's rights, and she spoke on 'Love, Courtship and Marriage' and the 'Degraded and Depressed Condition of Woman caused by Religion and Ignorance' to numerous audiences.[47] Her lectures over two decades spanned a wide range of political, feminist, and anti-religious topics, which showed off her encyclopaedic knowledge of Scripture and ability to ruthlessly dissect the arguments of her opponents. Holyoake described Law as 'the best debater of all the ladies on Freethought platforms' and although others felt that she was eclipsed after 1874 by the rising star of Annie Besant, Law was generally considered to be a talented, witty and courageous public speaker.[48]

In 1876 Harriet Law took over the editorship of the *Secular Chronicle,* declaring that from now on it would promote the 'atheist' position.[49]

Over the next three years, she defined this atheism in primarily negative terms through her opposition to all forms of religion. Her journalism suggests that she subscribed to a straightforward form of 'this-worldism', the simplified understanding of materialism common to many of the more militant Freethinkers, which insisted that man was shaped only by the natural world and that nothing beyond this existed or mattered. Law was equally critical of literalist evangelical forms of Christianity and of its more liberal manifestations. Rather than applaud the efforts of the liberal Anglican authors of *Essays and Reviews* (1860) to promote a historical approach to Scripture and question the doctrine of eternal punishment, Law simply declared that their more humane interpretation placed them outside the Christian Church.[50] Law posited an eternal battle between the forces of 'science' and those of 'religion' and dismissed as deluded those Christians who welcomed new developments in science and sought to reconcile them with a modified form of Christianity.[51] Religion, in her view, was opposed to humanity's natural thirst for knowledge and was used by the powerful as a form of social control.[52] Law's critique of Christianity was more concerned with pointing out Scriptural inconsistencies and the foolish reasoning of Church doctrine, than with putting forward an alternative Freethinking theology or metaphysics. Instead, her vision for an alternative society was firmly rooted in the material world and expressed through her commitment to 'socialism', 'republicanism' and 'utilitarianism'.[53]

Under Harriet Law's editorship, the *Secular Chronicle* took on 'Liberty, Equality and Fraternity' as its new motto. She also established a regular 'Ladies Page' dedicated to discussing 'those social, political and domestic matters that especially affect women' and to furthering their 'emancipation'.[54] Law was considered by her contemporaries to be firmly on the 'left' of the Freethought movement, and although she had been active in the agitation leading up to the 1867 Reform Act, her political commitments extended beyond the radical liberalism that characterised the mainstream of the Secularist organisations.[55] Law had been elected as the only female member of the general council of the First International in 1867 and in 1878 a biography of Karl Marx appeared on the front page of the *Secular Chronicle*.[56] The article noted the 'dread' with which the ruling class apprehended the International, and quoted with apparent approval the description of it given by the Spanish Minister of State, which maintained that it aimed to do away with the family, religion and the very social order upon which they were founded.[57]

Law also reported frequently on the progress of Socialism in Germany, particularly on the role of women in the Social Democratic

Party. 'When will the women of this country join the ranks of this civilising crusade?' she asked, pointing to her relative isolation as one of the few British women prominent in both Socialism and Secularism.[58] She appears to have supported Marx in the International, and she printed his reply to criticisms from the trade union leader and fellow International member George Howell, when he was refused publication elsewhere.[59] Yet Law's views also reflect the Owenite Socialism that still permeated the Secularist political outlook in the 1870s. Law applauded 'The highest and broadest kind of co-operation, as embodied in the communistic system of Robert Owen' and, as if in reply to the criticisms levelled by Marx, she maintained that Owen's writings on the land question were 'not from the pen of a Utopian philosopher, but are the utterances of an eminently practical man, who tested his theories.'[60] Law's Socialism was at odds with the radical individualism that dominated Secularism in the 1870s, powerfully advocated by Bradlaugh, who was a vocal opponent of Socialism. However, Law attempted to show her readers that a collectivist political vision did not have to contradict the pride that so many Freethinkers felt in their individual struggles to obtain an education and free themselves from the bondage of their religious upbringings. Instead, Law argued that 'communism (which is national co-operation) combines the strength of unionism, the zeal of patriotism, and resources of individualism …'.[61]

Harriet Law's daughters followed her into the Secularist movement. Florence Law (b. 1863) helped to establish the South London Ethical Society and Secular Sunday School in 1892, and was soon employed as its paid secretary.[62] In the 1870s, Harriet Teresa Law (c.1856–1941) was a frequent contributor to the *Secular Chronicle*, sharing her mother's radical politics and Freethinking views.[63] H. T. Law was a consistent critic of British imperialism as well as the Christian ideology that she believed motivated it.[64] In 1876 she re-printed H. M. Stanley's account of the massacre at Bambireh in Central Africa, and noted dryly that he was kindly 'giving the Aborigines a choice between bible and bullets.'[65] Yet H. T. Law maintained that all religion, not just Christianity, was to blame for imperialist atrocities and international conflict, for 'The history of a hundred generations proves that the Bible and the Koran have, by their precepts and examples, vitiated the minds of millions, and brought untold misery upon the world.'[66] This point was hammered home throughout the elder Law's editorship, and reports of the Turkish slaughter of Bulgarian Christians and discussions of the impending war with Russia never failed to point out that the Bible itself endorsed violence and therefore 'while men are influenced by religious prejudices those who differ from them will never be safe from outbursts of brutal violence.'[67] Taking this on board, H. T. Law was, like her mother, also a strong opponent of anti-Semitism.[68]

Although Harriet Law and her daughter were to the left of many Freethinkers and contemporary reform-minded readers, the *Secular Chronicle* printed an eclectic collection of views from across the radical spectrum. As well as Karl Marx, the 'Famous Freethinkers' series included biographies of William Cobbet, Charles Dickens, Giuseppe Mazzini and Louis Adolphe Thiers. Unfortunately, this did not achieve the desired result of higher circulation figures, and, after a couple of appeals for money, Harriet Law had to give up her editorship of the *Secular Chronicle* at the end of 1878, having lost £1,000.[69] As in the days of Sharples, Macauley and Martin, Freethinking feminists could still find themselves in dire financial straits. In response, one correspondent to the *Secular Chronicle* called for better economic support for the women of the movement, given the extreme sacrifices they made in deciding to take up the Secularist cause and the peculiarly vulnerable social and economic situation they found themselves in.[70]

Harriet Law retired from public life in 1879, possibly having been edged out of the Freethought movement by Bradlaugh, whose autocratic style she had always opposed. Law refused to become a member of the National Secular Society, despite being elected to (and turning down) the position of Vice President at a number of its annual conferences.[71] Instead, she became president of the Freethought League in 1869 and was one of the founders of the British Secular Union in 1877, both organisations independent of Bradlaugh.[72]

By contrast, Annie Besant's career as a Freethought lecturer flourished under the patronage of Charles Bradlaugh, with whom she formed a close partnership. Annie Besant (1847–1933) was born into an upper-middle-class family in London, whose financial prospects were damaged by the death of her father, a doctor, when Besant was five years old. Her mother was therefore grateful when a wealthy spinster, Ellen Marryat, offered to educate Besant. Marryat took the young Besant to live with her in Dorset, where she administered a strong dose of Anglican Evangelicalism combined with thorough grounding in Latin, French, German, history and geography. Annie Besant's genteel but extensive education contrasted with that of Harriet Law, who had been largely self-taught and whose main intellectual resource was the Bible.[73] Later in her teens Besant acquired a taste for the High Church ritual of the Oxford movement. When she was twenty she accepted an offer of marriage from the Rev. Frank Besant, though she later speculated that she had been more enamoured of his clerical status than his otherwise unexceptional personality.[74] They had two children – Digby, born in 1869, followed by Mabel in 1870. The marriage was an unhappy one that started to fall apart in 1871 when Besant began to undergo a crisis of faith prompted by the near-fatal illness of her daughter. In 1874 Besant left her husband and, taking only Mabel, went to live in London.

Besant had already published freethinking tracts before she encountered organised Secularism. She still considered herself a theist when she attended her first meeting of the National Secular Society, though, on meeting Bradlaugh 'We found that there was little real difference between our theological views, and my dislike of the name "Atheist" arose from my sharing in the vulgar error that the Atheist asserted "There is no God"', when in fact it could merely indicate an unwillingness to speculate on a matter for which it was impossible to come to an evidence-based conclusion.[75] It was not long, however, before Besant gave up all belief in a supernatural power and declared herself an atheist in the same vein as Bradlaugh. Besant began to contribute regularly to Bradlaugh's journal *The National Reformer*, under the name of Ajax, and Bradlaugh also organised her first public lecture in August 1874 on 'The Political Status of Women'.[76] Besant was soon renowned for her extraordinary powers of platform oratory, which, combined with her beauty and her exhaustive knowledge of theology and Scripture, won her a leading role in the Secularist movement. For the next ten years she toured the Freethought lecture circuit, combining attacks on the Christian Church with support for women's emancipation, on which she wrote numerous pamphlets and articles.

In 1877 Annie set up the Freethought Publishing Company with Bradlaugh in preparation for their re-publication of Charles Knowlton's 1832 birth-control pamphlet *Fruits of Philosophy*. Bradlaugh and Besant deliberately courted prosecution under the Obscene Publications Act in order to establish the right to circulate information about a cause they both supported. They lost the case but avoided imprisonment, and both felt they had successfully defended neo-Malthusianism and free speech. Success, however, came at a high price, for in 1878 Frank Besant succeeded in denying Annie custody of her daughter Mabel on the grounds that her views made her unfit to be a mother. In the 1880s Besant combined campaigning for Bradlaugh's right, as an atheist, to take his seat in parliament as MP for Northampton, with a developing interest in Socialism. In 1885 she became a member of the Fabian Society Executive and later supported Henry Hyndman's Social Democratic Federation. This placed a great strain on her relationship with Bradlaugh, and they engaged

Figure 1 Annie Besant, early in her Freethinking career (1878).

in a series of public debates over the future of Socialism, this time on opposing sides. In 1888 Besant again attracted national interest for her efforts in helping the match workers at the Bryant and May factory form the first all-women union. Besant's career as a Secularist ended finally in 1889 when she met Madame Helena Petrovna Blavatsky and converted to Theosophy.[77]

Kate Watts (1847/8–1924) was another leading female figure in the Secularist movement. She was one of the few prominent Freethinking feminists not to have converted from Christianity but to have been brought up by Freethinking parents.[78] The wife of the Secularist leader Charles Watts, she is best known for her supposed rivalry with Annie Besant, and in particular her opposition to Bradlaugh and Besant's decision to re-publish the Knowlton pamphlet.[79] Her *Reply to Mr. Bradlaugh* (1877) claimed that this was the first time she had appeared in print, though she embarked upon her lecturing career soon after.[80] In 1879 she wrote a series of articles in the *Secular Review* on 'The Education and Position of Women', attacking Christianity as the root of women's oppression and calling for better education and employment opportunities for women, which in turn would promote happier and more equal marriages.[81] Kate was promoted as the female figurehead of the anti-Bradlaugh faction; and while her husband branded the Bradlaughites mongers of smut, she cultivated a ladylike demeanour and primly condemned 'mannish' women's rights advocates.[82] Much of this was simply the rhetoric of internal division. Yet the need for greater respectability had long been voiced in the Secularist movement, and this in turn affected the role of its prominent female advocates.

It has been argued that the newly emerging Secularist organisations were deeply concerned to appear respectable, and to disassociate themselves from the accusations of sexual immorality that had haunted the Owenite movement.[83] The Secularist leaders did not wholly succeed in this, the movement retained a strong, if minority, tradition of libertinage throughout the century.[84] Moreover, the changes that Freethought culture underwent in the 1850s should not be overstated, since Owenite Freethinkers had also been concerned to stress that their critique of the marriage system was not intended to endorse sexual anarchy.[85] Nevertheless, the pressures on Freethinking feminists to conform to conventional feminine behaviour rose in response to increasingly entrenched notions of feminine domesticity. The marital status of leading Freethinking feminists at different points in the century is perhaps one indicator of this. In the 1830s and 1840s, Sharples and Martin both co-habited with men in free unions, whereas in the 1870s Watts and Law remained respectably married (although the fact that Harriet Law's husband was responsible for childcare suggests some continuation of older Owenite unorthodoxies into later Secularist domestic arrangements).[86] Annie Besant caused a scandal, just as Emma Martin had, by leaving her husband in order to become a Freethinker, yet unlike Martin and Sharples she never entered into a free union with Bradlaugh, despite their deep attachment.[87]

Not all of the women who contributed to the Secularist movement followed the path of public lecturer or are so easily identified with the tradition of militant agitator. Instead, women such as Sara Hennell and Sophia Dobson Collet participated in the movement as journalists and authors. Hennell and Collet occupied a more peripheral position within the Secularist organisations than those Freethinking feminists discussed so far, but although they never promoted themselves as 'party' women they nevertheless worked closely with its leaders. Sara Hennell (1812–99) was born into a liberal middle-class family in London. Her father had been a partner in a mercantile firm who died when she was young. Although he had insured his life for a sum that provided 'respectable maintenance to his widow and family', Hennell nonetheless described her childhood as one of 'straitened circumstances' if not actual poverty.[88] Hennell's family worshipped with the Unitarian congregation of Robert Aspland at Gravel Pit Chapel in Hackney, London. Unlike her brother, Charles Hennell, Sara Hennell was not sent away to school and so was denied 'instruction of a higher kind', but she was taught German, Latin, music, painting and drawing at home along with her sisters.[89] Informal religious and familial networks also supported Hennell's intellectual development. At 'after-supper conversations' she and her sisters would join in the 'critical discussion … habitual to us on all subjects that interested us', including 'the topic of Scripture history'.[90] It was in this environment that Hennell's religious views began gradually to shift towards Freethought, and in the 1830s she and her brother pursued a line of theological inquiry which led them to reject Unitarianism altogether. Charles went onto develop what he termed 'Christian Theism', which combined a belief in the God of nature or 'The Causing Mind' with respect for the morality of Christianity and in particular the figure of Jesus Christ.[91] But Sara Hennell moved beyond this to develop a highly distinctive form of natural religion that emphasised the continuing importance of faith in a post-Christian world.

In 1857 Hennell published her first book, *Christianity and Infidelity*, which took the form of a debate between the two viewpoints. In the guise of 'Infidel' Hennell put forward her own religious vision. Although she rejected all orthodox religions, she distinguished herself from 'some minds … which will simply rejoice in being freed from what to them was the tyranny of religion, and may well be called Atheistic in the negative sense'. Instead she defined herself as 'the idealist … the Pantheist, [who] conceives and therefore truly finds God everywhere.'[92] In subsequent publications she went on to reject all forms of theism and deism, insisting on the need for the free use of reason and arguing that all theological systems were nothing more than a projection of man's highest ideals. Yet she believed that doctrinal systems were needed to manifest this manmade religious feeling, and that the nineteenth century marked the next stage in the progressive development of 'general religion' so that a new theological framework would soon emerge to replace that of Christianity.[93] These beliefs positioned Hennell at the opposite end of the Freethought spectrum from atheists like Besant and Law, who rejected the idea of 'feeling' or 'faith' as autonomous forces, but her views remained within the scope of the Secularist movement. Hennell corresponded with George Jacob Holyoake in the 1850s and 1860s and requested that her works be reviewed in his journal *The Reasoner*, writing that she wished in particular to hear a 'Secularist' response.[94] Hennell had been interested in the woman question throughout her life, and her final work, *Present Religion*, discussed at length the relationship between her religious views and her vision of female emancipation. Hennell also wrote on this for the *Woman's Penny Paper* in the 1880s. She died at the family home in Coventry, presided over by her sister Caroline and Caroline's husband, the radical Charles Bray, in 1899.

Hennell's career draws attention to a point of intersection between popular, organised Freethought and the upper-middle-class intellectual milieu of 'honest doubters' typified by figures such as George Eliot and Francis Newman.[95] These were not distinct historical entities but over-lapping movements, although those higher up the social strata often sought themselves to disassociate their beliefs from the more vulgar secularism of organised Freethought.[96] Sara Hennell was a close friend of George Eliot, whose acquaintance with the Hennell and Bray families in Coventry provoked her own crisis of faith. Yet when Hennell recommended *The Reasoner* to Eliot, the author scorned the publication as 'imbecile' and sarcastically expressed her surprise at Hennell's 'friendly inclination towards it'.[97]

Sophia Dobson Collet (1822–94) was also born into these middle-class liberal dissenting circles, and was acquainted with both Hennell and Francis Newman.[98] In the 1840s she was close to many of the leading members of William Johnson Fox's South Place Unitarian chapel, which provided a central meeting point for metropolitan radicals of all shades, attracting Owenites, Unitarians, feminists and Freethinkers.[99] South Place was used as a venue for speakers with far more extreme Freethinking opinions than those of its radical Unitarian founders. Frances Wright, for example, was commissioned to give a series of lectures there in 1847, and the chapel was advertised every week in Holyoake's journal *The Reasoner* as a regular venue for Secularist events.[100] In 1864 the freethinking American preacher Moncure Daniel Conway took over as minister at South Place.[101] Conway knew many of the Secularists, including Sara Hennell and Sophia Dobson Collet, and when Besant left her husband she initially went to live with Conway and his wife.[102]

Through such networks Sophia made the acquaintance of George Jacob Holyoake, with whom she entered into regular correspondence. She was also a frequent contributor in the 1840s and 1850s to his journals

The Movement and *The Reasoner*, under the pseudonym 'Panthea'. Collet was perhaps the most 'religious' of all the Freethinking women in this study. Her rejection of the idea of an intelligent or personal God probably set her apart from the radical Unitarians at South Place Chapel, and yet in contrast to most Secularists, she argued that there was not sufficient evidence to rule out the possibility of a divine Creator.[103] The fact that she was a minority voice within organised Freethought did not dissuade her from offering frequent advice to its leaders, both in private letters to Holyoake, whom she bombarded with suggestions for 'further reading', and in her published critiques of the movement.[104] She defended Secularism, even in the face of criticism from William Johnson Fox, and argued that it was a profoundly moral movement.[105] Yet she believed that it was held back by the vulgar iconoclasm of men such as Charles Southwell and Richard Carlile. Instead, she championed the 'religious atheism' of Lionel Holdreth, another frequent contributor to *The Reasoner*, and urged the rest of the movement to move in this direction.[106]

Collet also contributed to the wider Freethought discussion of women's rights, and she published articles in *The Reasoner* in support of female education.[107] Like all Freethinking feminists, she condemned the oppression of women in Scripture and the subordinate position assigned to them by Christianity.[108] In the 1880s she was an active member of the Moral Reform Union, which campaigned for 'social purity' in the wake of the campaigns to repeal the Contagious Diseases Acts, and she also supported W. T. Stead when he was imprisoned for the undercover newspaper investigation he undertook in 1885, which entailed his procuring a young girl for the purposes of prostitution in order to expose the high levels of child prostitution in London.[109] Collet's religious views became increasingly orthodox as she grew older. She moved closer to the Christian Socialism of F. D. Maurice, probably from the late 1860s, and, following pressure from her sister, appears to have been baptised in 1870.[110] She did not lose interest in non-Christian forms of theism, however, and in the 1870s she published a number of works on the Hindu reform movement, the Brahmo Somaj. She died in her London home in 1894, mourned, among others, by her friend and leading feminist Frances Power Cobbe.

By the 1890s the only really prominent Freethinking feminist still based in the Secularist movement was Charles Bradlaugh's daughter Hypatia Bradlaugh Bonner (1858–1935). She and her sister Alice (1856–88) spent most of their childhood in Sussex with their mother whose 'intemperance' (alcoholism) had led to their parents' separation in 1870.

Charles nevertheless remained an attentive father, and when Alice and Hypatia's mother died in 1877 they came to live with him in London where they began to help mobilise support during the Knowlton Trial. Hypatia's first public speech was a protest against the obscenity charges levelled at Bradlaugh and Besant, calling for complete freedom of the press. Charles also arranged for her to take over many of the editorial and financial responsibilities of *The National Reformer* in case of his imprisonment. The Bradlaugh sisters remained active in the Freethought movement throughout their lives. After studying at University College London, where they were among the very first women students admitted in 1877, they began to study and then teach (Hypatia in Chemistry and Alice in French) at the Old Street Hall of Science.

In 1885 Hypatia met and married one of her students, Arthur Bonner, who had been the son of a non-conformist minister before converting to Secularism. Following their engagement Arthur was employed as Charles Bradlaugh's printer while Hypatia continued to work, even after she gave birth to her son, as Charles' secretary. She also kept up her Freethought lecture tours, which took her all over the UK. Her husband was supportive of women's rights, claiming that his initial interest in the Hall of Science was due to their employing female instructors at a time when it was almost unheard of for women to teach mixed-sex classes. The couple also decided that she should keep her own name after marriage, joining it with that of her husband, to signal her 'individuality' within their union.

The first years of Hypatia's marriage were blighted by the deaths of her son, her sister and her father in close succession, but she remained active in a wide range of political causes, especially penal reform, opposition to capital punishment and international arbitration. She wrote extensively on such issues in *The Reformer*, an independent Freethought journal which she edited from 1896 to 1904. *The Reformer* also reported regularly on the progress of the women's rights cause, though most of Hypatia's work for the suffrage was carried out through her active membership of the Women's Liberal Association rather than the national suffrage societies. Increasingly dissatisfied with George Foote and the National Secular Society, she joined the short-lived Freethought Federation in 1896. In 1905 she was employed as a Rationalist Press Association lecturer, later becoming the only woman on their Board. As a founding member of the Rationalist Peace Association, Hypatia opposed the outbreak of the war in 1914 although two years later she and J. M. Robertson signed a statement recognising it as a war of defence: terrible yet necessary.[111]

Freethinkers in the women's movement

Speaking at a Rationalist Press Association dinner in 1907, Hypatia Bradlaugh Bonner remarked that she was now 'the solitary specimen of the woman Freethought advocate'.[112] She was referring, however, only to the lack of women active in the Secularist Party, for there were still, as there had always been, a number of female Freethinkers and Secularists who chose to make the women's movement, rather than organised Freethought, their primary political base.[113] For example, Harriet Martineau's career as a prolific journalist and author, populariser of political economy, anti-slavery campaigner and women's rights advocate, is well known, but her freethinking beliefs have received less attention from historians. Like many other Freethinking feminists, it was financial necessity that first compelled Martineau into serious intellectual labour. Martineau (1802–76) was born into a middle-class Unitarian family in Norwich, the daughter of a cloth manufacturer, but in 1829 the family firm failed. She rejected work as a governess and decided instead to earn a living through her writing. Her career proved more successful and profitable than that of many of the other women studied here, and in 1832 she was able to move to London, where she enjoyed family connections in the same radical circles in which Hennell and Collet also moved. In 1851, Martineau publicly declared her atheism in *Letters on the Laws of Man's Nature and Development* and she later became a critical supporter of the Positivist philosophy of Auguste Comte.[114]

Although Martineau was never publicly associated with organised Freethought, the Secularist movement sought to benefit from her fame and to claim her as one of their own.[115] Female Secularists in particular looked to her as a pioneering figure. Harriet Law delivered a lecture on 'Harriet Martineau: the Great Heroine of Freethought' in 1877, while her daughter, Harriet Teresa Law, reviewed Martineau's autobiography for the *Secular Chronicle*.[116] The Freethinking feminist Florence Fenwick Miller (1854–1935) also took Martineau as a subject for one of her lectures.[117] Born in Hackney, Fenwick Miller irritated her comfortably-off parents by insisting on entering the medical profession at the age of seventeen. She studied at the Ladies' Medical College, an institution supported by a number of prominent Secularists, at a time when other universities were strongly resistant to allowing women to study medicine.[118] She had already lost her faith by this point, having begun at the age of thirteen to question the Anglicanism in which she had been raised, and she readily took up the Freethinking views of her teacher, the Secularist Dr Charles Drysdale. Drysdale took Fenwick Miller to the Dialectical Society – a debating society committed to freedom of thought and discussion – where she met Annie Besant and Charles Bradlaugh. Fenwick Miller's natural talent for public speaking soon became apparent, and she left medicine to pursue a career as a lecturer, speaking both in Freethinking venues and for the National Society for Women's Suffrage. In 1877 she was one of the first women to be elected to the London school board, where she remained until 1885 in spite of attempts to remove her after she publicly supported Besant and Bradlaugh's decision to publish the Knowlton pamphlet. Fenwick Miller was also a prolific journalist and between 1895 and 1899 she assumed editorship and proprietorship of the leading feminist periodical *The Woman's Signal*.[119]

Another freethinking feminist, Frances Power Cobbe (1822–1904), was quite atypical of the other women discussed here.[120] She was born into an Anglo-Irish landed family whose wealth allowed her to enjoy a standard of living inconceivable to women such as Harriet Law or even Sara Hennell.[121] Moreover, her conservative political views were strongly opposed to those of other Freethinking feminists.[122] Cobbe suffered a crisis of faith that began at the age of seventeen and lasted for four years, during which she discarded Anglicanism in favour of Agnosticism. Soon after, an encounter with the work of the American Transcendentalist Theodore Parker left her happily affirmed as a theist with a strong belief in the existence of a Divine Being, a moral law and an afterlife.[123] Nevertheless, when Cobbe informed her father of her new belief system, following the death of her mother, he banished her from the family home for a year and threatened to disinherit her. Despite her heterodox views and personal experience of persecution, Cobbe remained hostile to the organised Freethought movement. She disliked the materialist view of the world advanced by many Secularists and this intensified later in her life when she launched a crusade against the medical establishment and professional science.[124] It is also likely that Cobbe found the Secularist movement vulgar: Besant reported that her lecture on the 'Political Status of Women' had horrified Cobbe, who was in the audience at the Unitarian chapel where Besant spoke. Cobbe's objections were ostensibly metaphysical, but the strength of her complaint suggests that she was also repelled by the unrestrained attacks on Christianity contained in the lecture.[125] Nevertheless, Cobbe published a number of works discussing her freethinking religious beliefs, including her first book *The Theory of Intuitive Morals*, and Besant read Cobbe's essays during her own crisis of faith.[126] Both Annie Besant and Harriet Law also subsequently debated Cobbe on the subject of Freethought.[127]

In spite of a strong connection between Freethought and the women's movement, not every prominent woman who held Freethinking views became a feminist. At least one, Eliza Lynn Linton (1822–98), became one of feminism's most ardent opponents. In her youth, Lynn Linton had been a passionate defender of women's rights and had viewed herself as 'one of the vanguard of independent women', but from the late 1860s she became increasingly conservative and eventually turned against, what she termed, the 'shrieking sisterhood'. Lynn Linton was the daughter of an affluent Anglican clergyman who, after an intensely religious childhood, had lost her faith at the age of fourteen and remained an agnostic for the rest of her life.[128] She moved to London at the age of twenty-three, determined to find success as a writer. There she met George Eliot, whom she disliked, and Sara Hennell, who did not like her.[129] Eliza Lynn married the engraver and radical republican William James Linton (the marriage was a disaster), and through him became life-long friends with Holyoake.[130] Her 1872 bestseller, *Joshua Davidson*, contained a damning condemnation of the Established Church that was greatly enjoyed by both Holyoake and Bradlaugh, who admired her in spite of her anti-feminist position.[131]

Freethinking women were, on the whole, however, closely identified with feminism and strongly represented in the suffrage movement throughout the period. The Freethinking Elizabeth Wolstenholme Elmy (1833–1918) was never active in the Secularist movement, but she had strong links with it and in 1874 she married Ben Elmy, Vice President of the National Secular Society.[132] Wolstenholme Elmy was born in the Manchester area to a Methodist minister and his wife. Her parents did not believe in female education and after their death her guardians refused to allow her to attend Bedford Women's College, while her brother went off to Cambridge to begin a successful academic career. Orphaned at fourteen, Wolstenholme Elmy struggled to earn a living from the girls' boarding school that she established while still in her teens. She combined this with political activity, supporting the employment and education of women. From 1869 onwards her increasing inclination towards Freethought prevented her from taking up a prominent position in female educational institutions and in 1872 she gave up her school in Congleton in the realisation that it would not be possible to continue as a teacher once her heterodox religious beliefs had been made public.[133] Wolstenholme Elmy became acquainted with Annie Besant and Charles Bradlaugh, who came to stay with her and Ben Elmy at Congleton in 1876. On this occasion Wolstenholme Elmy was the victim of an attack by an angry 'Christian' mob who wished to drive the Secularists out of their village.[134]

Wolstenholme Elmy chose to dedicate her political career to women's rights, rather than to Secularism, though she remained critical of the role of religion in oppressing the female sex.[135] She campaigned for women's property rights, the repeal of the Contagious Diseases Acts and for women's suffrage. Between 1871 and 1874 Wolstenholme Elmy combined her commitment to freedom of thought with her concern for civil equality for women, working as paid secretary of the Vigilance Association for the Defence of Personal Rights. She and Ben Elmy both supported birth control and sex education for women, and in 1894 they published *The Human Flower*, one of the first sex education books for children.[136] In 1889 Wolstenholme Elmy founded the Women's Franchise League, which demanded the vote on equal grounds with men, in opposition to Lydia Becker and Millicent Garrett Fawcett's wish to campaign only for the enfranchisement of single women. Other Freethinking members included Florence Fenwick Miller and the leading US feminist Elizabeth Cady Stanton and her London-based daughter Harriet Stanton Blatch.[137] Wolstenholme Elmy left due to personal disagreements in 1890 to form the Women's Emancipation Union on a very similar political basis. This organisation also had a strongly Secularist membership including George Jacob Holyoake, his sister Caroline Holyoake Smith, and Lady Florence Dixie.[138]

As suffrage campaigns grew into a mass movement in the early twentieth century, Freethinking women were often to be found on its more radical fringes. The Women's Freedom League, which in 1907 split with the Pankhurst's Women's Social and Political Union in protest against their autocratic leadership, was supported by Alice Vickery (1844–1929) and her daughter-in-law Bessie Drysdale (1871–1950), both outspoken Secularists. Vickery's association with Freethought was longstanding. The daughter of a South London piano-maker, she began to earn her living while still in her teens as a pupil teacher, possibly at the Secularist William Ellis endowed school in Camberwell. In 1869 she began to study alongside Florence Fenwick Miller at the Ladies Medical College, under the tutelage of Charles Drysdale with whom she formed a free union. She gained a midwifery certificate in 1873 before travelling to Paris to qualify as a doctor, finally completing her training at the London Medical School for Women from 1877. That same year she testified in support of Besant and Bradlaugh during the Knowlton Trial and became a member of the Council of the newly formed Malthusian League. For the next twenty-five years the British birth-control movement was to be dominated by Alice, Charles, their son Charles Vickery-Drysdale and his wife Bessie Ingman Edwards.[139]

The Vickery-Drysdales were active within a sex radical milieu beginning to cohere towards the end of the nineteenth-century which overlapped (and also clashed) with the feminist and Freethought movements. Mona Caird (1854–1932), whose famous journalistic assault on marriage in the *Westminster Review* (1888) came to exemplify the sexual rebellion of the New Woman, was also a self-proclaimed Freethinker although she was not associated with any Secularist organisation.[140] Jane Clapperton (1832–1914) likewise condemned marriage, questioned the value of monogamy, and supported birth control. Like Caird, she was not aligned to any Freethought party, but she published books and articles arguing for Christianity to give way to a new non-theistic 'religion' of 'scientific meliorism' based upon humanity's ability to evolve, via correct educational and environmental conditions, towards a state of 'social love'.[141] Clapperton, Caird, and Vickery were all associated with the Legitimation League (est. 1893), which supported free unions between men and women and whose membership was heavily dominated by Secularists.[142] This later generation of Freethinkers served to bridge *fin de siècle* sex radicalism and the pre-war feminist *avant-garde*. Charles Vickery and Bessie Drysdale, for example, wrote for the feminist Free Love periodical *The Freewoman* (1911–13), as did Guy Aldred, Rose Witcop and Stella Browne, Freethinkers now better remembered as leading advocates of birth control in the inter-war period.

Conclusion

In spite of the very small numbers of women involved in organised Freethought, a strong female Freethinking tradition did exist and was promoted and celebrated by the movement as a whole. Women in the Secularist societies laid claim to the achievements of their Owenite predecessors, and the earlier image of the Freethinking feminist as a militant combatant in the war over religion was reproduced later in the century. It was their desire for knowledge, truth and reason that motivated these women to challenge the boundaries of acceptable womanhood and brave the social ostracism that often accompanied their public repudiation of religion. Whatever their educational backgrounds, prominent female Freethinkers all exhibited a passion for learning and a desire to disseminate their ideas as widely as possible. Freethinking feminists also remained prominent in movements for the suffrage, marriage reform and birth control later in the century, providing a thread of continuity between the Victorian women's movement and the often more sexually radical feminism of the early twentieth century. The next chapter begins with an exploration of how the women who form the subject of this study came to Freethought in the first place. They hailed mostly from religious backgrounds before experiencing a violent and life-changing 'conversion' to Freethought. Chapter 2 will discuss this process of 'counter-conversion' and explore how Freethinking feminists found themselves on the 'path to atheism'.

Notes

1 D. Nash, 'The Leicester Secular Society: Unbelief, Freethought and Freedom in a Nineteenth-Century City' (unpublished doctoral thesis, University of York, 1990), p. 226.
2 'Only the Secularists and O'Brianites appear to have accepted women at their clubs as of right ...'. Other radical clubs and societies catered primarily for men, whose wives and families might attend only at the weekend; see S. Shipley, *Club Life and Socialism in Mid-Victorian London*, History Workshop Pamphlets 5 (1971), pp. 21, 46.
3 E. Royle, *Radicals, Secularists and Republicans: Popular Freethought in Britain, 1866-1915* (Manchester: Manchester University Press, 1980), p. 246.
4 H. C. G. Matthew, 'Law [nee Frost], Harriet Teresa (1831–1897)', *Oxford Dictionary of National Biography* (online edn; Oxford University Press, 2004); *Secular Chronicle* (*SC*), 27 May 1877, p. 274.
5 Leicester Local Archive (LLA), Leicester Secular Society (LSS) Scrapbook 10D68/6, p. 4, emphasis added.
6 Leicester Secular Society specified that wives and children of male members could attend events and meetings for free, *Principles and Rules of the Leicester Secular Society* (Leicester: Geo Gibbons, 1884), p. 9.
7 Royle (1980), p. 130.
8 S. Budd, *Varieties of Unbelief: Atheists and Agnostics in English Society 1850–1950* (London: Heinemann, 1977), p. 50; Royle (1980), p. 250; Nash (1990), p. 227.
9 *The National Reformer* (*NR*), 12 January 1868, p. 27, 18 June 1871, p. 398. Quasi-religious rituals had long been part of Freethought culture. For an account of Secularist 'infant naming ceremonies', marriage ceremonies and burial services, see C. M. Davies, *Heterodox London: or, Phases of Freethought in the Metropolis* 2 vols (London: Tinsley Brothers, 1874) ii, 165–78.
10 *NR*, 7 February 1869, pp. 94–5.
11 LLA, LSS Minute Book 10D68/2, pp. 54–5.
12 *Ibid.*, p. 7.
13 *The Reasoner* (*Reasoner*), 16 November 1856, p. 159.
14 S. Morgan, 'Middle-Class Women, Civic Virtue and Identity: Leeds and the West Riding of Yorkshire, c.1830–c.1860' (unpublished doctoral thesis, University of York, 2000), p. 187.
15 Formally established January 1877.
16 *NR*, 10 January 1877, p. 28.
17 No other references to the Ladies Secular Association have been found in the sample surveys of Secularist journals carried out for this study.

18 *NR*, 24 October 1869, p. 268.

19 *Reasoner* 4: 94 (1848), pp. 222–4 [N.B. copies of *The Reasoner* held in the Bishopsgate Library for 1847–48 are not individually dated, only volume and number are listed.]; 29 July 1846, p. 141.

20 *NR*, 24 October 1869, p. 268, 16 May 1869, pp. 316, 27 June 1869, p. 411, 11 December 1870, p. 411.

21 LLA, LSS Scrapbook 10D68/6.

22 LLA, LSS Register of Members and Annual List Summary 10/D/68/15.

23 *NR*, 11 September 1870, p. 170.

24 For Frances Wright, see B. Taylor, *Eve and the New Jerusalem. Socialism and Feminism in the Nineteenth Century* (London: Virago, 1983), pp. 65–70; H. Heineman, 'Wright, Frances (1795–1852)', *Oxford Dictionary of National Biography* (online edn; Oxford University Press, 2004).

25 F. Wright, 'Lecture VI. Formation of Opinions', in F. Wright, *Course of Popular Lectures as Delivered by Frances Wright, in New York, Philadelphia, Baltimore, Boston, Cincinnati, St. Louis, Louisville, and other Cities, Towns and Districts of the United States. With Three Addresses on Various Public Occasions and a Reply to the Charges Against the French Reformers of 1789*, 4th edn (New York: Published at the Office of the Free Enquirer, Hall of Science, 1831) (first published 1828), pp. 127–49, 148.

26 F. Wright, *Fanny Wright Unmasked By Her Own Pen. Explanatory Notes. Respecting the Nature and Objects of the Institution of Nashoba and of the Principles Upon Which It Is Founded. Addressed to the friends of human improvement in all countries and of all nations*, 3rd edn (New York: C.N. Baldwin, 1830), p. 12.

27 There was a considerable amount of transatlantic dialogue between Freethinking feminists. Another prominent US figure was Ernestine Rose (1810–92), who came to England from Poland after rejecting the Jewish faith, and was involved in the Owenite movement before emigrating to the USA in 1836. For the next thirty years she was hailed as 'Queen of the Platform', active as a Freethought and feminist lecturer. She returned to England in 1869, where she remained until her death in 1892. Rose was friends with the leading US women's rights activist Elizabeth Cady Stanton, also a Freethinker and author of the *Woman's Bible* (1895/8), which was well received by Freethinking feminists in Britain. See C. A. Kolmerton, *The American Life of Ernestine L. Rose* (New York: Syracuse University Press, 1999); Y. Suhl, *Ernestine L. Rose: Women's Rights Pioneer* 2nd edn (New York: Biblio Press, 1990); *Reasoner*, 1 June 1856, p. 170, 8 June 1856, p. 181, 20 July 1856, p. 21, February 1871, pp. 21–2; Royle (1980), p. 250. For other US Freethinking feminists, see A. L. Gaylor (ed.), *Women Without Superstition. "No Gods– No Masters". The Collected Writings of Women Freethinkers of the Nineteenth and Twentieth Centuries* (Madison: Freedom from Religion Foundation, 1997); E. A. Kirkley, *Rational Mothers and Infidel Gentlemen: Gender and American Atheism, 1865–1915* (Syracuse, New York: Syracuse University Press, 2000).

28 T. Carlile Campbell, *The Battle of the Press, as Told in the Story of the Life of Richard Carlile* (London: A. & H.B. Bonner, 1899), p. 151.

29 *Isis*, 10 March 1832, p. 71, 7 April 1832, p. 136.

30 H. Bradlaugh Bonner, *Charles Bradlaugh: A Record of his Life and Work by his Daughter Hypatia Bradlaugh Bonner. With an Account of his Parliamentary Struggle, Politics and Teachings by John M. Robertson MP*, 7th edn (London: T. Fisher Unwin, 1908), pp. 19–20.

31 For the most detailed biographical account of Eliza Sharples, see Carlile Campbell (1899). See also E. Royle, 'Carlile, Elizabeth Sharples (1803–1852)', *Oxford Dictionary of National Biography* (online edn; Oxford University Press, 2004); H. Rogers, 'The Prayer, the Passion and Reason of Eliza Sharples: Freethought, Women's Rights and Republicanism', in E. Yeo (ed.), *Radical Femininity: Women's Self-Representation in the Public Sphere* (Manchester: Manchester University Press, 1998), pp. 52–78; H. Rogers, *Women and the People: Authority, Authorship and the Radical Tradition in Nineteenth-Century England* (Aldershot: Ashgate, 2000).

32 H. Rogers, 'Facing Her Public': The Actress, Eliza Macauley (1785–1837)' (unpublished manuscript), pp. 18–19.

33 Taylor (1983), p. 73.

34 *Isis*, 26 May 1832, p. 248.

35 B. Taylor, 'Macauley, Elizabeth Wright (1785?–1837)', *Oxford Dictionary of National Biography* (online edn; Oxford University Press, 2004). See also E. Macauley, *Autobiographical Memoirs of Miss Macauley* (London: the author, 1834); E. Macauley, *Autobiographical Memoirs of Miss Macauley written under the title of Elizabeth or "A Plain and Simple Tale of Truth"* (London: Charles Fox, 1835).

36 K. Gleadle, 'Chappellsmith, Margaret (1806–1883)', *Oxford Dictionary of National Biography* (online edn; Oxford University Press, 2004). For Chappellsmith's critique of religion at New Harmony, see *Reasoner*, 16 September 1857, p. 198; C. Kimberling, '"I am, dear sir, your grateful disciple Margaret Chappellsmith."', *Communal Studies. Journal of Communal Studies Association* 20 (2000), 26–44, 36–7.

37 E. Martin, *A Few Reasons for Renouncing Christianity and Professing and Disseminating Infidel Opinions* (London: Watson, 1850), p. 4.

38 G. Cowie & E. Royle, 'Emma Martin (1812–51), Socialist, Free Thinker and Women's Rights Advocate', in J. Bellamy & J. Saville (eds.), *Dictionary of Labour Biography* 12 vols (London & Basingstoke: Macmillan Press, 1972–) vi (1979), pp. 188–91.

39 G. J. Holyoake, *The Last Days of Mrs Emma Martin: Advocate of Free Thought* (London: J. Watson, 1851), p. 2; B. Taylor, 'Martin, Emma (1811/12–1851)', *Oxford Dictionary of National Biography* (online edn; Oxford University Press, 2004).

40 J. Belchem, *Popular Radicalism in Nineteenth-Century Britain* (London & Basingstoke: Macmillan Press, 1996), p. 82.

41 For the decline of Owenite feminism, see Taylor (1983), p. 276.

42 See D. Thompson, 'Women and Nineteenth-Century Radical Politics: A Lost Dimension', in J. Mitchell and A. Oakley (eds.), *The Rights and Wrongs of Women* (London: Croom Helm, 1976), pp. 112–38, 136–8; H. Rogers, 'Poetesses and Politicians: Gender, Knowledge and Power in Radical Culture, 1830–1870' (unpublished doctoral thesis, University of York, 1994), p. 23; Rogers (1998), pp. 69–74.

43 *NR*, 11 September 1870, p. 170; *SC*, 9 September 1877, pp. 121–2.

44 H. C. G. Matthew, 'Law [nee Frost], Harriet Teresa (1831–1897)', *Oxford Dictionary of National Biography* (online edn; Oxford University Press, 2004).

45 Alternatively known as 'Strict' or 'Particular', these Calvinist Baptists represented the Baptist mainstream in nineteenth-century England, outnumbering Arminian 'General' Baptists; see J. H. Y. Briggs, *The English Baptists of the Nineteenth Century* (Didcot: Baptist Historical Society, 1994).

46 E. Royle, 'Law, Harriet Teresa (1831–97), Feminist, Secularist and Radical', in Bellamy & Saville v (1979), pp. 134–6.

47 For example, in the same week in January 1869 Law performed this lecture at both Liverpool and Manchester; see *NR*, 31 January 1869, p. 78. The latter lecture was one of Law's earliest; see *NR*, 30 November 1861, p. 8.

48 *Agnostic Journal (AJ)*, 16 October 1897, p. 254. See also *SC*, 31 March 1878, p. 149.

49 *SC*, 2 January 1876, pp. 1–2.

50 *NR*, 30 November 1861, p. 8.

51 *SC*, 6 February 1876, pp. 66, 20 August 1876, p. 85.

52 *Ibid.*, 26 August 1877, p. 97.

53 *Ibid.*, 2 January 1876, pp. 1–2.

54 *Ibid.*

55 E. Royle (1980), p. 193; *The Shield of Faith*, September 1877, p. 129.

56 Karl Marx to Ludwig Kugelman, 12 December 1868, in D. Torr (ed.), *The Correspondence of Marx and Engels, 1846–1895. A Selection with Commentary and Notes* (London: Martin Lawrence Ltd, 1934), p. 255.

57 *SC*, 7 July 1878, pp. 1–3.

58 *Ibid.*, 31 March 1878, pp. 153–4.

59 *Ibid.*, 4 August 1878, pp. 49–50.

60 *Ibid.*, 2 January 1876, p. 1, 14 May 1876, p. 225.

61 *Ibid.*, 1 January 1876, p. 1.

62 *The Reformer*, 15 October 1897, p. 224, 15 January 1898, p. 330.

63 In fact, apart from the discrepancy of the initial 'T' and the mention of a surviving daughter in an obituary of Harriet Law, it would be impossible to identify their articles as the work of two separate authors. For H. T. L., see *AJ*, 16 October 1897, p. 254.

64 For Secularist anti-imperialism, see D. Nash, 'Taming the God of Battles: Secular and Moral Critiques of the South African War', in G. Cuthbertson, A. Grundlingh & M. Suttie (eds.), *Writing a Wider War: Rethinking Gender, Race and Identity in the South African War 1899–1902* (Athens, Ohio: Ohio University Press, 2002), pp. 266–86.

65 *SC*, 27 August 1876, pp. 100–101. See also *SC*, 17 September 1876, p. 221.

66 *Ibid.*, 3 September 1876, p. 113.

67 *Ibid.*, 10 September 1876, p. 121. See also *SC*, 3 December 1876, pp. 265–6.

68 *Ibid.*, 7 January 1877, pp. 13–4, 22 July 1877, p. 40, 14 July 1878, pp. 17–18.

69 *Ibid.*, 23 June 1878, p. 297.

70 *Ibid.*, 1 July 1877, p. 8.

71 *Ibid.*, 3 June 1877, p. 274.

72 Matthew (2004).

73 Royle (1979), p. 135.

74 For a full account of Besant's life, see A. Taylor, *Annie Besant: A Biography* (Oxford: Oxford University Press, 1992).

75 A. Besant, *Autobiographical Sketches* (London: Freethought Publishing Co., 1885), p. 90.

76 See E. Royle, 'Annie Besant's First Public Lecture', *Labour History Review* 57:3 (1992), 67–69.

77 For Annie Besant's later career as Theosophist, see J. Dixon, *Divine Feminism: Theosophy and Feminism in England* (Baltimore & London: Johns Hopkins University Press, 2001); as champion of Indian nationalism, see N. L. Paxton, 'Complicity and

Resistance in the Writings of Flora Annie Steel and Annie Besant', in N. Chaudhuri & M. Strobel (eds.), *Western Women and Imperialism. Complicity and Resistance* (Bloomington & Indianapolis: Indiana University Press, 1992), pp. 158–76.

78 She was the daughter of the Nottingham bootmaker William Nowlan and was born Eunice Kate; see E. Royle, 'Watts, Charles (1836–1906)', *Oxford Dictionary of National Biography* (online edn; Oxford University Press, 2004); K. E. Watts, *Mrs Watts Reply to Mr. Bradlaugh's Misrepresentations* (London: Co-operative Printing and Stationary Co., 1877[?]), p. 7.

79 Royle (1980), pp. 246–7.

80 *Secular Review (SR)*, 11 March 1877, p. 44; *SC*, 17 June 1877, p. 297, 2 September 1877, p. 118.

81 *SR*, 27 September 1879, pp. 193–4, 4 October 1879, pp. 212–14, 18 October 1879, pp. 246–7.

82 *SC*, 17 June 1877, p. 297; *SR*, 18 October 1879, p. 246.

83 Royle (1980), pp. 116–18, 253–4.

84 *Ibid.*, p. 118.

85 Taylor (1983), p. 48.

86 It was also reported that household chores were evenly divided between Margaret Chappellsmith and her husband; see Kimberling (2000), p. 38.

87 Florence Fenwick Miller was acquainted with both Bradlaugh and Besant and was certain that they were in love, though prevented from marrying; see London, Wellcome Library, F. Fenwick Miller, 'An Uncommon Girlhood' (unpublished auto-biography) GC/228, pp. 12–13 [NB the pagination for this work is inconsistent].

88 S. S. Hennell, *A Memoir of the Late Charles Hennell* (n.p., for private circulation, 1899), pp. 1–3.

89 *Ibid.*, p. 6; E. Jay, 'Hennell, Sara Sophia (1812–1899)', *Oxford Dictionary of National Biography* (online edn; Oxford University Press, 2004).

90 Hennell (1899), p. 12.

91 See C. Hennell, *An Inquiry Concerning the Origin of Christianity*, 3rd edn (London: Trubner and Co., 1870) (first published 1838); C. Hennell, *Christian Theism*, 3rd edn (London: Trubnor and Co., 1870) (first published 1839).

92 S. S. Hennell, *Christianity and Infidelity: An Exposition of the Arguments on Both Sides. Arranged According to a Plan Proposed by George Baillie Esq.* (London: Arthur Hall, Virtue & Co., 1857), p. 163.

93 See S. S. Hennell, *Thoughts in Aid of Faith, Gathered Chiefly from Recent Works in Theology and Philosophy* (London: George Manwaring, 1860); S. S. Hennell, *On Need of Dogmas in Religion. A Letter to Thomas Scott* (London: n.p., 1874); S. S. Hennell, *Present Religion as Faith Owning Fellowship with Thought*, 3 vols (London: Trubnor and Co., 1865, 1873, 1887).

94 Sara Hennell to George Jacob Holyoake, 30 May 1860, Manchester, Co-operative Union Archive (CUA), Holyoake Correspondence (HC) 1221.

95 For a discussion of the upper-middle-class milieu, see B. Willey, *Nineteenth-Century Studies: Coleridge to Matthew Arnold* (London: Chatto & Windus, 1949); R. Helmstadter & B. Lightman (eds.), *Victorian Faith in Crisis: Essays on Continuity and Change in Nineteenth-Century Religious Belief* (London & Basingstoke: Macmillan, 1990).

96 T. Larsen, *Crisis of Doubt* (Oxford: Oxford University Press, 2006), p. 15.

97 George Eliot to Sara Hennell, 28 July 1858, in G. Haight, *The George Eliot Letters* (London: Oxford University Press; Geoffrey Cumberlege, 1954), p. 473; Eliot and Hennell's theological paths diverged from the mid-1850s (Hennell could never sympathise with Eliot's Positivism) and by the end of the 1860s their friendship had come to an end; see Jay (2004).

98 George Eliot to Sara Hennell, 9 October 1843, Haight (1954), p. 161; Sara Hennell to Sophia Dobson Collet, 22 February n.d., 22 April 1857, 8 January 1888, London, Women's Library (WL), Papers of Clara Collet and Family (CCF) 7CCF [uncatalogued]. This collection contains extensive correspondence between Sophia Dobson Collet and Francis Newman from 1849 to 1893.

99 K. Gleadle, *The Early Feminists. Radical Unitarians and the Emergence of the Women's Rights Movement, 1831–51* (Basingstoke & London: Palgrave Macmillan, 1995), p. 6.

100 See, for example, *Reasoner*, 3 March 1858, p. 72.

101 Conway is described as an 'ethical preacher' in the *ODNB* and later became an agnostic, though he retained a deep reverence for religious feeling; see J. d'Entremont, 'Conway, Moncure Daniel (1832–1907)', *Oxford Dictionary of National Biography* (online edn; Oxford University Press, 2004).

102 Taylor (1992), pp. 60–5.

103 S. D. Collet, *George Jacob Holyoake and Modern Atheism. A Biographical and Critical Essay* (London: Trubnor and Co., 1855), p. 28.

104 Sophia Dobson Collet to George Jacob Holyoake, 17 February 1846, CUA, HC 157.

105 Sophia Dobson Collet to George Jacob Holyoake, 4 October 1845, CUA, HC 144.

106 S. D. Collet, *Phases of Atheism, Described, Examined and Answered* (Holyoake & Co.: London, 1860) p. 2.

107 *Reasoner* 4:91 (1848), pp. 175–6.

108 Collet (1855), pp. 42–3.

109 Gleadle (2004); Sara Hennell to Sophia Dobson Collet, 30 September 1889, 17 January 1892, WL, CCF.

110 Gleadle (2004); Collet wrote of her 'conversion' to her close friend Francis Newman in 1867, though his reply expressed frustration at her failing to clarify exactly what it was that she had come to believe and which aspects of Christianity she now considered true, see Francis Newman to Sophia Dobson Collet, 7 December 1867, WL, CCF.

111 A. Bonner & Charles Bradlaugh Bonner, *Hypatia Bradlaugh Bonner: The Story of Her Life* (London: Watts & Co., 1942); E. Royle, 'Bonner, Hypatia Bradlaugh (1858–1935)', *Oxford Dictionary of National Biography* (online edn; Oxford University Press, 2004); Royle (1980), pp. 40–1.

112 Bonner & Bradlaugh Bonner (1942), p.85.

113 Barbara Leigh Smith Bodichon, for example, one of the founders of first wave feminism, was also a Freethinker though this is not mentioned in her *ODNB* entry; see P. Hirsh, 'Bodichon, Barbara Leigh Smith (1827–1891)', *Oxford Dictionary of National Biography* (online edn; Oxford University Press, 2004).

114 R. K. Webb, 'Martineau, Harriet (1802–1876)', *Oxford Dictionary of National Biography* (online edn; Oxford University Press, 2004). See also H. Martineau, *Autobiography* 2 vols, 3rd edn (London: Smith, Elder & Co., 1877: repr. Farnborough: Gregg International Publishers Ltd, 1969); C. Roberts, *The Woman and the Hour.*

Harriet Martineau and Victorian Ideologies (London: University of Toronto Press, 2002).

115 J. Watts and Iconoclast (eds.), *Harriet Martineau*, Half Hours with Freethinkers 2:11 (London[?]: n.p., 1864); *SR*, 18 March 1877, pp. 49–50.

116 *SC*, 26 August 1877, p. 106, 10 June 1877, p. 279, 17 June 1877, p. 295.

117 F. Fenwick Miller, *The Lessons of a Life: Harriet Martineau. A Lecture Delivered Before the Sunday Lecture Society, St. George's Hall, Langham Place on Sunday afternoon, 11th March 1877* (London: The Sunday Lecture Society, 1877). Fenwick Miller later published a full biography of Martineau, see F. Fenwick Miller, *Harriet Martineau* (London: John H. Ingram, 1884).

118 J. M. Benn, *The Predicaments of Love* (London: Pluto Press, 1992) pp. 116–23, 135.

119 Fenwick Miller, 'An Uncommon Girlhood'; R. T. Van Arsdel, *Florence Fenwick Miller. Victorian Feminist, Journalist and Educator* (Aldershot: Ashgate, 2001).

120 S. J. Peacock, *The Theological and Ethical Writings of Frances Power Cobbe, 1822–1904* (Lampeter: The Edwin Mellen Press, 2002), p. 4.

121 F. Power Cobbe, *The Life of Frances Power Cobbe as Told by Herself. With Additions by the Author and Introduction by Blanche Atkinson* (London: Swan Sonnenschein and Co., 1904), p. 82.

122 L. Williamson, *Power and Protest. Frances Power Cobbe and Victorian Society* (London: Rivers Oram Press, 2005), p. 77.

123 *Ibid.*, pp. 93–9.

124 F. Power Cobbe, 'Magnanimous Atheism', *The Theological Review*, 59 (October 1877), 447–489; Williamson (2005), pp. 165–6.

125 Besant, *Sketches*, pp. 95–6; Royle (1992), p. 67.

126 Besant, *Sketches*, p. 62.

127 See H. Law 'Letter to Miss Frances Power Cobbe', *SC*, 21 October 1877, p. 197; A. Besant, *A World Without God. A Reply to Miss Frances Power Cobbe* (London: Freethought Publishing Co., 1885).

128 N. F. Anderson, 'Linton, Elizabeth Lynn (1822–1898)', *Oxford Dictionary of National Biography* (online edn; Oxford University Press, 2004).

129 E. Lynn Linton, *My Literary Life. Reminiscences of Dickens, Thackery, George Eliot, etc. With a Prefatory Note by Miss Beatrice Harraden* (London: Hodder & Stoughton, 1899), pp. 85, 92; N. F. Anderson, *Woman Against Woman in Victorian England. A Life of Eliza Lynn Linton* (Bloomington & Indianapolis: Indiana University Press, 1987), p. 43.

130 See Eliza Lynn Linton to George Jacob Holyoake, 1873[?], CUA, HC 2231.

131 *Ibid.*; G. Somes Layard, *Mrs Lynn Linton. Her Life, Letters, and Opinions* (London: Methuen & Co., 1901), p. 180.

132 S. S. Holton, 'Elmy, Elizabeth Clarke Wolstenholme (1833–1918)', *Oxford Dictionary of National Biography* (online edn; Oxford University Press, 2004).

133 E. Ethelmer, 'A Woman Emancipator: A Biographical Sketch', *Westminster Review*, 145 (April 1896), pp. 424–8, 426–7. Maureen Wright argued that Wolstenholme Elmy's conversion to Secularism was a gradual process, beginning at the age of seven, but that she firmly committed to a 'humanist and secularist creed' by 1871; M. Wright, 'Elizabeth Wolstenholme Elmy: A Biography' (unpublished doctoral thesis, University of Portsmouth, 2007).

134 *NR*, 8 October 1876, pp. 225–6.

135 Wolstenholme Elmy described Christian marriage as the 'ecclesiastical yoke'; see *Westminster Review*, 163 (May 1905), 513–29, 525–6. (I am grateful to Maureen Wright for drawing attention to this source.)

136 E. Ethelmer, *The Human Flower. A Simple Statement of the Physiology of Birth and the Relations of the Sexes*, 2nd edn (Congleton: Mrs Wolstenholme Elmy, 1894).

137 S. S. Holton, 'Now You See It, Now You Don't: The Women's Franchise League and its Place in Contending Narratives of the Women's Suffrage Movement', in J. Purvis & M. Joannou (eds.), *The Women's Suffrage Movement: New Feminist Perspectives* (Manchester: Manchester University Press, 1998), pp. 15–36.

138 M. Wright, 'The Women's Emancipation Union and Radical-Feminist Politics in Britain, 1891–99', *Gender & History* 22:2 (August 2010), 382–406. G. J. Holyoake's daughter, Emily Holyoake Marsh, was also active in the suffrage movement as a member of the International Women's Franchise Club; E. Crawford, *The Women's Suffrage Movement: A Reference Guide 1866–1928* (London: UCL Press, 1999); R. Samuel, 'The Bishopsgate Institute', *History Workshop Journal* 5:1, 163–72. Florence Dixie's aristocratic lifestyle set her apart from fellow Freethinking feminists, but she supported the cause and wrote the introduction to Joseph McCabe's *Religion of Women* (1905); see D. Middleton, 'Dixie [nee Douglas], Florence Caroline, Lady Dixie (1857–1905), *Oxford Dictionary of National Biography* (online edn; Oxford University Press, 2004).

139 L. A. Hall, 'Vickery, Alice (1844–1929)', *Oxford Dictionary of National Biography* (online edn, Oxford University Press, 2004); Benn (1992).

140 M. Caird, 'Marriage', Westminster Review, CXXX (1888), 186–201.

141 J. Hume Clapperton, *Scientific Meliorism and the Evolution of Happiness* (London: Kegan Paul, Trench & Co., 1885); S. M. Den Otter, 'Clapperton, Jane Hume (1832–1914)', *Oxford Dictionary of National Biography* (online edn; Oxford University Press, 2004).

142 Caird was a member of the Freedom of Press Defence Committee formed when the editor of the Legitmation League's journal, *The Adult*, was arrested for obscenity, *The Adult*, August 1898, p. 191. For Clapperton and Vickery, see *Adult*, January 1898, pp. 134–5, 138–40.

2

Counter-conversion: Freethinking feminists and the renunciation of religion

I n 1842, Emma Martin published a tract entitled *A Few Reasons for Renouncing Christianity and Professing and Disseminating Infidel Opinions*, in which she described her conversion away from the Baptism of her youth to a militantly atheist brand of Freethought. Before embarking upon a full account of this counter-conversion, Martin paused to explain the significance of her tale. 'But reader,' she asked, 'of what importance is it to you whether I am an infidel or Christian? None! Why then do I call your attention to the fact? For the simple reason that the causes which have produced my present state of mind have operated upon thousands of others.'[1] In publishing the story of her conversion to atheism, and in seeking to hold it up as a model for others, Martin employed a popular Freethought motif which placed the process of counter-conversion at the heart of the movement's analysis of both religion and freedom of thought. All but three of the women discussed in this study had been devout Christians before converting to Freethought.[2] In the first half of the nineteenth century, first Eliza Sharples and then Emma Martin wrote about their counter-conversions at length, and used their personal narratives in their propagandising for the Freethought movement. From the 1850s onwards, after the formation of Secularist societies and national institutional structures, Harriet Law and Annie Besant continued the tradition, and their account of their counter-conversions became a central part of their Secularist repertoire. Other women associated with the movement, such as Sara Hennell, and those on its periphery, such as Harriet Martineau, also made reference to their former Christian faiths and put forward their reasons for rejecting them. Similarly, agnostics such as Frances Power Cobbe and Eliza Lynn Linton, though standing outside organised Freethought, identified their conversion away from Christianity as a crucial turning point in their lives.

The term 'counter-conversion', rather than 'loss of faith', is used here to highlight how Freethinkers had rejected one worldview only to embrace another with equal fervour.[3] They renounced religion for a variety of reasons – because of inaccuracies found in the Bible which prevented them from accepting it as the Word of God; because supernatural dogmas could not be reconciled with modern scientific knowledge; and because they were repulsed by a God who could allow so much suffering to continue among His people. Yet the most important aspect of counter-conversion was that it generated an entirely new way of looking at and relating to the world. Drawing on older Enlightenment notions of mental awakening and the casting off of intellectual bondage, Freethinkers felt themselves to have acquired a new freedom to judge the world on their own terms and accept only those teachings and values which *they* deemed just. To question religion – still one of the most significant forces of social and moral authority in Britain – was a terrifying task. To have successfully found the courage to do so, to have survived the journey, and to realise that it was possible to be guided by moral frameworks of one's own making, was a profoundly empowering experience. It opened up a whole new vista of previously unquestioned rules and limitations imposed on the way one lived one's life which now might be challenged. Annie Besant described it thus:

> Once encourage the human mind to think, and bounds to the thinking can never again be set by authority. Once challenge traditional beliefs, and the challenge will ring on every shield which is hanging in the intellectual arena.[4]

The implications of this new-found intellectual freedom were especially important for female Secularists, whose experiences of feminist politicisation were closely bound up with the new anti-religious mindsets born out of their counter-conversions. For women, the counter-conversion process often appeared as a journey of self-realisation in which freedom from the intellectual bondage of superstition became a template for a more general emancipation from sexual oppression. Appropriating the genre of Christian spiritual biography to propagandise for unbelief allowed Freethinking women to reject a conventional feminine authorial voice in favour of the authoritative stance of religious commentator. Female counter-conversion narratives also, with striking frequency, linked the transition to unbelief with a challenge to patriarchal authority, whether domestic or spiritual, while some accounts offered explicitly feminist reasons for rejecting Christianity in favour of Freethought.

Counter-conversion also generated a particular way of under-standing and defining religion. Freethinkers' narratives aimed to show that religion was nothing more than error, a set of untrue beliefs founded upon ignorance and superstition. Emma Martin reiterated the arguments of David Hume and other Enlightenment thinkers, claiming that ancient man had invented tales of the supernatural in order to explain the workings of nature in a pre-scientific age.[5] Sara Hennell, on the other hand, followed the German philosopher Ludwig Feuerbach in arguing that religion was the projection of abstract human ideas onto a personified form. Although she took a positive view of the religious instinct, Hennell nevertheless insisted that it derived not from God but from man.[6] Freethinkers therefore described their counter-conversion as a primarily intellectual process, showing that it was possible to be argued out of religious belief.[7] Religion was in contradiction to truth and reason, they claimed, and once the pursuit of these nobler goals had begun, it was inevitable that they should eventually lead away from Christianity, no matter how dearly held the tenets of faith might be.

Freethinkers also developed psychological explanations to account for the personal religious experience of the individual,[8] arguing against the existence of an independent religious instinct and describing personal piety as merely an outlet for some other natural or psychological urge, such as a 'melancholy turn of mind' or sexual frustration.[9] In this, they adopted what modern commentators have described as an 'externalist' approach to religion, seeking to explain away religious beliefs by factors outside the belief-system itself.[10] Many thinkers have criticised this as too reductive. The philosopher William James, a contemporary of the later Secularist movement, condemned what he termed the 'intellectual' approach to religion, particularly the interpretation of religiosity as a manifestation of sexual frustration. He insisted on the need to examine the feelings, acts and experiences of believers as legitimate in and of themselves.[11] In the last decade many more scholars have begun to repeat the call to examine religion 'on its own terms', arguing against it being read as merely sublimated sexual desire or misplaced emotion rather than as a genuine expression of personal conviction.[12] Charles Taylor, in particular, has insisted that scholars should recognise an 'independent religious motivation' that cannot be explained away by external factors or in terms of its social function.[13] Meanwhile, many historians have begun to work with broader conceptualisations of religion, moving away from viewing it as a fixed set of doctrines or beliefs, toward an interpretation of it as a linguistic structure or overarching discursive framework.[14]

On this account, religion might continue to shape the 'mental horizons' of unbelievers long after they had forgone belief in God.[15]

In light of such developments in the historiography of religion, it would be foolhardy to take at face value Freethinkers' claims of a mental awakening that thereafter left them untainted by religion. Religious belief was of fundamental importance to many women in this period, and it is in this light that we must consider Freethinking feminists' decision to reject it. Christian beliefs and life in the Churches fundamentally shaped the process of counter-conversion and how Freethinking women chose to represent it. Counter-conversion accounts can also therefore be read as inverted spiritual autobiographies, in which it is possible to trace the continuing influence of religion on the Freethought stance. Yet real shifts of attitude and self-perception did occur and it is necessary to find a way to understand the relationship between counter-conversion and the religion it renounced while also taking seriously the transformative nature of the break with religion and the adoption of a Freethinking worldview.

Former faith: Freethinking representations of Christianity

A study of conversions to unbelief must begin in the world of serious religion. All the Freethinking women discussed here first encountered serious Christianity as very young children. Eliza Sharples described how her induction into the Methodist Church had begun 'at infancy' and how 'in that most strict attendance upon the ceremonies of religion I was educated'.[16] Accounts of women raised in the Baptist churches, from which Margaret Chappellsmith, Emma Martin and Harriet Law hailed, recall a similarly strict regime of daily prayers, church attendance, and frequent Bible study.[17] Nor was it only dissenting or evangelical churches that imposed upon their young members such severe religious training. Sara Hennell, who grew up in the theologically liberal Unitarian Church, was also subject to the early and pervasive influence of religion. She and her siblings would attend Sunday Chapel morning and evening, where Robert Aspland's sermons served to 'bite in the facts and actual words of the Bible in memory, leaving an indelible impression'.[18] Another Unitarian, Harriet Martineau, was, from the age of seven, required to memorise and then transcribe the weekly sermon delivered by the minister.[19] Annie Besant and Frances Power Cobbe, both raised in the Anglican Church, also testified to the constant presence of God throughout their childhoods. Frances Power Cobbe described how 'God was always to me the All-seeing Judge. His eye looked into my heart ... beholding all its naughtiness and little duplicities ... [this] was so familiar a conception that I might be said to live and move in a sense of it.'[20] Annie Besant's imaginative universe was also permeated by religious fervour. She described how tales of early Christian martyrs invaded her childish fancies, so that 'I would spend many an hour in day dreams, in which I stood before Roman judges, before Dominican Inquisitors, was flung to lions, tortured on the rack, burned at the stake …'.[21]

Given their deep absorption in religion from such a young age, it is not surprising to find Freethinking women frequently testifying to the strength and intensity of their former faith. When, in 1832, Eliza Sharples launched her Freethought lecturing career, her new persona as the 'Lady of the Rotunda' relied heavily upon an account of her recent and dramatic break with Methodism. Her first lecture, reported in her journal the *Isis*, began with the declaration that 'I have been full of superstition, but I trust that I have ceased to be so.'[22] There had been nothing in Sharples' previous religious conduct to suggest that she might soon be lost to infidelity. In fact she was among the most devoted members of her chapel: 'I prayed and sang spiritual songs until my health sank under the unnatural excitement … The strongest Methodism in religion was not too strong for me; I was a slave to it.'[23] Eliza Lynn Linton's account of her conversion from Anglicanism to Agnosticism described how her former faith had been so powerful that it was virtually tangible: 'I realised my faith as positively as if it had been a thing I could see and touch; my confirmation was a consecration; and when first I received the communion, I felt as if I had tabernacled the Lord in my own body …'.[24] Annie Besant's faith was also capable of making her 'tremble' so that 'I could scarcely control myself as I knelt at the altar rails'. As she later recalled, by the time of her confirmation her childish impressionability had given way to the heightened emotional state of adolescence, which, combined with ignorance about the adult world, made her the perfect candidate for devotion to the religious life. During this period, she seriously considered joining one of the Anglo-Catholic Sisterhoods.[25]

Of course there were many reasons why women who subsequently propagandised for Freethought would have wanted to emphasise the sincerity of their former faith. Firstly, they were keen to affirm their respectability in response to accusations that infidels, particularly female infidels, had left the Christian Church in order to satisfy their carnal desires. Eliza Sharples, countering the salacious rumours surrounding her relationship with Richard Carlile, insisted that she was but 'a simple country girl' who was 'counted respectable by religious people when among them'.[26] It was also necessary for Freethinking women to prove that their decision to reject their former faith was not due to mere dilettantism or any lack of commitment, but because religion, in the end, was unable to satisfy their search for 'Truth' and morality. The Freethought mission was a deadly serious endeavour, characterised not by indifference to religion but by a powerful sense of moral duty, to cleanse society of superstition and to build a new world based upon Secularist principles. Thus, Eliza Sharples claimed that she had tried religion, given it a fair chance, but ultimately found it wanting. 'I have been a religious woman in the full sense of that word', she declared in her Ninth Discourse at the Rotunda, 'Was I then the wiser or the happier? ... If that were heaven, or the road to it, I have known it, and will not miss it in the end, if I do not find a better. I will do nothing unworthy of it; and if I fail to improve on it, I will return.'[27] Emma Martin's tract on *Renouncing Christianity* insisted that it was precisely her former dedication to religion that qualified her to mount her subsequent critique, and it was this that made her a true 'infidel'.

> No one now can be said to reject that with which he is unacquainted ... consequently those persons who do not receive Christianity, because its study is too troublesome or its practice inconvenient – the butterflies of society who sport in the sunshine of the moment, cannot be correctly termed infidels.[28]

Martin maintained that she had become an infidel not because she had been *unwilling* to receive the grace of God; to the contrary, she had earnestly sought it, and 'nay more [I] believed that I had received it'. Yet, like Eliza Sharples, she ultimately concluded that Christianity was not worth striving for.[29]

By portraying their former faith as strict in its indoctrination and all-consuming in its practice, Freethinking women also contributed to a Freethought critique that sought to brand Christianity as joyless, masochistic and philistine. This tendency is most marked in the conversion accounts of women from evangelical backgrounds. Eliza Sharples, for example, favourably compared Roman Catholicism (which at least permitted its believers to 'dance of a Sunday evening') to 'the character of reformed religion [which] has been to make life a scene of repentance throughout, in sackcloth and ashes, and tears, for imaginary sins that never had reality ...'.[30] Emma Martin retrospectively mused that it had probably been her 'melancholy turn of mind' that had inclined her towards religion. Although she had joined the Particular Baptists with great hopes for finding 'sympathy of soul' and 'communion of heart' her encounter with the reality of 'church meetings' soon sobered her expectations, and instead she discovered a petty, unsympathetic and narrow-minded community.[31] Harriet Teresa Law, possibly drawing on her mother's account of the religion of her youth, referred to the years G. J. Holyoake spent in the Baptist Church as a period during which 'the should-have-been buoyancy of youth was absorbed in the gloom of religion'.[32] Annie Besant mocked her younger self, who, in the belief that she was 'a decidedly pious girl', 'looked on theatres (never having been to one) as traps set by Satan for the destruction of foolish souls; I was quite determined never to go to a ball … the little prig that I was …' The adult Besant was also critical of the effects that a 'sense of sin' and 'contrition for man's fallen state' had had upon her younger self, claiming that 'the total effect of Calvinistic training was to make me somewhat morbid …'.[33]

However, in spite of the undoubted propaganda pay-off of emphasising the intensity of their past religious fervour, it is also necessary to believe Freethinking women when they claimed that their faith had been important to them. Religion had acted as a powerful presence in their lives almost since birth. The stories, rituals and symbols of the Christian Church had fundamentally shaped their intellectual, emotional and spiritual worlds. Undoubtedly, Freethinking women found the domination of their lives by religion repressive, as they later went on to claim. However, as the ever-increasing historiography on women and religion continues to demonstrate, religion could provide women with an extraordinary source of strength in both their personal and political spheres of action.[34] Of course, when women in the Freethought movement recounted their counter-conversions they were concerned to present them as an ultimately positive experience, yet some of them also acknowledged that they were making a sacrifice. Frances Power Cobbe admitted,

> For a long time my intense desire to remain a Christian predominated, and brought me back from each return to scepticism in a passion of repentance and prayer to Christ to take my life or my reason sooner than allow me to stray from his fold.[35]

Annie Besant also recorded the anguish caused by the loss of faith, declaring that 'There is in this life no other pain so horrible. The doubt seems to shipwreck everything, to destroy the one steady gleam of happiness …'.[36] She also acknowledged the possible benefits of believing 'in the existence of a Being who is always at hand to remedy your mistakes, and to save you from the painful consequences of your actions'.[37] Perhaps Harriet Martineau best summed up the difference in outlook required once the decision to reject one's religion had been made. Writing to George Henry Atkinson in 1848 regarding their soon-to-be-published correspondence, in which Martineau explicitly avowed her atheism, she commented that 'this book is, I believe, the greatest effort of courage I ever made'. Others had suggested to Martineau that publishing her radical views on political economy, the 'woman question', or Mesmerism had been more daring authorial ventures. And yet, for Martineau, the publication of *Letters* was by far the most daunting, not because of its subject matter, but because, when her former works had been published, she had still believed in a God who would support her. 'Then I believed in a Protector who ordered me to do that work, and would sustain me under it: and, however I may now despise that sort of support, I had it then, and have none of that sort now.'[38]

The path to atheism: Freethinking representations of counter-conversion

The conversion experiences described by the women studied here all followed a similar pattern, in which intellectual inquiry and independent study played a central role. Eliza Sharples was first 'roused ... to enquiry and reflection' by the 'cry of persecution' directed at Richard Carlile. She presented her subsequent conversion as arising from intellectual investigation: 'I sought his books – I found them; I learned something by reading them ...'[39] Eliza Sharples' daughter, Theophila Carlile Campbell, later confirmed her mother's account when recalling the events leading up to Sharples' reincarnation as 'Lady of the Rotunda'. Carlile Campbell described how Sharples had accidentally come across copies of Richard Carlile's paper the *Republican* while staying at a cousin's house. 'She began reading them with avidity' which soon turned into 'instructive astonishment'. Sharples was persuaded of the worthlessness of her former faith by the power of words and arguments alone, so that 'In those writings the ignorance and errors of her past life were told to her as by a magician.'[40]

The story of Emma Martin's rejection of Baptism in favour of atheism became one of the best-known counter-conversion narratives of the Freethought movement. At the age of twenty-six Martin decided on a whim to attend a lecture by the Owenite Alexander Campbell in her home town of Bristol. She found herself listening with 'riveted attention', at first 'astonished and delighted' to hear Campbell's condemnation of the very same 'evils of our present social system' that had always concerned her, particularly 'the degraded condition of women'.[41] However, the following night she became increasingly outraged as Campbell denounced the evils of religion, finally challenging him to a series of debates in which she set about defending her faith in the face of Socialist critique. Emma Martin devoted the next few months to private study, with the intention of arming herself with the evidence to refute Owenite arguments once and for all. Reading the Bible for the first time in a spirit of inquiry rather than the 'prayer spirit' encouraged by the churches, Martin began to notice that it was full of inaccuracies and inconsistencies.[42] Her very public conversion to infidelism followed shortly and must have been a valuable publicity coup to the Owenites, occurring as it did in the course of a series of platform debates.[43] Yet Emma Martin always maintained that her decision to leave her husband, her home town and her former religion and to join the Freethinking Owenites in London, had very little to do with personal loyalties or sympathies. Instead, she had been compelled to take the course she did, whether she liked it or not, by the logic of her own reasoning. She always maintained that only 'fanatics' refused to investigate the intellectual foundations of their beliefs, but that if one wished to become, like herself, 'a free-enquirer after truth', one had to be prepared to 'proceed with ... investigations even though they should lead ... to conclusions very different from those ... expected ...'.[44]

Harriet Law's conversion experience was virtually identical to that of Emma Martin. Law's initial encounter with Freethinkers was also as a devout 'religionist'. George Jacob Holyoake recalled his first meeting with her in the early 1850s at the Philpot Street Secular Hall. Holyoake had been employed to speak on Secularism, and afterwards Harriet Law rose from the audience to challenge him with Christian arguments. According to Holyoake, her rhetorical skill was, even then, impressive.[45] However, after attending lectures by Charles Southwell, Bradlaugh and other leading Secularists, Law was eventually convinced by their arguments and lost her former faith.[46] Her personal conversion experience became a central theme in her lecture repertoire, and she spoke all over Britain on the subject of 'How I became a Secularist'.[47]

Sara Hennell's account of her brother Charles' loss of faith can also be read as describing Sara's own journey from the liberal Unitarian belief-system of Robert Aspland's chapel to a form of Freethought. It began in April 1836 when their sister Caroline was shocked to discover on her honeymoon that her husband, the prominent radical Charles Bray, was a Freethinker. Charles Hennell promised Caroline that he would provide her with an answer to her husband's attacks on Christianity, and the family began to investigate the 'truth' of their religious beliefs as if they represented an intellectual puzzle that could be 'solved' through rational inquiry. Charles thus declared that he would 'examine' religion 'as he would any other subject in which he had no concern'. Sara recalled how 'every evening the great family Bible was spread open before him and studied with ... intense interest ... He sought diligently for every information that could throw light on his subject.' Despite their liberal approach to Scriptural interpretation, Unitarian congregations during the 1830s continued to uphold a number of orthodox Christian doctrines. The Hennell family examined these doctrines one by one, and eventually concluded that they could not stand up to reasoned intellectual inquiry. Towards the end of 1836, Sara and her sister Mary began to doubt the truth of Christ's miracles, the proof of which, recorded Mary in her journal, 'is shaken for the present in my mind, and Sara's too ... the inquiry "what is truth?" is a most anxious one'.[48] In 1838, by the time Charles came to publish the findings of his and his sisters' investigations, they had also come to reject the truth of the Resurrection. The belief-system with which they were left – that later Sara went on to modify into her own distinctive form of Freethought – they entitled *Christian Theism*.[49]

Harriet Martineau's journey away from her former Unitarianism towards atheism and freethought was also characterised by study and a puzzling out of the intellectual conundrums presented by Christianity. When she was only eight years old, Martineau began to wrestle with the problem of how humans could be blamed or rewarded for their conduct if God had already predetermined their fate. These initial doubts were brushed aside by an older brother, who told her that she was too young to understand such things – a dismissal to which Martineau later attributed her subsequent passion for finding out the truth herself through independent inquiry.[50] By the time she was nineteen years old she had 'studied the Bible incessantly and immensely ... getting hold of all the commentaries of elucidation I could lay my hands on'. After many years of theological study of this kind, which led her to move gradually further and further away from the religion in which she had been raised, Martineau, at the age of forty-two, concluded that it was not possible to comprehend 'the scheme, or nature, or fact of the universe' in terms of a divine being.[51] Far from being comforted by a theologically liberal attitude to interpreting Scripture, Harriet Martineau found throughout her life that this aspect of Unitarianism actually intensified her intellectual doubts as to the truth of her early faith. Unitarianism's flexible approach to the less palatable doctrines of orthodox Christianity meant that, unlike many of the Freethinking women discussed here, Martineau 'never suffered more or less from fear of hell' and 'did not, at any time ... believe in the devil'. She was thus spared the gloom and doubt recalled by many other Freethinking women when they described their religious pasts. Instead, however, she suffered from 'a covert sense that it was taking a monstrous liberty with the Gospel to pick and choose what made me happy'.[52]

Of all the women in this study, the ever-prolific Annie Besant produced the most detailed and comprehensive account of her conversion to atheism. In fact, she began to write articles on the subject even before she had fully renounced Christianity, and in 1877 she collected together these early writings and re-published them under the title *My Path to Atheism*, which charted the development of her crisis of faith.[53] Besant's *Autobiographical Sketches* of 1885 also provided a lengthy account of her break with Christianity and she structured her narrative around this turning point in her life. Besant had first experienced doubt as a young child when, in order to mark the feast of Easter, she decided to compare all four Gospel accounts of the Crucifixion and Resurrection, only to find that they contradicted each other.[54] The young Annie stifled such misgivings and they were not to return again until early adulthood, provoked by the near death of her two young children from whooping cough. This time Besant decided to confront her doubts, and made up her mind 'to investigate, one by one, every Christian dogma, and never again say "I believe" until I had tested the object of faith'.[55] She read the Broad Church theologians F. D. Maurice and F. W. Robertson, and the unorthodox preacher Stopford Brooke, and visited one of the fathers of the Oxford Movement, Edward Pusey, all of whom failed to provide her with a satisfactory answer to the queries generated by her studies.[56] There were four issues that particularly concerned her:

I.   The eternity of punishment after death.
II. The meaning of 'goodness' and 'love' as applied to a God who had made this world with all its evil and its misery.
III. The nature of the atonement of Christ, and the 'justice' of God in accepting a vicarious suffering from Christ, and a vicarious righteousness from the sinner.
IV. The meaning of 'inspiration' as applied to the Bible, and the reconciliation of the perfection of the author with the blunders and immoralities of the world.[57]

'Step by step,' Besant 'renounced the dogmas of Christianity' until at last she gave up her most cherished belief – the doctrine of the Deity of Christ – and declared herself no longer a Christian but a Theist.[58]

In 1872 Besant began to associate with the freethinking clergyman Charles Vosey, who, in a high profile case, had been deprived of his clerical living for refusing to retract statements questioning the divinity of Christ.[59] He encouraged her to read the works of Theodore Parker, Francis Newman and Frances Power Cobbe.[60] She also met the freethinking theist publisher Thomas Scott, who invited her to his salon in Upper Norwood, South London, also frequented by Freethinkers such as Charles Bray and Sara Hennell. Scott began to commission from Besant some of the articles that later appeared in *My Path to Atheism*.[61] Meanwhile, Annie's refusal to continue to receive communion in her husband's parish church led to their separation, and she moved to London in 1873. Soon afterwards she attended a National Secular Society meeting, where Charles Bradlaugh laid to rest her concerns about the vulgarity of organised Secularism and assured her that the movement welcomed members who were still uncertain of their views on the Divine. The decisive break with theism came when she began to write for *The National Reformer* and Thomas Scott refused to publish any more of her work. By the time Besant delivered her first lecture in August 1874 she had declared herself an atheist and taken up arms in the name of Secularism.[62]

The pattern of these accounts, it should be noted, was replicated by male Freethinkers. From her study of biographies of Secularists between 1850 and 1965, Susan Budd concluded that the majority of Secularists of both sexes had been actively and sincerely religious in their former lives, and that many of them had, like Emma Martin and Harriet Law, been Sunday school teachers prior to their conversion. Chance encounters with proselytising infidels were commonly the cause of initial doubts. Like Emma Martin and Harriet Law, Charles Bradlaugh had challenged Freethinkers to debate when, as an ardently religious adolescent and star pupil of his Sunday school, he stumbled across them preaching in Bonner's Fields. Other causes included confusion over discrepancies in the Scriptures, which male Freethinkers had studied as ardently and thoroughly as the women in the movement. Male Freethinkers also testified to the sincerity and the emotional intensity of their early religiosity and to the morbidity that evangelical piety encouraged.[63] Freethinking feminists were, therefore, both contributing to and following an established set of narrative practices designed to promulgate 'best practice' in the loss of faith. Historian Timothy Larsen has recently shown that a significant minority of Freethinkers converted back to Christianity after periods of activism in the Secularist movement, leading other Freethinkers to call into question the authenticity of their initial counter-conversion.[64] Freethinking women would therefore have felt an extra imperative to describe their conversions according to a set pattern in order to reassure their audiences, and perhaps even themselves, of the sincerity of their renunciation of religion.[65]

Counter-conversion as a religious narrative?

Infidel stories of counter-conversion were strongly indebted to Enlightenment notions of mental awakening, the irresistible force of truth and so forth, but they also owed much to the longstanding genre of spiritual autobiography, which remained a cornerstone of dissenting and evangelical devotional literature throughout the eighteenth and nineteenth centuries. Quakers, Baptists, Methodists and Evangelicals wrote and published accounts of their spiritual awakenings, which were widely distributed and read. For the women emerging from these groups into Freethought, the framework provided by the conversion narrative would have been a familiar and readily accessible structure in which to recount their transformations. From this perspective, counter-conversion narratives might be read as simply an inversion of Christian conversion accounts and the wider genre of spiritual biography.[66] There are many similarities between the two kinds of narrative; the Freethinkers' use of counter-conversion to affirm the sincerity of their religious renunciation reflected the origins of the Christian conversion account, which had begun in seventeenth-century radical religious sects as a way of giving public and 'authentic' account of how a believer came to be numbered among the elect.[67] Freethinkers emphasised the importance of extensive reading and studying to their counter-conversion, wishing to counter-pose the rational and intellectual nature of their path to unbelief, to superstitious and emotional religious fervour. Yet such intellectual activity was not particular to the process of losing one's faith, but also characterised the conversion accounts of Christian women.[68] Moreover, the Freethinkers' description of being carried along by the power of reason 'to conclusions very different from those expected', echoed aspects of the Christian conversion process, whereby the believer, having subjected herself to God, would be born again through the power of His grace.

However, if counter-conversions are read simply as the mirror image of Christian conversions, perceiving Freethought to be an inverted Protestant sect, we risk losing sight of the force of Freethinkers' repudiation of religion. The current insistence among historians of religion that we take seriously the religious beliefs of people in the past, should apply equally to anti-religious views. Counter-conversion should not be reduced to metaphor or delusion. Renouncing religion was often a painful and traumatic experience, entailing the loss of status, community and sometimes even family. Freethinkers thought long and hard about the reasons for rejecting each one of the Christian doctrines, and the conclusions they reached regarding the non-divinity of Scripture and the capricious immorality of God placed them fundamentally at odds with Christian thinkers. Attention to similarities of process must not, therefore obscure the intellectual content of Freethought which, as far as any contemporary Christian or Freethinker was concerned, clearly distinguished it from all other 'religious' organisations.

Rather than conceptualise the relationship between Christianity and Secularism as one of replication, it is more useful to borrow Charles Taylor's idea that the intellectual structures of nineteenth-century Protestantism determined the form taken by the Victorian crisis of faith. This approach allows a consideration of how the path to unbelief took routes laid down by antecedent forms of Christian belief, while also allowing for the fact that the doubting Christians who followed this path eventually arrived at an entirely new destination. For example, nineteenth-century Protestantism was a prepositional form of religion, that is, one in which membership required adherence to articles of faith such as the doctrine of the Atonement, the Resurrection or the Divinity of Christ.[69] Its evangelical forms, especially, emphasised the need to conform to all the tenets of a particular church. Therefore, once a believer had convinced herself that any of these doctrines were wrong, she often felt compelled to renounce her faith wholesale.[70] Frances Power Cobbe certainly felt that it had been her Evangelical upbringing that had encouraged her to reject religion more decisively than she might have done, for 'Evangelical Christianity presented itself as a thing to be taken wholly or rejected wholly.'

> Had anything like modern rationalising theories of the Atonement, or modern expositions of the Bible stories, or finally modern loftier doctrines of disinterested morality and religion, been known to me at this crisis of my life, it is possible that the whole course of my spiritual history would have been different ...[71]

It is also apparent how the frequency with which Freethinkers cited the Bible and its inconsistencies as the source of their initial doubts reflected the influence of the Evangelical Revival and its emphasis on Scripture.[72] Annie Besant maintained that 'most inquirers ... before they have read any heretical works ... will have been awakened to thought by the discrepancies and inconsistencies of the Bible itself. A thorough knowledge of the Bible is the ground work of heresy.'[73] Frances Power Cobbe described how the forms of Christianity could continue to structure one's outlook even after its content had been rejected. '[T]here was Christian sentiment and the results of Christian training in all that I felt and did,' she recalled, 'I could no more have cast them off than I could have leaped off my own shadow. But of dogmatical Christianity there was never any more.'[74] In light of this emphasis upon the influence of the intellectual structures of religion upon unbelief, it also becomes possible to identify how different Christian denominations shaped the way former adherents experienced counter-conversion. For example, female Freethinkers from evangelical backgrounds tended to adopt far more intransigent and 'atheistic' forms of Freethought than the ex-Unitarians Sophia Dobson Collet, Sara Hennell and Harriet Martineau, who all developed more subtle and sympathetic critiques of Christianity.

Serious Christianity did not only shape the manner of its repudiation, but in some cases actually stimulated unbelief. The insistence upon the sincerity of personal belief and the refusal to accept any disjunction between outward conformity and inner faith meant that even slight doubts about the truth of the Gospels could prompt endless self-interrogation and profound uncertainty. Annie Besant stopped receiving communion long before she was certain of her atheism, in spite of the fact that this enraged her husband and led to her eventual expulsion from the family home. The emphasis within serious Christianity on the importance of an intense and personal faith in God was also a determining factor in provoking Besant's crisis of faith in the first place. It was precisely because she had achieved a powerful sense of God as her ever-present companion that Besant began to doubt his worth. She described how, when her children almost died from whooping cough, her 'intense faith in [Christ's] constant direction of affairs' turned against her, for it was impossible to feel anything other than revulsion for a God who, existing as a 'living reality' in her day-to-day life, could allow innocent children to suffer so.[75]

The emphasis on a personal relationship with God was accompanied by the importance Protestants placed on the right of private judgement – that is, the insistence that the truth of Scripture and the grace of God had to be apprehended by the believer herself rather than through a priestly mediator. As all the counter-conversion accounts discussed here testify, the imperative to inquire and reach one's own conclusions about the claims of Christianity played a pivotal role in the Freethinking feminists' paths to unbelief. Sara Hennell recalled how she and her brother had come into conflict with the minister of their former chapel, Robert Aspland, when they finally renounced Unitarianism. In fact, all they had been guilty of, she maintained, was following Aspland's 'own constant injunction to think always for ourselves and take our faith from no other person's teaching'.[76] Yet, as this account also reveals, Sara Hennell's eventual Freethinking stance represented a significant break with the church of her youth, for Aspland from then on treated her and her brother with the contempt due to heretics. In recognising the religious resonances of Freethought, therefore, we must at the same time be careful to respect

contemporary distinctions between Christianity and Secularism, orthodoxy and heterodoxy, even with the knowledge that such definitions
were relative and unstable. The women who feature here took a difficult
journey along a path to atheism, one that often entailed sacrifice and
persecution, and felt themselves to have arrived at a very different place
from where they had started. Their new Freethinking stance represented
an important enough shift in worldview to propel them to question other
aspects of their lives, including women's position in Christianity and
society at large.

Counter-conversion as a feminist narrative?

In publicly recounting their renunciation of religion Freethinking feminists appropriated a distinctively masculine narrative.[77] Their accounts
followed the same pattern as those of male Secularists, presenting themselves as independent-minded agents engaged in traditionally 'male'
acts of reading, intense study, and rebellion against authority. They thus
represented a radical departure from the dominant form of nineteenth-
century women's autobiography, which tended to describe the self in
terms of relationships to family and friends.[78] The disruptive potential
of seizing upon a masculine mode of life-writing was increased further
by their use of an *inverted* form of spiritual biography. Freethinking
accounts of spiritual turmoil and inner torment subverted the Christian
conversion narrative, leading to the conclusion that religion was false;
that rather than struggling against one's doubts one should follow them
through; and that unbelief rather than union with God should be the
outcome of this critical spiritual journey. In the counter-conversion
narratives of Freethinking women, subversion of the religious norms of
spiritual biography was paralleled by subversion of female norms – so
that, by narrating the story of their counter-conversion, Freethinking
feminists were also invoking the possibility of a transformation of
women's roles and social status.

The enlightened, knowledgeable and authoritative authorial voice
of the 'convert' autobiographer assumed by Freethinking women had
well-entrenched masculine associations. Loss of faith was seen as a manifestation of an intellectual and moral maturity which some Freethinkers
regarded as a male prerogative. 'Atheism', as one leading Freethinker put
it, was 'natural to man in his intellectual and moral manhood.'[79] This
outlook owed much to debates within Christianity from the seventeenth
century onward, in which proponents of 'rational' Christianity criticised
religious 'enthusiasm', which they saw as expressing humanity's more

immature or primitive urges. This critique of religious enthusiasm had a highly gendered element, with intense religiosity equated with female childishness and emotional incontinence. In declaring themselves to have acquired the necessary level of maturity to throw off their former faith, Freethinking women were therefore defying deeply entrenched notions of female subjectivity. By continually recounting their counter-conversion experiences and imploring others to follow them, Freethinking women affirmed that there was nothing in the female nature that compelled women to remain in 'thrall' to religion. Both Eliza Sharples and Emma Martin reminded their audiences that they too had once been in their position – 'slaves' to religion – but that simply through 'serious consideration of Christianity' and rational examination of Scripture – a course that was open to any woman – they had achieved an enlightened state of maturity.[80]

Freethinking feminists thus described their former faith as a state of dependence, and the independence of mind conferred by Freethought as a form of liberation. In a letter to Francis Power Cobbe, Harriet Law argued that the realisation of God's non-existence was a 'glorious discovery' in which they should 'rejoice', for 'If Atheism is true then the Bible is false; and man is no longer an unholy outcast, a degraded and *dependent* fallen being.'[81] In a review of Harriet Martineau's autobiography, Harriet Teresa Law described how Martineau had been ashamed of her need to 'acquiesce' in God's will, and that her renunciation of religion was a realisation that the only 'support' she required was to be found within.[82] Harriet Martineau herself attributed the vestigial and 'prejudiced' religious beliefs that remained prior to her conversion to atheism as a result of her failing to deal 'truly with my own mind' and instead 'trying to gain strength of conviction by vigour of [someone else's] assertion'.[83] Having finally rid herself of this state of dependency and declaring her atheism to the world, Martineau experienced an intoxicating sense of liberation, describing herself as 'a free rover on the bright, breezy common of the universe'.[84] The act of thinking independently, of deciding upon the Truths of Scripture for oneself, was, for women, an extremely ambitious and radical one. When Annie Besant declared that 'I should never again say "I believe" where I had not proved,' she effectively asserted her right to systematically examine the intellectual and moral foundations upon which the whole of society was founded, and to trust only her own reason and judgement.[85] Many Freethinking women thus used the vocabulary of emancipation to describe their renunciation of religion. Eliza Sharples' daughter likened her mother's conversion to a re-birth: 'her quiet and peaceful past was falling away from her, like loosened garments from her shoulders, to be left behind her as she steps into the new life'.[86] Annie Besant felt that the emotional torment entailed by her loss of faith was nevertheless a price worth paying for 'the joy of freedom, the joy of speaking out frankly and honestly each thought … I revelled in the liberty I had bought'.[87]

The link between freedom from religion and freedom from patriarchal authority was implicitly drawn in many Freethinking women's counter-conversion stories.[88] Eliza Sharples, for example, had lost her 'indulgent, attentive and intelligent father' about two years before she fled her paternal religion to become Richard Carlile's infidel missionary.[89] Sharples' father had not only been a 'devout churchgoer' but had also worried greatly that the beauty of his favourite daughter might bring about her ruination, and as a result had attempted to keep her as much as possible 'in the seclusion of her own room, sewing and reading'. Theophila Carlile Campbell maintained that, had it not been for the death of Sharples' father, she might never have converted to infidelism, although Campbell did not explain whether this was due to the increased freedom Eliza enjoyed after his death or because her grief had caused her to reassess her former faith.[90] Soon after her decision to renounce the Methodism of her youth, Sharples' conversion to infidelism became mixed up with her love affair with Richard Carlile, and was thus marked by a change of allegiance from one man to another.

Emma Martin's conversion entailed a more complete bid for independence from patriarchal authority. Although she did not include it in her own account of her *Reasons for Renouncing Christianity*, it was well known among Owenite Freethinkers and their opponents that soon after coming over to the infidel camp, Martin had left her husband, 'whose company it was a humiliation to endure', and taken her three daughters to live in London. She subsequently formed a free union with another Freethinking Owenite, Joshua Hopkins.[91] Similarly, it was only when Annie Besant decided that she could no longer call herself a Christian that her fraught and unhappy relationship with her husband the Rev. Frank Besant finally came to an end. Up until this point she had been attending weekly church services in order to maintain an appearance of respectability, though, as already mentioned, she had ceased to receive communion. According to Besant's version of events, just as she had decided to renounce Christianity *in toto*, Frank delivered an ultimatum: 'It was resolved that I should either resume attendance at the Communion, or should not return home: hypocrisy or expulsion – such was the alternative. I chose the latter.' Annie Besant's brother offered her a place in his house providing she give up her heretical friends, but

Besant chose independence over financial security and male protection, asserting that 'being freed from one bondage, nothing was further from my thoughts than to enter another'.[92]

Although Freethinking women tended to avoid drawing explicit links between their repudiation of religion and their rejection of patriarchal authority, the connection did not escape the notice of the wider Freethinking public. Constance Howell's novel, *A More Excellent Way*, was published in 1888, and describes the counter-conversion of Agatha Hathaway.[93] Agatha is of a higher social standing than many of the women studied here, and, because of the need to protect her family's good name, she never openly advocates the Freethought cause. Nevertheless, Howell's account of her counter-conversion follows what, by the end of the century, must have appeared as a fairly set pattern: bored in her marriage to the Collector of one of the North West Indian provinces, Agatha begins to read sceptical works such as Renan's *Life of Christ* and, as the result of this sustained intellectual inquiry, loses her former faith. Agatha's announcement of her loss of faith leads her to argue with her husband for the first time. He commands that she keep her beliefs secret and continue to practice as a Christian, but Agatha refuses, though she is later compelled to obey her husband for fear that he will take her son away from her.[94] Agatha eventually separates from her husband and it is only after his death that she feels completely free to pursue her commitment to the Freethought cause. The depiction of Agatha's story in *A More Excellent Way* shows how women's conversion to Freethought could become popularly associated with rebellion against a male authority figure.[95]

Some Freethinking women took a more explicitly political tack, claiming that they had rejected religion because it enforced male power over women. Emma Martin confessed that she had been long troubled by the 'degraded condition of women' and when she first heard Campbell speak it was his support for female emancipation which most 'delighted' her.[96] Harriet Law had also begun to rage against the oppression of women prior to her conversion to Freethought, and it was later claimed that it was this nascent feminism which led her to begin to question the truth of Scripture when she found herself unable to accept St Paul's injunction against women speaking in the church.[97] Annie Besant's counter-conversion narrative portrayed the Church of England as an institution in which an all-male clerical hierarchy jealously guarded their exclusive access to knowledge and power, and where women were expected to exist in a permanent state of spiritual submission. At an advanced stage in her crisis of faith, when she began to doubt even the divinity of Christ,

Annie Besant decided to ask for help from the Rev. Edward Pusey, who in her youth she had greatly admired as one of the founders of the Oxford Movement. Besant's account presented her former self as the archetypal rebellious woman: 'hot, eager, passionate in my determination to know, resolute not to profess belief while belief was absent – but very little of that meek, chastened, submissive spirit to which he was accustomed in the penitents wont to seek his counsel ...'. Pusey's response, however, was to refuse Besant the intellectual enlightenment she so desperately sought, claiming that she had 'read too much already' and that she ought simply to pray. Besant recalled that Pusey had treated her 'as a penitent going to confession', when in fact she was 'an enquirer after truth', thus deliberately contrasting the image of the submissive Christian with that of the confident and liberated female Freethinker.[98]

Conversion and the women's movement

Conversion as a feminist narrative was not, of course, limited to the Freethought movement. Women in early twentieth-century struggles for the suffrage frequently described their politicisation in such terms, whereby the decision to join the Cause was shown to bring about a whole new way of living.[99] Here too, historians have grappled with whether such experiences ought to be read as 'religious' or 'political' and how we should understand the distinction between the two. Was suffragette militancy, for example, a form of religious displacement, attracting those who might formerly have found an outlet for their enthusiasm in the churches?[100] Should we understand the religious symbolism so frequently employed by suffragettes as the remnants of a general shift from 'religious' to 'secular' approaches to reform within the women's movement at the turn of the century?[101] Was religious language simply a convenient way to articulate the 'political' desire for sexual emancipation?[102] Most recently, historians have begun to argue that spirituality needs to be recognised as a political site in and of itself. The reconfiguration of the sacred or the development of a new spirituality was, therefore, as important a *political* act for feminists as the demand for the franchise.[103]

Such an approach is also helpful to understanding the relationship between Freethinking feminists and the wider women's movement. For Secularist women, the renunciation of religion was crucial to how they both experienced and articulated their emancipation. It would therefore seem that their feminism was very differently situated from those Christian feminists who found religion a liberating force or from those increasingly drawn to new forms of esoteric spirituality such as

Theosophy. Yet if religion is conceptualised as the broad political terrain upon which different forms of feminism were constituted, it is possible to view these various feminist currents within a common framework. It is no longer necessary to define feminism's relationship with religion in this period solely in terms of 'for' and 'against'. Rather, we understand the desire to redefine the religious landscape as central to all of these feminist projects, despite their being pursued to very different ends.

This also offers us new way of approaching Annie Besant's conversion from Secularism to Theosophy. Many Freethinkers viewed it as a betrayal of the principles of rationality, evidence-based thinking, and independent judgement – principles which, as we have just seen, were also central to her feminism. Yet Besant maintained that she remained true to the 'intellectual state' of Freethought, continuing a journey of 'mental discovery' which led her to Theosophy. This conversion, much like her earlier renunciation of Christianity, was the result of 'years of close and strenuous study both of physiology and psychology', and her account of *Why I Became a Theosophist* devoted a number of passages to discussing scientific phenomena which the Secularist creed of materialism proved incapable of explaining. Even Theosophy's most outlandish doctrine (belief in the existence of a Brotherhood of teachers of Theosophy 'who have devoted their lives to the study of Occultism and have developed certain faculties which are still latent in ordinary human beings') was justified on a rational basis. Besant claimed that 'persons who are interested in the matter can see these people, cross examine them, and form their own conclusions as to the value of their evidence' (though she admitted that her own belief was based upon 'second hand evidence'). Thus, Besant was able to claim that her endorsement of Theosophy represented a seamless transition rather than a radical break with her Freethinking worldview.[104]

Despite adopting a set of new beliefs which other women in the Secularist movement would have found abhorrent, Besant remained true to the central tenets of their feminist project in the sense of continuing to assert her right to re-define her relationship to knowledge, authority and the divine. She remained an active advocate for women's rights, and many of the new women members who joined the Theosophical Society (TS) after Besant became President in 1907, were themselves prominent feminists. Theosophists were also, like the Secularists, often critical of Christianity as a key site of women's oppression.[105] This is not to say, however, that Besant's conversion to Theosophy was irrelevant to her feminist politics. Most strikingly, she withdrew her support for birth control in line with the TS's preference for spiritual relations between men and women. Theosophy's denigration of crude materialist forms of science entailed, in general, a very different view of free unions and sexual freedom than that encouraged by the Freethought movement's celebration of the reality of the physical world.[106] Annie Besant's successive conversions suggest, therefore, the need for a conceptual framework which allows for a detailed study of how individuals' religious views intersected with their feminism while keeping in mind that such processes relied upon broader intellectual structures which Freethinkers, Christians and even Theosophists could hold in common.

Conclusion

Counter-conversion narratives reveal much: about the relationship between religion and Secularism; about the gendered dynamics of belief and unbelief; and about the feminism of women in the Freethought movement and how they sought to present it in the public arena. We need to study counter-conversions for what they tell us about the intellectual, psychological and political motivations behind the organised Freethought movement – many of which can be understood in terms of the Christian faith that it rejected. Read as personal accounts, the counter-conversion narratives of female Freethinkers highlight the centrality of religion to the lives of women in this period. Read as public propaganda, they portray religion as a set of untruths that could be argued away by honest minds. Counter-conversion narratives were nevertheless heavily indebted to the religious viewpoints they rejected. Furthermore, in the case of female Freethinkers it is also possible to identify a gendered dynamic at play, as questions of religion and anti-religion became bound up with ideas about liberation from male authority. Yet, for Freethinking feminists, counter-conversion was not simply a metaphor for a more important kind of intellectual shift or political awakening. They really had undergone a painful and traumatic experience during which everything they had previously believed was first doubted, then questioned, and eventually challenged and renounced. The agony they suffered at having to reject religious figures, doctrines and articles of faith that had previously served as a source of comfort was only too real. And yet also real was the at first slowly dawning, and then intoxicating, sense that a world that had previously been defined according to the teachings of some higher authority, was now theirs to judge, participate in, and seek to change as only they saw fit.

While the counter-conversion narrative offered possibilities to women seeking to assert themselves as independent agents, Secularist ideology in general could at times pose problems for feminists. The counter-conversion narrative was itself problematic in that it imposed an end point upon the stories of the women who told them. Conversion to Secularism brought with it liberation and enlightenment, but there was little scope for recounting one's experiences of the Secularist movement after this point and, in particular, any problems these women might face as participants within that movement. The next chapter, therefore, will take up the stories of Freethinking feminists after the moment of conversion, to explore what it was like for women to be members of such a male dominated movement and how they were able to rise to public prominence within it.

Notes

1 E. Martin, *A Few Reasons for Renouncing Christianity and Professing and Disseminating Infidel Opinions* (London: Watson, 1840–1850[?]), p. 3.

2 Kate Watts, Hypatia Bradlaugh Bonner and Harriet Teresa Law, daughter of Mrs Harriet Law, had been born into Freethinking families.

3 The term is taken from W. James, *The Varieties of Religious Experience. A Study in Human Nature Being the Gifford Lectures on Natural Religion at Edinburgh in 1901–1902* (London, New York & Bombay: Longmans, Green & Co., 1902).

4 A. Besant, *Autobiographical Sketches* (London: Freethought Publishing Co., 1885), p. 86.

5 E. Martin, *Baptism, A Pagan Rite. Or a Mythological Essay Proving the Existence of This Ceremony in the Most Remote Ages, with an Exposition of the Materials Used in Its Celebration Being Earth, Water, Fire, Air, Blood, etc. And the Subjects of its Administration in Various Times and Countries, Being Not Only Adults and Infants But Also God's Religious Symbols, Buildings, Bells. By Emma Martin, Formerly a Member of a Baptist Church* (London: n.p. 1844), pp. 7–9, 11, 13.

6 S. S. Hennell, *Thoughts in Aid of Faith, Gathered Chiefly from Recent Works in Theology and Philosophy* (London: George Manwaring, 1860), p. 60.

7 As Susan Budd has shown, ethical and political considerations also played a part in leading Freethinkers to reject religion, but these were not emphasised as much in Freethinkers' own accounts; S. Budd, *Varieties of Unbelief: Atheists and Agnostics in English Society 1850–1950* (London: Heinemann, 1977), pp. 106–22.

8 For a detailed analysis of the religious urge see J. Barker, *Confessions of Joseph Barker. A Convert from Christianity. [Reprinted from* The Reasoner, *Nos 646–9]* (London: Holyoake & Co., 1858), p. 14.

9 For melancholia, see Martin, *Renouncing Christianity*, p. 4. For painting former faith in eroticised tones, see G. Somes Layard, *Mrs Lynn Linton. Her Life, Letters, and Opinions* (London: Methuen & Co., 1901), p. 31.

10 The term 'explanatory' is used to describe this approach in D. M. Wulff, *Psychology of Religion. Classic and Contemporary* (New York & Chichester: John Wiley & Sons, 1997), p. 14.

11 James (1902), pp. 10, 29–31. J. M. Robertson reviewed James' work in *The Reformer* defending the position of those James' dismissed as 'medical materialists', *Reformer*, 15 August 1904, pp. 485–98.

12 P. Mack, 'Religion, Feminism and the Problem of Agency: Reflections on Eighteenth-Century Quakerism', in S. Knott & B. Taylor (eds.), *Women, Gender and Enlightenment* (Basingstoke & New York: Palgrave Macmillan, 2005), pp. 434–59, 437; P. Mack, *Heart Religion in the British Enlightenment: Gender and Emotion in Early British Methodism* (Cambridge: Cambridge University Press, 2008). See also S. S. Holton, 'Feminism, History and Movements of the Soul: Christian Science in the Life of Alice Clark (1874–1934)', *Australian Feminist Studies* 13:28 (October 1998), 281–94; J. de Vries, 'More than Paradoxes to Offer: Feminism, History and Religious Cultures', in S. Morgan & J. de Vries (eds.), *Women, Gender and Religious Cultures, 1800–1940* (Abingdon: Routledge, 2010), pp. 188–210, 204; S. Williams, 'Is There a Bible in the House? Gender, Religion and Family Culture', in Morgan & de Vries (2010), pp. 11–31, 14.

13 C. Taylor, *A Secular Age* (Cambridge, MA & London: The Belknap Press of Harvard University Press, 2007), p. 437.

14 See for example S. Williams, 'Religious Belief and Popular Culture: A Study of the South London Borough of Southwark c.1880–1939' (unpublished doctoral thesis, University of Oxford, 1993); S. Williams, 'The Language of Belief: An Alternative Agenda for the Study of Victorian Working-Class Religion', *Journal of Victorian Culture* 1:2 (Autumn 1996), 303–17; C. G. Brown, *The Death of Christian Britain. Understanding Secularisation, 1800–2000* (London: Routledge, 2001).

15 S. Morgan, *A Passion for Purity: Ellice Hopkins and the Politics of Gender in the Late-Victorian Church* (Bristol: Centre for Comparative Studies in Religion and Gender, 1999), p. 26. See also E. Jay, 'The Return of the Culturally Repressed – Religion and Women', *Nineteenth-Century Studies*, 17 (2003), pp. 1–12, 5.

16 *Isis*, 11 February 1832, p. 7.

17 M. Farningham, *A Working Woman's Life. An Autobiography* (London: James Clarke & Co., 1907), p. 19, 32.

18 S. S. Hennell, *A Memoir of the Late Charles Hennell* (n.p., for private circulation, 1899), p. 5. Author's emphasis.

19 H. Martineau, *Autobiography* 2 vols, 3rd edn (London: Smith, Elder & Co., 1877: repr. Farnborough: Gregg International Publishers Ltd, 1969) i, p. 33.

20 F. Power Cobbe, *The Life of Frances Power Cobbe as Told by Herself. With Additions by the Author and Introduction by Blanche Atkinson* (London: Swan Sonnenschein & Co., 1904).

21 A. Besant, *An Autobiography* (London: T. Fisher Unwin, 1893), p. 42.

22 *Isis*, 11 February 1832, p. 2.

23 *Ibid.*, 11 February 1832, p. 7.

24 Layard (1901), p. 31.

25 Besant, *Sketches*, p. 23.

26 *Isis*, 10 March 1832, p. 71, 3 March 1832, p. 55.

27 *Ibid.*, 31 March 1832, p. 113.

28 Martin, *Renouncing Christianity*, p. 3.

29 E. Martin, *God's Gifts and Man's Duties. Being the substance of a lecture delivered by Emma Martin at the Hall of Science in Manchester, October 1, 1843, to which is*

added an address to the Minister, members and congregation of that chapel; and a letter acknowledging the receipt of "The Sinner's Friend" which had been presented to her by that gentleman (London: J. Watson, 1843), p. 11.

30 *Isis*, 3 March 1832, p. 55.

31 Martin, *Renouncing Christianity*, p. 4.

32 *Secular Chronicle (SC)*, 11 November 1877, p. 230.

33 Besant, *Sketches*, pp. 23, 20.

34 For the historiography, see Introduction. See also Farningham (1907), p. 280 for a contemporary account illustrating this point.

35 Cobbe (1904), p. 89.

36 Besant, *Sketches*, p. 54. Jane Clapperton similarly referred to the 'intellectual heavings' the loss of faith entailed as 'intensely painful'; J. Clapperton, 'Agnosticism and Women: A Reply', *The Nineteenth Century* 7:39 (May 1880), 840–44, 841.

37 A. Besant, *The Gospel of Christianity and the Gospel of Freethought* (London: Charles Watts, 1877), pp. 7–8.

38 Martineau (1877) ii, p. 345.

39 *Isis*, 10 March 1832, p. 66.

40 T. Carlile Campbell, *The Battle of the Press, as Told in the Story of the Life of Richard Carlile* (London: A. & H.B. Bonner, 1899), pp. 149–50.

41 Martin, *Renouncing Christianity*, pp. 4–5.

42 *Ibid.*, p. 5.

43 Jackie Latham suggests that Martin's conversion may have been slower and more gradual than Martin's own account implies, revealing that Martin corresponded with the mystic and 'sacred socialist' James Pierrepont Greaves in 1840, and that in September of that year she defended the principle of a 'First Cause' in a lecture. By 1841, however, it appears that Martin had passed through this brief period of deism to affirm her materialist atheist principles; see J. E. M. Latham, 'Emma Martin and Sacred Socialism: the Correspondence of James Pierrepont Greaves', *History Workshop Journal* 38 (1994), 215–17.

44 E. Martin, *Baptism*, p. 3.

45 *Agnostic Journal (AJ)*, 16 October 1897, p. 254.

46 E. Royle, 'Law, Harriet Teresa (1831–97), Feminist, Secularist and Radical', in J. Bellamy & J. Saville (eds.), *Dictionary of Labour Biography* 12 vols (London & Basingstoke: Macmillan Press, 1972–) v (1979), pp. 134–6.

47 For example, see *The National Reformer (NR)*, 14 November 1879, p. 317.

48 Hennell (1899), p. 32

49 Hennell (1899), p. 35; C. Hennell, *An Inquiry Concerning the Origin of Christianity … To which is added Christian Theism. Third People's Edition of Both Works* (London: Trubner and Co., 1870) (first published 1839).

50 Martineau (1877) i, p. 44.

51 *Ibid.*, pp. 103, 185.

52 *Ibid.*, p. 39.

53 The earliest essay in the collection, 'On Inspiration', was written in 1870, the opening essay on the 'Deity of Jesus of Nazareth' 'was written just before I left the Church of England, and marks the point where I broke finally with Christianity'. See A. Besant, *My Path to Atheism* (London: Freethought Publishing Co., 1877).

54 Besant, *Path to Atheism*, p. vi; Besant, *Sketches*, p. 34. Both Frances Power Cobbe and Eliza Lynn Linton, also brought up in the Established Church, recorded very similar childhood experiences of doubt sparked off by incredulity over Bible stories. Cobbe's came at the age of eleven when she was shocked to discover herself unconvinced by the miracle of the loaves and fishes, while Linton at fourteen years old was suddenly unable to believe in the Virgin Birth after noting its similarities with the myths of women impregnated by the gods of the classical world; see Cobbe (1904), pp. 86–7; Layard (1901), p. 37.

55 Besant, *Path to Atheism*, pp. iv–vii.

56 Besant, *Path to Atheism*, p. vii; Besant, *Sketches*, pp. 55, 65–66.

57 Besant, *Sketches*, p. 55.

58 Besant, *Path to Atheism*, p. vii; Besant, *Sketches*, pp. 62–65, 69.

59 Vosey subsequently went on to found the Theistic Church.

60 Besant, *Sketches*, p. 62.

61 A. Taylor, *Annie Besant: A Biography* (Oxford: Oxford University Press, 1992), pp. 46–9, 55–57.

62 *Ibid.*, pp. 70–3, 83.

63 S. Budd, 'The Loss of Faith: Reasons for Unbelief Among Members of the Secular Movement in England, 1850–1950', *Past and Present* 36 (1967), 106–25; S. Budd (1977), p. 123; S. A. Mullen, *Organised Freethought: the Religion of Unbelief in Victorian England* (New York: Garland, 1987). For male conversion narratives, see G. J. Holyoake, *The Trial of George Jacob Holyoake on an Indictment for Blasphemy, Before Mr. Justice Erskin, and a Common Jury at Gloucester – August 15, 1842* (London: Printed for Anti-Persecution Union by Thomas Paterson, 1842), pp. 20–1; *The Reasoner* (*Reasoner*), 2 September 1855, p. 179; G. J. Holyoake, *The Last Trial for Atheism in England. A Fragment of Autobiography*, 5th edn (London: N. Trubnor & Co., 1878), p. 52; G. J. Holyoake, *My Religious Days* (1901) London: Bishopsgate Library, George Jacob Holyoake Archive; H. Bradlaugh Bonner, *Charles Bradlaugh. A Record of his Life and Work by his Daughter Hypatia Bradlaugh Bonner. With an Account of his Parliamentary Struggle, Politics and Teachings by John M. Robertson MP*, 7th edn (London: T. Fisher Unwin, 1908), pp. 8–12.

64 T. Larsen, *Crisis of Doubt* (Oxford: Oxford University Press, 2006).

65 A comparison can be made with Freethinkers' deathbed accounts. It was particularly important that Freethinkers should be recorded as having had a peaceful death in order to counter rumours that they had renounced their unbelief at the final moment and asked for God's forgiveness; see D. Nash, '"Look in Her Face and Lose Thy Dread of Dying": The Ideological Importance of Death to the Secularist Movement in Victorian England', *Journal of Religious History* 19 (1995), 158–80. For the 'public uses' of Freethinkers' biographies, see D. Nash, '"The Credulity of the Public Seems Infinite": Charles Bradlaugh. Public Biography and the Battle for Narrative Supremacy in Fin de Siècle England', *Journal of Victorian Culture* 7:2 (Autumn 2002), 239–62.

66 Though not referring directly to the Freethought movement, historians and literary critics have noted the importance of conversion narratives to nineteenth-century biography, as well as how accounts of loss of faith tended to mirror the rhetorical structures of Christian conversions; see F. Turner, 'The Victorian Crisis of Faith and the Faith that was Lost', in R. Helmstadter & B. Lightman (eds.), *Victorian Faith*

in Crisis. Essays on Continuity and Change in Nineteenth-Century Religious Belief (London & Basingstoke: Macmillan, 1990), pp. 9–38, 10; J. D. Barbour, *Versions of Deconversion. Autobiography and the Loss of Faith* (Charlottesville & London: University Press of Virginia, 1994), p. 4.

67   E. Graham, H. Hinds, E. Hobby & H. Wilcox (eds.), *Her Own Life. Autobiographical Writings by Seventeenth-Century Englishwomen* (London & New York: Routledge, 1989), pp. 3–4.

68   L.Peterson, *Traditions of Victorian Women's Autobiography. The Poetics and Politics of Life Writing* (Charlottesville & London: University Press of Virginia, 2000), p. 45.

69   Taylor (2007), p. 4.

70   C. Taylor, *Sources of the Self. The Making of the Modern Identity* (Cambridge: Cambridge University Press, 1989), pp. 403–4.

71   Cobbe (1904), pp. 89–90.

72   This point is made by Budd, who noted that 'The two books most frequently mentioned as being important to deconversion were the Bible and Paine's *Age of Reason*', Budd (1977), p. 107.

73   Besant, *Path to Atheism*, pp. v–vi.

74   Cobbe (1904), p. 93.

75   Besant, *Sketches*, p. 50.

76   Hennell (1899), p. 12.

77   For a discussion of 'crisis of faith' literature as 'deeply masculine', see J. Dean, *Religious Experience and the New Woman: The Life of Lilly Dougall* (Bloomington & Indianapolis: Indiana University Press, 2007), pp. 47–8.

78   This has been noted of Cobbe and Martineau's spiritual autobiographies; Peterson (2000), p. 27, 64.

79   Barker (1858), p. 14.

80   *Isis*, 18 February 1832, pp. 21, 68; Martin, *Renouncing Christianity*, p. 3.

81   *SC*, 21 October 1877, p. 197, emphasis added.

82   *SC*, 1 July 1877, pp. 9–10.

83   Martineau (1877) ii, p. 186.

84   Martineau (1877) i, p. 116.

85   Besant, *Sketches*, p. 55.

86   Carlile Campbell (1899), p. 155.

87   Besant, *Sketches*, p. 85.

88   See, H. Rogers, 'Poetesses and Politicians: Gender, Knowledge and Power in Radical Culture, 1830–1870' (unpublished doctoral thesis, University of York, 1994), p. 54; Fix Anderson (1987), pp. 18–19; S. J. Peacock, *The Theological and Ethical Writings of Frances Power Cobbe, 1822–1904* (Lampeter: The Edwin Mellen Press, 2002), p. 28; B. Caine, 'Feminist History and Feminist Biography', *Women's History Review* 3:2 (1994), 247–61, 256–7.

89   *Isis*, 31 March 1832, p. 113.

90   Carlile Campbell (1899), p. 148.

91   G. J.Holyoake, *The Last Days of Mrs Emma Martin. Advocate of Free Thought* (London: J.Watson, 1851).

92   Besant, *Sketches*, pp. 74–5.

93 C. Howell, *A More Excellent Way* (London: Swan Sonnenschien, 1888). Despite a lack of biographical information available for Howell, it is likely that the character of Agatha Hathaway contains at least some autobiographical elements for Howell was also the author of two educational works for the children of Freethinkers – *A Biography of Jesus Christ. Written for Young Freethinkers* (London: Freethought Publishing Co., 1883) and *The After Life of the Apostles. Written for Young Freethinkers* (London: Freethought Publishing Co., 1884) – subjects on which Agatha Hathaway is also said to have published; see Howell (1888), pp. 61–2.

94 For this, Howell must have drawn on Annie Besant's account in *Autobiographical Sketches*, published three years previously, of how she was deprived custody of her daughter ostensibly for failing to give her a religious education.

95 Howell (1888), pp. 16–17, 37, 56.

96 Martin, *Renouncing Christianity*, p. 5.

97 E. Royle, 'Law, Harriet Teresa (1831–97), Feminist, Secularist and Radical', in J. Bellamy & J. Saville (eds.), *Dictionary of Labour Biography* 12 vols (London & Basingstoke: Macmillan Press, 1972–) v (1979), pp. 134–6, 135; *The Freethinker*, 8 August 1897, p. 502.

98 Besant, *Sketches*, p. 34.

99 J. de Vries, 'Transforming the Pulpit: Preaching and Prophecy in the British Women's Suffrage Movement', in B. Mayne Kienzle & P. J. Walker (eds.), *Women Preachers and Prophets Through Two Millennia of Christianity* (Los Angeles: University of California Press, 1998), pp. 318–34, 322; K. Hartman, ' "What made me a suffragette": the New Woman and the new (?) conversion narrative', *Women's History Review* 12:1 (2003), 35–50.

100 This is suggested by Brian Harrison, *Peaceable Kingdom: Stability and Change in Modern Britain* (Oxford: Clarendon Press, 1982), pp. 44–5.

101 C. Midgley is among those historians who have identified such a shift occurring more generally; see 'Women, Religion and Reform', in S. Morgan and J. de Vries (eds.), *Women, Gender and Religious Cultures in Britain, 1800–1940* (Abingdon: Routledge, 2010), pp. 138–58, 154.

102 This approach has been criticised by J. Dixon, *Divine Feminine: Theosophy and Feminism in England* (Baltimore: The Johns Hopkins University Press, 2001), p. 2.

103 M. Vicinus, *Independent Women: Work and Community for Single Women, 1850–1920* (London: Virago, 1985), pp. 251–2, 259; Dixon (2001), p. 3.

104 A. Besant, *Why I Became a Theosophist* (London: Freethought Publishing Company, 1889).

105 Between 1900 and 1910 two thirds of new members were women. Prominent feminist members included Mona Caird (a member from 1904 to 1909) and Charlotte Despard (a member from 1899 to 1934); Dixon (2001), pp. 68, 156.

106 Many Theosophists advocated abstinence from all sexual relationships, though Dora Montifiore and Edith Lanchester, both of whom were members of the TS in the 1890s, were also advocates of free unions; Dixon (2001), pp. 172–3.

3

Preachers of truth: women's activism in the Secularist movement

I n 1855, only a few years after the first Secularist societies were established, George Jacob Holyoake published an article calling for women to play a prominent role in the new movement. Women, he argued, possessed the necessary 'self-command' and 'intellectual strength' to enable them to participate in the public realm; to 'conquer in that domain of disinterested and unnoticed purpose where manly genius has been held to be supreme'. He took as an example the recently deceased Emma Martin, describing her as an exemplary member of the Secularist 'party', a 'true propagandist' who understood her part in the 'corporate body'. Holyoake encouraged other Freethinking women to follow Martin in becoming 'teacher[s] of the public', a role readily assumed by those female lecturers, journalists and writers in the Secularist movement.[1] In otherwise male dominated political, religious and intellectual arenas the foremost principles of Freethought – a spirit of free inquiry and commitment to the free dissemination of knowledge – provided openings for women to assume a powerful and public role. They employed the ideal of 'free inquiry' in particular, to legitimate their involvement in religious controversy and to challenge the authority of the priesthood. Knowledge became a weapon in the hands of these female Freethinkers, who fused the Secularist attack on the Christian monopoly on Truth with the struggle of women to participate in the public sphere.

'Public free discussion ...'

Despite the relatively extensive range of activities and different types of roles on offer to women in the Freethought movement, only a tiny number of female Secularists took up these opportunities. This was due not to formal restrictions but because to publicly assert oneself as a Freethinking woman seriously contravened acceptable codes of female conduct. Historians have extensively discussed the obstacles to women's entry into the public sphere in the nineteenth century, when dominant constructions of womanhood placed significant restrictions upon their participation in national and pressure-group politics especially.[2] Public speaking in particular represented, in the words of Florence Fenwick Miller, 'the very head and front of our offending … It was the last degree of "unsexing," forgetting the proper delicacy of womanhood.'[3] The cultural injunction against heated exchange between men and women was so strong that even feminists such as Frances Power Cobbe cautioned against women participating in 'angry' debates or discussions in which they would have to respond to contributions and questions from male members of the audience.[4]

Yet such warnings, along with the proliferation of more conservative 'angel in the house' rhetoric, occurred in response to the gradual incursion of small groups of women into a wide range of 'public' activities over the course of the century. It may have been unusual, in the 1840s and 1870s respectively, for women such as Emma Martin or Florence Fenwick Miller to speak in public, but it was not unheard of.[5] Since the early 1800s women had been lecturing and writing for a number of social and political causes, including the abolition of slavery, temperance, prison reform and extensive philanthropic endeavours.[6] In the first half of the century the Owenite and Chartist movements had provided a radical platform for women, while later in the nineteenth and early-twentieth century increasing numbers of women became active in campaigns for education, employment and the suffrage. But it was in the name of Christianity that most women in the nineteenth century would have gained their first experience of activity outside the home – as district visitors, fundraisers, missionaries and even as preachers. While many Christian churchmen attacked female advocates of Freethought for their usurpation of masculine 'public' roles and insisted that their Church would never allow its women to 'walk in breeches or wear a beard'[7], some of those Christian women were in fact becoming preachers themselves.[8]

The Church was only one of many sites during this period in which different and competing voices struggled to be heard. The nineteenth and early twentieth century witnessed multiple attempts to democratise a variety of public institutions and political arenas. Successive movements for franchise reform meant that formal political structures became more inclusive, while those who continued to be excluded from them fought even harder for their right to have their say on pressing social and political issues of the day. 'Public opinion' began to be taken into account in elections, thus increasing the power of the press, which in turn acted as an alternative arena in which women and working-class men – excluded from government to varying degrees – could participate.[9] The periodical press in particular was characterised by polemical rhetoric and reactive dialogue between competing voices and opposing views.[10] Public meetings took on a similar function when, from the 1780s, campaigners began to use them to promote a variety of social and political causes. By the 1830s and 1840s the mass outdoor public meeting had become a crucial aspect of Chartist activity, and public meetings remained important to campaign politics throughout the century, forming an essential part of metropolitan radicalism.[11] Such meetings tended to be formally committed to free and fair debate between opposing sides, in the belief that the public could then decide for itself which case was the most convincing.[12] This period also witnessed the battle for a free press, and in the 1830s the Freethinkers Richard Carlile and Henry Hetherington were imprisoned for the publication of unstamped newspapers.[13] When the campaign was renewed in the late 1840s George Jacob Holyoake sat on the Newspaper Stamp Abolition Committee alongside Sophia Dobson Collet's brother Collet Dobson Collet, and both men remained committed to repealing the 'taxes on knowledge' until the final duty was removed in 1869.[14]

Organised Freethought was therefore part of a world in which widening access to ideas was not only valued but also politically charged. The Secularist movement distilled this commitment to freedom of expression into the principle of free inquiry, an ideal that had been an important strand of anti-religious worldviews from the seventeenth century onwards, and which became a defining characteristic of nineteenth- and early twentieth-century Freethought.[15] Rather than look foremost to economic or political means, Freethinkers believed that society would be transformed by liberating the popular mind from the bonds of superstition. 'Public free discussion,' declared Richard Carlile, 'is the only system of purification in society – the only system that abates wrong bias, and strengthens right and wrong.'[16] Freethinkers maintained that 'Truth' would inevitably reveal itself providing knowledge was allowed to disseminate freely. The public life of Freethought – its meetings, lectures, publications and its press – was fundamentally shaped by this spirit of free inquiry, and by an insistence upon rational disputation, openness, and clarity of language. In the 1820s, Freethought culture was built around a profoundly democratic vision of 'a community of free and equal speakers' in which no hierarchy or privilege of speech existed.[17] Such a vision persisted into the second half of the century, re-invigorated by J. S. Mill's philosophical liberalism, which saw free discussion as 'the highest guarantee of public truth'.[18] Secularist societies were committed to totally open platforms, so that by the end of the century their venues had hosted Anarchists, Socialists, Positivists, Ethicists and Christians.[19] A typical Freethought meeting might consist of a lecture, followed by a discussion in which the audience could participate and direct questions at the speaker. Another popular format was the set-piece debate between a Freethinker and a Christian, also followed by general discussion. Such practices reinforced the Freethought commitment to democratic access to knowledge and, in a movement which boasted such a high number of self-taught members, the right of every individual to engage with and contribute to ideas.[20]

Thus Freethinkers did not advocate freedom of discussion for its own sake. Their commitment to eradicating ignorance was a political and moral one. According to Holyoake, the 'self-thinker' followed truth 'wherever he may find it, and wherever it may lead', not out of 'caprice or wantonness' but in order 'to find out the law of humanity, the conditions of human progress, and the nature of human duty ... Our object is to promote personal morality.'[21] Enforced ignorance was therefore both evil in itself and the cause of all other forms of suffering. Frances Wright surveyed the penitentiaries, poor houses, drinking and gambling that afflicted society and, in asking 'what is the cause of all this?' declared the answer to be 'Ignorance! Ignorance! There is none other.'[22] Harriet Law agreed, maintaining that the biblical figure of Eve ought to be rehabilitated on the grounds that, in partaking of the forbidden fruit; she had removed the evil of ignorance 'which must be admitted as the greatest of all evils.'[23]

As Harriet Law's statement suggests, the spirit of free inquiry connected with ideas about women's access to widening arenas of intellectual and political activity. It therefore had important implications for women's ability to participate as thinkers, speakers and writers in the Freethought movement itself. The commitment to freedom of discussion at the very least precluded an explicit exclusion of female members from Secularist public platforms. Small numbers of Freethinking women were able to negotiate a prominent role for themselves in arenas of public talk and writing, which challenged dominant Christian notions of womanhood. The culture of free inquiry and the hyper-rationalist rhetoric that accompanied it encouraged women to assume a gender-neutral and even 'masculine' public persona so that Freethinking lecturers and writers presented themselves not as feminine subjects but as 'preachers of truth'. While this challenged traditional (and subordinate) notions of femininity, it could also act as a barrier to women's full integration into the Secularist movement. Some women therefore sought to influence the intellectual framework and future direction of organised Freethought away from polarised understandings of the highly gendered categories of 'faith' and 'reason'.

Public talk

Public meetings and lectures were central to Freethought activism and Secularist branch culture, with their national press regularly reporting local meetings in detail. These meetings were part of a world of public talk in which the more formalised lectures by campaigning organisations jostled for space alongside itinerant street speakers of every political and religious stripe. Secularist activities took place in many arenas: some were held in purpose-built venues such as the Old Street Hall of Science and the John Street Institute in London, or the Secular Hall in Leicester, but it was also common for the upstairs rooms of pubs to be rented for the evening. Many Freethought lectures and debates took place in the open air, since Secularists were constantly refused bookings at indoor venues because of their unorthodox views. In the streets of London's poorer districts and in popular outdoor spaces such as Bonner's fields in East London, Secularists competed with Christian preachers for the same audiences.[24] This was a world in which different voices and views struggled – sometimes violently – to be heard, and the female Freethought lecturer was seen as a highly controversial, provocative and embattled figure. In the 1820s, during her lecture tour of America, Frances Wright set the tone for subsequent generations of Freethinking public women when she ascended the platform (dressed in bloomers) in defiance of attempts by her Christian opponents to prevent her from speaking. Wright made much of the opposition she faced, recording how the clergy of New York had circulated 'inflammatory placards and pamphlets, in which the object of the lecturer was represented to be nothing short of universal insurrection of the people'. In response to these 'ribald slanders and incendiary threats' against her 'reputation and person as a woman', Wright portrayed herself as a martyr to the cause of truth and, with a firm sense of the importance of her task, compared herself to both Socrates and Jesus.[25]

On the other side of the Atlantic, English Freethinking women used similar modes of self-representation in order to manage an equally rowdy lecture circuit. Wright's fellow Owenites Emma Martin and Margaret Chappellsmith were chased out of town by angry mobs, and their encounters with male clergymen frequently led to abusive exchanges and expulsion from meetings. Martin spent time in a Scottish gaol for expressing her Freethought opinions in too trenchant a manner.[26] Later in the century, both Harriet Law and Annie Besant encountered very similar reactions.[27] They lectured to audiences of both men and women, sometimes numbering up to a thousand, and it was not unusual for the venue to be filled well over capacity so that frequently 'every nook and cranny of [the] Hall was literally crammed'.[28] When Law and Besant lectured in areas that did not have a large Secularist base their audiences were often made up of hostile Christians. In 1869 Harriet Law travelled to the Newcastle area to deliver a lecture 'On Chinese Missions'. The hostility Law faced from the crowd was so great that even the Christian reporter from the *Gateshead Tribune* sympathised with her:

> Mrs Law rose. Her doing so was the signal for a scene which baffles description. As a spectator it seemed to me as if all the beasts, clean and unclean, in Noah's ark were let loose ... Mrs Law stood, meanwhile, as quiet as a model in Rembrandt's studio, looking half Joan of Arc, half the Widow Brownrigg, and a little bit of the Lancashire lass with her clogs on. Dr. Gregson, as chairman, rose and [said] ... that, as an Englishman, he was ashamed of the conduct of a meeting towards a woman.[29]

Harriet Law, however, had no need of the protection of the chairman, for she was used to such scenes and more than capable of dealing with them herself.

> Mrs Law said that there was only one man annoying her, and if all the others kept quiet, she defied one man to prevent her from being heard ... Mrs Law's virtual challenge to tackle the pre-eminent disturber of her peace, if all others kept quiet, turned the meeting at once in her favour. She assailed Mr. Vasey ... in trenchant style.[30]

As in this instance, female lecturers were not exempt from the Secularists' insistence on free discussion in public meetings, and, as with the case of Harriet Law and Mr Vasey, they were frequently called upon to answer questions and attacks from male members of the audience. At Annie Besant's first public lecture, contributors in the ensuing debate climbed up beside her onto the platform to say their piece. Since it was her first time lecturing, Charles Bradlaugh stepped in once to answer a point for her, but otherwise she was left to defend her argument.[31]

Harriet Law and Annie Besant also engaged in public debates with male opponents, where the atmosphere often resembled that of a football match complete with rival teams of supporters to cheer on their respective sides. When Rev. J. H. Gordon lectured in Darlington on 'The Gospel according to Secularism, and Secularism according to the Gospel' he allowed Law time to reply, and 'A great crowd had gathered in the knowledge that Law was to attend this lecture ... Mrs Law ... was loudly applauded by her partisans on entering the hall, as were the lecturer and local ministers.'[32] Law, like Emma Martin in the 1840s, had probably posted bills around the town, advertising her intention of attending the meeting, for Freethought lecturers were well aware of the publicity value of a showdown between a furious Christian and a 'trenchant' female advocate of Freethought. Secularist audiences could cause just as much trouble for the Christian speaker as his supporters could for the Freethinker. When Annie Besant debated William T. Lee on the question 'Christianity or Secularism; which is the better system for man' in 1888, Lee's transcription of the debate described how at one point he was engulfed by jeers and shouts from the audience – 'I did not say that Hallam – (dissent) – I did not say – ("You did," and hisses) – I did not say that – (cries of "Liar," "You did," and great uproar).' However, Besant declared herself outraged on behalf of her opponent at this affront to free speech, and informed the lecture hall that, though she was used to 'unruly' audiences, 'I can conceive of nothing so fatal to discussion as the kind of interference that has been going on during the last speech.'[33]

Sometimes the usual rowdiness of the 'unruly' meeting might escalate into a more serious form of violence; both Law and Besant found their persons in danger on at least one occasion. In 1870 Law was in the middle of delivering a lecture on 'Martin Luther and Thomas Paine' when sand and small pebbles began to be thrown at the windows of the hall by residents of Hebden Bridge who had gathered outside. At first Law ignored this disturbance and continued to lecture, but soon the beams supporting the building began to be hammered 'by some person with a huge stone' and the vibrations almost caused the large clock to fall off the wall onto the audience below. Law, however, persevered with her lecture and managed to finish it. But 'upon the exit of the lecturer, she was literally mobbed.' She just managed to reach her lodgings for the night unharmed, but on the following day, when she returned to give a second lecture, 'the crowd closed in upon her, notwithstanding the efforts of the police, and the lady received a blow in the right eye struck by a man's fist, causing her great pain for a length of time ... the mob was estimated by some at 2,000.'[34]

Besant's worst experience was at the village of Congleton, near the home of Elizabeth Wolstenholme Elmy and Ben Elmy, with whom she was staying in 1876. She had lectured at Congleton the previous year but had encountered nothing more threatening than a band outside the lecture hall repeatedly playing *God Save the Queen*. This time, however, the violence began almost immediately with 'a tremendous hooting and yelling ... heard outside'. The mob smashed the windows of the building where she was lecturing and 'some specially cowardly scoundrel ... [threw] some hard substance which struck Mrs Besant ... a rather sore blow on the back of the neck'. As Law had found at Hebden Bridge six years before, the mob was determined to follow the female lecturer back to her lodgings, where 'the senseless bigots kept up the same terribly, ear-splitting, headache-inducing provoking noise, until about midnight'. The following day Elizabeth Wolstenholme Elmy was hit by a volley of stones which left a serious gash on her forehead, and Bradlaugh was compelled to wrestle with one of the opponents to prevent him from interrupting Besant's lecture. However, like Harriet Law at Hebden Bridge, Besant succeeded in finishing her speech and felt that the forces of Freethought had triumphed.[35]

Some Freethinkers were anxious that the carnival atmosphere created by the more adversarial forms of debating would brand the Freethought movement common and unrespectable. This especially concerned Holyoake from the 1850s, in his attempt to build a more positive and constructive version of Secularism. In 1855 *The Reasoner* published a set of helpful hints to the young speaker, the first of which was to 'strictly avoid anything vulgar ... do not study witticisms to excite vain laughter'.[36] Holyoake also published a guide to public speaking and debate, in which he argued that the lecturer should be treated, and behave, as a professional with 'as much dignity as any trade'.[37] Holyoake was perhaps influenced by his associate Sophia Dobson Collet. Collet also had strong views on the future direction of Secularism and its need to cast off its reputation for vulgarity and belligerence. In 1846, as Holyoake prepared to take on a Christian opponent in public debate, Collet wrote to remind him that 'courtesy with the clergy, not only with personal intercourse, but in discussion, is especially called for from you in these sorts of meetings ...'. And she rebuked him for 'that constant tone of disparagement in which you speak of nearly everything connected with the clergy – a tone traditional among freethinkers'.[38] Concern to avoid vulgarity translated, in the case of female lecturers, into an increased pressure to conduct oneself in a 'ladylike' manner. Writing in 1897, Holyoake recalled that both Harriet Law and Annie Besant had adopted the 'defiant and loud' tones of his arch-enemy Charles Bradlaugh, who had himself been an advocate of more populist styles of debate. Holyoake concluded that this 'unwomanly' tone of speech was unsuitable for them and had resulted in them losing their 'engagingness' as speakers.[39]

Freethinkers who wished for a respectable movement were particularly critical of those who undertook painstakingly detailed deconstructions of all the inaccuracies and disparities to be found in Scripture, arguing that this approach made Secularism into a wholly negative philosophy.[40] Well established Secularist meetings often acquired a resident 'Christian Evidence questioner' ready to engage in combative debates in which entertainment took precedence over intellectual rigour. Historians have also been critical of this aspect of Freethought culture, whereby 'the search for reason and truth was abandoned for the enjoyment of the fight'.[41] This populist mode of discussion, with its emphasis on the Bible, can however be read as a particularly democratic and inclusive form of intellectual exchange, given that any man or woman with a basic understanding of Scripture would have possessed the knowledge required to participate in such debates. This was especially important for the women in the audience, the vast majority of whom would have been denied elite educations but were very likely to have been brought up with a thorough and detailed religious education. Leading female Freethought lecturers possessed extensive theological knowledge that often far exceeded that of the clergymen they debated. Yet for semi- and self-educated women such as Harriet Law, who first encountered Secularist ideas in a 'dark' and 'shady' room just off the Mile End Road in the East End of London, it is surely extremely significant that she was immediately able to participate in the discussion as a result of being armed with the basic 'Christian arguments' provided by her Baptist upbringing. It was because of the democratic potential of these Scriptural debates that they continued throughout the century in spite of criticisms from some elements within the leadership. When Bradlaugh joined the ranks of the Secularist leadership in the 1860s, he was able to capitalise on this, and used his considerable oratorical skill to revive the big set-piece debate between Atheist and Christian.[42]

The right of any individual to interpret, and even to dismiss, Scripture as they saw fit was, of course, a direct challenge to the authority of the Churches. For a woman to do so represented an even more radical transgression of both religious authority and acceptable modes of feminine conduct. Freethinking women thus encountered especially strong opposition from Christians. In 1876 Harriet Law accompanied Bradlaugh to debate with the leader of the Christian Evidence Society, Bishop Cloughton. On finding that Harriet Law was also to be on the platform, Cloughton complained that 'although he came prepared to listen to men who challenged the truths of the gospel, he never imagined that he should be called upon to meet a *woman* who had the effrontery to do the same.'[43] Some Christian commentators maintained that the act of speaking publicly on matters of religion served to un-sex Freethinking women. An exchange of letters in the *Huddersfield Daily Examiner* revealed a Rev. Telford to have been telling lies about Harriet Law, and attempting to cover up his slander by claiming that it was in fact a man he referred to. When he was called upon to explain his deception Telford claimed that the only reason he had become confused about the sex of the Freethought lecturer was 'because there was so little of the "woman" about her whole address and deportment ... that but for her attire I could scarcely imagine she was of that class whom we are proud to designate "woman"'.[44] St Paul's prohibition on women speaking in the Church was frequently invoked against female Freethought lecturers. When Annie Besant debated with William T. Lee he accused her of failing to answer the question put to her, but joked that he hoped she had finally learnt the lesson of the Apostle 'Let the women learn in silence'.[45]

Freethinking feminists believed St Paul's injunction to be the main cause of all the restrictions placed on women playing an active public role, both inside and outside the Church. Florence Fenwick Miller claimed that:

> it is undoubtedly the case that the clergy of every denomination have been the most 'vehement and vitriolic' opponents of women as public speakers; partly, of course, because of the lead given by Paul and partly, one cannot but suspect, from a spice of jealousy themselves as by far the largest professional class of public speaker.[46]

An article in *The National Reformer* entitled 'St. Paul vs. Mrs Fawcett', similarly condemned St Paul for the 'violence' he expressed 'towards anything like freedom of thought and action in women'.[47] It was claimed that Harriet Law's loss of faith had been sparked off by initial doubts about the Pauline injunction, and she continually contrasted the silence imposed on Christian women with the freedom and equality of female Freethinkers.[48] When Bishop Cloughton complained about having to debate with a woman, Law retorted that of course the Christian Evidence Society would never have allowed females to attend *their* annual meeting, from fear that women might use their 'brains and tongues' to 'disconcert' the Episcopal authority.[49] In 1876 she attacked the undemocratic structures of the Perfectionist sect, claiming that, by prohibiting women from speaking at its annual conference, its ministers were merely attempting to ensure that their authority would not be questioned.[50] The contrast between the 'sad meekness' of the Christian woman and the free and intellectually equal Freethinking woman was an important part of the female Freethought lecturer's public persona, in outright defiance of dominant Christian ideas about woman's proper role.[51]

Because their movement by default opposed all Christian teachings, Freethinking women found it far easier to reject the Pauline injunction than their Christian sisters, some of whom were struggling to re-interpret St Paul's epistle in order to justify a greater public role for women in the churches and in society at large.[52] The right to speak out against the injustice of their own position, and to contribute to moral and social improvement, was one of the main demands of the feminism of this period. Many, especially middle-class, women focused upon this imposed silence as one of the primary forms of their oppression. Florence Fenwick Miller, for example, recalled how in the 1870s endless debates took place in which young men held forth upon the subject of 'Woman', while 'no young woman ever rose up and intervened'. Fenwick Miller 'burned within' at such injustice until one day by chance she was called upon to deliver a lecture and found that the words simply flowed forth.[53] Fenwick Miller went on to bask in the atmosphere of the Dialectical Society – frequented by numerous Freethinkers – where 'the ideal of the duty of freedom of thought … and courageous frankness in expression of such truth as one apprehended, profoundly appealed to my intellectual and moral character'.[54] Annie Besant experienced a similar 'longing to find outlet in words' and, in her autobiography, she equated her eventual assertion of her right to speak with the subversion and usurpation of the authority of the Church. Her 'first lecture' was performed in an empty church when, one day finding herself alone in her husband's parish, she climbed into the pulpit and assumed the role of the minister. 'I shall never forget,' she recalled, 'the feeling of power and delight that came upon me as my voice rolled down the aisles.'[55]

By the beginning of the twentieth century many more women were beginning to find a voice – speaking up for their rights and joining the women's movement in ever larger numbers. Yet in the Secularist movement the heyday of the infamous female lecturer had passed, and Hypatia Bradlaugh Bonner remained the only prominent woman on the Freethought lecture circuit. This was due in part to the shifting social and intellectual basis of Freethought. As freethinking views became more broadly accepted within educated society, the confrontational style employed by Law and Besant in the 1860s and 1870s seemed less and less relevant.[56] Progressive intellectuals increasingly professed a desire for a less embattled and less mechanistic approach to religious critique than that offered by the National Secular Society. The Freewoman editor Dora Marsden, for example, held deeply heterodox views with regards to both Christian doctrine and sexual morality, yet she was critical of Secularist Guy Aldred's preoccupation with revealing the inaccuracies of Scripture. 'Christian origins are not proved by true or false data', she wrote, for 'spiritual values cannot be gauged save by the spirit sense'.[57] The longstanding current of 'positive' Freethought found new voice among middle-class thinkers such as Jane Clapperton and Karl Pearson, who argued for Freethought to be construed as a new religion in itself – free from the trappings of Christian myth but still respectful of the 'infinite'.[58] Yet Karl Pearson's wish to move away from 'coarse satire' and purely 'negative action' also indicated the expropriation of an arena of

Figure 2 Leicester Secular Hall (1877)

knowledge which had, by virtue of its marginalisation, become democratised to the extreme.[59]

The gradual mainstreaming of Freethought also had implications for the role of female lecturer. By 1907 it was possible for Hypatia Bradlaugh Bonner to give a drawing-room lecture to middle-class professionals without her Secularist connections causing too much scandal.[60] Yet in acquiring a more respectable audience, the Freethought female lecturer also lost the radical edge that had permitted her to challenge many of the strictures of polite femininity. Hypatia Bradlaugh Bonner cultivated a far less adversarial public image than the Secularist platform ladies of previous decades. Reports of her lectures appearing in *The Reformer* never contained details of violent opposition or savvy comebacks. According to her husband, she 'made no efforts to cultivate the art of oratory … her object was to convey information and awaken thought, and she was much more concerned to marshal facts in orderly sequence and to present the case at issue fairly'.[61]

Performing on Freethought platforms in the 1890s and 1900s still required tenacity and courage, but these ceased to be the defining characteristics of its female lecturers.[62] The Freethinking feminist legacy of rowdy, aggressive and confrontational 'assault on public space' is more easily traced to the early twentieth suffrage movement. The tactics of militants and non-militants alike are clearly comparable to those of the Secularist preachers earlier in the period. Especially if we define open-air speaking and newspaper-selling, along with more extreme attacks on private property, as part of a broad spectrum of direct action rather than view 'militancy' as a new invention of the Women's Social and Political Union (WSPU).[63] Through such activities women imposed both their bodies and their political demands on public arenas from which they had been excluded or made invisible. The suffrage movement gained much of its potency from the novelty of well-dressed middle-class women marching through muddy streets, forming crowds and confronting policemen.[64] Yet the Freethinking lecturers of previous decades also recognised the power of publicly transgressing the boundaries of acceptable femininity.

Freethought was only one current within a broader nineteenth-century radical culture which historians have now shown made an important contribution to twentieth-century franchise campaigns. There are nevertheless striking similarities between Freethinkers invading church services and suffragettes disrupting parliamentary meetings, between the violence meted out by crowds of angry Christians and that endured by suffragists who took their message to the streets. The 'War

Against the Church' launched by the WSPU in 1913 included mass walk-outs, interrupting sermons with shouts of 'votes for women', and even burning down churches.[65] Such activities can hardly have failed to strike a chord with some of the older generation of Secularists, whose experiences and memories provided a crucial link through successive waves of feminist struggle.

Public writing

Delight in public speaking was not, of course, shared by all Freethinking women; some preferred to make a public contribution to the cause in written form, by way of numerous secularist and feminist journals and pamphlet series, as well as in monographs, essays and novels; and public speakers too sometimes published as well as lectured. Sophia Dobson Collet and Sara Hennell avoided speaking in public and restricted their activities to writing – both of them publishing monographs on the philosophy of Freethought. Collet also contributed articles, reviews and poems to *The Reasoner* in the 1840s and 1850s under the pseudonym 'Panthea', while Hennell had a brief foray into journalism in the late 1880s when she contributed a series of articles to *The Women's Penny Paper*. Harriet Law, Annie Besant and Hypatia Bradlaugh Bonner worked as journalists as well as lecturers, and edited leading Secularist periodicals. Annie Besant followed Emma Martin and Frances Wright in publishing her lectures in pamphlet form, which sometimes led to written exchanges or 'tract wars' with her Christian opponents. Collet, Hennell, Law, Besant and Bradlaugh Bonner were part of a wider community of 'women of letters' – those who took advantage of the expansion of publishing to earn a living as writers in a variety of media – pamphlets, tracts, books, literary reviews and essays.[66] Journalism in particular was one of the few professions open to women during this period, because it did not require specialist or formal training.[67] George Eliot and Harriet Martineau both launched their successful writing careers as contributors to the periodical press, and by 1862 Frances Power Cobbe believed that writing was already an established area of work for middle-class women.[68] A feminist press also emerged in the second half of the century, beginning with the *English Woman's Journal* (est. 1858) and then the *Victoria Magazine* (est. 1863), so that by the 1880s a range of 'female advocacy' journals existed, including campaign organs such as *The Shield* and the *Women's Suffrage Journal*, and the more general *The Women's Penny Paper* and *The Woman's Signal*. Florence Fenwick Miller took over as editor of this last paper in October

1895, following her success as the author of the regular column 'Ladies Notes' in the *Illustrated London News*.[69]

Women wanting to succeed as professional writers nevertheless had to overcome significant obstacles. Throughout the nineteenth century, particularly in the later decades with the rise of the 'New Journalism' that focused on sensationalist exposés and risky undercover work, writing for the press continued to be a male-dominated occupation. Writing on non-fictional or political topics was considered particularly unsuitable for women. It was often argued that women writers of all kinds were incapable of impartiality and objectivity, producing instead overly emotional and scatter-brained 'gush'.[70] Women thus adopted a variety of strategies to overcome their anomalous position. Assuming a male pseudonym, or taking advantage of the practice of publishing articles anonymously (common still in the 1860s), was often useful.[71] Sara Hennell used the designation S. S. instead of her full first name in the hope that her work would be read as having been written by a man. 'If you can avoid giving me a feminine designation in public I shall be glad', she asked Sophia Dobson Collet, who had been reading her drafts, 'My publisher knows me only as S. S. and I like the incognito as far as may be, but I do not want to make a secret of it.'[72] Perhaps this masculine persona helped the reviews of Hennell's first book *Christianity and Infidelity* (1857), in which she was often referred to as 'Mr. Hennell' and praised for her 'lucid and temperate' style.[73] Hennell was irritated when her sex was revealed the same year that her first book was published. She became even more annoyed when friends offered comfort by assuring her that her work did not read in the least as though it had issued from a female pen.[74]

Sophia Dobson Collet's use of a pseudonym was not because she wished to disguise her sex (Panthea was a clearly feminine designation), but more likely because she was worried about associating herself publicly with an unrespectable Freethought press. In 1849 Francis Newman, who later went on to contribute to *The Reasoner* himself, expressed his surprise that Collet should want to write for such an 'avowedly Atheistical and Socialist' publication. In light of this, Collet's eagerness to direct the Freethought movement towards greater sobriety and respectability becomes more understandable. She began to consider using her own name from 1855 onwards, perhaps because she finally judged the new Secularism to have successfully thrown off its previous connotations of vulgarity and sexual immorality.[75]

Women writing about Freethought were operating in a particularly male dominated arena – that of theological disputation. Their work is perhaps best described as 'anti-theology' given the frequency with which they engaged with contemporary theological debates and took the deconstruction of Christian doctrine as one of their primary themes. Even Harriet Law and Annie Besant's most populist and polemical works abounded with discussions of historical disputes of Scriptural interpretation and the latest biblical criticism. Sophia Dobson Collet discussed a variety of theological and freethinking perspectives in detail in *George Jacob Holyoake and Modern Atheism* (1855) and *Phases of Atheism* (1860), and her later interest in Hindu reformism led her to write *Indian Theism and its Relation to Christianity* (1870). Sara Hennell published a number of extremely complex philosophical works. *Christianity and Infidelity* (1857) drew on the writings of a wide range of Christian theologians to put the case for and against revealed Christianity, with the second half of the book dedicated to a discussion of her Pantheist beliefs. Hennell went on to explore the work of the great Anglican theologian Bishop Butler in her 1859 *Essay on the Sceptical Tendency of Butler's 'Analogy'*, which later attracted the attention of Prime Minister W. E. Gladstone.[76] A talented linguist, Hennell was well acquainted with German developments in biblical criticism and philosophy, and she used the work of Ludwig Feuerbach to develop her vision of religious progress, which she argued for in the three volumes of *Present Religion* (1865, 1873, 1887).

In engaging with doctrinal debates rather than with more traditionally feminised areas of religious knowledge such as devotion, conduct and worship, Freethinking feminists stood apart from the many other women active in contributing to religious thought during this period. They were mounting a direct challenge to the churches' often explicit barring of women from the traditional genres of theology, which (as John Ruskin famously declared) remained the 'one dangerous science for women – one which they must indeed beware how profoundly they touch'.[77] As a result of such transgression, Freethinking feminists faced significant opposition from male critics who continually called their intellectual ability into question. The anti-infidel organ *The Shield of Faith* reviewed a tract sarcastically entitled *The Scholarship of Secularism*, whose author criticised Besant for using inaccurate quotations from Calvin. The reviewer agreed, commenting that 'The lady – though one of "culture" – when challenged about this, makes matters worse in her attempt at justification …'.[78] In another issue the reviewer of Besant's contributions to the *Freethinker's Text-book* referred to her as 'the little busy B' before accusing Besant of merely regurgitating the work of leading male Freethinkers. 'Of original criticism she is quite innocent,' the reviewer condescended, 'and she is more to be commended for her industry than for her logic.'[79]

Female Secularists responded by utilising the Freethought principle of free inquiry to justify their right to engage with theology. They competed with their Christian opponents over who could appear more knowledgeable and demonstrate the greatest amount of 'objective' evidence in support of their arguments. Annie Besant boasted that her adolescent studies of the early Church Fathers 'served me well in many of my later controversies with Christians who knew the literature of their Church less well than I'.[80] Besant and Law's extremely detailed refutations of Christian doctrine were absolutely crucial to them fulfilling their mission as 'bearers of truth'. Great attention needed to be paid to every theological dispute and Scriptural inconsistency to ensure that 'truth' was established each and every time. The Christian Church could not deny them this right to pronounce upon the truths of Christianity, whether or not theology was a science usually reserved for men.[81]

Yet women in the Secularist movement were well aware of the controversial nature of their writing about a subject that was not only dominated by male theologians but also practised mainly by Churchmen. The Freethought challenge to Christianity was, in the hands of women, amplified by a female challenge to the male authority of the Church. Freethinking women capitalised on this by usurping and then subverting traditional genres of clerical writing. For example, the Christian sermon (which consisted of taking a scriptural text, dividing it, and speaking on its various heads) was a form of writing particularly associated with the ministry.[82] Freethinking women appropriated this form, and, in their critiques of Christian commentators, often reprinted a particular sermon or theological text, and then dissected it with their own criticisms and comments. Harriet Law regularly employed this practice in the *Secular Chronicle*, which critiqued the latest thoughts of prominent Christians by reprinting them complete with Law's irreverent and sarcastic interjections. In her *Essay on the Sceptical Tendency of Butler's Analogy*, Sara Hennell similarly used her critique of Butler to put forward her own ideas, quoting from his work and then inserting her own thoughts in parenthesis. Sara Hennell also used this *Essay* to reflect playfully upon the anomaly of her position as a (Freethinking) woman daring to take on and contradict such a well-regarded (orthodox) theologian. The first passages of the book lavish praise on the talents and fame of Butler, building up his reputation as one of the greatest Christian thinkers of his time before proceeding to demolish his arguments. Many Freethinking feminists, like Hennell, revelled in the '*anti*' aspect of their work – developing style of 'theological' engagement that valorised the desire to dismantle and deconstruct, sometimes (though not in every case) at the expense of generating an alternative Freethinking philosophy.[83] Such 'critique' was not wholly negative, in that it was informed by the 'positive' Secularist values of the right to freely inquire and to think independently. In becoming its champions Freethinking feminists were, however, challenging feminised norms of knowledge production at a most profound level.

Freethinking women's anti-theological efforts were better received inside the Secularist community, even when, as in the case of Sophia Dobson Collet, they were critical of some elements of the movement's leadership. That Collet, a self-defined 'Theist', felt able to comment on the state of modern atheism was in itself a testament to the Freethought commitment to free discussion.[84] Her book *Modern Atheism* began with an apology for the 'presumption' of a 'novice' such as herself attempting to persuade atheists of her religious beliefs.[85] Collet's initial attempt at feminine modesty was belied, however, by the rest of the work, in which she took on the ambitious task of proving that Holyoake was not the atheist he claimed to be, but was in fact 'gradually, but unmistakeably, "moving towards a God possible"'. Collet then went on to define Secularism's 'main purpose' as establishing 'a common ground on which persons of differing faith may work together for human welfare and happiness'. Her insistence that Secularists should avoid conflict with Christians and instead show them that 'our sympathy with them as men is greater than our difference from them as theologians', was in strong disagreement with those who continued to favour a more adversarial approach.[86] However, it appears that most Secularists accepted Collet's right to seek to determine the future direction of the Secularist movement. Holyoake's review in *The Reasoner* was generally favourable, if a touch patronising in its tone, declaring that 'The feeble sentimentality of the earlier writings of the authoress has given place to clear vigour and often striking thoughts. Those who read her book will be informed by her able and original treatment of the whole question in her little volume.' Holyoake took Collet's discussion of his own 'religious' views seriously enough to dedicate the January Sunday morning lectures to responding to them.[87] Collet was given further space in *The Reasoner* to reply to Holyoake's critique of her work.[88] When Collet published *Phases of Faith* in 1860, there ensued a similarly serious discussion of her ideas among *The Reasoner*'s contributors and readers. This time, Collet's advice was even more directive, declaring that the 'religious atheism' of Lionel Holdreth offered the only hope for the future of the Secularist movement.[89] The anonymous reviewer for *The Reasoner* believed *Phases of Faith* to be 'The best, the fullest and the fairest account of the aspects of Atheistic thought in England.'[90]

Gender and Freethought discourse

The Freethought spirit of free inquiry and their vision of themselves as preachers of truth could provide Freethinking women with a gender-neutral role. '[T]ruth has no sex', declared Frances Wright, and therefore as 'teachers of the public' Freethinking women had only to do one thing:

> to throw wide the gates of our understanding; to dare the exercise of our intellectual faculties, and to encourage in others, as in ourselves, a habit of accurate and dispassionate investigation.[91]

Women active in Victorian reform politics referred to their sex in a variety of ways to justify their public activities, speaking as mothers, moral guardians or as innocents against corruption.[92] Freethinking women instead took on the part of 'free inquirer after truth', deflecting attention away from their sex. Harriet Law was praised in the *Secular Chronicle* for possessing 'logical abilities' and a 'hard, cold and logical' mind that was the reverse of 'womanly weakness'.[93] Notably, the Secularist press tended not to report upon the sex of the speaker in its reports of female Freethinkers' lectures but instead to focus on their words.[94] When Kate Watts first launched her career as a lecturer, she referred to her youth, rather than her sex, as a possible disability before going on to stress that she had been raised a Freethinker and could therefore boast a 'long time' with the movement – adherence to Freethought principles provided all the credentials she needed.[95] Freethinking feminists therefore remained apart from more 'essentialist' or 'sex-specific' arguments that gained currency in large parts of the early twentieth-century suffrage movements.[96] In contrast to the emotive appeals of contemporaries such as Christabel Pankhurst, Hypatia Bradlaugh Bonner was praised for her straightforwardly rational tone: 'Deeply as she felt upon many of the themes she discussed, she never allowed either her hatreds or her admirations to tempt her into over-emphasis ... her appeal was invariably the appeal to reason ...'[97]

This apparently egalitarian approach was not without problems. On the one hand, Freethought culture freed women from conventional womanly roles. On the other, the Freethought valorisation of science and reason, contrasted with emotion and superstition, carried with it highly gendered connotations, whereby traditionally 'feminine' qualities were precisely those which Freethinkers opposed. As a result, some female Freethinkers challenged this polarisation of feeling or faith and reason and used their theological writings to attempt to re-shape the philosophical framework of Secularism, asserting the continuing importance of feeling or emotion in a post-religious world. Even before Collet had come to adopt some loose form of Christianity in the late 1860s, and while she still rejected the idea of a personal Creator, she was critical of the organised Freethought movement for what she perceived to be its cold, hard materialism.[98] Although Collet agreed with the Freethinkers that morality could exist independently of religion, she nevertheless argued that religious 'feeling' had an important part to play in the morality of the individual. To ignore this, as she believed Holyoake and other Secularists had, was to ignore the profound effect that 'the perception of religious reality' had on the moral consciousness of the individual. Collet defined 'faith' or religious 'feeling' as existing autonomously from the intellect and she argued in favour of the position of the more 'religious atheists', such as Lionel Holdreth, that 'the mind may be entirely persuaded of the untenability of Theism; but the intellectual conviction in such cases is at war with the whole bent of the soul' which 'feels the need of the Divine with a keenness that *cannot* be suppressed'. [99] Collet did not reject the Freethought commitment to the pursuit of truth through independent inquiry but re-defined the concept to allow it to incorporate religious sentiment. There were, she argued, two kinds of truth, the 'truth' revealed by intellect and the 'truth' revealed by faith. 'The religious instinct is to me so vividly a reality,' she insisted, 'that no intellectual difficulties can destroy or diminish my conviction that it is the presage of deep Truth.'[100]

Sara Hennell also wrestled with the relationship between feeling, faith and reason. She agreed with the majority Freethought view that reason and faith were not reconcilable within a Christian frame-work, or rather that Christianity stifled the use of reason. When some Christians, such as Bishop Butler, did accept that reason had a role to play within Christianity, such a belief immediately set them on the path to scepticism. 'Until the nature of the relation between these two faculties [faith and reason] is discovered,' she wrote, 'there must necessarily continue the old mischievous antagonism between the different parts of our nature.'[101] Thus Hennell did not deny the emotional or spiritual side of the individual but believed that it was as important an element of human 'nature' as reason. The 'feeling' of loss and distress that often accompanied one's rejection of religion was, she argued, to be examined and valued, 'instead of endeavouring, as we often do, in all honesty, to crush into silence, treating it as a mere remnant of superstition.' Hennell continued to maintain that while truth and reason were central princi-ples, they should be seen as a means to more spiritual ends; 'intellectual satisfaction is not in itself our real want ... what we require of our reason is to furnish us with a clear perception of so much sustaining truth that our moral sentiments may be able to repose upon it – a basis for our faith.'[102] Jane Clapperton also sought to retain the value of 'religious feelings' within a freethinking or agnostic framework that was entirely reconcilable with the findings of modern science. Male theologians, she argued, from all religious perspectives remained preoccupied with the 'object' of religion, whether this was the sun and the moon, ghosts and souls, the Holy Trinity or the Unitarian God. Clapperton, by contrast, asserted the need to focus on the 'feeling' aroused by such objects – an 'emotional bearing on life' that could be valued free from theology or dogmatic disagreements.'[103]

Florence Fenwick Miller was concerned that portrayals of Secularism as divorced from feeling had especially negative implications for women. In her lecture on Harriet Martineau, Fenwick Miller discussed the predicament of the intellectual woman. Already, by virtue of their ability to think and study, women such as her were accused of lacking emotion. Florence strongly refuted this 'commonplace supposition', using her medical knowledge to insist that it was founded upon 'ignorance of both physiology and the facts'. Society at large often condemned learned women, whereas the Freethought movement celebrated them. Yet, according to Fenwick Miller, Freethinkers were also often equally guilty of presuming that 'emotions are crowded out of the mind by the development of the intellect'.

> I am not sure but that the most fatal mistake made by the party who would free mankind from superstition and priestcraft is not the very fact that they neglect and skim over such subjects [e.g. the emotions].

Religion appealed to the masses because it provided 'rites and ceremonies' to reflect the human 'sympathies' and mark the passages of life – birth, marriage and death. Therefore, 'if there is an impression abroad that the Religion of Humanity is the blasphemy of individual emotion; if it is believed by the masses that only priestcraft recognises and hallows the most solemn occasions of life; then indeed will priestcraft flourish'. Women in particular would be deterred from joining the Freethought movement, given the already existing injunction against their participating in the life of the mind. It was therefore imperative that the Secularists accept the importance of feeling.[104]

Conclusion

Freethinking women were at the forefront of Victorian women's attempts to participate in political, religious and intellectual public arenas. As lecturers, authors and journalists they rose to prominence in a world where attempts to democratise public institutions led to a proliferation of competing voices – though not all of them had an equal chance of being heard. The Freethought opposition to Christianity was in part a struggle for cultural authority over the right to proclaim upon questions of truth, morality and the regeneration of society. Freethinking women participated in this struggle, using the Freethought principle of free inquiry to justify their even more radical attempts as women to usurp the role of the churches as moral and intellectual guides. Driven by the imperative to preach the truth they faced down numerous efforts by their Christian opponents to silence them and appealed instead to the right to free discussion and free dissemination of knowledge. Within the Secularist movement itself, these principles ensured that public platforms in both the lecture hall and the press were, at least formally, open to women. Freethinking feminists were able to carve out public personas distinctive to the wider women's movement because they relied upon neither a feminised Christian moral agenda nor a sex-specific political vision. In doing so, they contributed to a substratum of feminist identity – self-consciously rebellious and at times derisive of traditionally female qualities – which re-emerged particularly strongly in the pages of *The Freewoman* from 1911 to 1913 and in post-war *avant-garde* feminist circles more generally.[105]

Only tiny numbers of female Freethinkers, however, were able to assume the 'masculine' role of Secularist preacher. The ultra-democratic Freethought ideal of a free community of speakers opened up space for women to participate, but its utopian blindness to structural inequalities that might prevent them from assuming such a masculine persona meant that only the bravest women could take advantage of it. While some women used their theological writings to challenge the opposition between faith and reason or thought and feeling, the polarised way in which the Secularist movement at large conceived of these highly gendered categories had important implications for how Freethinkers defined womanhood and sexual difference. The following chapter will go on to discuss how such contradictions influenced the feminism that emerged from the Secularist movement.

Notes

1   *The Reasoner* (*Reasoner*), 6 May 1855, p. 41.
2   For a recent discussion of the 'gender asymmetry' that continued to structure 'public' (national) politics into the second half of the nineteenth century, see K. Gleadle,

Borderline Citizens: Women, Gender and Political Culture in Britain, 1815–1867 (Oxford: Oxford University Press, 2009), p. 90.

3   *The Woman's Signal*, 4 January 1894, p. 4.

4   J. Schroeder, 'Speaking Volumes: Victorian Feminism and the Appeal of Public Discussion', *Nineteenth-Century Contexts* 25:2 (2003), 97–117, 100, 109.

5   Fenwick Miller claimed that the big shift occurred between the late 1870s (when she made her first speech) and the 1890s (when she wrote an article surveying the progress made by women during this twenty-year period); see *The Woman's Signal*, 4 January 1894, pp. 4–5.

6   For middle-class women's 'public activities', see A. Summers, *Private Lives, Moral States. Women, Religion and Public Life in Britain 1800–1930* (Newbury: Threshold Press, 2000); S. Morgan, *A Victorian Women's Place: Public Culture in the Nineteenth Century* (London: Tauris Academic Studies, 2007).

7   *The Shield of Faith*, July 1877, pp. 95, 97, March 1877, p. 34.

8   Female preaching continued in a sporadic manner after the Wesleyan Methodists banned it in 1803, but in the 1860s the evangelical revival prompted a renewal; O. Anderson, 'Women Preachers in Mid-Victorian Britain: Some Reflections on Feminism, Popular Religion and Social Change', *The Historical Journal* 12:3 (1969), 467–84. It has recently been argued that the 1803 ban did not entirely eradicate female preaching in the Wesleyan Methodists, while Bible Christians and Primitive Methodists kept the tradition of female itinerancy alive until the early 1850s; see J. M. Lloyd, *Women and the Shaping of British Methodism: Persistent Preachers, 1807–1907* (Manchester: Manchester University Press, 2009). For women in other denominations, see S. Mumm, '"I Love My Sex": Two Late Victorian Pulpit Women', in J. Bellamy, A. Laurenca & Gill Perry (eds.), *Women, Scholarship and Criticism. Gender and Knowledge c.1790–1900* (Manchester: Manchester University Press, 2000), pp. 204–21; J. Holmes, 'Women Preachers and the New Orders: Women Preachers in the Protestant Churches', in S. Gilley & B. Stanley (eds.), *World Christianities, c. 1815–1914* (Cambridge: Cambridge University Press, 2005), pp. 84–93, 88–9.

9   B. Onslow, *Women of the Press in Nineteenth-Century Britain* (Basingstoke: Macmillan, 2000), pp. 16, 35.

10   H. Fraser, S. Green & J. Johnston (eds.), *Gender and the Victorian Periodical* (Cambridge: Cambridge University Press, 2003), pp. 1–3.

11   C. Tilly, *Popular Contention in Great Britain, 1753–1834* (Cambridge, MA: Harvard University Press, 1995), pp. 357–60; S. Shipley, *Club Life and Socialism in Mid-Victorian London*, History Workshop Pamphlets 5 (1971).

12   For example, the Chartist Robert Lowery insisted that the best way to campaign was to call a public meeting so that 'the public might judge for itself'; see B. Harrison & P. Hollis (eds.), *Robert Lowery: Radical and Chartist* (London: Europa, 1979), pp. 144–7 (I am grateful to Janette Martin for drawing attention to this source). Ticketing and other procedures could of course be used to exclude people from, and therefore control debate within, public meetings. See also J. Epstein, *Radical Expression: Political Language, Ritual and Symbol in England, 1790–1850* (Oxford: Oxford University Press, 1994); J. Meisel, *Public Speech and the Culture of Public Life in the Age of Gladstone* (New York: Columbia University Press, 2001); R. Stephen, *The People's Charter: Democratic Agitation in Early Victorian Britain* (London: Merlin,

2003). For lecturing, see J. Martin, 'Itinerant Lecturing and Popular Political Oratory in Yorkshire and the North East in the Age of Chartism, 1837–1860' (unpublished doctoral thesis, University of York, 2010).

13 J. H. Wiener, *The War of the Unstamped. The Movement to Repeal the British Newspaper Tax, 1830–1836* (Ithaca & London: Cornell University Press, 1969).

14 Many of those active in the campaigns for a free press in the 1830s went on to play a central role in the formative years of the Secularist movement; see D. Nash, 'Unfettered Investigation – the Secularist Press and the Creation of Audience in Victorian England', *Victorian Periodicals Review*, 28:2 (Summer 1995), 123–35.

15 Epstein (1994), p. 112.

16 Quoted in Wiener (1969), pp. 133–4.

17 Epstein (1994), p. 114.

18 Nash (1995), p. 124.

19 D. Nash, 'Secularism in the City: Geographies of Dissidence and the Importance of Radical Culture in the Metropolis', in M. Cragoe & A. Taylor (eds.), *London Politics, 1760–1914* (Basingstoke & New York: Palgrave Macmillan, 2005), pp. 97–120, 114. See also D. Nash, 'The Leicester Secular Society: Unbelief, Freethought and Freedom in a Nineteenth-Century City' (unpublished doctoral thesis, University of York, 1990), p. 141.

20 D. Nash, *Secularism, Art and Freedom* (Leicester, London & New York: Leicester University Press, 1992), p. 139.

21 *Reasoner*, 10 September 1854, p. 161.

22 F. Wright, 'Lecture III. Of the More Important Divisions and Essential Parts of Knowledge', in F. Wright, *Course of Popular Lectures as Delivered by Frances Wright, in New York, Philadelphia, Baltimore, Boston, Cincinnati, St. Louis, Louisville, and other Cities, Towns and Districts of the United States. With Three Addresses on Various Public Occasions and a Reply to the Charges Against the French Reformers of 1789*, 4th edn (New York: Published at the Office of the Free Enquirer, Hall of Science, 1831) (first published 1828), pp. 63–84, 81.

23 *The National Reformer* (*NR*), 4 April 1869, p. 223.

24 For a fascinating description of the world of public talk, see A. Davin, 'Socialist Infidels and Messengers of Light', in T. Hitchcock & H. Shore (eds.), *The Streets of London from the Great Fire to the Great Stink* (London: Rivers Oram Press, 2003), pp. 165–82.

25 F. Wright, 'Reply to the French Reformers of the Year 1789', in Wright, *Lectures*, pp. 227–31, 227; F. Wright, 'Introductory Address', in Wright, *Lectures*, pp. 13–16, 13–14.

26 Martin invaded Christian meetings in Manchester and in Paisley in 1844; see E. Martin, *The Missionary Jubilee Panic and the Hypocrites Prayer. Addressed to the Supporters of Christian Mission* (London: Hetherington, 1844); *The Movement*, 18 December 1844, p. 463.

27 Royle (1979), p. 135; E. Royle 'Annie Besant's First Public Lecture', *Labour History Review*, 57:3 (1992), 67–69.

28 *NR*, 30 May 1869, p. 350, 21 February 1869, p. 125.

29 Quoted in *NR*, 4 April 1869, p. 218.

30 *Ibid*.

31   C. M. Davies, *Mystic London: or Phases of Occult Life in the Metropolis* (London, 1875, repr. *Labour History Review*, 57:3, 1992), p. 71.

32   *Secular Chronicle (SC)*, 18 June 1876, pp. 288–9.

33   *Christianity or Secularism: Which is the Better System for Man? Being a verbatim report of a public debate held in the Olympia Hall, Plymouth, on Monday and Tuesday evenings, Sept. 24th and 25th, 1888. Between Mrs Annie Besant (of the National Secular Society) and Mr. William T. Lee (of the Three Town's Christian Evidence Society; and Missioner at the Exeter Street Hall, Plymouth)* (Plymouth: W.F. Westcott, London: John Kensit, 1888), pp. 81–6.

34   *NR*, 28 August 1870, p. 143.

35   *Ibid.*, 8 October 1876, pp. 225–6.

36   *Reasoner*, 8 April 1855, p. 12.

37   G. J. Holyoake, *Rudiments of Public Speaking and Debate: or Hints on the Application of Logic* (London: J. Watson, 1852). See also, G. J. Holyoake, *On Lecturing: Its Conditions and Character* (printed for private circulation, 1851[?]) Manchester, Co-operative Union Archive (CUA), George Jacob Holyoake Collection (GJHC).

38   Sophia Dobson Collet to George Jacob Holyoake, 1 February 1853, CUA, Holyoake Correspondence (HC), 561.

39   *Agnostic Journal (AJ)*, 16 October 1897, p. 254.

40   See, for example, *Secular Review (SR)*, 11 February 1877, p. 10.

41   S. Budd, *Varieties of Unbelief: Atheists and Agnostics in English Society 1850–1950* (London, Heinemann, 1977), p. 48.

42   For debates over style and tone of meetings and the Biblical focus, see E. Royle, *Radicals, Secularists and Republicans. Popular Freethought in Britain, 1866–1915* (Manchester: Manchester University Press, 1980), pp. 116–7, 152. The Freethinker W. S. Ross was particularly critical of what he believed to be the lack of education and vulgarity of Bradlaugh's followers.

43   *SC*, 21 May 1876, p. 237.

44   *SC*, 27 October 1878, p. 200.

45   Besant, *Christianity or Secularism*, p. 10.

46   London, Wellcome Library, F. Fenwick Miller, 'An Uncommon Girlhood' (unpublished autobiography), GC/228, pp. 12–3, 8–9 [NB the pagination for this work is inconsistent].

47   *NR*, 18 June 1871, p. 396–7.

48   *The Freethinker*, 8 August 1897, p. 502.

49   *SC*, 21 May 1876, p. 237.

50   *SC*, 5 March 1876, p. 105.

51   Fenwick Miller, 'Uncommon Girlhood' , p. 3. In 1870 the Northampton Secular Society attempted to arrange a debate between Harriet Law and 'a lady Christian advocate' named Mrs Sturgis. Their belief in the greater freedom of Freethinking women was, however, vindicated, when Mrs Sturgis refused the invitation and thus proved herself 'prudent' in matters of 'discussion', *NR*, 3 July 1870, p. 10.

52   Although many Christians continued to oppose female preaching, by the 1860s there were considerable numbers among them who supported women's right to preach. For Christian debates on how to interpret biblical passages forbidding female preaching, see J. Butler (ed.), *Woman's Work and Woman's Culture. A Series of Essays* (London:

Macmillan and Co., 1869), pp. xlviii, lviii–lix; Anderson (1969), pp. 478–9; J. H. Y. Briggs, *The English Baptists of the Nineteenth Century* (Didcot: The Baptist Historical Society, 1994), pp. 278–9; Mumm (2000), p. 206.

53 Fenwick Miller, 'Uncommon Girlhood', pp. 12–16.

54 *Ibid.*, p. 3.

55 A. Besant, *Autobiographical Sketches* (London: Freethought Publishing Co., 1885), p. 72.

56 George Strandring commented on this shift in style in *The Reformer*, 15 March 1897, pp. 11–13.

57 *The Freewoman*, 18 April, 1912, p. 424.

58 J. H. Clapperton, *Scientific Meliorism and the Evolution of Happiness* (London: Kegan Paul, Trench & Co., 1885), pp. 409–24; K. Pearson, *The Ethic of Freethought: A Series of Essays and Lectures* (London: T. Fisher Unwin, 1888), pp. 13–32.

59 Some Ethical Societies promoting this more positive form of freethought, for example, were 'socially out of reach' to more working-class Secularists; Royle (1980), p. 42.

60 'Report of Mrs Bradlaugh on Women Suffrage', London, Bishopsgate Library, Charles Bradlaugh Archive 2770.

61 A. Bonner & C. B. Bonner, *Hypatia Bradlaugh Bonner: The Story of Her Life* (London: Watts & Co., 1942), pp. 39–40.

62 According to her biography, Hypatia had her first experience of heckling from a hostile audience some time in the 1890s, when she lectured in the mining town of Stanley, County Durham, *ibid.*, p. 91.

63 Christabel Pankhurst of the WSPU claimed that militant tactics first began to be used in 1905 when she and Annie Kenney disrupted a Liberal Party political rally in Manchester, yet historians have recently pointed to the origins of militancy in the radical suffragists' campaigns of previous decades; S. S. Holton, *Feminism and Democracy. Women's Suffrage and Reform Politics in Britain 1900–1918* (Cambridge: Cambridge University Press, 1986); H. L. Smith, *The British Women's Suffrage Campaign, 1866–1928* (Harlow: Pearson Education Ltd., 2010), p. 35; Wright (2010). Holton also argues that neither the militants' nor the constitutionalists' practices remained static, while even constitutional forms of agitation required great bravery and provoked violence, pp. 36–7, 44.

64 See M. Vicinus, *Independent Women: Work and Community for Single Women, 1850–1920* (London: Virago, 1985), Chapter 7.

65 J. de Vries, 'Transforming the Pulpit: Preaching and Prophecy in the British Women's Suffrage Movement', in B. Mayne Kienzle and P. J. Walker (eds.), *Women Preachers and Prophets Through Two Millennia of Christianity* (Los Angeles: University of California Press, 1998), pp. 318–34, 326.

66 B. Caine, 'Feminism, Journalism and Public Debate', in J. Shattock (ed.), *Women and Literature in Britain, 1800–1900* (Cambridge: Cambridge University Press, 2001), pp. 99–118.

67 Fraser et al. (2003), p. 13.

68 *Ibid.*, p. 13; Onslow (2000), p. 31.

69 R. T. Van Arsdel, *Florence Fenwick Miller. Victorian Feminist, Journalist and Educator* (Aldershot: Ashgate, 2001).

70 Arnold Bennet's guide for women journalists identified 'lack of restraint' and 'gush' as particularly feminine characteristics, see Onslow (2000), p. 32. See also Fraser et al. (2003), p. 130.

71 Onslow (2000), p. 21; Fraser et al (2003), p. 27.

72 Sara Hennell to Sophia Dobson Collet, 22 February n.d., London, Women's Library (WL), Papers of Clara Collet and Family (CCF) 7CCF [uncatalogued].

73 'Reviews of S. S. Hennell's *Christianity and Infidelity*', in S. S. Hennell, *Essay on the Sceptical Tendency of Butler's 'Analogy'* (London: John Chapman, 1859).

74 Sara Hennell to Sophia Dobson Collet, 22 April 1857, WL, CCF.

75 Sophia Dobson Collet to George Jacob Holyoake, 25 April 1855, CUA, HC 759.

76 W. E. Gladstone, 'Bishop Butler and His Censors', *The Nineteenth Century* 38 (July 1895), 715–40.

77 J. Ruskin, 'Of Queens' Gardens' (1865), quoted in J. Melnyk (ed.), *Women's Theology in Nineteenth-Century Britain. Transfiguring the Faith of their Fathers* (New York & London: Garland Publishing, 1998), p. xii. Victorian women created their own theological cultures in religious periodicals such as *The Christian World Magazine* (1866–87) and *The Monthly Packet* (1851–95), yet they continued to be denied the right and the expertise to *directly* interpret Scripture and publicise their conclusions; J. Melnyk, 'Women, Writing and the Creation of Theological Cultures', in S. Morgan and J. de Vries (eds.), *Women, Gender and Religious Cultures in Britain 1800–1940* (Abingdon: Routledge, 2010), pp. 32–53. See also, Mumm (2000), p. 204. Jacqueline de Vries noted that Frances Power Cobbe, having authored a number of theological and ethical works, was a rare exception to this – in fact, as this chapter shows, Cobbe was part of a wider tradition of freethinking female 'theologians'; see J. de Vries, 'Review of S. Peacock, *The Theological and Ethical Writings of Frances Power Cobbe, 1822–1904*', *Albion: A Quarterly Concerned with British Studies* 35:4 (Winter 2003), 692–94.

78 *The Shield of Faith*, January 1877, p. 10.

79 *Ibid.*, March 1877, pp. 25–6.

80 Besant, *Sketches*, p. 26.

81 See, for example, Law's debate with the Rev. J. Campbell, *NR* 28 February 1869, p. 141, 14 March 1869, p. 172.

82 C. Krueger, *The Reader's Repentance. Women Preachers, Women Writers and Nineteenth-Century Social Discourse* (Chicago: University of Chicago Press, 1992), p. 58.

83 As discussed earlier in this chapter, Freethinkers such as Jane Clapperton preferred to promote a more positive alternative philosophy of Freethought. Sophia Dobson Collet's *Modern Atheism* and Sara Hennell's three-volume *Present Religion* also attempted to develop alternative ethical systems.

84 Collet did not feel that her religious views excluded her from the Secularist movement, believing that the readership of *The Reasoner* consisted of 'persons whose notions of theology differ as the hues of the rainbow', see Sophia Dobson Collet to George Jacob Holyoake, 25 April 1855, CUA, HC 759.

85 S. D. Collet, *George Jacob Holyoake and Modern Atheism. A Biographical and Critical Essay* (London, Trubner and Co., 1855), no page.

86 Collet (1855), pp. 24–5.

87 *Reasoner*, 30 December 1855, p. 313.

88 *Ibid.*, 6 January 1856, p. 6.

89 S. D. Collet, *Phases of Atheism, Described, Examined and Answered* (Holyoake and Co., London, 1860).

90 *Reasoner*, 3 June 1860, pp. 181–2.

91 Wright, 'Lecture II', in *Lectures,* p. 42.

92 Epstein (1994), p. 133–4; Onslow (2000), p. 16; Fraser et al. (2003), pp. 43–4.

93 *SC*, 26 November 1876, pp. 255–6.

94 According to Helen Rogers, reports of Chartist women's speeches in the earlier part of the century, in both the mainstream and radical press, tended to do the opposite and focus upon the sex of the female speaker. A 'chivalrous' reception of female speakers – which drew attention to and justified their anomalous involvement as women in a public campaign – was common to both the Chartist platform and the campaign to repeal the Contagious Diseases Acts later in the century, H. Rogers, 'Any Questions? The Gendered Dimensions of the Political Platform', *Nineteenth-Century Prose* 29:1 (Spring 2002), 118–132, 120, 125–6.

95 *SR*, 11 March 1877, p. 44.

96 Holton (1986), Chapter 1.

97 Bonner (1942), pp. 39–40.

98 Collet praised Keshub Chunder Sen because he was free from 'that coarseness of fibre of the Western mind which brings everything into logical formula'; S. D. Collet, *Indian Theism and its Relation to Christianity* (London: Strahan & Co., 1870), p. v.

99 S. D. Collet (1860), pp. 4–10.

100 S. D. Collet (1855), p. 2.

101 Hennell (1859), p. 28.

102 S. S. Hennell, *Thoughts in Aid of Faith, Gathered Chiefly from Recent Works in Theology and Philosophy* (London: George Manwaring, 1860), pp. 56, 59, 2.

103 J. Clapperton, *Scientific Meliorism and the Evolution of Happiness* (London: Kegan Paul, Trench & Co., 1885), p. 417.

104 F. Fenwick Miller, *The Lessons of a Life: Harriet Martineau. A Lecture Delivered Before the Sunday Lecture Society, St. George's Hall, Langham Place on Sunday afternoon, 11th March 1877* (London: The Sunday Lecture Society, 1877), pp. 12–13.

105 Editors of *The Freewoman* were particularly critical of the respectable suffrage movement, which they believed continued to subscribe to many traditional feminine values such as 'the realisation of the will of others, and not their own' instead of 'the instinct for self-realisation, the instinct for achievement in their own purposes', *The Freewoman*, 14 December 1911. See also L. Delap, *The Feminist Avant Garde: Transatlantic Encounters of the Early Twentieth Century* (Cambridge: Cambridge University Press, 2007).

4

Infidel feminism: feminism in the Freethought movement

T he Secularist movement was home to a distinctively Freethinking brand of feminism, which viewed Christianity as the primary cause of women's oppression. Freethought ideology prompted a re-definition of womanhood which could lead to far reaching and radical suggestions for transforming woman's role in society. Secularists' renunciation of religion necessarily entailed a rejection of the notion of 'God-given' sexual characteristics. The resulting need to find new criteria by which to understand sexual difference led to extensive discussions within the movement, producing a variety of answers – some more radical and more feminist than others. The question of woman's 'religious nature' was at the centre of these debates, for if Freethinkers were to argue that Christianity was woman's greatest oppressor, they needed also to address the problem of why the majority of women continued to flock to the churches. The belief that women were, for whatever reason, more susceptible to religious influence than men could, in a movement which valued science and reason above all else, tend toward a misogyny that sat uncomfortably alongside a professed commitment to women's rights. Nevertheless, considerable space had been opened up to consider the role of social or 'environmental' factors in determining what had previously been thought of as inherent feminine qualities. Some female Freethinkers continued to push for a fundamental re-thinking of what it meant to be a woman, arguing that they too were capable of strength of mind, intellectual maturity and independent thought – qualities so crucial to the Freethinking identity.

Secularists were particularly interested in analysing the origins of women's oppression, believing that any improvement in women's status was tied to the gradual secularisation of society. They argued that the Judeo-Christian Scriptures had enshrined woman's subordination and that, historically, the rise of Christianity had signalled a significant decline in the status of women. The detrimental effects of this could still be felt in the present day and it was religion, especially Christianity, which was responsible for all existing inequalities between men and women. Freethinkers directed their arguments against the popular assertion that Christianity had 'elevated' womankind. They drew on earlier Enlightenment histories of civilisation, which treated women's position in society as a measure of human progress. Ideas of race and empire permeated both Christian and secular definitions of progress and female emancipation, but in denying that women were better off under Christianity Freethinkers sometimes challenged 'imperial feminism'. Freethinkers also engaged with Christian feminists, those who wanted to re-interpret Christianity to show that it was compatible with women's rights. This represented a much more serious challenge to 'infidel feminism', one that went to the heart of debates on women and religion, rights and authority. Biblical teachings on the position of women and the role of female characters in the Bible continued to be a very important element of the Woman Question into the twentieth century, engaging Christian feminists, Christian commentators from a variety of theological perspectives, and Freethinkers. At stake in these sometimes seemingly pedantic and repetitive debates were fundamental questions about the compatibility of religion with women's rights, the possibility of re-interpreting ancient texts according to 'modern' values, the impact of the rise of science and rationalism on the role of women, and – perhaps most importantly – from what authority feminists derived their claims for equality.

Re-defining 'woman'

When most contemporary attitudes toward gender were still strongly influenced by Christianity, Secularism's rejection of the idea of God-given masculine and feminine characteristics opened up space for different ways of thinking about sexual difference. In seeking new criteria by which to explain gender roles, Freethinkers came to define 'woman' in a variety of ways. Their anti-religious stance often encouraged Freethinkers to take up the argument that apparent differences between men and women were not inherent to their sex but resulted primarily from environmental factors. Owenite feminists had drawn on Mary Wollstonecraft's denunciation of the deforming character of women's upbringing, and applied the Owenite doctrine of circumstance (the belief that the individual was determined entirely by her environment) to argue for a radical transformation of gender roles.[1] These critiques of the presumption of innate sexual inferiority were closely related to the Freethinking rejection of Original Sin and the belief in the potential perfectibility of humankind[2]: writing in 1832, Eliza Macauley explained how 'it is only very lately that I have fully understood his [Owen's] doctrine of circumstances', and this had prompted her to pen an 'Essay' questioning the doctrine of Original Sin and 'human depravity'. She argued that the belief that men and women were inherently sinful was a form of oppression and enslavement, for it deprived individuals of both their capacity for virtue and thus their responsibility for sin; 'the idea of native depravity is paralysing to every feeling of virtue, for it debases man to the condition of slave'. The doctrine of Original Sin, argued Macauley, denied the individual the freedom to fully develop her character and human potential. These religious arguments led naturally on to discussion of female oppression, and Macauley's reference to enforced 'retarded growth' closely paralleled Wollstonecraft's argument that oppressive circumstances worked to deform the female character.[3] Although Macauley did not directly compare the oppression of humanity by God to that of women by men, the link was implied, for her article finished with the assertion that, in breaking out of 'the pale which slavish custom provides' women would be able to 'hold a more honourable rank in the scale of creation'.[4]

Later in the century, some Secularists opposed the entire notion of natural sexual difference. An article appearing on the 'Ladies Page' in Harriet Law's *Secular Chronicle* claimed that it had not 'as yet been proved that a man differs from a woman' and as a result women should have full rights and duties in the governance of the polity. In discussing whether men and woman had natural and different talents, the author denied that any skill was definitely the domain of a particular sex. Even weaving and knitting, generally seen as something women had a special talent for, were acquired habits. The article concluded with what it claimed were the words of Plato; 'There is no function, my friend, among the entire members of our state that is peculiar to woman ... but natural talents are indiscriminately diffused through both, and the woman naturally shares in all offices the same as man.'[5] In 1874, in her first public lecture, Annie Besant also set out to challenge ideas about woman's 'natural inferiority' and thus also the existence of supposedly innate female characteristics. In answer to those who claimed that women were 'naturally unfit for the proper exercise of the franchise' she cautioned that '[w]e must however analyse this natural inferiority of women'. The evidence emerging from such an analysis did not support the notion that women suffered from 'mental weakness', 'susceptibility to influence' and 'unbusinesslike habits', for women such as Mary Somerville, 'Mrs Evans'

(George Eliot), Frances Power Cobbe and Harriet Martineau (the last three being women professing unorthodox religious beliefs) showed themselves quite capable of competing on an equal basis with men. Moreover, Besant argued, it was impossible to know what woman's true nature really was until she had been freed from those repressive social conditions that restricted her natural development and deformed her character, for 'it is difficult to judge what power a person may have when he is never permitted to exercise it'.[6]

However, a spectrum of views on woman's natural character existed within the Secularist movement. Sara Hennell's belief in religious progress led her to develop a theory of 'natural sexhood'. Hennell argued that men and women possessed 'different moral standpoints' and that the two sexes could be distinguished by a 'constitutional antagonism' that made possible the 'enhancement' of their respective qualities through the proximity of contrasting characteristics in the opposite sex.[7] She therefore concluded that 'women who hope to be integrally like men' should be 'reckoned mere monstrosities'.[8] Hennell attempted to link the 'dualism' inherent within 'sexhood' to metaphysical concepts of 'balance' and 'opposing dualism' in the universe, and defined certain of these concepts as either 'masculine' or 'feminine'.[9] However, despite the vagueness which hindered Hennell's attempts to discuss sexual difference at an abstract or metaphysical level, she was clear that her own understanding of masculine and feminine qualities was quite at odds with conventional definitions.[10] Just as her theological views were decidedly idiosyncratic, so were the conclusions she drew from her theory of 'natural sexhood'. Her belief in distinctive female characteristics did not, therefore, lead Sara Hennell to glorify conventional femininity. She was dismissive of worries that the 'new women', enjoying the expanded opportunities offered to their sex towards the end of the nineteenth century, would become 'manly women'. 'I resent,' she wrote, 'as you and most of us do, that women who attend public meetings, speak on platforms, and claim the Suffrage, should be charged with dishonouring their womanhood' and she even defended 'for the sake of health and convenience', those women who chose to dress in a masculine style.[11]

Freethought was not, however, full proof against more conventional thinking on gender. In *Woman, Her Glory, Her Shame and Her God* (1894), the leading Freethinker W. S. Ross (a.k.a. Saladin) argued that although the conditions of society or the 'superstructure' did shape the behaviour of men and women, ultimately this did not affect the 'foundation' of their sexual characteristics, which 'it is beyond the power of the school teacher and banker to radically affect'.

There are ineradicable traits of man which education and all it involves can neither make nor mar. And all that is lovely in woman – her unconquerable devotion, the immeasurable depths of her affections – are hers, whether she wear the cap of maid-servant or the diadem of a queen.[12]

Ross was tapping into a popular discourse on womanhood which emphasised differences between men and women while celebrating woman's superior moral qualities. Christian writers took a leading role in promoting what historians have called 'domestic ideology', which simultaneously sought to elevate woman while insisting upon the complimentary (rather than equal) roles of the sexes. But the religious associations of this ideal of womanhood did not prevent some Freethinkers from echoing many of its assumptions. Joseph Barker, for example, claimed that 'If woman is to be happy, she must have a happy home', for the home provided a sanctuary from 'the storms of commercial or political life' and was precious therefore to men as well as to women. Yet woman, unlike man, found her natural habitat in the home, so that although 'a happy home is much even to a *man* ... to a *woman* it is everything ...'.[13] Ross similarly wrote that, 'The home is woman's realm, the family are her subjects whom she sways over with the sceptre of love...'[14] The desire of some Freethinkers to assure their audience that the Secularist movement posed no threat to that bastion of morality – the home – could limit the radical implications of an anti-religious vantage point on the question of sexual difference and lead to a more conservative articulation of woman's nature.

Continued support for the idea of innate sexual differences could also lead some Freethinkers to assert that women were naturally more religious than men. Joseph McCabe, for example, argued in *The Religion of Woman* (1905) that 'woman' possessed a number of distinctive and innate characteristics. Women were naturally more conservative than men, providing a force for stability to complement man's force for change. Because they were 'more imaginative, more emotional and more sensitive to suggestion' than men, women were therefore also more susceptible to religious influence.[15] Freethinkers' discussions of female religiosity related to a broader debate about woman's relationship to religion and the feminisation of the churches and Christian organisational structures. This was accompanied by a mass of writings by Christian commentators and devotional writers on woman's role as moral guardian and her greater capacity for communion with God, an idea that was at the heart of Victorian domestic ideology.

Like Christians, Freethinkers believed that women now made up the majority of practising Christians and formed the churches' last defence against a rising tide of secularism. This made the struggle to emancipate women all the more important. Thus Kate Watts wrote of how

> Christianity has received many deadly blows owing to the discoveries which a proper investigation of science has brought to light; but the deadliest of all will be struck when women can be brought to see their true position, when they refused to be treated as slaves, and demand the rights which belong to them as they do to man.[16]

Freethinkers believed that Christianity was the main cause of female oppression, both historically and in contemporary society. The question of why so few women were attracted to the Freethought movement while they continued to attend Christian services in large numbers was therefore particularly vexing. Kate Watts expressed the bewilderment (and no doubt irritation) felt by the entire movement when she wrote that, 'It has ever been a source of wonder to me how women could be such devout believers in a creed which places them in a position which, in many instances, is scarcely above the level of the brute.'[17]

Why were women so vulnerable to the blandishments of the churchmen? Some Freethinkers recognised the social pressures and cultural conditions that made women more likely to embrace religion – they were less educated and more needy of clerical solace because of the injustices they faced due to their sex, it was suggested.[18] Yet Secularist criticism of women's exploitation by the Priesthood could easily shade into hostile accounts of women themselves. The female mind was portrayed as less intellectually rigorous, less critical, and, most importantly, less rational than that of men. Discussions of the need to attract more women to Secularism often assumed that women preferred the ritualistic, emotional and sensual forms of worship offered by the churches to the scientific and rational organisational practices of the Secular societies. In 1868 Austin Holyoake suggested that local societies ought to hold Secular ceremonies in order to encourage women to join. 'The … female,' he claimed, 'is moved and controlled almost exclusively through the feelings or emotions.'[19] Kate Watts also intimated that the majority of women lacked the intellectual and critical rigour required by the Freethought movement. 'The explanation suggested to my mind,' she wrote, when considering the question of female religiosity, 'is that, as a rule, women have never studied the subject [of religion], and are quite content to follow blindly in the path their mothers and grandmothers had travelled before them.'[20]

In the work of W. S. Ross, the suggestion that women were susceptible to religious influence due to some fault of their own developed into full-blown misogyny. He focused on how religion had deformed women's characters and 'enfeebled their minds with superstitions [so] that we have a world full of ninnies ... Where we might have had millions of women proper we have only giggling gawkies.'[21] Women's own stupidity was to blame for their inability to recognise Christianity as their oppressor:

> Have fourteen centuries of the numbing moral narcotic left you so stupid and spiritless that you cannot resent the dishonour done to you by this Galilean Tarquin? Are you too deeply drugged and so intellectually dead that you feel no impulse to set your heel upon the neck of this poisonous viper of faith?[22]

In spite of its formal commitment to women's rights the Freethought movement could also act as home to a brand of misogyny that was enhanced, rather than undermined, by its anti-religious ideology. This continued into the twentieth century, when some Freethinkers employed emerging ideas of social progress and modernity to imply that women were backward or lagging behind enlightened male society which by now had thrown off tiresome Church allegiance.[23]

Yet some Freethinkers continued to insist upon woman's intellectual capacity for Freethought and denounced any idea that she was inherently destined to remain in thrall to religion. In 1880 Bertha Lathbury published an article in *The Nineteenth-Century* hostile to female Freethinkers, outlining the harmful effects of Agnosticism for women. 'The strength of women lies in their heart,' she insisted. 'Intellectual courage is rarely one of their virtues', and thus women's renunciation of religion entailed far greater sacrifice and more intense suffering.[24] The following month, however, Jane Clapperton published a reply asserting that, as one of 'a considerable band of women agnostics in this country' she knew it *was* possible for women to 'gain in intellectual courage' and live a rewarding life as Freethinkers. Many women did indeed possess that 'earnestness of nature and intelligent spirit of inquiry' necessary to free oneself from religious tutelage. Clapperton acknowledged that, in the present time, women did often have stronger emotions than men, but denounced the idea that 'women will always remain exactly [as they are] now – that ... the essential nature of the sex is unchangeable'. On this question, she insisted, 'agnostics take a different and much more hopeful view. Human nature is to them infinitely modifiable ...' and thus changes to 'outward conditions' (presumably the improved education for which so many other Freethinking feminists were campaigning) would enable women to release themselves from religion and embrace freethinking values.[25]

The presence of Freethinking women in these debates serves as an important reminder that the history of gender and religion during this period cannot be narrated entirely within a framework of 'secular man' and 'spiritual woman'.[26] Such binary notions did exert a powerful influence over both Freethinkers and Christians, and historians themselves have often re-inscribed such assumptions when discussing the low level of female involvement in Freethought organisations.[27] In noting that women were more open to joining the Ethical Societies or esoteric religions that began to emerge towards the end of the century, they imply that women were more inclined to enjoy aesthetic forms of worship and spiritualised understandings of the world over the intellectual debates and materialist analyses offered by the Secularist movement.[28] We should, however, guard against such essentialist understandings of 'masculine' or 'feminine' forms of spirituality.[29] The gender dynamics of Secularism were not straightforwardly 'feminist' and did at times reproduce dominant ideas about women's inherently spiritual nature. Yet, as the history of female Freethinkers testifies, it did provide a space in which a handful of women were able to embody radically disruptive, *anti*-spiritual visions of womanhood.

Religion as the root of women's oppression

Religion above all else, claimed the Freethinkers, was to blame for the subordination of women (both historically and in the present day), and the Bible was the founding text of sexual oppression. In her first month as editor of the *Secular Chronicle*, Harriet Law declared that 'the Bible does assign women a distinct, and what is worse, a subordinate sphere. And renders her subject to man in nearly every relationship of her life.'[30] As many other Freethinkers went on to argue, woman's subject position was enshrined at the very start, when God had formed Eve as a 'helpmeet' for Adam, or, in the words of Freethinkers, as an 'after-thought', 'a last resort'.[31] That the Bible then made Eve responsible for the Fall and the emergence of evil into the world served to legitimate her subsequent mistreatment at the hands of men and society at large.[32] Scriptural teachings were also responsible for women's subordinate position in marriage, for as punishment for eating of the tree of knowledge God had pronounced that women should be subject to their husband's will.[33] Annie Besant wrote a pamphlet condemning *God's Views on Marriage* in the Old Testament, and pointed elsewhere to New Testament passages that confirmed woman's submission to her husband's authority.[34] Moreover, as Sophia Dobson Collet pointed out, the situation of married women hardly improved under Christianity, in spite of the fact that 'Christ forbade Jewish husbands to abuse their power of summary divorce', since this still left women without any rights so that 'the innocent wife must ever be bound to the brutal husband ...'.[35] St. Paul, in particular, was condemned as 'a thorough misogynist' for his belief that 'the sole object of marriage is the prevention of irregular indulgence'.[36] This denigration of marriage, it was argued, was disrespectful to women and ruled out the possibility of equal and respectful heterosexual partnerships.[37]

The Freethinking feminist attack on religion was framed as a response to '[o]ne of the favourite claims put forward on behalf of the Bible by believers in its inspiration ... that the position of women in society has been improved by its acceptance'.[38] Here Besant was referring to the proliferation of historical accounts of women's changing role in society, which identified Christianity as the key factor in the 'elevation' of their position over the centuries. These histories were Christianised versions of Enlightenment accounts, which had identified the status of 'woman' as a measure of human progress and civilisation.[39] In 1812, Robert Aspland, minister at the Unitarian Chapel that Sara Hennell had attended for much of her early life, published *The Beneficial Influence of Christianity on the Character and Condition of the Female Sex*, which argued that the spread of Christianity after the collapse of the Roman Empire had promoted morality and ended practices harmful to women such as divorce and polygamy.[40] A few years later Francis Augustus Cox's *Female Scripture Biography* (1817) integrated his discussion of female biblical figures into a broader historical framework which similarly examined the position of women in terms of a stage-by-stage progress of civilisation. 'The morals of women', he argued, 'are indicative of the state of society in general, and of the estimation in which they are held in particular.' He first examined woman's position in the 'Pagan nations of Antiquity', including the Greeks, Egyptians and Celts, where they were subject to polygamy, seclusion and infanticide. Next he looked at 'the state of women' in modern-day 'Savage, Superstitious and Mahometan countries', which included Catholic Europe. Cox concluded that Protestantism alone had rescued women from degradation and had acted as the driving force of civilisation.[41] By the 1840s such ideas had proliferated to the extent that Sarah Lewis, in her best-selling *Woman's Mission*, devoted a few paragraphs to a 'rapid historical sketch' which likewise proved that 'The rescue of this [female] half of the human race was henceforth the ascertained will of the Almighty', so that anywhere Christianity triumphed the work of Providence acted to elevate the position of women.[42]

In response to these Christian histories of womanhood, Freethinkers provided an alternative historical account of women, religion and progress. They too accepted the premise of Enlightenment historians that woman's position was an indicator of social progress: 'the welfare of woman is the welfare of man,' declared Joseph Barker. 'If she be elevated, man rises; if she be degraded, man falls...'[43] Harriet Law agreed that 'the progress of the human race cannot be very rapid while the education of one half is either neglected, or conducted upon unsound principles ... the world's progress will be accelerated a thousand fold by [female] emancipation.'[44] Harriet Law and her fellow Freethinkers viewed Christianity not as a progressive but as a reactionary force, detrimental to civilisation and therefore also to the emancipation of women. They inverted the Christian historical narrative to demonstrate that 'It is the business of the Bibleites to obstruct the revolt of the female and to prevent, if possible the forces of Evolution and Civilisation from giving woman her freedom.'[45] Whereas some Christian writers claimed that women in classical antiquity had been mistreated as a result of those societies' depraved sexual practices,[46] Freethinkers argued that the introduction of Christianity into the Pagan world had led to a significant decline in the status of women. Sara Hennell insisted that 'The old Roman matron was, relative to her husband, morally as high as in modern Italy.'[47] Francis Newman had made an identical argument in *Phases of Faith* (1850) where he also maintained that Christianity had had a retrogressive impact on the social position of women in the Germanic Pagan tribes.[48]

This freethinking critique remained a feature of feminist writing into the late nineteenth and early twentieth century. In 1897 Mona Caird published a collection of essays attacking the existing marriage system, which included an extended historical account of the oppression of women by the Christian churches.[49] In 1905, Joseph McCabe wrote the most systematic and comprehensive Freethought account of the history of women, which drew heavily on themes developed earlier in the movement. McCabe agreed that women in the Pagan world had been better off before the introduction of Christianity, which, under the command of St Paul, had actively repressed proto-feminist movements in early Christian societies. He then went on to discuss medieval Europe, arguing that women had suffered greatly under monasticism but had also not 'gained much' by the Reformation, before finishing with an analysis of women's position in modern British society.[50] Debating the impact of Christianity upon woman's position remained pertinent to discussions of legal rights up until the First World War. McCabe's work, for example, was referred to in 1912 in the feminist periodical *The Freewoman*, in an article advocating divorce law reform.[51]

Freethinkers subscribed to a linear understanding of progress similar to that employed by their Christian opponents, but which identified Secularism as the final stage in the development of humanity. While most of them agreed that women's position had gradually improved over the course of history, they argued that this had occurred in direct proportion to the weakening of the Christian Church.[52] This secular conception of progress had more feminist potential than its Christian counterpart in maintaining that the final stage of civilisation had not yet been arrived at, and therefore the struggle for a better society was ongoing. Thus, in opposition to some Christian commentators who argued that, thanks to Christianity, modern British women now occupied a privileged position,[53] Freethinkers were compelled to be more critical of the role of women in contemporary Christian society.[54] Joseph Barker asked, 'How is woman treated now, in our land of Bible and Churches? She is denied the opportunity of obtaining a suitable education. In no country of Europe, and in no state of the American republic, is woman allowed to share the same educational advantages as man.'[55] Similarly, Joseph McCabe contrasted the Pagan Egyptian woman of Ancient times with her counterpart in Boston USA c.1850, and concluded that the position of the former was in fact more favourable.[56]

Contemporary notions of race and empire profoundly influenced the concepts of stadial progress and civilisation which both Christians and Freethinkers employed in their histories of women.[57] For Christian commentators, the oppression of women under Islam, or in 'savage' colonised nations, was taken as proof that they occupied a less advanced stage of civilisation.[58] The belief that Christianity had elevated women was taken up by missionaries, who called upon Christian women to liberate their less fortunate sisters in heathen lands.[59] From 1860 onwards, as British imperialism gained momentum, these primarily religious discourses became bound up with more 'secular' ideas about racial superiority.[60] Such ideas became hugely influential in the women's movement, where demands for British women's rights were justified in terms of their ability to contribute to the imperial project and raise up the women of colonised nations, especially those in India.[61] Freethinking feminists also at times expressed orientalist assumptions about women in the 'East'. Sophia Dobson Collet's interest in the Brahmo Somaj, and her admiration for Rammohun Roy and Keshub Chunder Sen, led her to take an interest in the position of women in India, and she supported campaigns for female education, against child marriage, and for mixed-sex worship.[62] Collet's

lengthy and melodramatic description of Rammohun Roy's early experience of women's oppression associated 'the lot of ... women ... a tissue
of ceaseless oppressions' with the general backwardness of India in the
early days of the century.[63]

Secularist opposition to the Christian values of Empire, especially
the missionary spirit, could, however, sometimes lead them to turn a
discourse of progress and civilisation against the British government.
Though their definition of progress – which counter-posed Western
Enlightenment rationalism and science to 'primitive' superstition – was
also implicated in contemporary imperialist discourses,[64] their opposition to Christian statehood necessitated a more critical evaluation of
the kind of 'progress' brought to colonised nations. Secularists therefore accused the proponents of Empire of not living up to a standard of
enlightenment and civilisation that they claimed to bring to the 'infidel'
nations.[65] In particular, they challenged that aspect of 'imperial feminism' which cited the superiority of Protestantism. Christianity, they
argued, was hypocritical in its claim to value women more highly than
the heathen religions. Many Freethinkers, although professing hatred
for all forms of superstitious religion, tended to portray Christianity
as the worst. Lady Florence Dixie believed that although 'every superstitious religion, more or less, enslaves women ... there are none more
potent than those emanating from the Bible precept...'.[66] Joseph Barker
condemned the practice of polygamy in Islamic countries but argued
that this was in fact the legacy of Christianity, for 'Mahometanism' was
'both the legitimate and consistent offspring of the Bible'.[67] Ross attacked
Christian missions for using the language of women's rights to garner
support for their expansion:

> [T]he Christian missionary pretends that the women of the regions
> he is sent to bring under the influence of the "blessed Gospel" are
> unspeakably vile and immoral. This falsehood suits his trade. If the
> women of England could not be induced to believe that the women of
> "heathen countries" are more vile and immoral than they, they would
> decline to subscribe to the missionaries' income.[68]

Annie Besant also challenged the prevailing assumption that Christian
women were better off than their heathen sisters, and even argued that
Christianity was no less guilty of the degraded sensuality that its proponents lamented was the mark of Islam and Hinduism.

> [T]he degraded position assigned to women by Christianity led to
> their still further degradation at the hands of the superior sex. In
> Christendom the brothel took the place of the harem, and women

sacrificed to men's passions did not receive from the Christian even the protection, shelter, food and clothing which were freely given by the Oriental and the Turk.[69]

Opposition to Christianity could sometimes, therefore, encourage Freethinkers to challenge imperialist assumptions of cultural superiority.

Women and Scripture

Freethinkers' condemnation of the Bible as the founding text of woman's oppression was part of a wider debate on women's role and representation in Scripture.[70] In 1876 Harriet Law noted how this subject had occupied the 'platforms' of both feminists and anti-suffrage campaigners throughout the land.[71] Christians used Scripture to answer the Woman Question in a variety of ways. The Baptist writer Clara Balfour clearly framed her book on *The Women of Scripture* (1847) as an intervention into the debate on woman and her role, stating her wish to add to the growing collection of works 'treating of the moral capabilities, moral qualities, and social responsibilities of woman'.[72] As an organised women's movement began to emerge in the second half of the century, many of those involved in it sought to modify and reinterpret Scripture in order to prove that it was compatible with their feminist principles. In doing so, they came into conflict not only with anti-feminist Christians but also with Freethinking feminists, and the Bible debates on women continued to form an important part of wider discussions of the Woman Question right up to the First World War.

The Victoria Discussion Society (VDS) provided a forum in which Freethinkers and Christians of a variety of feminist perspectives came to discuss these questions. The VDS was established in 1869 by the women's rights activist Emily Faithfull, and lasted until 1875. Faithfull, the daughter of an Anglican clergyman, had worked for the *English Woman's Journal* in the 1850s and had been close to Barbara Leigh Smith Bodichon, Bessie Raynor Parkes and Emily Davies.[73] Faithfull continued to support the women's cause actively throughout the 1860s and 1870s, founding the women-only Victoria Press and lecturing on behalf of women's rights in England and the USA. Although Faithfull was a committed Christian, one of the founding aims of the VDS was 'to induce a free interchange' between representatives of 'all shades of opinion'.[74] Faithfull would later claim that its greatest achievement was that it brought together 'earnest people who could never otherwise have met, and enabled them to compare their varied experiences'.[75] The varying 'shades of opinion' represented at the society appear to have included those of both

Christians and Freethinkers. When the society was first launched, *The National Reformer* ran an article urging Secularists to attend so that they might show that 'Freethinkers are not behind-hand in these questions [of women's rights].'[76] Attendees in the first six months included the radical freethinking Malthusian Charles Drysdale, the Christian and anti-Malthusian Dr Elizabeth Blackwell, and Sophia Dobson Collet's friend, the Hindu reformer, Keshub Chunder Sen.[77]

Time and time again members of the VDS argued over whether women's rights could be reconciled with Christianity. Emily Faithfull affirmed on a number of occasions that 'If I could not reconcile this [women's rights] movement with the highest Christian rule, I would never say another word in its favour.'[78] Yet she did not deny the fact that some members of the churches were wholeheartedly opposed to female emancipation. In 1871 Faithfull reported on a sermon by the Rev. Charles Dunbar in which he proclaimed, 'In advocating this movement for the "equality and rights of women" few people will deny that they are acting in defiance of the revelation from God given them through St. Peter and St. Paul.'[79] Faithfull condemned Dunbar's sermon as an example of the 'vials of clerical wrath which are poured upon' the women's movement. In 1884 she once again attacked the 'theological Rip Van Winkles' who used arguments from the Bible, 'supposed to be unanswerable, and therefore crushing', to deny women's emancipation.[80] In fact, Faithfull was called upon so often to confront Christian opponents of women's rights that she developed a stock answer, which she reproduced, word for word, in a variety of publications.[81] Yet Faithfull did not believe that such examples of Christian anti-feminism meant that the religion itself was incompatible with support for women's rights. Instead, she argued for a different interpretation of Scripture which denied the legitimacy of teachings that seemed to endorse the subjection of women.

In doing so Faithfull focused on the same passages of Scripture as did Freethinkers when demonstrating the Bible's hostility to female emancipation – in particular St Paul's command that wives should submit to their husbands. Faithfull argued that St Paul's text needed to be examined in its historical context. He was, she maintained, deeply concerned to treat with sensitivity the indigenous customs and culture of the Greeks to whom he was writing. It was therefore 'only natural that an Apostle … should urge Greek converts to be "keepers at home" in days when no respectable matron or maiden ever left the house save for religious festivals.'[82] Moreover, if nineteenth-century readers were to accept Paul's teachings on female subordination, they should also accept his command 'Slaves, obey your masters.' Faithfull maintained that Paul's writings should not be interpreted as laying down the law for modern-day conduct, but as representing the values and prejudices of his time. Christians in the nineteenth century should be more concerned with interpreting the 'spirit' of Scripture, and she frequently reminded her readers that the Bible also taught that 'the letter killeth, [while] the spirit giveth life'. According to Faithfull, the 'spirit' of Scripture was clearly in favour of female emancipation: God's command that all His children fulfil their talents surely indicated a support for women's employment and education, and God Himself represented a merging of mascu-line and feminine characteristics.[83] Thus Faithfull's feminist defence of Christianity relied upon the more liberal approach to biblical criticism that was gaining ground in the nineteenth century, and which focused on the spirit rather than the letter of Scripture.

Lydia Becker, president of the National Society for Women's Suffrage, also adopted a liberal approach to Scriptural interpretation when she defended the principle of female suffrage against those who opposed it on religious grounds. In 1875 Mr Leatham MP delivered a speech to his Huddersfield constituents in which he opposed the enfranchise-ment of women, and declared that 'the experience of ages, sanctioned by Revelation, has assigned a distinct sphere to man and woman which clearly meant that God had not intended for women to vote'.[84] Leatham's use of religious arguments to justify his anti-suffrage stance had been a subject of discussion for some months already in the *Women's Suffrage Journal*, edited by Lydia Becker.[85] Leatham's speech at Huddersfield prompted Becker to refute his arguments in more detail, and to give Scriptural grounds for her claim that Christianity supported women's rights. Becker accused Leatham of assuming 'the function of a Pope' in declaring that his interpretation of Scripture was the only possible correct interpretation. She threatened that 'we fear there might be found some obstinate Protestants among women who would refuse to resign the right of private judgement on a question which primarily concerns themselves'. Like Emily Faithfull, she went on to insist 'that Revelation was not meant to teach practical politics any more than it was meant to teach physical science ... why then should men appeal to Revelation on the question of enfranchising women householders?'.[86]

Arguments over the manner in which Scripture should be inter-preted were therefore a crucial determining factor in the debates over whether the Bible assigned women a subordinate sphere. An article in the *Contemporary Review* discussed the importance of developments in biblical criticism to women's rights debates. E. Lyttleton's 'Women's Suffrage and the Teaching of St Paul' (1896) argued that 'some years ago the majority of English Christians would have been unwilling to make use of the researches of Jewish or other scholars ... in such a way as to detract from the binding force of each particular injunction contained anywhere in the Bible'. As a result, Lyttleton claimed, passages such as those in which St Paul prohibited women from speaking in the churches would have been interpreted to imply their exclusion from all public activities, especially parliamentary politics. However, once the need to approach the Scriptures as historical documents, steeped in the values of their own time, had been widely accepted, it was possible to show that Paul's injunctions regarding women were simply a reflection of the 'backward' 'rabbinical' attitudes of the time and not a true Christian teaching which must be adhered to.[87] Just as Lyttleton had described, Emily Faithfull and Lydia Becker's liberal Anglican beliefs enabled them to overcome the problem posed to feminists by those Scriptural passages that appeared to proscribe a subordinate role for women by simply arguing that these should not be read literally. In contrast, a literalist approach to the interpretation of Scripture clearly revealed God's teachings to be in stark opposition to the claims of the women's rights movement. Just such an interpretative approach informed the Freethinking feminist critique of Christianity, unsurprisingly since many Freethinkers had been raised in evangelical churches that, at least until the end of the nineteenth century, tended to favour a literalist reading of the Bible. In insisting that this was the only way in which Scriptural teachings on women could be understood, Freethinking feminists found themselves in strange company. For this was also the claim of some of the most virulent enemies of the women's movement.

The Freethinking feminist case against the Bible was, for example, put to the VDS, not by a Secularist, but by the seasoned misogynist and anti-suffrage campaigner James McGrigor Allan. In July 1870 McGrigor Allan presented a paper to the VDS entitled 'A Protest Against Woman's Demand for the Privilege of Both Sexes'.[88] He later published his arguments in the monograph *Woman Suffrage, Wrong in Principle* (1890), which also responded to many of the arguments made against him by other members of the VDS.[89] In this publication McGrigor Allan attacked Faithfull's liberal approach to Scriptural interpretation which allowed her to ignore clear statements in the Bible affirming female subordination.[90] He contrasted what he termed Faithfull's inconsistent and illogical arguments to those of Freethinking feminists, who honestly and openly repudiated the Bible as the founding text of female oppression. McGrigor Allan praised 'the late Mrs Emma Martin, a Deistical writer of considerable ability ... The most consistent advocate of

Woman Suffrage I ever heard ... Mrs Harriet Law [and] ... Mrs Besant, an avowed Atheist.'[91] 'Such advocates,' he claimed, 'are quite consistent and set an example of candour and honesty to Woman Suffrage advocates professing Christianity.'[92] McGrigor Allan was so impressed by the 'candour' and 'honesty' of Freethinking 'platform ladies' that he devoted numerous pages to laying out their case against the Bible:

> Freethinkers see clearly and admit frankly that the Old Testament and New Testament are totally opposed to Sexual Equality; that the Bible distinctly declares man's supremacy, and calls him the head of the woman. Freethinkers do not here prevaricate, compromise nor tamper with the plain, obvious, meaning of Scripture. Adopting Sexual Equality, they consequently ignore and repudiate the Bible, and believe that something they call 'progress' will enable them to 'elevate' woman in direct defiance of Christianity or religion, natural or revealed.[93]

McGrigor Allan praised Harriet Law for her insistence on treating the Bible as the literal word of God, despite disagreeing with her conclusion that as a result of its clear misogyny it should be discarded *in toto*. 'It is to her credit,' he wrote, '(as compared with professedly Christian advocates of sexual equality) that she did not tamper with the plain meaning of Scripture. *She* made no attempt to quibble away or distort the obvious sense of the words "Let the woman learn in silence with all subjection".'[94] McGrigor Allan did such a good job at pointing out the crucial distinction between Freethinking feminism and mainstream Christian feminism, to the great benefit of the former, that Holyoake advertised *Woman Suffrage, Wrong in Principle* in *The Reasoner*.

The distinction between Freethinking and Christian feminists was articulated most clearly by Harriet Law in her critique of Lydia Becker's response to Mr Leatham MP. Law had obviously been following the exchanges in the *Women's Suffrage Journal* between Leatham and Becker, and she published her own commentary on the debate in the *Secular Chronicle* the following week.[95] Harriet Law applauded Lydia Becker for 'courageously' following Mr Leatham onto the 'elastic pages' of the Bible to 'fight the battle' of women's rights. Unfortunately, Law wrote, 'the gallant MP is quite right; the Bible *does* assign women a distinct, and what is worse, a subordinate sphere', and she went on to quote a number of Scriptural passages as evidence. However, Law's advice to Lydia Becker moved the debate on women and religion beyond the usual dispute over differing interpretations of Scripture, to draw a far more radical conclusion. To give her Christian sister credit, Law wrote, 'Miss Becker returns to Leatham the only answer a believer in inspiration can', that Scripture should not be interpreted literally and should not be used to determine political or social questions. Yet Law felt that even this was a weak response, for why should women's emancipation depend upon what was written in the Bible at all? '[W]e who do not believe in Divine inspiration ... beg to ask if we are to wait for political emancipation, until Tory theologians agree to give a new interpretation to an old book ... We answer, no!' Harriet Law therefore rejected any possible limitation of women's emancipation as determined by religion, custom or any authority beyond women themselves.[96] Her position here contrasts with that of Christians such as Lyttleton, who, in defending women's right to the suffrage in the face of a conservative and literalist reading of Scripture, nevertheless suggested that the Bible implied some limits upon the extent of women's emancipation. It was one thing, Lyttleton maintained, to reject 'rabbinical teachings' with the aid of a more sophisticated approach to Scripture, but 'quite another thing to dissent from [Paul's] broad views of human nature and history' which also implied a somewhat subordinate or at least circumscribed role for women. 'Surely,' Lyttleton asked, 'all deference to authority ceases entirely when we choose to discard opinions which were formed in such a way by so great a teacher.'[97]

Scripture remained an important site of feminist debate into the twentieth century. But the opposition (posited by Freethinking feminists such as Harriet Law) between Freethinking and Christian, feminist and anti-feminist interpretations became increasingly difficult to maintain. With the emergence of a host of new spiritualities and heterodox religions, Scripture seemed to offer more, not less, potential for highly personal, heterodox and feminist interpretation. Henrietta Muller, for example, the editor of *The Women's Penny Paper* who later joined the Theosophical Society, believed the '[re-]interpretation of the Bible to be central to the paper's policy of expounding women's cause in the press'. Throughout 1888, the paper published a series of Scriptural readings and critiques by women of varying theological and religious perspectives, the majority of which affirmed that the Bible might be reclaimed as a feminist text. Muller, a friend and correspondent of Elizabeth Cady Stanton, was open to the Freethinking feminist critique of the Bible's more patriarchal passages. She welcomed contributions from Sara Hennell, maintaining that her work was among the most 'original thought of women about the Bible'. Yet she also made sure to distance herself and the *Penny Paper* from Hennell's total rejection of Scripture's divine origins.[98] Even in the increasingly open and multivarious religious culture of the *fin de siècle* Secularist women therefore continued to occupy a distinctive position.[99]

More than a decade later, Dora Marsden, editor of *The Freewoman*, likewise distinguished her heterodox religious views from those of her Secularist women correspondents, insisting that Christian dogmas and 'questions of the soul and destiny' remained of central importance to her feminist vision. Freethinking feminists continued to write into *The Freewoman* insisting on the need to reject the Bible *in toto*, but their arguments seemed less compelling in an age when the religious terrain had opened up to the degree that that Marsden was now able to embrace a radical feminist and Free Love morality yet remain within a broadly Christian framework.[100]

Conclusion

A look at the 'infidel feminism' of the Secularist movement reveals the extent to which the Woman Question during this period was framed by religion. But debates over whether woman's nature and role was determined by God; whether she was innately more religious than man; whether Christianity or Secularism were of more benefit to her; and whether the Bible granted her rights or not, all hinged on fundamental questions of women's agency in their struggle for emancipation. The implications of Secularist ideology in this regard could be problematic, for the woman oppressed by religion might also be seen as the woman stupefied by it. In this sense, the secular idea of progress could present women's emancipation as beyond the control of women themselves. On the other hand, the Freethought critique of religion also opened ways of envisaging a greater degree of agency for women in their own struggle for freedom. Firstly, the rejection of Original Sin and God-given sexual characteristics afforded control over the development of one's own character and behaviour in the world. Secondly, Secularism rejected all moral and intellectual authority beyond one's own conscience. It thus presented the possibility for women to demand their rights without having to justify them according to male-defined standards (including religion). The next chapter will go on to show how this infidel feminism was put into practice in the campaigning women's movement.

Notes

1 B. Taylor, *Eve and the New Jerusalem. Socialism and Feminism in the Nineteenth Century* (London: Virago, 1983), p. 25.

2 The belief in human perfectibility and environmentalism was also an important current within Unitarianism, and hence in the feminism of radical Unitarians in

the first half of the nineteenth century; see K. Gleadle, *The Early Feminists. Radical Unitarians and the Emergence of the Women's Rights Movement, 1831–51* (Basingstoke & London: Palgrave Macmillan, 1995), pp. 6, 11.

3   See M. Wollstonecraft, *A Vindication of the Rights of Woman* (1792) Chapters 1–2; Rogers argues that Macauley must have been acquainted with the work of Wollstonecraft; see H. Rogers, 'Facing Her Public: The Actress, Eliza Macauley (1785–1837)' (unpublished manuscript), p. 12.

4   *The Crisis*, 16 June 1832, p. 49, 7 July 1832, p. 66.

5   *Secular Chronicle (SC)*, 30 January 1876, p. 49. The Ladies Page was usually written by Law, though on occasion left anonymous.

6   A. Besant, *The Political Status of Women* 3rd edn (London: Freethought Publishing Company, 1874[?], repr. J. Saville (ed.), *A Selection of the Social and Political Pamphlets of Annie Besant. With a Preface and Biographical Notes by John Saville*, New York: Augustus M. Kelley, 1970), pp. 6–7. Here Besant made similar arguments to J. S. Mill in *The Subjection of Women* (1869). Clearly arguments of this kind were not the sole preserve of the Freethought movement and, by the 1870s, were also being made within the mainstream women's movement, but Freethought 'theology' complemented and encouraged an environmentalist view of sexual difference.

7   *The Women's Penny Paper (PP)*, 23 February 1889, p. 7; S. S. Hennell, *Present Religion as Faith Owning Fellowship with Thought* 3 vols (London: Trubnor and Co., 1865, 1873, 1887) iii (1887), p. 337.

8   *PP*, 20 July 1889, p. 5.

9   *PP*, 10 August 1889, p. 4.

10 Hennell's incredibly dense and confused style was commented upon by the reviewer for the *Penny Paper*, who said of *Present Religion* that 'The literary style is certainly unfortunate. Miss Hennell has clothed a beautiful child in most ugly garments.' *PP*, 29 June 1889, p. 10.

11 *PP*, 23 February 1889, p. 7.

12 Saladin [W. S. Ross], *Woman, Her Glory, Her Shame and Her God*, 2 vols (London: W. Stewart and Co., 1894[?]) i, p. 57.

13 J. Barker, *What Has the Bible Done for Woman?* (London: Barker & Co. [186?]), p. 10.

14 Ross, *Woman*, i, pp. 61–2.

15 J. McCabe, *The Religion of Women. An Historical Study, with an Introduction by Lady Florence Dixie* (London: Watts & Co., 1905), pp. 15, 60.

16 *SR*, 27 September 1879, p. 193.

17 *Ibid.*, p. 193.

18 *The Reasoner (Reasoner)*, 4 July 1869, p. 10. This motif had been common within Freethought at least since the beginning of the century. Frances Wright complained that 'the neglected state of the female mind' placed women at the mercy of the Priesthood, whose 'very subsistence depends, of necessity, upon the mental and moral degradation of their fellow creatures'; F. Wright, 'Preface', *Course of Popular Lectures as Delivered by Frances Wright, in New York, Philadelphia, Baltimore, Boston, Cincinnati, St. Louis, Louisville, and other Cities, Towns and Districts of the United States. With Three Addresses on Various Public Occasions and a Reply to the Charges Against the French Reformers of 1789* 4th edn (New York: Published at the Office of the Free Enquirer, Hall of Science, 1831) (first published 1828), pp. 8–9.

Sara Hennell was more willing to countenance the inherent religiosity of women, but saw this as a positive. She believed that now, with the ushering in of the new religious order, 'for the first time in human history ... The Maker now seems to say in the hearts of women that for the future with *them* he will deal directly.' See *PP*, 20 July 1889, p. 5.

19 *NR*, 12 January 1868, p. 27. See a similar debate a few years later, *NR*, 18 June 1871, p. 398, 2 July 1871, p. 15.

20 *SR*, 27 September 1879, p. 193.

21 Ross, *Woman*, ii, p. 420.

22 *Ibid.*, ii, p. 346.

23 See, for example, the female correspondent in *Freewoman*, 18 April, 1912, p. 496; F. J. Gould, *Will Women Help? A Appeal to Women to Assist in Liberating Modern Thought from Theological Bonds* (Rationalist Press Association Ltd; London: Watts & Co., 1900), Chapter 1.

24 B. Lathbury, 'Agnosticism and Women', *The Nineteenth Century* 7:38 (April 1880), pp. 619–27, 620, 626.

25 J. Clapperton, 'Agnosticism and Women: A Reply', *The Nineteenth Century* 7:39 (May 1880), 840–44

26 The need to move beyond this binary within the study of gender and religion more generally is pointed to as one of the key challenges now facing historians in this field; see S. Morgan & J. de Vries, 'Introduction', in *Women, Gender and Religious Cultures in Britain 1800–1940* (Abingdon: Routledge, 2010), pp. 1–10, 8; J. Dixon, 'Modernity, Heterodoxy and the Transformation of Religious Cultures', in S. Morgan & J. de Vries (2010), pp. 211–30, 212.

27 In 1892, for example, one Christian woman countered G. W. Foote's indictment of Christianity as 'Woman's Worst Foe' with the assertion that Secularism was 'so bare and sterile a thing' that even Annie Besant had abandoned its 'materialistic utilitarianism' for the more emotional culture of the Theosophical Society, *Anti-Infidel*, June 1892, p. 12.

28 See E. Royle, *Radicals, Secularists and Republicans. Popular Freethought in Britain, 1866–1915* (Manchester: Manchester University Press, 1980). pp. 249–50; D. Burfield, 'Theosophy and Feminism: Some Explorations in Nineteenth-Century Biography', in Pat Holden (ed.), *Women's Religious Experience* (London: Croom Helm, 1983), pp. 27–56, 35–6.

29 For this argument, see J. Dixon, *Divine Feminine: Theosophy and Feminism in England* (Baltimore: The Johns Hopkins University Press, 2001), p. 6.

30 *SC*, 9 January 1876, p. 17; Sara Hennell agreed that the 'myth' of female inferiority was introduced by 'Hebrew supernaturalism'; Hennell (1887), p. 289.

31 Ross, *Woman*, i, pp. 4–5; F. Neale, 'Is Woman Indebted to the Bible?', in *British Secular Union Almanack for 1879* (London: Charles Watts, 1879), p. 33; see also Barker (186?), p. 3.

32 *SC*, 9 January 1876, p17; Neale (1879), p. 34; McCabe (1905), p. 26.

33 Barker (186?), p. 4.

34 A. Besant, *God's Views on Marriage. As Revealed in the Old Testament* (London: Freethought Publishing Co., 1890); A. Besant, *Marriage; As It Was, As It Is and As It Should Be* (New York: A.K. Butts, 1879), p. 7.

35   S. D. Collet, *George Jacob Holyoake and Modern Atheism. A Biographical and Critical Essay* (London: Trubnor & Co., 1855), pp. 42–3.

36   Ross, *Woman*, i, p. 9.

37   Neale (1879), p. 34. For other attacks on Paul see *NR*, 21 January 1877, p. 38; A. Besant, *Woman's Position According to the Bible* (London: Besant & Bradlaugh, 1885).

38   Besant (1885), p. 1.

39   For discussion of Enlightenment stadial histories of women and civilisation, see S. Sebastiani, '"Race", Women and Progress in the Scottish Enlightenment', in S. Knott & B. Taylor (eds.), *Women, Gender and Enlightenment* (London: Palgrave Macmillan, 2005), pp. 75–96, 78–9. For their use by nineteenth-century feminists, see J. Rendall, *The Origins of Modern Feminism. Women in Britain, France and the United States, 1780–1860* (Basingstoke: Palgrave, 1985), pp. 20–32; Gleadle (1995), pp. 64–7; C. Midgley, 'Anti-Slavery and the Roots of "Imperial Feminism"', in C. Midgley (ed.), *Gender and Imperialism* (Manchester: Manchester University Press, 1999), pp. 161–79.

40   Gleadle (1995), p. 66. For the trend for nineteenth-century Christian writers to write histories of the positive influence of Christianity on women; see also Davidoff & Hall (1987), p. 115; C. Midgley, *Feminism and Empire. Women Activists in Imperial Britain, 1790–1865* (London & New York: Routledge, 2007), esp. Chapter 1. Midgley was the first to properly acknowledge the extent of nineteenth-century Christian writings on the beneficial influence of Christianity on women and to explore them in depth. Her account, however, focuses on the cross cultural comparisons made in these histories rather than on their view of Christianity as a force for historical progress.

41   F. A. Cox, *Female Scripture Biography: Including an Essay on What Christianity has Done for Women* (London: Gale & Fenner, 1817), pp. ii–xxi.

42   S. Lewis, *Woman's Mission* 7th edn (London: John W. Parker, 1840) (first published 1839), pp. 43–5; see also A. Monod, *The Christian Woman: Her Place and Power* (London: T. Nelson & Sons, 1861[?]), p. 8, which argued that 'Nothing truly distinguishes the savage state from the civilised, the east from the west, paganism from Christianity … than the condition of woman.'; C. L. Balfour, *The Women of Scripture* (London: Houlston & Stoneman, 1847), p. 4.

43   Barker (186?), p. 1.

44   *SC*, 2 January 1876, p. 1.

45   F. Dixie, 'Introduction', in McCabe (1905), pp. 5–9, 6.

46   See Cox (1817), pp. vi–xiv; Lewis (1839), p. 15; Angell James (1852), pp. 5–6.

47   S. S. Hennell, *Christianity and Infidelity: An Exposition of the Arguments on Both Sides. Arranged According to a Plan Proposed by George Baillie Esq.* (London: Arthur Hall, Virtue & Co., 1857), p. 80. Hennell's particular vision of religious and moral evolution led her to take a far less accusatory approach to Christianity's treatment of women than many other Freethinkers. Because Hennell believed that Providence determined that the position of women should evolve and improve over time until a final stage of 'perfection' and equality had been reached, she viewed the treatment of women in the ancient Judeo-Christian texts as inevitable and therefore as almost excusable. Hennell applied the rule of liberal Anglican Biblical criticism – that Scripture should be understood as the product of a particular time and place – to explain the oppression of women under Christianity. Although Hennell believed that in the modern day, 'The thought that God, with moral attributed, had expressly

laid out that women should in this way be made over to the brutal masterfulness of men ... must surely be fatal to any moral reverence we could pay Him', she was tolerant of *historical* Christian attitudes towards women. She even intervened in a debate in *The Women's Penny Paper* on the 'View of Women in the Bible' in defence of Scripture, arguing that once the Bible was accepted as a collection of manmade documents it became clear that its position on the role of women was inconsistent, for although Genesis argued for their subordination, elsewhere appeared 'the divine fact that woman, just as man, was made in God's image'. Although Hennell appears to have been the only female Freethinker to have taken this more sympathetic approach, her views serve as a reminder of the extent to which Freethinkers' 'theological' beliefs shaped their feminism; see Hennell iii (1887), p. 295; *PP*, 15 December 1889, p. 6.

48 F. Newman, *Phases of Faith* (London: Watts & Co., Rationalist Press Association, 1907) (first published 1850), p. 78; see also Neale (1879), p. 33; Ross, *Woman*, ii, p. 345.

49 M. Caird, *The Morality of Marriage and Other Essays on the Status and Destiny of Woman* (London: George Redway, 1897), pp. 41, 73, 81.

50 McCabe (1905), pp. 26, 36, 28, 40, 47.

51 Its author, ESP Haynes, was a supporter of the Rationalist Press Association and referred to McCabe as his 'friend'; S. M. Cretney, 'Haynes, Edmund Sidney Pollock (1877–1949)', *Oxford Dictionary of National Biography* (online edn.; Oxford University Press, 2004); *The Freewoman (Freewoman)*, 4 January 1912, p. 127. See also Guy Aldred in *Freewoman*, 18 January 1912, pp. 178–9.

52 *SR*, 14 June 1888, p. 17; see also Barker (186?), p. 17

53 Midgley (2007), p. 27.

54 This was even the case with individual Freethinkers who lacked a genuine commitment to women's emancipation but who nevertheless found themselves arguing in favour of greater freedom for women. In spite of Ross's patent dislike of women, the logic of Freethought hostility to Christianity and its impact on the condition of women compelled him to condemn the treatment of women in modern-day Christian society and to support a vague notion of increased emancipation.

55 Barker (186?), p. 12.

56 McCabe (1905), p. 17.

57 Sebastiani (2005), pp. 76–7, 87.

58 See, for example, F. Close, *The Female Chartists' Visit to the Parish Church. A Sermon Addressed to the Female Chartists of Cheltenham. Sunday, August 25th, 1839. On the Occasion of their Attending the Parish Church in a Body* (London: Hamilton, Adams and Co., 1839), pp. 5–7; Lewis (1840), pp. 146–7.

59 C. Midgley, 'Can Women Be Missionaries? Envisioning Female Agency in the Early Nineteenth-Century British Empire', *Journal of British Studies* 45:2 (2006), 335–58, 349, 350.

60 Midgley (2006), see also C. Midgley, 'From Supporting Missions to Petitioning Parliament: British Women and the Evangelical Campaign against *Sati* in India, 1813–30', in K. Gleadle & S. Richardson (eds.), *Women in British Politics 1760–1860: The Power of the Petticoat* (Basingstoke: Macmillan, 2000), pp. 74–92. Midgley identified these as the forerunners to Burton's 'imperial feminism'.

61 A. Burton, *Burdens of History: British Feminists, Indian Women, and Imperial Culture, 1865–1915* (Chapel Hill & London: University of North Carolina Press, 1994), pp. 5, 2, 8.

62 S. D. Collet, *Indian Theism and its Relation to Christianity* (London: Strahan & Co., 1870), pp. 22–3. By the time Collet began to take an interest in Indian women she had already re-converted to some loose form of Christianity.

63 S. D.Collet, *The Life and Letters of Raja Rammohun Roy. Compiled and Edited by the Late Sophia Dobson Collet and Completed by a Friend* (London: Harold Collet, 1900), p. 17 It should be noted that this might not have come directly from the pen of Sophia Dobson Collet since it was completed and published after her death. The language used to describe the position of women on the Indian subcontinent is the most extreme, but not out of place with earlier work by Collet on the subject.

64 See discussion of the 'Anglo-centric emphasis' of Bradlaugh's opposition to British rule in India; D. Nash, 'Charles Bradlaugh and the Many Chameleon Destinations of Republicanism', in D. Nash & A. Taylor (eds.), *Republicanism in Victorian Society* (Thrupp, Stroud: Sutton Publishing, 2000), pp. 106–24, 117–18.

65 D. Nash, 'Taming the God of Battles: Secular and Moral Critiques of the South African War', in G. Cuthbertson, A. Grundlingh & M. Suttie (eds.), *Writing a Wider War: Rethinking Gender, Race and Identity in the South African War 1899–1902* (Athens, Ohio: Ohio University Press, 2002), pp. 266–86, 267, 273; see also G. Claeys, *Imperial Sceptics: British Critics of Empire 1850–1920* (Cambridge, Cambridge University Press, 2010), pp. 43–5, 192. For a sustained anti-imperialism motivated by a Secularist position see Harriet Law's articles in the *Secular Chronicle*.

66 F. Dixie (1905), p. 6.

67 Barker (186?), p. 6.

68 Ross, *Woman*, ii, p. 316.

69 A. Besant, *Is Christianity a Success?*, pp. 2, 5. Freethinkers frequently contrasted Eastern religions favourably with Christianity, or used the 'oriental gaze' to condemn Western Christendom. See for example, 'Hindoo Toleration Instructive to Christians', *Reasoner*, 5 August 1855, p. 149.

70 For parallel debates in the US women's movement, see discussion of the publication of Elizabeth Cady Stanton's *The Woman's Bible* (1895), D. Spender; 'Introduction', in E. Cady Stanton, *The Woman's Bible: The Original Feminist Attack on the Bible* (Glasgow: Polygon Books, 1985), i–v; K. Kern, *Mrs Stanton's Bible* (Ithica & London: Cornell University Press, 2001), pp. 1–2.

71 *SC*, 9 January 1876, p. 17.

72 Balfour (1847), p. iii. Balfour was one of a number of nineteenth-century female biographers of women in Scripture who, although they were not overtly 'feminist' nevertheless contributed to a more 'woman-centred' reading of the Bible. Their work emphasises the extent to which Scripture was, during this period, a key arena for discussions of womanhood and female attempts to participate in the male-dominated disciplines; see R. Styler, 'A Scripture of their Own: Nineteenth-Century Bible Biography and Feminist Bible Criticism', *Christianity and Literature* 57:1 (Autumn 2007), 65–85. For the broader context of female interpretation, see C. de Groot & M. A. Taylor, *Recovering Nineteenth-Century Women Interpreters of the Bible* (Boston: Brill Leiden, 2007).

73 J. Stone, *Emily Faithfull: Victorian Champion of Women's Rights* (Toronto: P.D. Meany, 1994).

74 *Ibid.*, p. 77.

75 E. Faithfull, *Three Visits to America* (Edinburgh: D. Douglas, 1884), p. 100.

76 *The National Reformer* (*NR*), 31 October 1869, p. 279.

77 *The Victoria Magazine* (*VM*), September 1870, pp. 395–419.

78 *Ibid.*, July 1870, pp. 354–5.

79 *Ibid.*, August 1871, p. 358.

80 Faithfull (1884), p. 106.

81 For examples of this stock reply, see Faithfull (1884), pp. 106–7; *VM*, July 1870, pp. 354–5, August 1871, pp. 356–8.

82 *VM*, July 1870, pp. 354–5.

83 *Ibid.*, July 1870, p. 355.

84 Quoted in *Women's Suffrage Journal*, 1 January 1876, pp. 1–5.

85 *Ibid.*, 1 June 1875, p. 79.

86 *Ibid.*, 1 January 1876, pp. 1–5.

87 E. Lyttleton, 'Women's Suffrage and the Teaching of St. Paul', *Contemporary Review* (May 1896), 680–91.

88 *VM*, July 1870, pp. 318–56.

89 J. McGrigor Allan, *Woman Suffrage, Wrong in Principle and Practice. An Essay* (London: Remington & Co., 1890). The earliest copy held by the British Library is from 1890 but the work was obviously published earlier, as it was advertised in *The Reasoner* in the 1870s.

90 In the discussion of his paper at the VDS he argued that this overemphasis on the role of 'private judgement' would logically conclude with the position of 'the infidel who repudiates the whole of it because none of it commends itself to his "private judgement"', *VM*, July 1870, p. 241.

91 McGrigor Allan (1890), pp. 11–12.

92 *Ibid.*, pp. 27–8.

93 *Ibid.*, p. 28.

94 *Ibid.*, pp. 28–9.

95 *SC*, 9 January 1876, p. 17.

96 *Ibid.*, p. 17.

97 Lyttleton (1896), pp. 688–9.

98 *PP*, 15 December 1888, p. 6.

99 For this argument and a more in-depth account of *fin de siècle* Bible debates, see N. Hetherington, 'Biblical Interpretation and Women's Rights in the Late Nineteenth-Century British Women's Advocacy Press', *Women's History Review* (forthcoming 2013).

100 *Freewoman*, 6 June 1912, p. 59. See also 23 May 1912, 6 June 1912.

5

Freethinking feminists and the women's movement

I n the autumn of 1869, the Freethinking feminist Elizabeth Wolstenholme Elmy left the Social Science Congress determined to fight the Contagious Diseases Acts. Wolstenholme Elmy was encouraged by the Congress voting to oppose the Acts, which introduced the state regulation of prostitution by forcing women suspected of soliciting to undergo medical checks and possible detention in 'lock hospitals'. Yet instead of heading a repeal campaign herself she put forward her friend Josephine Butler, whose married status and religious piety provided her with the necessary cloak of respectability to speak on a subject well beyond the pale of middle-class womanhood. That a self-proclaimed atheist and Secularist should have played such an important part in initiating a campaign that became renowned for its religious fervour and Christian moralism is an irony rarely noted or explained. While historians have long recognised the importance of Christianity to feminism in the second half of the nineteenth century, anti-religious or freethinking ideas have never received more than a brief mention. Historians of feminism have either passed over or misrepresented the freethinking views of certain leading feminist figures, while studies of the Freethought movement have tended to represent its support for female emancipation as disconnected from the organised women's movement.[1] In fact, the women's rights and Freethought movements shared an intellectual and political inheritance, and Freethought and wider feminist networks frequently overlapped. Freethinking individuals were central to promoting the first feminist organisations in the middle decades of the century, and female Secularists continued to actively contribute to the women's movement over the course of the century. The contribution made by Freethought to nineteenth-century feminism – at both an organisational and ideological level – needs, therefore, to be acknowledged. Nevertheless, the unorthodox and unrespectable nature of their beliefs meant that Freethinking feminists at times found themselves marginalised within women's rights organisations. Despite many inter-connections and similarities between Freethought and 'mainstream' feminism, various religious and anti-religious perspectives could also influence women's rights activism in very different directions.

Freethinkers and (Christian) feminists both utilised a language of rights and of women's reforming mission, though by the second half of the nineteenth century Secularists tended to support the more radical current within the women's movement. In spite of the Christianised aspect of the campaign against the Contagious Diseases (CD) Acts, many Freethinkers became involved and some happily embraced its moral crusading rhetoric. In fact, the Secularist movement shared the sense of moral imperative that infused this more overtly Christian-identified campaign. Freethinking feminists also, however, developed a distinctively 'Secularist' critique of the CD Acts, blaming the evils of prostitution on the hypocrisy of the Christian marriage institution. The Freethinking emphasis on the sanctity of individual private judgement and moral autonomy also shaped attitudes towards the social purity campaigns that came out of repeal work, deterring some Secularists from endorsing the more repressive aspects of this movement. Remaining true to a longstanding, ultra-democratic tradition, Freethinking feminists tended to cohere around the radical fringes of the new suffrage organi-sations emerging in the early 1900s. The legacy of their commitment to female enfranchisement, which stretched back to the beginning of the nineteenth century, was, however, evident across the twentieth-century suffrage movement – informing many of its supposedly novel political practices.

Freethinkers and feminists: a shared inheritance

The organised campaign for women's rights from the late 1850s onward – what its adherents dubbed 'the Cause' – is generally seen to have emerged out of three main ideological currents. The first of these was an Enlightenment tradition of natural rights, which early feminists such as Mary Wollstonecraft had sought to extend to women. The rise of evangelicalism or 'serious Christianity' was another contributing factor, whereby ideas about woman's mission and woman's greater moral capacity provided women with a sense of self-worth, spiritual motivation and ideological justification for the expansion of their public activities. The final ideological current channelled into 'the Cause' was utopian socialism, which early on in the century developed a critique of the ways in which private property and the institutions of marriage and the family perpetuated the subordination of the female sex.[2] These intellectual and political discourses overlapped with and fed into each other so that, for example, the suffrage campaign not only made the 'Enlightened' argument for women's equal rights with men but also claimed, in language drawn from evangelical writings on women, that a female role in the polity was necessary for the moral improvement and social reformation of society.[3]

The same pro-woman arguments also influenced Freethinking feminism, and organised Freethought, like the women's movement, became a forum in which these three ideological currents converged. Freethought emerged directly out of the utopian Socialist tradition, while its identification with an Enlightened tradition of the 'Rights of Man' was clearly evident in the strong support that Secularists lent electoral reform and Republican campaigns in the 1850s, 1860s, and 1870s.In addition, organised Freethought expressed that powerful sense of moral mission that has traditionally been associated with and attributed to the serious Christianity of the Victorian era. Freethought support for a multiplicity of reform movements, ranging from anti-Sabbatarianism to land reform to Irish Home Rule, was motivated by a sense of moral purpose which rivalled that of the most pious evangelical philanthropist. This no doubt reflected the evangelical backgrounds of many Freethinkers, so that the two movements shared not only an organisational but also, in some ways, a moral culture. In 1866, an article on 'The Necessity of Reform' in *The National Reformer* described the Freethinking sense of moral 'enthusiasm' thus:

> some persons ... want truth and not falsehood. They are Reformers: they know that they have their appointed work, which is, according to their capacity, to root out the tares that blight the growth of humanity, and to sow the seeds of progress – a work in which the consciousness of doing good upholds them...

Freethinkers, therefore, were very susceptible to the militant moralism and powerful reforming zeal that characterised so much of the Victorian and early twentieth-century women's rights campaigns.[4]

Secularism and the women's movement developed in tandem. The latter is usually considered by historians to have begun with the founding of the *English Woman's Journal* (*EWJ*) in 1858 by Barbara Leigh Smith Bodichon and Bessie Raynor Parkes, and their campaigning for the extension of women's educational and employment opportunities.[5] The name and idea for such a journal had in fact first been mooted by

George Jacob Holyoake as early as 1847 in an article in *The Reasoner* entitled 'Hints to the Advocates of the Rights of Women', in which he called for the founding of a journal devoted to discussing the 'woman question'. Holyoake argued that such a journal should be run by and for women, who, he believed, needed to lead their own struggle for emancipation.[6] Holyoake had initially contacted the Owenite feminist Catherine Barmby about the possibility of editing the proposed *EWJ*. Though Barmby and her husband Goodwyn showed much interest in this project it was postponed on account of a recent bereavement in Catherine's family and was never taken up by them again.[7] The idea for a women's journal lay dormant until 1857, when Bessie Raynor Parkes began to correspond with Holyoake about purchasing a suitable magazine for the purpose.[8]

Bessie Raynor Parkes and Barbara Leigh Smith Bodichon had both been brought up in 'radical unitarian' circles, which was possibly how they came to know Sara Hennell and Sophia Dobson Collet, and Parkes and Bodichon had once joined Hennell and George Eliot for a summer holiday in 1853.[9] Bodichon held freethinking religious views, and although she was not involved in the organised Freethought movement, both she and Parkes were acquainted with Holyoake, read the Secularist press and kept up to date with the activities of 'Secularist Ladies'.[10] Matilda Hays, who was co-editor with Raynor Parkes on the *EWJ* until 1862, worked with Eliza Ashurst, daughter of the freethinking radical lawyer and close friend of Holyoake, Richard Ashurst.[11] Sarah Lewin, secretary and book-keeper at the *EWJ* was friends with Sophia Dobson Collet, and the two of them once presented Holyoake with a new writing desk as a sign of their admiration.[12] Such close links between the newly emerging Secularist movement and the *EWJ* meant that the activities of the latter were advertised in *The Reasoner*, and their respective readerships probably overlapped.[13]

Freethinkers continued to lend their support as these small organisational initiatives gained momentum over the following decades to become national networks campaigning on a variety of women's rights issues. The Secularist Elizabeth Wolstenholme Elmy was central in initiating many of these campaigns. In 1865 she set up the Manchester Board of School Mistresses, which aimed to promote better education and formal qualifications for female school teachers in order to improve their pitiful pay and the quality of education in girls' schools. Wolstenholme Elmy's idea was soon taken up across other towns in the north-west of England and, together with campaigners such as Anna Jemima Clough, who went on to found Newnham College at Cambridge, Wolstenholme Elmy organised a series of advanced lectures for women in the region during 1867. That same year the North of England Council for Promoting the Education of Women was founded, with Josephine Butler as its president.[14] Feminist issues were also, at this time, taken up in the Secularist press and local Secular societies. In 1866 one of Harriet Law's most popular lectures was on the 'Degraded and Oppressed Condition of Woman Caused by Religion and Ignorance'. This lecture was particularly well-received on the lecture circuit covered by the 'North of England Secular Society', the same area in which Wolstoneholme Elmy, Clough, and Butler were organising. In choosing to lecture on this subject, Law had an explicitly activist agenda, for she claimed to want not just to expose the 'ignorance' and lack of education for women but also to 'stir up public opinion' and to call on her audience to act 'to remove this monstrous anomaly' of women's inequality.[15]

Education was a particularly important cause for Freethinking feminists because of their belief that ignorance (manifested in religion) was the root of all society's ills. In 1869, Mrs Lipsham, an especially active member of the Liverpool Secular Society, travelled to Manchester to deliver a lecture on 'Female Education', while Louisa Wade lectured on the same subject to a Secularist audience at Mile End, and argued that girls should receive exactly the same education as their brothers.[16] Wade also supported extended employment opportunities for women, but she advanced more radical arguments than either Bodichon or Raynor Parkes, insisting that women were capable of being lecturers, professors, artists, politicians, physicians and even judges – an argument which succeeded in 'delighting an appreciative and numerous audience' of fellow Freethinkers.[17] The campaigning efforts of Freethinking women were regularly and approvingly reported in the Secularist press, which also provided favourable publicity for Elizabeth Wolstenholme Elmy's other two main projects – securing the right of married women to own property and the campaign against the CD Acts.

Christian feminists, however – those who made up the majority of the women's movement – were not always so keen to associate their struggle with Secularism. The early women's movement was desperately concerned to convince people of its respectability, and associations with unorthodox religious views could pose a serious threat to its reputation.[18] Although Raynor Parkes was happy to read and 'enjoy' *The Reasoner* and even to ask that it publish some translations of hers, she was careful to ensure that her name was never printed in its pages, reminding Holyoake to 'carefully suppress' all mention of her.[19] As Raynor Parkes' religious views became increasingly orthodox and inclined towards Catholicism, she began to refuse to publish anti-clerical articles by Bodichon's husband in the *EWJ*. Elizabeth Garrett, one of the first British women to qualify as a medical doctor, felt that the *EWJ*'s connections with unorthodox religious thought were enough to brand it 'almost atheistic'.[20]

Garrett also kept her distance from the Female Medical Society (FMS), which was established in 1862 with the aim of training women in midwifery and in the treatment of diseases of women and children. The Society was supported by George Jacob Holyoake and *The National Reformer* and later employed the neo-Malthusian Charles Drysdale as a teacher. The Freethinking feminists Florence Fenwick Miller and Alice Vickery also trained there. Its atheistical and Malthusian associations, however, meant that the FMS occupied a marginal position in the campaign to allow women to enter the medical profession.[21] The FMS was superseded by the London School of Medicine for Women, founded by Sophia Jex-Blake in 1874. Alice Vickery enrolled at the LSMW in 1877 to complete her medical training, but the following year Jex Blake attempted to expel her and fellow students Katherine Mitchell and Julia Swaagman. Swaagman and Mitchell were, like Vickery, freethinking members of the Malthusian League and Swaagman had joined Vickery on Bradlaugh and Besant's defence committee during the Knowlton Trial. In the end, they were permitted to remain as students but only on condition that they remove their names from the Council of the League.[22]

The atheistic views of Elizabeth Wolstenholme Elmy were also a source of embarrassment, and her recent biographer believes that Wolstenholme Elmy's absence from the feminist historiography has been a direct result of the 'abhorrence' that many in the women's movement felt for her Secularist beliefs. When Elizabeth's partner Ben Elmy began to join her in campaign work, he was met with a notable degree of suspicion and even outright hostility due to his Secularism.[23] One supporter of the campaign to repeal the CD Acts, Henry Wilson, wrote that the Wolstenholme Elmys were part of a general trend of 'lawlessness and disrespect for recognised authority ... not in accordance with God's word.'[24] Elizabeth Wolstenholme Elmy's associations with Freethought were as much of a factor as her free union with Ben Elmy in leading to her period of ostracism.[25] Secularists were well aware of their precarious position in the movement and in 1874 Annie Besant reported on anti-Secularist feeling at a meeting to support the removal of women's electoral disabilities. 'Nothing', she warned, 'would be more suicidal than the policy of shutting out the Secularists from the movement, and of thus strengthening the feeling which already makes some true Radicals shrink from giving the suffrage to women, lest they should thereby bring back the reign of ignorance and superstition.'[26] In spite of an overall shared approach to women's rights, there were occasions when Freethinking feminists like Besant found themselves struggling to unite divergent elements among the Secularists and the women's movement.

The campaign to repeal the Contagious Diseases Acts

The campaign to repeal the Contagious Diseases Acts was one of the defining causes of the nineteenth-century women's movement. It combined a liberal commitment to personal liberty with middle-class philanthropic concern for the 'fallen sisterhood' and a feminist critique of the sexual double standard.[27] The Ladies' National Association to Repeal the CD Acts (LNA) (est. 1869) was headed by Josephine Butler, whose inspirational leadership soon came to dominate the entire movement. Butler's main motivation for leaving her work in women's education to take up arms against the CD Acts was her intense religious faith and commitment to Evangelical Anglicanism.[28] Under her leadership the repeal movement assumed a Christianised identity which influenced how it was perceived by both contemporaries and historians.[29] Edward Royle suggested that as a result of the repealers' associations with Christian piety Freethinkers kept their distance from the campaign, even when they basically agreed with its demands. According to Royle, 'The Contagious Diseases Acts proved extremely difficult, and many a freethinker must have brought out the felicific calculus of his utilitarian ethical system.'[30] Royle therefore implied that the moral fervour of the LNA and its supporters was at odds with and alien to the rational scientific approach of the Freethought movement.

While Royle was right that some Freethinkers were uncomfortable with the overtly Christian tone of the campaign, he did not account for the fact that many Secularists *were* actively involved in it.[31] Before an organised campaign had been formed, it was the freethinking Harriet Martineau who had published a series of four letters against the regulation of prostitution in 1863 in the *Daily News*.[32] It was not until 1869 that the public agitation against the CD Acts was launched at the Social Science Congress, where the freethinking Francis Newman supported Charles Bell Taylor's paper against the Acts and also expressed his disappointment that women had not been admitted to the meeting so that they might voice their concern at 'the iniquity proposed to be perpetrated upon their sisters'.[33] Elizabeth Wolstenholme Elmy had been present at the Congress and played a crucial part in the formation of the women's repeal campaign. Josephine Butler, who went on to lead the LNA at Wolstenholme Elmy's request, had been in Europe at the time of the Congress. Wolstenholme Elmy, however, was able to fill her in on the legal situation and make the arguments in favour of the pressing need for a campaign, for despite the fact that Butler and Wolstenholme Elmy were from 'theologically opposing poles' they were nevertheless able to unite in their quest for justice for women.[34]

The repeal campaign was therefore of immediate interest to the Secularist movement, who began straight away to debate the implications of the Acts. Soon after the launch of the public agitation against the Acts at the Social Science Congress in Bristol, *The National Reformer* declared its pages open to discussion of this most sensitive yet pressing question. The Secularist principle of freedom of discussion and free dissemination of knowledge committed the movement to providing a platform for an otherwise controversial and potentially unrespectable feminist campaign.[35] The editorial note attached to an article on 'The Contagious Diseases Acts by a Social Reformer' acknowledged that the decision to speak about the Acts would be deemed by some to contravene social customs but that the Secularist commitment to Truth compelled *The National Reformer* to disregard such conventions. 'We feel that the insertion of this article may draw down upon us a torrent of indignant vituperation,' it claimed, 'but we insert it because at present no other journal dare...'[36] The 'Social Reformer', who in a later article revealed herself to be a woman, put forward a series of feminist arguments against the Acts which became common in the repeal campaign. She condemned the notion that prostitution was a 'public necessity'; lamented the plight of the 'women, poor and friendless, who loathe the very trade they ply'; maintained that poverty rather than vice drove women into prostitution; and expressed outrage at the current law's persecution of the 'weakest sex' rather than their 'seducers'. The only part of her article that was not in conformity with the later mainstream movement was the suggestion that prostitution was exacerbated by restraints placed on early marriages – an argument usually made in favour of birth control.[37]

The 'Social Reformer' soon received a reply from another Freethinker, who signed himself T. S. B., and who was also 'very glad that you have opened the columns of your paper to discussion on this most important subject.' T. S. B employed the ideas of political economy and utilitarianism – both important elements of the Freethought ideological inheritance – to argue in favour of the CD Acts. He maintained that it was impossible to raise the wages of working women, as the 'Social Reformer' had suggested, without interfering with Free Trade. 'We must take things as they are,' he advised, 'not as they ought to be. Prostitution exists and must be treated accordingly ... then we must consider how to mitigate some of the great evils attending it.'[38] The 'Social Reformer' sent an immediate and strongly worded reply, which maintained that support for repeal was the only true feminist and Secularist position on the subject:

> I am not greatly surprised that your correspondent takes the view he does, for it is a painful fact that the great majority of the male population are looking forward to the measure as one offering 'advantages' and 'security', and no doubt this is through the "masculine view" of the question.[39]

And yet, '*as a real Secularist*, and one desirous of being worthy of that name, I strongly object to dealing with matters so vastly important in such a compromising manner...'[40] In her view, the Secularist position demanded a clear moral response to the CD Acts that left no room for the 'felicific calculus' of a utilitarian moral system.

Other Freethinking feminists went on to utilise traditional Freethought arguments in favour of repeal. Annie Besant was also aware that some Secularists supported the CD Acts on utilitarian grounds. In *The Legalisation of Female Slavery in England* (1876) she rebuked these sections of the movement, asserting that 'the Secular party, as whole, has a duty with regard to this subject which it has somewhat failed to discharge.' The Secular party naturally supported 'the promotion of national morality, of national health, and ... the inalienable rights of the individual liberty of women as well as men'; it must, therefore, support the repeal of the Acts.[41] Elizabeth Wolstenholme Elmy distributed a pamphlet that demonstrated that the CD Acts were in no way compatible with 'Necessarian Philosophy'. The pamphlet's author, who called herself 'A Necessarian', addressed 'both friends and foes', who insisted that 'the Contagious Diseases Acts are the natural fruit of the creed I profess'. She countered their arguments, not by condemning a utilitarian approach to morality as such, but by maintaining that the 'necessity' of male sexual satisfaction was no such thing, and that 'chastity is not opposed to health'. She challenged the utilitarian supporters of the Acts in their own terms. 'Do you suppose that instinct, irresistibly impelling to vice, on which you rest your case, to be common to both sexes, or peculiar to your own? If you take the former view of it, then to be logical you must grant to all women the licence you claim for yourselves.'[42]

Some Freethinkers also became actively involved in organising and campaign work. William Shaen, a public supporter of Secularism who had given legal advice to both Bishop Colenso and the Rev. Charles Vosey when the Church had threatened to expel them for their freethinking beliefs, was chairman of the National Association to Repeal the Contagious Diseases Acts from 1870 to 1886.[43] In 1875 Ben Elmy, Elizabeth Wolstenholme Elmy's husband and Vice-President of the National Secular Society, was recommended by the freethinking Emilie Venturie to succeed her as editor of the repeal campaign's journal *The Shield*.[44] London's radical and Secular clubs also opened their doors to the repealers, who made the rounds lecturing on the evils of the Acts.[45] But of course the campaign was also made up of 'those with whom religion takes the lead, and with whom virtue and the laws of God are the paramount interests.'[46] The male leadership of the anti-CD Acts campaign generally consisted of wealthy industrialists and merchants from the industrial north from Non-conformist and Quaker churches.[47] In the Ladies Association, of the twenty-two women whose religious background is known, twelve were Quakers, four belonged to Non-conformists sects, four were agnostics or atheists, and two were Anglicans.[48] Tensions arose between London-based Freethinkers and Unitarians involved in the campaign, and evangelical bases of support in the north. Many Christians were not always happy to have a movement already tinged with unrespectability tarnished further by associations with infidelism. In spite of significant Freethought involvement in the campaign's organisation, there were times when their rejection of Christianity excluded Freethinkers from its activities. Josephine Butler maintained in her memoirs that 'We never asked of our adherents what their religious views or non-views were', yet Ursula Bright and Emilie Venturie were denied access to a 'joint conference of Christian bodies' organised by Butler to discuss opposition to the Acts.[49]

Besant, despite her support for the repeal campaign, complained about the proliferation of 'Christian cant upon this subject.'[50] Prostitution had been enshrined as the 'great social evil' during the evangelical revival of the 1850s, and the repeal campaign continued to frame the issues in terms of Christian morality.[51] Freethinkers found themselves campaigning alongside the like of Francis Close, Bishop of Carlisle, who had been the scourge of Owenites and Chartists in the 1830s and 1840s in Cheltenham, and had played a central role in the prosecution for blasphemy of George Jacob Holyoake. Yet some Secularists were happy to contribute to the repealers' moralistic critiques of sensual gratification and the libertine cynicism of those who supported the Acts.[52] Francis Newman, for example, in a letter to Sophia Dobson Collet, inveighed against the 'Medico-Military schemes of glorifying military impurity as Medical Wisdom ...'[53] Annie Besant willingly appropriated the language of the evangelical Christian mission, referring to the 'noble hearted missionary Mrs Josephine Butler' and 'her crusade through Europe'.[54] In her series of articles on *Female Slavery*, Besant lapsed into sentimental eulogies to the 'domestic ideal' that elsewhere she criticised, proclaiming 'our reverence for the home ... which forms the healthy and pure nursery for the next generation of citizens'. She sentimentalised the 'fallen women' as 'poor ruined creatures'; 'Each one might have been the centre of a happy home, the mother of brave men and women who would have served the Fatherland, and we have made them *this*.'[55] Similarly, in a paper given at an international convention for the 'Abolition of State Vice', William Shaen declared that 'The unwritten Common Law of England embodies the sound principle that everything that is an offence against public morality is unlawful.'[56]

The similarities between Freethought repeal rhetoric and that of their Christian colleagues show that it is impossible to attempt to characterise the Secularists' response to the CD Acts as one of utilitarian and libertarian distaste for the repealers. In fact, Freethinkers in the campaign combined an 'evangelical' morality with a radical libertarian political agenda. Annie Besant moved seamlessly from political appeals to 'Liberty' to moralistic protests against the ruination of fallen innocents. Unlike Christian repeal campaigners, however, she also called for 'more reasonable marriage laws', by which she meant greater freedom of divorce and the availability of birth control to encourage early marriage.[57] Similarly, *The National Reformer*'s correspondents of 1869 (the 'Social Reformer' and the 'Necessarian'), in making their distinctively Secularist attacks on the CD Acts, also began to raise questions of female sexuality, sex outside marriage and other means of making 'early marriage' possible (i.e. birth control). The greater degree of individual and sexual freedom that some in the Secularist movement were prepared to countenance had important implications for their approach to the repeal movement and subsequent 'social purity' campaigns.

Social purity was the umbrella term for a broad set of campaigns against prostitution and 'vice' that emerged from the CD repeal movement in the 1880s. Social purity activists engaged in rescue work, agitated to increase the age of consent, and in some cases, campaigned for the closure of brothels and prosecution of brothel owners. The social purity organisation the National Vigilance Association (NVA) supported the Criminal Law Amendment Act (1885), which allowed for the forcible closure of all brothels and the prosecution of anyone renting accommodation to a suspected prostitute. Others who had been involved in the repeal campaign, however, opposed these clauses of the Act and were repelled by what they saw as the repressive and authoritarian direction taken by some social purity organisations. The Vigilance Association for the Defence of Personal Rights (PRA)[58], which had also grown out of the repeal campaign, strongly opposed these passages of the Criminal Law Amendment Act, claiming that it restricted the freedom of prostitutes in a similar manner to the CD Acts. Secularists played a prominent part in this organisation. George Jacob Holyoake addressed the PRA in 1877, while Elizabeth Wolstenholme Elmy was employed as its secretary. In an article for its journal in 1886 she pointed out that the closure of brothels had made many prostitutes homeless, making them liable to be arrested as vagrants, which could lead to a period of imprisonment far longer than that implemented under the CD Acts. Moreover, once in prison, these women would be subject to the same 'internal examinations' that the supporters of social purity had spent sixteen years campaigning against.[59]

Not all Secularist repealers opposed social purity. William Shaen became a founding member of both the Social Purity Alliance and the Moral Reform Union (MRU). Sophia Dobson Collet and Sara Hennell both strongly supported W. T. Stead (founder of the NVA) in his sensationalist journalistic crusade against the 'white slave trade', which contributed to the passing of the Criminal Law Amendment Act in 1885. Collet financially supported Stead's family while he served a term in prison for the procurement of prostitutes as a result of his undercover work.[60] Annie Besant and Charles Bradlaugh had initially been critical of Stead's sensationalist and illegal tactics, though Besant subsequently formed a strong friendship with him – sharing his crusading zeal when it came to questions of Socialist and labour agitation – whilst Stead, in 1877, had publicly supported Besant during the Knowlton Trial.[61] It is not, therefore, possible to draw a clear line between the broadly termed 'social purity' movement and those who maintained a consistent commitment to the defence of personal liberty. Josephine Butler, for example, was a member of the Moral Reform Union and a strong supporter of the PRA, as was the freethinking Francis Newman. The Moral Reform Union combined its commitment to purifying the public world with a belief that this required improved knowledge on questions of 'moral reform', and for this reason it also published Elizabeth Wolstenholme Elmy and Ben Elmy's works on sex education.[62]

Yet both religious and political perspectives played a role in shaping the dispute over the Criminal Law Amendment Act of 1885. Those who campaigned for the outlawing and closure of brothels were not simply prudes or conservatives, but also engaged in articulating a radical feminist rejection of male centred sexual norms.[63] At the same time, however, the strong Christian faith of the majority of social purity campaigners fundamentally shaped their vision of a purified public and private world.[64] This vision of purity, combined with their experience of middle-class philanthropic missions to the urban poor, led these activists to support repressive measures and to justify the surveillance and forced 'rehabilitation' of prostitutes. Those Freethinkers who identified more closely with the social purity movement – Newman, Collet and Hennell – were also those at the more religious end of the Freethought spectrum, while the strongest opposition to the repressive elements of the Criminal Law Amendment Act came from atheists in the Secularist movement.

In the 1890s many of the Freethinkers clustered around the PRA were also involved in the Legitimation League (est. 1893), which campaigned for the legal protection of children born outside marriage and, subsequently, for the right to form 'Free Love' relationship untrammelled by institutional regulation.[65] The Legitimation League's journal, *The Adult*, opposed both state regulation and state prohibition of prostitution, and continued to provide space for Freethinking feminists to argue that the Church, Christian marriage and male domination (rather than prostitutes themselves) were to blame for dividing women 'into two sets, trained to detest each other'.[66] The editor of *The Adult* also condemned the National Vigilance Association's campaign to close down brothels and theatres in the West End which only forced women to work on the streets in even more vulnerable conditions.[67] G. W. Foote, President of the National Secular Society, also criticised this campaign for ignoring the economic causes of prostitution, while the Freethinking editor of *The Present Day*, Thomas Barrett, attacked those 'sickly bodies, the "Social Purity", the "Gospel Purity", the Moral Reform Union, the White Cross Society' supported by 'religious persons of the Salvation Army type'.[68] Thus, the Secularist rejection of the moral authority of Christianity, the commitment to a radical liberal tradition and the emphasis on the moral autonomy of the individual could at times point away from the more repressive interpretations of social purity.[69]

Secularism and the suffrage

The demand for female enfranchisement was raised in freethinking circles long in advance of the emergence of a national campaign in the 1860s. The Owenites had supported women's right to vote, and some radical Unitarians supported women's suffrage in the 1830s and 1840s and pushed for it to be adopted as part of the Chartists' list of demands.[70] Older Freethinkers such as Sophia Dobson Collet and Sara Hennell would, therefore, have already been familiar with the arguments when they began to be advanced with renewed vigour in the 1860s. The nation-wide campaign for women's suffrage began as part of wider agitation for franchise reform around the first Reform Bill of 1866, when John Stuart Mill attempted to attach an amendment to remove any distinction on grounds of sex.[71] The leading Secularist journal of this time, *The National Reformer*, also identified female suffrage as an important aspect of its general support for franchise reform and lent its editorial support to the committees set up to petition in favour of the amendment. Elizabeth Wolstenholme Elmy was among the first signatories of the London committee, of which Caroline Stansfeld (another of the Ashurst sisters) was also a member. Wolstenholme Elmy also set up the Manchester committee and, as its first secretary, almost single-handedly collected over 300 of the 1,499 signatures on the petition that Mill presented to the House of Commons on 7 June 1866.[72] Two weeks later, in the midst of the wider reform agitation, *The National Reformer* devoted its front-page article to argue for the inclusion of women's suffrage in the Bill. Its author expressed wholehearted support for Mill's amendment and the petition presented by the women's suffrage committees, and inveighed more generally against 'the aristocracy of sex'.[73] In 1867 the various local committees came together to form the National Society for Women's Suffrage, and in 1870 it began to publish its own *Women's Suffrage Journal*, the first edition of which listed the Secularist lecturer Louisa Wade and a 'Mrs Bradlaugh' as members of the London society.[74] Over the next two decades the Secularist press regularly published reports of the suffrage societies' committee meetings and public lectures.[75]

When the first petitions for female suffrage began to be circulated, the question was already being avidly discussed in numerous Secular societies and radical clubs around the country, reports of which were then published in the national Secularist press. On the whole, the appointed lecturer tended to be in favour of full political rights for women. Christopher Charles, for example, argued at the Birmingham Secular Club and Institute in 1870 that there was absolutely no reason for 'denying the largest half of the human race their "rights"', while Mr Conway of Cleveland Hall, London maintained that, given the chance, there was no reason why women should not show themselves to be perfectly capable politicians.[76] However, opposition to women's suffrage did exist among rank and file members, and reports of meetings record members of the audience arguing that women's place was in the 'domestic circle' and that her involvement in politics would lead to the neglect of her family duties.[77] There were also occasions on which distinctively Freethinking arguments were employed to oppose political rights for women, with Secularists always returning to the thorny question of 'woman and her religion'. Mr G. Bill, for example, argued against Christopher Charles at the Birmingham Secular Society, claiming that to grant women the vote would be to severely damage the Secularist project. 'He referred to some of the weaknesses of women, especially as they had always been the tools of priesthood, and completely in their power, and had wrought much mischief to mankind as a result.'[78] The leading Secularist W. S. Ross railed against the oppression of the female sex by Christianity, and yet he also opposed the enfranchisement of women on the grounds that they were too susceptible to the influence of the clergy and that their votes would be used to elect Christian candidates.[79]

Most Victorian Freethinkers, however, were in agreement with the National Society for Women's Suffrage in utilising a language of equal rights that harked back to the Enlightenment. In 1870 *The National Reformer* journalist H. V. Mayer began his article on 'Woman Suffrage' with the assertion that 'As a lover of liberty I would have woman free as well as men … Freedom is everyone's birthright, no matter what the condition or sex.' Mayer also referred to the 'long axiom' of 'English liberals' that there should be no taxation without representation.[80] Annie Besant's pamphlet on marriage reform also invoked natural rights in support of female suffrage: '[T]he rights of man have become an accepted doctrine, but unfortunately, they are only the rights of *man*, in the exclusive sense of the word. They are sexual and not human rights … Women, as well as men "are born free and equal in rights"' and had as much claim to the franchise.[81]

However, Freethinkers also discussed the question of women's suffrage in the context of a more general extension of the franchise as heralded by the 1866 and 1867 Reform Bills. The National Secular Society was allied to the Reform League, which lent its tentative support to William Gladstone's 1866 Bill proposing a limited extension of the suffrage. Most Secularists, however, even those who thought it wise to support the Bill, advocated a far wider suffrage and rejected the idea of a property test.[82] The more radical Secularists went even further and, like Harriet Law, 'rather rejoiced' at the defeat of the 1866 Bill in the hope that a subsequent general election would enable the people to rally and force through a more extensive measure of reform. In a speech just before the final reading of the 1866 Bill, Harriet Law advocated votes for women in the context of her broader commitment to full universal suffrage.[83] Law was subsequently a key figure in the events in Hyde Park in July 1866, when large numbers of police attacked the pro-democracy demonstrators who were trying to get into the park. As crowds began to gather outside Hyde Park, Law 'was called upon to address those assembled' before a rush was made by her supporters to force their way through the gates. Mrs Law somehow 'overcame one of the stern policemen guarding a smaller gate, and gained admittance to the park'. There she 'was obliged to keep continually talking, being carried in triumph from place to place ... delivering ... a very fervid address on the political and social rights of the people'.[84]

Harriet Law's adventures were reported in *The Times*, and must have horrified the more conservative members of the recently formed London committee for women's suffrage, who wished to keep the campaign for the female franchise separate from the agitation surrounding the Reform Bill. Emily Davies had from the start been wary of attempting to organise mass support, preferring to use personal influence to lobby individual MPs. Davies expressed great concern regarding the 'radical proclivities' of some of those on the London committee, and after the Hyde Park riots she wrote to Barbara Bodichon in a panic, insisting that 'It will clearly not do to identify ourselves too closely with Mill'. As a result of the differing political outlook of its members, the London Committee re-formed in 1867, its more conservative supporters withdrawing, allowing the radicals to take the lead.[85]

The question of *how* to pose the demand for women's suffrage became a longstanding source of disagreement and division in the movement. Not only did leading figures such as Emily Davies, Frances Power

HYDE PARK RAILINGS THROWN DOWN IN 1866.

Figure 3 Hyde Park railings thrown down during 1866 Reform Bill Agitation. Harriet Law participated in this demonstration, addressing protestors on the need for universal suffrage and votes for women.

Cobbe, Millicent Garrett Fawcett and Lydia Becker fail to challenge the property qualification – thus excluding many working-class women from their campaign – they also wanted to limit themselves initially to asking for the vote for single women.[86] By contrast, most Freethinking feminists remained true to the tradition of Harriet Law in calling for female enfranchisement on the same grounds as men and wedding it to a broader struggle for democracy. The Women's Franchise League (est. 1889) and the Women's Emancipation Union (est. 1891), both founded by Wolstenholme Elmy and attracting a strongly Secularist membership, campaigned for the vote for married as well as single women and pursued new sources of support among the emerging Socialist and labour movements.[87]

Such organisations cohered and made visible a current of 'democratic suffragists' or 'radical suffragists', which continued as an important political force in the twentieth-century suffrage campaigns. Some historians have argued that the distinction between democratic suffragists, and those who preferred to separate 'votes for women' from broader political demands, provides a more meaningful frame of analysis than that of constitutionalist vs. militant.[88] Much of the initial political direction of the Women's Social and Political Union (est. 1903) derived from these earlier radical suffragist organisations.[89] The WSPU was not initially founded as a 'militant' alternative to the National Union of Women's Suffrage Societies (est. 1897), but emerged in response to the feeling that alliance with progressive and labour movement forces might prove more politically effective than non-partisan lobbying. As the NUWSS and the WSPU developed over the next ten years, Freethinking feminists and other democratic suffragists might be found in one or the other. Alice Vickery, for example, had been a subscriber of the NUWSS in the 1890s and then the WSPU before splitting off to form the Women's Freedom League along with Bessie Drysdale in 1907 in protest at the increasingly undemocratic leadership of the Pankhursts.[90] Hypatia Bradlaugh Bonner, on the other hand, abhorred the militant tactics of the WSPU and pursued most of her suffrage campaign work through the National Women's Liberal Association. Yet she too believed that women should not separate their support for the vote from their wider political views and support for democracy and adult suffrage.[91]

Conclusion

Freethought needs to be written back into the history of organised feminism. The first organisational initiatives that went into forming a women's rights movement emerged from Freethinking circles, and the subsequent efforts that many Freethinking feminists put into the day-to-day work of women's rights campaigning should be duly acknowledged. Attempts by their contemporaries to marginalise them from histories of the movement need therefore to be redressed in future historiography. It should also be noted that Secularists active in the women's movement were motivated as much by their Freethinking beliefs as they were by a commitment to women's rights, or rather that these two intellectual currents were intertwined. Freethought principles such as the importance of the moral autonomy of the individual, the eradication of ignorance as the key to social improvement and the commitment to free discussion no matter how controversial the subject, all played a crucial role in the development of feminist thought. The women's movement was undoubtedly a predominantly Christian one, as the hostility that Secularists sometimes faced clearly signified. Nevertheless, in spite of the respectable and pious image that its leaders sought to promote, the women's movement was never far away from a more dangerous world of radicalism and irreligion. As a result, a radical current (represented by Harriet Law in Hyde Park or Elizabeth Wolstenholme Elmy in her insistence on votes for married women) persisted and had an important impact upon twentieth-century suffrage politics.

A focus on Freethinkers in the women's movement also provides a richer account of the 'reforming' spirit of this period. The Secularist support for the CD Acts repeal campaign demonstrates that the militant moralism normally associated with evangelical Christianity was not limited to religious contexts, and that it was often combined with a supposedly 'secular' language of personal rights. At the same time, tensions could flare up between 'purity' and 'liberty', and feminism and libertarianism. Religious differences were certainly a factor in the debates over social purity and the Criminal Law Amendment Act. While the commitment to individual freedom enabled some Secularists to see the flaws inherent within repressive 'purity' legislation, at other times this could lead away from support for women's rights. The editor of *The Present Day*, after condemning the religious aspect of the social purity movement and the failure of Christian morality to engage with the real, economic causes of prostitution, also criticised the Personal Rights Association for supporting the Married Women's Maintenance Act in Case of Desertion (1886). This, he claimed, wrongly allowed the state to interfere in sexual relations, and a commitment to the freedom of the individual ought to take precedence over any concern for the plight of women left destitute when deserted by their husbands.[92] This Freethinker was also a strong supporter of 'Free Love', based on the premise that only men and women themselves could decide with whom to form a union and for how long this should last. He was not, however, particularly concerned with the systemic inequalities which made this a far more attractive prospect for men than for women.[93] Thus, the contradictions and conflicts between feminism and Freethought that existed in the campaigns to repeal the CD Acts become even more apparent in an examination of attitudes to sexual morality – the subject of the next chapter.

Notes

1 Elizabeth Wolstoneholme Elmy's Secularism has only recently been studied; see M. Wright, 'Elizabeth Wolstenholme Elmy: A Biography' (unpublished doctoral thesis, University of Portsmouth, 2007); M. Wright, *Elizabeth Wolstenholme Elmy and the Victorian Feminist Movement: The Biography of An Insurgent Woman* (Manchester: Manchester University Press, 2011). Her anti-religious views were first noted as significant by S. S. Holton, 'Free Love and Victorian Feminism: The Divers Matrimonials of Elizabeth Wolstenholme and Ben Elmy', *Victorian Studies* 37:2 (Winter 1994), 199–222, 203–5. Banks noted the influence of Barbara Bodichon and Harriet Martineau's Unitarian upbringings on their subsequent support for women's rights but makes no mention of the Freethinking views they adopted in adulthood; O. Banks, *Faces of Feminism. A Study of Feminism as a Social Movement* (Oxford: Basil Blackwell, 1993) (first published 1981), p. 30. Frances Power Cobbe has been misrepresented as a 'Unitarian'; see R. Watts, 'Rational Religion and Feminism: the Challenge of Unitarianism in the Nineteenth Century', in S. Morgan (ed.), *Women, Religion and Feminism, 1750–1900* (Basingstoke: Palgrave Macmillan, 2002), pp. 39–52, 46. In fact, Cobbe attended only one Unitarian service of which she was highly critical; see F. Power Cobbe, *The Life of Frances Power Cobbe as Told by Herself. With Additions by the Author and Introduction by Blanche Atkinson* (London: Swan Sonnenshein & Co., 1904), pp. 104–5.

2 R. Strachey, *The Cause. A Short History of the Women's Movement in Great Britain* (London: G. Bell & Sons Ltd, 1928), pp. 12–3, 30–2, 44. These three ideological currents were also identified in J. Rendall, *The Origins of Modern Feminism. Women in Britain, France and the United States, 1780–1860* (Basingstoke: Macmillan Education, 1985); Banks (1993).

3 S. S. Holton, *Feminism and Democracy. Women's Suffrage and Reform Politics in Britain 1900–1918* (Cambridge: Cambridge University Press, 1986), pp. 9–14, 17; Gleadle also stressed how 'different feminisms blurred and overlapped'; K. Gleadle, '"Our Several Spheres": Middle-Class Women and the Feminisms of Early Victorian Radical Politics', in K. Gleadle & S. Richardson (eds.), *Women in British Politics 1760–1860. The Power of the Petticoat* (Basingstoke: Macmillan Press, 2000), pp. 134–52, 139–40.

4 For Enlightened influences see E. Royle, *Radicals, Secularists and Republicans. Popular Freethought in Britain, 1866–1915* (Manchester: Manchester University Press, 1980), pp. 193–206. For 'evangelical' moralism see *The National Reformer* (NR), 13 May 1866, pp. 290–1.

5   B. Caine, *English Feminism 1780-1980* (Oxford: Oxford University Press, 1997), p. 88. See also J. Rendall, '"A Moral Engine"? Feminism, Liberalism and the English Woman's Journal', in J. Rendall (ed.), *Equal or Different: Women's Politics 1800-1914* (Oxford: Basil Blackwell, 1987), pp. 112-38.

6   *The Reasoner (Reasoner)* 3:63, pp. 429-37. [N.B. Copies of *The Reasoner* held in the Bishopsgate Library for 1847-48 are not individually dated, only volume and number are listed.]

7   Goodwyn Barmby to George Jacob Holyoake, 1840s[?], Manchester, Co-operative Union Archive (CUA), Holyoake Correspondence (HC), 339.

8   Bessie Raynor Parkes to Austin Holyoake and George Jacob Holyoake, 15 December 1857, CUA, HC 971.

9   K. McCormack, 'Bessie Parkes' *Summer Sketches*: George Eliot as Poetic Persona', *Victorian Poetry* 42:3 (2004), 295-311, 295.

10 Parkes wrote to Holyoake thanking him for copies of *The Reasoner* which she had 'enjoyed'. See Bessie Raynor Parkes to George Jacob Holyoake, 30 January 1857, CUA, HC 888.

11 L. Merrill, 'Mathilda Hays (1820-1897?)', *Oxford Dictionary of National Biography* (online edn.; Oxford University Press, 2004).

12 Sophia Dobson Collet to Eleanor Holyoake, 15 April 1847, CUA, HC 199; J. McCabe, *Life and Letters of George Jacob Holyoake* (London[?]: Watts, 1908), p. 119.

13 For example, see the advertisement of the *EWJ*'s women's employment registry in *Reasoner*, 8 April 1860, p. 58.

14 S. S. Holton, *Suffrage Days. Stories from the Women's Suffrage Movement* (London & New York: Routledge, 1996), pp. 16-17.

15 *NR*, 1 April 1866, p. 204. Law was still delivering this lecture in 1869; see *NR*, 12 December 1869, p. 382.

16 *NR*, 24 October 1869, p. 268, 11 December 1870, p. 396.

17 *NR*, 16 May 1869, p. 316. Female employment was the 'key issue' of the *EWJ* and it argued that women should have entry to the middle-class occupations of commerce and trade, though by mid-1862 Parkes was beginning to retreat from her former position and claim that she never wished for women to act as the main bread-winner; see Rendall (1987), pp. 120-4.

18 Caine (1997), p. 97.

19 Bessie Raynor Parkes to George Jacob Holyoake, 30 January 1857, CUA, HC 888.

20 Rendall (1987), p. 135.

21 See James Edmunds to George Jacob Holyoake, 22 July 1869, CUA, HC 1876; *NR*, 3 July 1870, p. 7. Millicent Garret Fawcett was critical of the LMA because it did not have a charter and could not therefore confer degrees upon its female students. She and Elizabeth Garrett maintained that women should instead campaign to receive a medical education on an equal basis with men in the existing medical schools. However, their opposition was also coloured by their desire not to be associated with the Malthusian practices (birth control) advocated by many of its Freethinking supporters; M. Benn, *The Predicaments of Love* (London: Pluto Press, 1992) pp. 123, 131.

22 Benn (1992), pp. 141-3.

23 Wright (2007), pp. 3, 6, 111. Elmy appeared alongside Wolstenholme Elmy on public platforms, speaking against the CD Acts in the early 1870s; Wright (2007), pp. 94-5.

24 *Ibid.*, p. 112.

25 *Ibid.*, pp. 112–114.

26 *NR*, 20 December 1874, pp. 389–90.

27 For the most comprehensive account of this movement, see J. Walkowitz, *Prostitution and Victorian Society. Women, Class and the State* (Cambridge: Cambridge University Press, 1980).

28 Helen Mathers has argued that Butler should be understood as a liberal evangelical; H. Mathers, 'The Evangelical Spirituality of a Victorian Feminist: Josephine Butler, 1828–1906', *Journal of Ecclesiastical History* 52:2 (April 2001), 282–312.

29 Anne Summers has argued that the repeal campaign was made possible by a distinctive form of Protestantism that was able to incorporate liberal support for civil and individual rights in a manner that proved impossible to more conservative forms of Protestantism found elsewhere in Europe; A. Summers (2006); A. Summers, 'Introduction: the International Abolitionist Federation', *Women's History Review* 17:2 (April 2008), 149–52.

30 E. Royle (1980), p. 251.

31 *Ibid.*, pp. 251–2.

32 Walkowitz (1980), p. 77.

33 E. Pears (ed.), 'Contagious Diseases', in *Transactions of the National Association for the Promotion of Social Science. Bristol Meeting 1869* (London: Longmans, Green, Reader & Dyer, 1870), pp. 428–51, 450.

34 Wright (2007), p. 88, 68.

35 Despite the best efforts of the repealers to promote themselves as guardians of the nation's morals, they were condemned for introducing a 'filthy subject' into public debate and on occasion their meetings were attacked; see H. Rogers, 'Any Questions? The Gendered Dimensions of the Political Platform', *Nineteenth-Century Prose* 29:1 (Spring 2002), 117–29, 126. Some feminist leaders, including Millicent Garrett Fawcett and Emily Davies, deliberately kept their distance from the campaign; O. Banks, *Becoming a Feminist: The Social Origins of 'First Wave' Feminism* (Brighton: Wheatsheaf, 1986), p. 64.

36 *NR*, 19 December 1869, p. 394.

37 *Ibid.*, pp. 394–5.

38 *Ibid.*, 9 January 1870, p. 26.

39 *Ibid.*, 30 January 1870, p. 76.

40 *Ibid.*, Emphasis added.

41 A. Besant, *The Legalisation of Female Slavery in England. Reprinted from* The National Reformer, *June 4th 1876* (London: Besant & Bradlaugh, 1885), p. 2.

42 A Necessarian, *The Contagious Diseases Acts and the Necessarian Philosophy* (Manchester: Ireland & Co., 1871), pp. 3, 5, 16.

43 M. J. Shaen (ed.), *William Shaen. A Brief Sketch. Edited by his Daughter M. J. Shaen* (London: Longmans, Green & Co., 1912), p. 53.

44 Wright (2007), p. 112.

45 Walkowitz (1980), p. 102.

46 *First Annual Report of the Ladies National Association for the Repeal of the Contagious Diseases Acts*, quoted in Walkowitz (1980), p. 94.

47 Walkowitz (1980), p. 101.

48 *Ibid.*, p. 122.
49 *Ibid.*, pp. 122–3.
50 Besant, *Female Slavery*, p. 2.
51 Walkowitz (1980), pp. 103, 131.
52 Walkowitz (1980), p. 102.
53 Francis Newman to Sophia Dobson Collet, 8 January 1892, WL, CCF.
54 Besant, *Female Slavery*, p. 1.
55 *Ibid.*, pp. 2–3, 4.
56 W. Shaen, 'What Are the Limits of Legitimate Legislation on the Subject of Prostitution? A Paper Read Before the Section of Legislation of the First International Congress of the British, Continental, and General Federation for the Abolition of the State Regulation of Prostitution, Held in Geneva, September 17–24, A.D., 1877', in M. J. Shaen (ed.), *William Shaen*, p. 79.
57 Besant, *Female Slavery*, p. 6.
58 This became known as the Personal Rights Association (PRA) to distinguish it from the National Vigilance Association.
59 *Journal of the Vigilance Association for the Defence of Personal Rights*, 15 March 1886, pp. 25–6.
60 Francis Newman to Sophia Dobson Collet, 15 December 1885; Sara Hennell to Sophia Dobson Collet, 30 September 1889; Sara Hennell to Sophia Dobson Collet, 17 January 1892, WL, CCF; L. Bland, '"Purifying" the Public World: Feminist Vigilantes in Late Victorian England', *Women's History Review* 1:3 (September 1992), 397–412, 400–1; K. Gleadle, 'Collet, Sophia Dobson (1822–1894), *Oxford Dictionary of National Biography* (online edn.; Oxford University Press, 2004).
61 A. Nethercot, *The First Five Lives of Annie Besant* (Rupert Hart-Davis, London, 1961), pp. 259–60; *NR*, 6 September 1885, p. 141.
62 'The founding "objects" of the MRU are 1. To study, and confer upon, all subjects which especially affect the moral welfare of the young. 2. To collect, sell, distribute, or publish Literature for Moral Education. 3. To consider how best to carry out practical measures for the reform of public opinion, law and custom, on questions of sexual morality', *The Moral Reform Union, Fifth Annual Report. From April 3rd 1886–April 27th 1887* (London: Moral Reform Union, 1887), p. 1.
63 S. Jeffreys, *The Spinster and Her Enemies. Feminism and Sexuality 1880–1930* (London: Pandora Press, 1985). See also M. Jackson, *The Real Facts of Life: Feminism and the Politics of Sexuality c. 1850–1940* (London: Taylor & Francis, 1994). Lucy Bland agreed that social purity feminists should not be dismissed as conservatives, but wished also to emphasise 'the contradictory aspects of social purity, in particular the racist assumptions and the contribution made by social purity to the policing of the working class'; see L. Bland, *Banishing the Beast. English Feminism and Sexual Morality, 1885–1914* (London: Penguin Books, 1995), p. xviii.
64 See Bland (1992) p. 397; S. Morgan, *A Passion for Purity: Ellice Hopkins and the Politics of Gender in the Late-Victorian Church* (Bristol: Centre for Comparative Studies in Religion and Gender, 1999).
65 A. Humpherys, 'The Journal that Did: Form and Content in The Adult (1897–1899)', *Media History* 9:1 (2003), 63–78, 63.
66 *The Adult*, March 1898, p. 30, September 1897, pp. 30–2.

67 *Ibid.*, March 1898, p. 30.

68 Royle (1980), pp. 251–2; *The Present Day*, October 1886, p. 33.

69 Briefly comparing the political views of Christian and Freethinking feminists, Banks noted that 'Freethinkers were much more interested in autonomy...'; Banks (1986), pp. 151–2.

70 B. Taylor, *Eve and the New Jerusalem. Socialism and Feminism in the Nineteenth Century* (London: Virago, 1983), pp. 180, 218–19, 270. Sophia Dobson Collet's brother, Collet Dobson Collet, and Richard Ashurst were members of William Lovett's National Chartist Association, which was open to women and strongly supported women's rights. It does not appear that either Sophia Dobson Collet or the Ashurst sisters were themselves members though Collet did play the piano at some of its functions; see Gleadle (2000), pp. 140–1. By 1867 Sophia Dobson Collet believed that women who did not exercise their municipal vote did not deserve it and ought not therefore to have the parliamentary vote, though she supported the principle of the latter; Francis Newman to Sophia Dobson Collet, 1 April 1867, London, Women's Library (WL), Papers of Clara Collet and Family (CCF), 7CCF [uncatalogued].

71 J. Rendall, 'The Citizenship of Women and the Reform Act of 1867', in C. Hall, K. McClelland & J. Rendall, *Defining the Victorian Nation: Class, Race, Gender and the British Reform Act* (Cambridge: Cambridge University Press, 2000), pp. 119–78, 119.

72 Holton (1996), p. 21.

73 *NR*, 24 June 1866, pp. 393–4.

74 *Women's Suffrage Journal*, 1 March 1870, p. 8.

75 See, for example, *Secular Chronicle (SC)* 2 January 1876, p. 5; *NR*, 25 December 1870, p. 410.

76 *NR*, 12 June 1870, p. 381, 25 February 1866, p. 124.

77 See for example, *NR*, 25 February 1866, p. 124, 18 September 1870, p. 190.

78 *NR*, 12 June 1870, p. 381.

79 Royle (1980), p. 249.

80 *NR*, 4 December 1870, pp. 354–5.

81 A. Besant, *Marriage; As It Was, As It Is and As It Should Be* (New York, A.K. Butts, 1879), p. 4.

82 *NR*, 29 April 1866, pp. 257–8.

83 *NR*, 6 May 1866, p. 285. Law's husband Edward Law opposed her from the audience and argued against universal suffrage on the grounds that the great mass of people were not yet fit to understand their political duties and properly exercise the suffrage.

84 *NR*, 29 July 1866, p. 72.

85 Holton (1996), p. 23.

86 Holton (1994), p. 202, 207; H. L. Smith, *The British Women's Suffrage Campaign 1866–1928* (Harlow: Pearson Education Ltd, 2010), pp. 12–13.

87 S. S. Holton, 'Now You See It, Now You Don't: The Women's Franchise League and its Place in Contending Narratives of the Women's Suffrage Movement', in J. Purvis & M. Joannou (eds.), *The Women's Suffrage Movement: New Feminist Perspectives* (Manchester: Manchester University Press, 1998), pp. 15–36; M. Wright, 'The Women's Emancipation Union and Radical-Feminist Politics in Britain, 1891–99', *Gender and History* 22:2 (August 2010), pp. 382–406.

88 Holton (1986), p. 4.
89 Sylvia Pankhurst attributed the Women's Franchise League great importance as a forerunner of the WSPU; see Holton (1998), p. 15.
90 F. Hilary, "'Dare to be Free!": The Women's Freedom League and its Legacy', in S. S. Holton & June Purvis (eds.), *Votes for Women* (London: Routledge, 2000), pp. 181–202.
91 A. Bonner & Charles Bradlaugh Bonner, *Hypatia Bradlaugh Bonner: The Story of Her Life* (London: Watts & Co., 1942), pp. 84–5; *The Reformer*, 15 August 1899, pp. 467–70. Hypatia supported Charles Dilke's 1907 Bill for adult suffrage; see 'Report of Mrs Bradlaugh Bonner on Woman Suffrage' (1907), London, Bishopsgate Library, Charles Bradlaugh Archive 2770.
92 *The Present Day*, July 1886, pp. 13–14, October 1886, pp. 33–4.
93 *Ibid.*, Aug 1886, p. 20, October 1886, pp. 29–30.

6

Freethought and Free Love?
Marriage, birth control and sexual morality

Questions of sex were central to Secularism. Even those Freethinkers who desperately sought respectability for the movement found it impossible to avoid the subject, for irreligion was irrevocably linked in the public mind with sexual license. Moreover, the Freethought movement had, since the beginning of the nineteenth century, been home to some of the leading advocates of sexual liberty, birth control and marriage reform. A complex relationship existed between these strands of sexual dissidence – sometimes conflicting, at other times coming together to form a radical, feminist vision of sexual freedom. If a 'Freethinking' vision of sexual freedom existed, it certainly did not go uncontested by others in the movement. Nevertheless, the intellectual and political location of organised Freethought made it fertile ground for a radical re-imagining of sexual norms and conduct.

The Freethought renunciation of Christianity necessarily entailed a rejection of the moral authority of the Church, particularly its role in legitimising sexual relations. Secularists were therefore required to find a new basis for morality, and questions of sex were at the centre of this project to establish new ethical criteria. In some cases Secularists' rejection of Christian asceticism and their emphasis on the material world could also lead to a positive attitude to physical passions in both men and women. The central Freethinking principle of free enquiry necessitated a commitment to open discussion of sexual matters, and while this often generated a great deal of anxiety, the majority of the movement's leadership supported the need for free discussion.

The furore surrounding George Drysdale's publication of *Elements of Social Science* in 1854, provides one way into understanding the complex dynamics of Secularist debates on sex. This book, anonymously authored by the Freethinker George Drysdale, proved enormously influential in Victorian debates on prostitution, female sexuality, marriage and birth control.[1] The distinctively anti-religious arguments put forward by Drysdale in favour of promiscuous sexual relationships, 'preventative checks' (birth control) and female emancipation, reveal the importance of Freethought ideology in developing libertarian thinking on sex during this period. Yet the reaction of the wider Freethought movement to *Elements of Social Science* was mixed to say the least; it provoked considerable opposition in some quarters and led Secularists to discuss questions of sex with renewed intensity. *Elements* raised two issues in particular that were already of great importance to the Freethought movement – a critique of the institution of marriage and Neo-Malthusian support for birth control.

Freethinking feminist attacks on marriage stretched back to the early decades of the nineteenth century, when Richard Carlile published *What is Love?* (1826) and formed a moral union with Eliza Sharples in 1832. In the 1830s and 1840s this critique was further developed by the Owenites, who saw the eradication of Christian marriage and traditional familial structures as a pre-condition of female emancipation. This more radical opposition to patriarchal family institutions is usually believed to have disappeared from feminist circles after the collapse of the Owenite movement, after which the mainstream women's rights movement favoured a more moderate and respectable campaign for marriage reform. It is argued here, however, that in continuing to provide a forum in which less conventional ideas about relations between men and women could be discussed, the Freethought movement kept alive the Owenites' more radical feminist vision.

Freethought support for birth control began in the 1820s, and was brought to public attention in 1877 when Annie Besant and Charles Bradlaugh were tried for the publication of Charles Knowlton's birth control pamphlet, *Fruits of Philosophy*. Their highly publicised trial saw the re-emergence of many of the same tensions and arguments in the Secularist movement that had arisen over the publication of Drysdale's *Elements*. The relationship between Neo-Malthusianism and feminism was not a straightforward one, and it was their support for birth control that most clearly divided Freethinking feminists from the rest of the women's rights movement. When, in the 1880s and 1890s the possibility of greater sexual freedom outside conventional marriage began to be discussed more openly in the wider women's movement, this more radical discourse drew heavily on older Freethinking arguments.

The Bible of the Secularists? George Drysdale's *Elements of Social Science*

In 1862 Harriet Law lectured at Brighouse, where she debated with the Rev. J. Clarke on the properties of matter. Towards the end of the debate, Clarke claimed that Secularism had no true basis for morality and that, without the Christian system of future rewards and punishments, there was nothing to prevent him from murdering his wife and children in the pursuit of self-interest. Harriet Law replied that Secularism was in fact more moral than Christianity, that it believed in the inherently 'noble qualities' of mankind, and that the Bible itself was full of the most immoral vices. Clarke, evidently put out by the quick-wittedness of his female opponent, then 'endeavoured to ruin the character of Mrs Law, to ruin her reputation, and insinuated that her mission was for accomplishing the most immoral purposes'.

> He read aloud in the coarsest manner, nearly all the most exciting passages contained in Mr Barker's *Review* of the *Elements of Social Science*, and, like him, dwelt with peculiar gusto on those parts which tickle the fancy of sensual natures ... he not only did this but said that the book was written by one of Mrs Law's party, and that she was going about the country pretending to lecture on 'The Degradation of Women, caused by Religion and Ignorance', but her real object was to indoctrinate her sex with the principles and the practices of the *Elements of Social Science*.[2]

The arguments put forward by Clarke would have already been familiar to Harriet Law, who keenly followed and contributed to the furore over the publication of the *Elements of Social Science*. In fact, her encounter with the irate Rev J. Clarke followed a familiar pattern: a debate on materialism closely followed by a discussion of whether Secularism was capable of supporting a system of morality independent from Christianity; the elision of morality in general with sexual morality in particular; the association of Secularism with the arguments put forward in the *Elements*; and the assumption that Freethinking feminism was a by-word for an extreme form of sexual libertarianism. Harriet Law's response, to which I will return, forcibly challenged such assumptions. Yet these same themes emerged again and again in the scandal surrounding the *Elements of Social Science*.

Physical, Sexual and Natural Religion (re-named *Elements of Social Science* in subsequent editions) was first published in 1854 by 'a student of medicine'. Its original title aptly indicated the connection between the author's Freethinking beliefs and his rejection of conventional sexual morality. George Drysdale was a Freethinking doctor from an upper-class family who later went on to write regularly for *The National Reformer* under the initials G. R., though his authorship of *Elements* was not revealed until after his death.[3] *Elements* opened with an attack on how the Christian religion elevated the 'spiritual' side of human nature to the detriment of the 'physical', so that 'the sexual appetites and enjoyments' were denigrated and repressed. The Christian Church, complained Drysdale, regarded it as 'a great merit to crucify the bodily lusts'. Instead, he espoused a new kind of 'physical religion' which looked to 'animal' nature as its guide. Physical religion would abolish Christian asceticism, doing away with 'all flimsy veils of morbid modesty, shame, and indolence …'.[4] Sexual desire, Drysdale argued, should be gratified without shame and regular exercise of the sexual organs was essential to good health. (He listed and described the variety of diseases in both men and women that were, he believed, caused by lack of sexual activity.)

Drysdale's favouring of the physical world over the spiritual was clearly part of his Freethinking worldview. He believed that the nineteenth century was witness to 'the greatest revolution which has ever taken place, or which perhaps ever will take place, in human Belief. This great change is the progress from a Supernatural to a Natural Religion.' The Secularists were identified as the true bearers of this Natural or Physical Religion, which held that all states of mind as well as states of the body were determined by physical laws. Morality itself was a 'science' and should be governed by the laws of nature.[5] Thus Drysdale's Freethought led him to argue for a complete overhaul of conventional sexual morality, since under the current system – in which marriage to a single person was for life, sexual intercourse outside marriage was forbidden, and sex was likely to lead to pregnancy – it was impossible fully to exercise one's sexual desires in conformity with the laws of nature. Instead, men visited prostitutes while women wasted away from 'green sickness' and other ailments caused by enforced celibacy. Again, 'the authority of supernatural religion' was blamed for this repressive system, which had 'been inseparably interwoven with the Christian and Hebraic beliefs'. For, as Drysdale wrote, 'there is scarcely anything on which so much stress is laid in the Old and New Testament as the institution of marriage'.[6] By contrast, Drysdale believed that men and women should be able to have sexual relationships free from both the sanction of marriage and the disapproval of society, claiming that, 'If a man and a woman conceive a passion for each other, they should be morally entitled to indulge it.' In the early years of one's life, from puberty onwards, promiscuous sexual experimentation should be permitted and boys and girls taught to enjoy one another's company. Later on, one might form longer-lasting attachments, but it should not be assumed, as the Christian institution of marriage did, that love was 'constant and unvarying', and Drysdale believed that couples should remain with one another only as long as their love and sexual desire lasted. Drysdale stressed that in envisaging this new system of sexual relations, he was not merely advocating easier divorce, but '*a far more radical change* ... before love can be rendered sufficiently attainable by all human beings ...'.[7] Unwanted pregnancy – the obvious obstacle to the free indulgence of sexual desire – would be overcome by the use of 'preventative checks' (birth control).[8]

Drysdale's 'physical, sexual and natural religion' was not an amoral libertinism; instead *Elements* articulated a moral code founded upon longstanding Freethinking principles. A commitment to the democratic dissemination of knowledge led Drysdale to provide a detailed and frank description of the sexual organs, reproduction, and venereal disease. For he believed that, especially in women, religiously inspired notions of 'innocence', 'purity' and 'delicacy' had prevented people from protecting themselves against disease. [9] Drysdale's attack on the current system of marriage was also motivated by his commitment to women's emancipation: marriage not only kept women legally and financially dependent upon men but also embodied a sexual double standard that prohibited women from fulfilling their sexual desire (which he insisted was as strong as that of men).[10] A more open practice of sexual relations, he maintained, would be more moral than the present one, for it would put an end to the 'licentiousness' and 'deception' that currently afflicted modern marriages, replacing it with 'happiness', 'virtue' and 'moderation'. Prostitution would no longer be necessary and friendship would develop more easily between men and women, once the compulsory element had been removed from their relationships.[11] Birth control was to be lauded because it 'put the two sexes almost on a par in sexual freedom', allowing a woman 'to indulge her sexual desires, with the same exemption from the after consequences as man ...'.[12] Drysdale's advocacy of 'preventative intercourse' also arose from his endorsement of Malthusian economics, which identified over-population, particularly overly-large families among the working class, as the cause of poverty. Large sections of *Elements of Social Science* were devoted to an exposition of the Malthusian theory of over-population and the decimating effects of poverty upon the working class. Drysdale fervently hoped that the birth control techniques he recommended in the book would ultimately put an end to such misery, and he dedicated *Elements* to 'the Poor and the Suffering'.[13]

Elements of Social Science was therefore very much a product of nineteenth-century Freethought, and the success of the work depended largely on the Secularist press and publishing industry. Publishers had shied away from the manuscript until the Freethinking Edward Truelove took it on, and the book received its first favourable reviews in the Secularist press, which advertised it thereafter. When Truelove died in 1898 George Standring, another Secularist, took over its publication.[14] However, in spite of the fact that Drysdale presented *Elements* as a Secularist work, the publication of his book had an explosive and extremely divisive effect on the movement. Drysdale's views on sexual morality were not only deeply shocking by Christian standards, but the explicitness with which they were expressed also exceeded anything previously written on the subject in Freethinking circles. Moreover, *Elements* was published just at the point when George Jacob Holyoake was attempting to present Secularism as a respectable movement, renouncing the title of 'infidelism' and its dangerous connotations of sexual immorality that had done so much to tarnish the reputation of Owenite Freethinking feminism.[15] Many Freethought leaders were shocked by the explicit tone and content of *Elements* while at the same time recognising the sincerity of its author's intentions. They thus found themselves torn between their commitment to freedom of discussion and their desire for a newly forged respectability. The *Investigator* gave a favourable review, but emphasised the courage it took to mention such a work in print, claiming that it was only their Secularist beliefs that compelled them to take this risk.[16] George Jacob Holyoake also had reservations, particularly regarding the original title *Physical, Natural and Sexual Religion*, for he feared that the term 'sexual' might confuse it with pornography and that the reference to 'religion' wrongly mixed up 'theology' with 'physiology'. Nevertheless, Holyoake concluded that *Elements* served a valuable purpose in providing the poor with information which was usually only available in 'high, expensive … volumes' and that the real crime lay with those who refused discussion of birth control, for this 'was a prudery as criminal as vice itself'.[17]

Freethinkers agonised over their endorsement of Drysdale's *Elements*, not because they lacked courage or were only half-heartedly committed to freedom of discussion, but because they were dealing with a question that was of central importance to the future of the Secularist project. How the movement approached questions of sex was fundamental to their wider mission to prove that morality could exist independently from religion. In the same year that *Elements* was published, Holyoake sought to explain the significance of the title he had chosen for his new movement.

'Freethought', he wrote, denoted '*how* we think', while 'Secularism' was the result and the object of such freethinking, a positive embodiment of the 'truths' of humanity and progress revealed by freedom of thought. 'Our object [as Secularists] is to promote personal morality.' Secularists rejected Christian morality because they believed that it endorsed vice: 'It sees wives beaten, but puts forth no hand to divorce poor women from brutes.' In declaring that, 'By Secularism we do not mean sensualism, nor do we mean prudery' Holyoake was therefore attempting to tread a very fine line, to carve out an alternative path for Freethought which allowed it to be just as morally upstanding as Christianity.[18]

In the debates over the publication of *Elements* Holyoake continued to steer this careful path. On the one hand, he gave *Elements* a relatively favourable review and agreed to advertise it (under a different title). At the same time he published in *The Reasoner* a series of articles by Francis Newman which took the moral hard-line on questions of sexual morality and implicitly condemned Drysdale's book, without mentioning it by name. Newman identified the emergence of a group of young and confident Freethinkers 'who feel their own power to refute as errors and mere prejudices many things counted as sacred in the past, and still dogmatically upheld by the churches ...'. But he cautioned against the exhilaration felt by those who had thrown off the tutelage of religious authority, on the grounds that it could lead to foolhardiness in matters of morality. Newman went on to strongly defend celibacy for the unmarried and, in a thinly veiled reference to *Elements*, accused anyone who questioned its importance of seeking to 'corrupt (if he can) our wives and sisters.'[19] In a later article he called upon working men to wreak 'vengeance' on all those who preached a doctrine of Free Love and who sought to persuade women that 'seduction' would cause them no harm.[20] Following this series of articles, Holyoake published an editorial distancing himself from the harsh moralistic tone of some of Newman's writings, while at the same time celebrating the fact that since their publication no one could be in any doubt as to the respectable 'moral temper' of Freethought.[21] Holyoake thus hoped that the newly founded Secularism had succeeded in riding out the potentially detrimental impact of Drysdale's work without betraying any of its fundamental principles.

Yet in 1861 organised Freethought was again to be divided over the *Elements of Social Science*. Charles Bradlaugh had praised Drysdale's book from its early days (his advocacy gaining it the title 'Bible of the Secularists') and he published a sympathetic review in *The National Reformer* in 1860.[22] Joseph Barker, who at this time co-edited *The National Reformer* with Bradlaugh, strongly opposed the book, and when Bradlaugh proposed the founding of a Malthusian League in 1861, Barker left in protest and set up the rival General Secular Reformers Society.[23] In his new journal, *Barker's Review*, he condemned Bradlaugh's 'Unbounded License Party' and re-published Francis Newman's series of articles from *The Reasoner*.[24] Barker also delivered a number of public lectures entitled 'The TWO CLASSES OF FREETHINKERS, their different views and aims with regard to *Morals*' in which he defended 'the Bible or the Hebrew notions of chastity'.[25] In spite of the fact that Drysdale's work had drawn on many of the principles and intellectual traditions that clustered around organised Freethought, the revulsion which both Newman and Barker felt for *Elements* suggests that there was by no means a straightforward correlation between Freethought and a libertarian approach to sexual morality. As the previous chapter demonstrated, the militant moralism that fuelled Newman and Barker's outrage was as characteristic of the Secularist viewpoint during this period as Drysdale's belief in the need to disseminate knowledge among the masses.[26] The debates that took place in *The Reasoner* in 1855 and in *Barker's Review* in 1861 reveal a wide spectrum of attitudes among Freethinkers.[27] Sophia Dobson Collet wrote to say that she wished the Secularist leaders would publicly distance themselves from 'the bad men of your own party' – presumably Drysdale – though she also criticised Newman for the unforgiving tone of his moralism.[28] Holyoake claimed that nine-tenths of those who responded to Newman's articles were in favour of them, although the selection of published correspondence also contained letters complaining that Newman had not properly considered the harmful effects of the current marriage laws and from one person who proudly declared all 'fidelity' to be '*immoral*' and '*unnatural*'.[29] Joseph Barker also printed numerous letters praising him for 'exposing' the *Elements of Social Science* and thus saving the correspondents from the terrible fate of accidentally reading it![30]

Some historians have laid great emphasis on how a mid-century turn to respectability produced far more conservative thinking on sexual morality among Freethinkers.[31] Michael Mason, especially, argued that Secularism was central to pushing what he called an 'anti-sensualist' agenda in Victorian debates on sexuality which promoted self-control or 'repression' rather than sexual liberation. While Mason rightly identified a strong current of anti-libertarian attitudes to sexuality within the Secularist movement, I want here to challenge his assumption that the intellectual culture of Freethought as a whole can be characterised simply as 'anti-sensualist', a category which is itself problematic in attempting to understand debates on sexuality during this period. Mason did not explain why, if Secularist ideology was the main bearer of anti-sensualist opposition to libertarian and libertine visions of sexuality, the very people that he identified as pushing for a more positive attitude to sexual liberation – Richard Carlile, George Drysdale, Charles Bradlaugh and Annie Besant – were also Freethinkers and Secularists.[32] There were a number of aspects of Secularist ideology easily lent to arguing for a libertarian break with traditional sexual morality, and it is therefore necessary to understand the many disagreements that arose regarding Freethought and Free Love also in relation to the Secularist movement's feminism.[33]

Harriet Law, militant atheist, feminist and socialist, was also a vocal opponent of George Drysdale's *Elements of Social Science*. When the Rev. J. Clarke attempted to smear her as an immoral proponent of the work, she claimed to be deeply insulted. In fact, Harriet Law had already publicly 'repudiated' the book in a previous issue of *The National Reformer*, and she declared herself to have nothing to do with 'that party' (presumably Bradlaugh's faction) which had endorsed it.[34] So why did Harriet Law, positioned on the left of the Secularist movement, oppose Drysdale's libertarian and ostensibly feminist work? Part of the answer can be found in the report of her encounter with Clarke in *The National Reformer*, which noted that, in spite of Law's protestations and public condemnation of *Elements*, 'The tales that have been afloat since Mr. Clarke's dastardly attack on Mrs Law's character and mission are too sickening to dwell upon. They are the result of his premeditated intention to ruin her character, and hence destroy her influence.'[35] In pursuing a highly public career as lecturer, denying the truths of the gospels and advocating women's rights, Harriet Law was already guilty of numerous transgressions. This made her particularly vulnerable to accusations of sexual impropriety – accusations which, if they stuck, would not only damage her reputation in the eyes of the Christian public, but might also place her career in jeopardy within the Secularist movement itself. It is perhaps not surprising, therefore, that she should have sought to distance herself from such a controversial work. In Law's case, the familiar Secularist technique of claiming to be more moral than the Christian was not simply a political defence of the movement but a personal defence of her reputation. Harriet Law compared *Elements* to the Bible and maintained that she would have been equally ashamed to be seen carrying about either of them. *The National Reformer* approvingly reported that, in responding to Clarke, Mrs Law had 'exhibited the superiority of a Secularist's morality over that practised by a Christian.[36] More, therefore, is required than a simplistic recourse to 'anti-sensualism' to explain why otherwise 'progressive' individuals might have been hostile to libertarian attacks on conventional sexual morality. Harriet Law's feminism might also have motivated her opposition to Drysdale, and this ongoing tension between feminism and sexual libertarianism was evident in wider Freethought discussions of marriage reform and birth control.

Marriage, divorce and Free Love

George Drysdale's attack on the Christian institution of marriage, and in particular his critique of the way it enslaved women, may have provoked a dramatic response but it in fact drew on a pre-existing Freethought tradition that would have been familiar to his Secularist readership. In previous centuries, unorthodox thinking in religious matters had often gone hand in hand with a rejection of conventional sexual morality. Freethinking libertines, such as the deist Peter Annet (1693–1769), had called for an end to laws in matters of love – championing divorce and proclaiming that 'Passion requires Liberty above all Things'.[37] Richard Carlile drew upon such works for *What is Love?*, while taking a more woman-centred approach. He condemned the 'artificial ties' of Christian marriage, which acted as 'shackles' on 'the simple enjoyment of a passion', while at the same time arguing that woman's right to sexual enjoyment was equal to that of man. Carlile did not advocate promiscuous inter-course, but thought that unions between men and women should be founded on the promise, 'You shall have me to yourself just as long as you treat me well and can really love me; when that feeling ceases, we had better part and seek new matches.'[38] A few years later, Carlile formed a moral union with the Freethinking feminist Eliza Sharples on precisely these lines.

The Owenite attack on 'Marriages of the Priesthood' also drew on these older critiques but fused them with a far more explicit and coherent feminist agenda.[39] Emma Martin's lectures in the 1840s on 'The Rights and Present Condition of Women' and 'Marriage and Divorce' argued that marriage under Christianity and capitalism was all too often a commercial transaction amounting to nothing more than legalised prostitution. She demanded that the present marriage system be aban-doned altogether, in favour of love unions, liberal divorce laws for both sexes and communal living arrangements in which all labour, including housework and childcare, would be divided equally between the sexes.[40] Margaret Chappellsmith also lambasted Christian marriage as a gross hypocrisy, and pointed to 'the vast number of brothels and prostitutes' that existed in spite of the lip service paid to the doctrines of 'chastity and conjugal fidelity'. Once women were granted economic independence, they would no longer be the victims of this corrupt system. Chappellsmith also maintained that the communal living advocated by the Owenites, 'by its certainty of producing abundant wealth and equal distribution, does away with all restraint upon marriage from pecuniary considerations, and does away with all temptation to form marriages from any other motive other than affection'.[41]

Freethinking Owenite feminists rejected both a repressive Christian morality *and* a libertine interpretation of their demand for a more liberal system of marriage. Emma Martin re-defined 'chastity' as 'equally distant from the erratic flights of passion, as from conventional abstinence'. She asserted that 'celibacy' was not 'natural' and condemned 'the interests of religion' for requiring 'the monitions of nature to be stifled'. Nevertheless, Martin also insisted that 'true love favours monogamy', and that the Owenite definition of 'chastity' was compatible with 'the cultivation of family affections and the discharge of marriage obligations'. Martin rejected the right of religious authorities to sanction or condemn women's sexuality via the means of 'false ceremonies' and argued instead for female sexual autonomy. A woman's chastity 'was of the mind' not dependent upon the 'law' or 'circumstance', so that, for example, a woman who had been raped did not become unchaste. Only the woman herself, as the person with the knowledge as to whether she truly loved her partner, could determine whether she was acting chastely.[42] Margaret Chappellsmith also insisted that 'the unions which would be formed under the new and rational arrangements' would be 'happy and lasting'.[43] However, in spite of attempts by Owenite feminists to present their new vision of sexual relations as both moral and chaste, there was no escaping the fact that they were advocating an extremely radical overhaul of conventional sexual morality. They not only faced fierce attacks from their Christian opponents on this subject, but were also confronted by the fears of working-class women that an end to marriage laws would leave them vulnerable to seduction, exploitation and abandonment.[44]

Freethinking feminists kept this libertarian feminist vision alive in the middle decades of the century. From the 1850s, feminists in the Secularist movement continued to critique Christian marriage institutions and after 1855 this became part of a broader and more sustained campaign for marriage reform organised by the women's rights movement.[45] Many of the arguments put forward by Freethinkers were in tune with those being made within the mainstream feminist movement. Harriet Law lectured throughout the 1860s and 1870s on the subject of 'Love, Courtship and Matrimony, greatly misunderstood and why', arguing that men and women should allow friendship to develop before embarking upon marriage, and that if women were better educated unions between the sexes could become equal partnerships.[46] The need for intellectual companionship and equality in marriage was also an important theme of Annie Besant's very first lecture on *The Political Status of Women* in 1874, and of Kate Watts' series of articles on female education which appeared in the *Secular Review* in 1879.[47] There was agreement across the Freethought and women's movements on the need for greater female autonomy and independence in marriage. Sara Hennell insisted that 'The girl adequately brought up must be at once fit to be married, and fit to live profitably alone' and she condemned the idea that a married couple should become 'one' in the eyes of God. 'The kind of love to be hoped for,' she argued, 'has to ... [cease] to merge the womanhood of the wife into the character of a mere adjunct to the man's nature.'[48] Such a belief motivated the campaign for the right of married women to hold property, which involved many Freethinking women, including Elizabeth Wolstenholme Elmy, who sat on the Married Women's Property Committee.[49] In 1878 and 1880 Annie Besant and Wolstenholme Elmy were the first women to publicly raise the issue of marital rape, causing an outcry soon responded to by the rest of the women's movement.[50]

Throughout this period, the Freethought movement continued to provide a space for debating the more controversial subjects of divorce, monogamy and Free Love – subjects that the mainstream women's movement generally felt unable to discuss. Freethinkers had necessarily to reject the Christian conception of marriage as an irreversible union of two people under God, and in disallowing the fundamental premise of the current marriage system they found themselves free to imagine different ways of organising relations between the sexes. Secularists began to trace the historical development of the marriage institution. In 1870 a review in *The National Reformer* of Richard Harte's *Laws Relating to Marriage* paid special attention to his historical account, which argued that monogamy had only emerged as a result of changing economic conditions which caused polyandry and polygamy to become obsolete. The review strongly supported Harte's view that divorce was perfectly permissible and in accordance with 'the moral and physical necessities of human beings'.[51] Sara Hennell also set out to show how the prevailing system of Christian marriage was the result of the development of a system of private property. Polygamy had given way to monogamy in order to ensure that property was kept within the family. Monogamy had not, therefore, been initially conceived out of respect for connubial love or the wifely role, but from 'the gross covetousness of clutching firmly by worldly property'.[52] Modern 'Christian marriage' was, according to Hennell, merely a sentimentalised version of the commercial transactions that had taken place in earlier societies, so that 'the idea of sale and purchase in fact lurks throughout our own form of marriage contract'.[53] Having deprived Christian marriage of its sacred status, Freethinkers were compelled to consider whether it should be replaced with a different system and if so, what this should be.

The term 'free union' could mean many things. In rejecting the religious ceremony of marriage, Freethinkers had by default to accept the legitimacy of some form of free union, though they fiercely debated how such unions should be defined and organised. George Jacob Holyoake, in spite of his anxiety to proclaim the respectability of Secularism, remained committed to the need for more liberal divorce laws and the right of men and women to form unions free from the sanction of Church and State. In 1855 he wrote in *The Reasoner* that marriage might well be very 'respectable' but since the 'legal restrictions which marriage imposes upon women are so disrespectful … marriage itself is not entitled to much respect'. Holyoake was primarily concerned for the security and freedom of women, in both marriages and free unions. Divorce under the existing system should be allowed in order that women might escape abusive husbands, while if an alternative system of civil contracts were established it ought to ensure provision for children in the case of separations. However, Holyoake also opposed the current marriage laws because they introduced compulsion and coercion into relationships. 'We have not so poor an opinion of love,' he commented, 'as to agree to the doctrine that the policeman or the magistrate is necessary to enforce the attachment which affection has formed'. Holyoake maintained that marriage became 'odious' when it was made a 'tyranny', and divorce for incompatibility of temperament should therefore also be permitted. He concluded that 'we … have as much respect for the unmarried, as the married, *provided always* the affection is single, sincere, pure, honourable to relatives, and just to offspring'.[54]

Francis Newman, however, took a very different position on the subject of free unions. He maintained that in all societies throughout history, 'unchastity' – defined as sexual relations outside life-long marriage – guaranteed the 'degradation' of women. No man could ever love a woman, he believed, who had herself loved another, and women themselves would become destitute if their husbands were permitted to cast them off as soon as their attentions strayed elsewhere.[55] However,

Newman did acknowledge that 'our existing laws do press hardly upon wives' who were unable to escape from 'tyrant' husbands, and he therefore struggled to imagine a morally viable alternative. Newman considered the case of Emma Martin, who had defied the law and left her abusive husband to live in a free union with another man. After much deliberation, Newman concluded that he could not condemn Martin's actions, and yet he also believed that some kind of institutional body was required to determine which relationships were 'just and sacred' and which were merely 'promiscuous'. Newman's concerns arose from the recognition that, in contemporary society, 'Marriage is *not* ... a union of those who are like and equal ... the man has more to gain, the woman to lose: for many reasons the woman needs *protection* by society ...'[56]

Later in the century, some female Freethinkers continued to advocate free unions and freer divorce laws, even when this led to their marginalisation within the broader women's movement. Annie Besant believed that it was possible for both virtue and happiness to flourish under a more liberalised system of marriage laws. Besant employed the familiar Freethought technique of assuming the moral high ground from which to advocate practices that the majority of people would perceive as dangerously immoral. She insisted that she 'reverenced' marriage before going onto explain that:

> marriage is different as regarded from the Secularist and from the Christian point of view ... [the Secularist] regards marriage as something far higher than a union 'blessed' by a minister; he considers also that marriage ought to be terminable like any other contract, when it fails in its object and becomes injurious instead of beneficial.[57]

Loveless marriages, Besant argued, led to immoral practices, whereas 'More reasonable marriage laws would ... tend to lessen prostitution. Reasonable facility to divorce would tend to morality.'[58] This was to reiterate arguments put forward by the Owenite feminists in the 1830s and 1840s and George Drysdale in the 1850s – that the binding nature of the marriage contract produced vice by encouraging men to seek their pleasure among prostitutes, making women the victims of deception and disease. This argument took on a new significance in the context of the campaigns against the Contagious Diseases Acts, given that one of the campaign's main concerns was that 'innocent' wives were catching venereal diseases from their husbands. However, Besant drew a far more radical conclusion than many of her fellow repealers in the women's movement. She argued that chastity was not a solution to the problem of prostitution, for it denied the natural expression of sexuality:

'the enforcement of celibacy on vigorous men always results in libertinage, whether among celibate priests or celibate soldiers'. Moreover,
she proclaimed that '[the Secularist] does not despise human passion,
or pretend that he has no body; on the contrary, reverencing nature, he
regards physical union as perfecting the union of the heart and mind
...'.[59] Annie Besant claimed that she 'differed considerably' from the
views on marriage expressed in the *Elements of Social Science*, but she
can nevertheless be found making similar claims for a positive view of
sexuality and the need for the marriage bond to rest upon love and affection rather than religious or state authority.[60]

Annie Besant separated from her husband when she became a
Freethinker, but unlike Emma Martin thirty years previously, never
formed a free union with another man. Alice Vickery and Charles
Drysdale formed a secret free union around 1870 but let it be assumed that
they were legally married, for any public avowal might have spelt the end
of Vickery's medical career.[61] However, another Freethinker, Elizabeth
Wolstenholme Elmy, did openly form a free union with Ben Elmy, the
Vice President of the National Secular Society, the main opposition to
which came from fellow feminists. The leaders of the women's movement
rejected any liberalisation of divorce laws, and Millicent Garrett Fawcett
declared that 'People ... who think that marriages should be dissolved
at will ... are in effect anarchists ... none of the leaders of the women's
movement in England have ever countenanced for a moment anarchic
methods or anarchic aims'.[62] When Wolstenholme Elmy became preg-
nant, fellow women's rights campaigners eventually pressured her into
marrying Ben Elmy. Yet even this did not satisfy, and on her return to
political activity after the birth of her son in 1875 Wolstenholme Elmy
became the subject of an orchestrated campaign against her continuing
public association with feminist organisations. Lydia Becker voted for her
removal from the Married Women's Property Committee in Manchester
(the motion failed), and also suggested to the meeting that the registry be
checked to ensure that Wolstenholme Elmy's marriage really had taken
place! Fawcett wrote privately to Wolstenholme Elmy condemning her
conduct and asking her to remove herself from activities in order to
prevent any further damage to the suffrage movement.[63]

On the whole, it seems that Freethinking feminists were more willing
than their Christian sisters in the women's movement to at least tolerate
and consider alternative modes of organising sexual relations. Historian
Barbara Caine has described how the Victorian feminist movement,
having consciously decided to take a cautious approach to questions of
sexual morality, omitted any reference to Mary Wollstonecraft from their

writings. This was, of course, because Wollstonecraft had conducted pre-marital affairs and had given birth to an illegitimate daughter.[64] By contrast, Harriet Law was happy to print a large portrait of Mary Wollstonecraft on the front page of the *Secular Chronicle* in 1878, accompanied by an enthusiastic biography written by Harriet Teresa Law.[65]

Figure 4 Mary Wollstonecraft as headline news in the *Secular Chronicle* (1878).

Feminist ambivalence over the degree of marriage reform that should be advocated was, however, motivated not simply by a desire to keep up appearances, but also by the concern that unregulated sexual activity would leave women vulnerable to sexual exploitation, abandonment and financial destitution. Without reliable birth control and adequate education and employment opportunities, such concerns were not easily dismissed. Victorian society often justified the double sexual standard on the grounds that the male sexual drive was stronger than that of the female and could not therefore be so easily suppressed. The Matrimonial Act of 1857, for example, permitted men to divorce their wives for adultery but did not grant the same right to women. Supporters of the Contagious Diseases Acts similarly argued that male sexual desire made prostitution a necessary evil. The feminist response was to argue that, rather than make women the victims of male passion, men should conform to the same standards of chastity as women. They therefore often favourably contrasted sexual self-restraint with unbridled physical passion. Within such a context, it becomes possible to understand how the more conservative views of Francis Newman and Sophia Dobson Collet regarding free unions, and the refusal of Harriet Law to endorse the libertarianism of George Drysdale, could co-exist in the Freethought movement with a drive towards a freer vision of sexuality. It certainly suggests that 'anti-sensualism' was a more complex phenomenon than mere puritanism.

From the late 1880s onwards, however, there developed a greater openness in the women's movement towards wholesale attacks on the marriage system which went beyond criticism of its present-day abuses to condemn the institution in its entirety.[66] One of the most infamous contributions to this debate was Mona Caird's 1888 article for the *Westminster Review*, which provoked a furious response in the *Daily Telegraph* inviting 27,000 items of correspondence on the question 'Is Marriage a Failure'.[67] Caird condemned Christian marriage and argued that 'the ideal marriage should be free' – a 'private transaction' uninhibited by Church and State for two individuals to form and dissolve at will. Yet her argument also rested upon her freethinking outlook, drawing on older Secularist critiques of the pernicious effects of Christianity on the historical position of women. Caird, for example, argued that the reason for the present day denigration of women's sexuality could be traced back to the medieval Church, which had presented woman as a source of sin. The Reformation, far from improving the situation, had merely endorsed a marriage system which turned woman into man's private property.[68]

The influence of Freethought was clearly evident in almost all *fin de siècle* radical circles moving towards a greater openness to free unions.

Mona Caird's *Westminster Review* article referred to the work of Karl Pearson, author of *The Ethic of Freethought* (1888), who, like Caird, held freethinking views without feeling the need to formally associate himself with the organised Secular party. Pearson was also the founder of the Men and Women's Club, formed in 1895 to discuss relations between the sexes with the stated intention of doing so 'from the historical and scientific as distinguished from the theological point of view'. Not all members of the Club were convinced by arguments for ending marriage, though its Secretary Maria Sharpe began to support free monogamous unions after undergoing a crisis of religious faith in the late 1880s.[69] Mona Caird's notorious article also referred to Jane Clapperton's recently published book *Scientific Meliorism* (1885). Like Caird, the freethinking Clapperton condemned existing marriages as 'an artificial sham' and called for future partnerships based upon a 'free' transaction which could be dissolved should the 'bonds of affection' be severed.[70] Such renewed interest in free unions did not, however, mean an end to the earlier concerns of both Freethinkers and feminists about the fate of women and children under a new and freer system. In the 1880s Sara Hennell advocated a new form of 'natural marriage' to replace that of the Church, whereby a woman would no longer be 'given away' by her father but instead make a declaration that she was to be married to a man of her own choice. Yet she concluded that duty towards the couple's children necessitated that the contract should be binding, even if 'affective passion' disappeared.[71] Jane Clapperton, on the other hand, thought '[d]issolution of marriage before parentage occurs ought to be a very simple affair, requiring only the expressed desire of both parties', while after the birth of the first child divorce should still be permitted yet be made 'more difficult and carefully guarded by society'.[72]

In 1893, when free unions were becoming a viable reality for a tiny radical minority, the Legitimation League was formed to secure legal recognition and protection for children born outside of Christian marriage. In 1895, however, its annual meeting controversially voted to expand its remit to include campaigning for the right to form free unions. The League emerged from a distinctly freethinking milieu, closely connected to the Personal Rights Association in which many Secularists had been active. The freethinking lawyer Wordsworth Donisthorpe became the second President of the League (resigning in 1895) and Jane Clapperton, Alice Vickery and Charles Drysdale were also associates.[73] In 1897 the League launched a journal entitled *The Adult*, which variously identified itself as 'A Journal for the Advancement of Freedom in Sexual Relationships', 'A Crusade Against Sex-enslavement' and, finally, 'A Journal of Sex'.[74]

The Adult justified its extreme subject matter on grounds of free discussion and free dissemination of knowledge – employing a rhetoric that had been refined over the generations within the Freethought movement: 'Frankness, before all things, is necessary if we are to wrench from the clutches of the Past any of the lessons it may hold in its grasp' declared editor George Bedborough, noting that 'Readers of The Adult are invited to criticise the suggestions, arguments and opinions published in this journal.'[75] 'Free Thought and Free Love' became a popular topic for discussion in the pages of *The Adult*, with the self-proclaimed Free Lovers now declaring that organised Freethought had become too cautious on the question. In 1897 one contributor, Lucy Stewart, noted that although 'it is frequently asserted from the Christian Evidence platform that Secularists believe in free love', in reality most Secularists prefer to disassociate themselves from it out of a slavish desire to be '*respectable*'.[76] Bedborough likewise commented that, 'judged by their attitude towards the free love movement there seems little difference between the average parson and the average Freethought leader'. He approvingly reviewed a pamphlet authored by Orford Northcote, a frequent contributor to *The Adult*, which provided a history of the relationship between Freethought and Free Love over the course of the nineteenth century and accused the existing Secularist leaders of betraying this proud tradition.[77]

The Free Lovers were, to some extent, justified in claiming that Secularists preferred to disassociate themselves from the vigorous support of free unions proclaimed by *The Adult*. *The Freethinker* (edited by the NSS President G. W. Foote) formally supported the Legitimation League and the right of *The Adult* to voice its opinions, but simultaneously remarked that 'the world wants more *discipline* instead of more *freedom* in sexual relationships'.[78] J. M. Robertson permitted Free Love advocates to write for *The National Reformer*, while stressing that such views did not reflect the editorial line.[79] *The Reformer*, however, declined to advertise the Legitimation League's meetings in its 'Directory of Reform Societies'. Its editors, Hypatia and Arthur Bradlaugh Bonner, wrote to *The Adult* in 1897–98 to state that they had been 'entirely in sympathy' with the Legitimation League when it was originally founded, but could not condone its new policy of *positively* advocating Free Love.[80]

Had, then, the Freethought leadership of the 1890s renounced the movement's earlier commitment to fighting for 'free utterance of opinion'? By the end of the century prominent Free Lovers were more likely to come from a broadly unaffiliated freethinking milieu rather than directly from the ranks of organised Freethought. And with the explosion of a radical press, encompassing a vast range of heterodox political currents, sex radicals no longer relied so heavily upon Freethinking publishers and periodicals to circulate their views.[81] It is, however, important not to allow the rhetoric of *The Adult* to over-determine our understanding of the Secularists' respectability. In fact, Freethinkers' views on marriage still positioned them firmly beyond the pale of conventional, even radical, morality.[82] In 1898 Charles Watts, while professing to deplore 'loose views' on the question, nevertheless 'frankly advocated' divorce by mutual consent.[83] Hypatia Bradlaugh Bonner may have found *The Adult* distasteful, but she published in her own newspaper affectionate endorsements of the 'pure' free unions formed by Mary Wollstonecraft and George Eliot. She remained true to the longstanding Freethought position that to remain married once love and happiness had gone was, in the words of one of her contributors, 'the most revolting crime that a man and a woman can commit'.[84]

The arguments between the Secularists and *The Adult* were less about clearly wrought differences of opinion, and more about contested definitions of the terms 'free union' and 'Free Love'. At the Legitimation League's annual meeting for 1897, George Bedborough, editor of *The Adult*, was asked to define 'freedom in sexual relationships'. He initially declined to do so, clearly aware of the contentious and potentially divisive effects this could have. Two months later, however, he clarified his position in *The Adult* by stating that 'Freedom merely means the absence of external restraint, and Free Love implies dispensing with the interference of the lawyer and the priest in sexual relationships.'[85] None of this was at odds with the Secularist position, and Charles Watts claimed to have 'great sympathy for free-love' if taken to mean that 'there should be proper means whereby the man and the woman should separate'.[86] Yet some contributors to *The Adult* took this celebration of freedom to imply a far more fundamental break with monogamy. Orford Northcote, for example, argued that the natural 'mutability of sex love' ought to be embraced rather than resisted, while Lucy Stewart declared that although most couples would probably continue to practise monogamy, it was important not to judge those who engaged in more fleeting connections.[87]

Feminist concerns played an important role in deterring some Freethinkers from what could become a distinctly male-centred vision of Free Love. Orford Northcote, for example, suggested that prostitution might be justified under present circumstances since there were so few adequately liberated 'free women' to satisfy the wants of those brave men who had managed to 'throw off the prison of monogamy'.[88] The Secularist leadership continued to make 'the old argument' that some form of contract in heterosexual relations was required to protect the woman. *The Freethinker* declared that: 'a man who neglects his wife and children, whatever he be, is no Secularist.'[89] Prominent Freethinkers in the 1890s thus backed away from an endorsement of 'fanatical' Free Love, but they did not reject it wholesale.[90] Their movement remained closely associated with campaigns for greater freedom in sexual relations, and part of the reason *The Adult* paid so much attention to the Secularists was precisely because their rank and file continued to be the most likely recruits to the Free Love cause.[91] Despite his criticisms of the Freethought leadership, Orford Northcote informed them in 1898 that: 'How you act in the coming struggle, largely depends the issue.'[92] The Secularist movement continued, at the end of the nineteenth century, to be recognised as a necessary and powerful ally in the Free Love cause.

Birth control

THE KNOWLTON TRIAL

Prominent birth control advocates had, since the beginning of the nineteenth century, almost invariably been Freethinkers and had found most support for their ideas within the Freethought movement.[93] Richard Carlile's *Every Woman's Book or What is Love?* (1826) was one of the earliest practical guides to contraception. Freethinkers also authored the other leading nineteenth-century works on birth control. Robert Owen's son, Robert Dale Owen, published *Moral Physiology* in 1830 and the American doctor Charles Knowlton wrote *Fruits of Philosophy* in 1832. Both of these continued to be published and circulated in Britain by Secularist publishers over the course of the century. Freethinking beliefs occupied a central place in these early writings on birth control. Richard Carlile's description of sponges and the withdrawal method sat alongside a critique of Christian symbolism, while for Charles Knowlton the 'philosophical' part of his treatise (which argued that the celibacy practised by monks and nuns was harmful since 'reason' taught us not to 'war against' nature), was as important as his explanation of the zinc syringe as a means of avoiding conception.[94] Leading figures in the Secularist movement continued to support birth control in the ensuing decades. Emma Martin's 'private physiological lectures to ladies', which she began in 1845 after training as a midwife, sought to educate women about their reproductive functions and probably included advice on how to avoid unwanted pregnancies.[95] George Jacob Holyoake and his brother Austin had published Knowlton's book long before Besant and Bradlaugh were prosecuted for its publication, and Austin Holyoake had himself written a birth control tract entitled *Large or Small Families* which referred to previous Freethought works on the subject, including George Drysdale's *Elements of Social Science*.[96] Drysdale, writing as G. R., had lent his support to the first 'Malthusian League' established by Charles Bradlaugh in 1861, and although the League was short-lived, articles on Malthusian economics and sometimes on preventative checks regularly appeared in *The National Reformer* throughout the 1860s.[97] When Annie Besant and Charles Bradlaugh republished Knowlton's *Fruits of Philosophy* in 1877 their introduction emphasised the long tradition of Freethinking support for birth control, asserting that 'for the last fifty years the book has thus been identified by Freethought, advertised by Freethinkers, published under the sanction of their names and sold in the headquarters of Freethought literature'.[98]

The trial of Annie Besant and Charles Bradlaugh on charges of obscenity for the publication of Charles Knowlton's *Fruits of Philosophy* thus represented the culmination of a long relationship between Secularism and birth control advocacy. In 1876 a Bristol bookseller, Mr Cook, was arrested for selling copies of the Knowlton pamphlet published by the leading Secularist Charles Watts, to which Cook had added lewd illustrations. Watts was subsequently charged with publishing an obscene work. He initially planned to defend Knowlton's book in court, but on closer reading and on hearing of Cook's illustrations, he changed his mind and pleaded guilty. Besant and Bradlaugh were furious at what they saw as a capitulation to the enemies of free speech.[99] After breaking off all business connections with Charles Watts and dismissing him from sub-editorship of *The National Reformer*, Besant and Bradlaugh established their own Freethought Publishing Company and set about publishing a new edition of *Fruits of Philosophy*, with notes by 'the author of the *Elements of Social Science*'. They did not fully endorse all the medical advice contained in the Knowlton Pamphlet, believing scientific expertise to have advanced since its original publication, but they justified their decision to republish on the grounds that 'free discussion ought to be maintained at all hazards … so that the public, enabled to see all sides of the question, may have the materials for forming a sound judgement'.[100] Besant and Bradlaugh were fully aware that such action would lead to their prosecution and they intended to make the re-publication of the Knowlton Pamphlet a test case for freedom of the press. They were arrested in June 1877 and their trial, for which they both conducted their own defence, received an enormous amount of attention within and beyond the Secularist movement. Besant and Bradlaugh were found guilty by the jury and were sentenced to six months' imprisonment, but their sentence was subsequently revoked on a technicality.

During the 'Knowlton trial', Annie Besant and Charles Bradlaugh were both celebrated and condemned by their fellow Secularists. Most rank and file activists supported them as champions of free speech and freedom of the press, suggesting that by this period the majority of the movement supported the practice of birth control, at least within marriage.[101] Moreover, even those Secularists who denounced Bradlaugh and Besant's decision to publish were in some cases actually in favour of birth control. Kate Watts' *Reply to Mr. Bradlaugh's Misrepresentations* (1877) condemned the President of the National Secular Society for his authoritarian style of leadership and for his unjust dismissal of her husband, who had been genuinely concerned to avoid tarnishing the good name of Freethought with an unworthy publication. But Kate Watts did not declare herself opposed to birth control itself, and in fact concluded that 'to a certain extent the subject matter [of the Knowlton Pamphlet] is good, but … I did not like the style'.[102] G. W. Foote similarly objected to Bradlaugh's failure to consult the rest of the National Secular Society before launching headlong into a highly public and controversial trial. Yet he too professed himself in favour of preventative checks as a means of controlling population.[103] George Jacob Holyoake and Harriet Law both sat on the platform at the first Secularist meeting called to protest against Bradlaugh and Besant's decision to republish, but ultimately chose to remain neutral on the question. Neither of them attempted to distance themselves from the shock waves of scandal that emanated from the trial by voicing any opposition to birth control.[104] On the other hand, conservative concerns for respectability did influence elements of opposition to the re-publication of *Fruits of Philosophy*. Harriet Law made clear that she 'did not approve' of the Knowlton Pamphlet and said that her experience as a 'propagandist' had led her to conclude that the association of Freethought with 'literature of the class to which the book in question belongs' made it harder to convince people of the principles of Secularism.[105] Foote felt that the Secularist commitment to free discussion did not extend to a subject as delicate as population control, and that Freethinkers damaged their reputation by encouraging such a debate among the general public rather than restricting it to medical experts.[106]

Early campaigns for birth control were not necessarily motivated by enthusiasm for women's rights or a desire for greater sexual freedom. Neo-Malthusians were, as the name suggests, primarily concerned with the propagation of Malthusian economics in an attempt to convince the poor to limit the size of their families. As a result, there also existed a long tradition of working-class, and later Socialist, opposition to birth control, on the basis that Malthusianism implied that the workers themselves were to blame for their poverty.[107] The vast majority of Bradlaugh and Besant's 1877 defence and subsequent Malthusian League propaganda consisted not of the feminist case for a woman's right to avoid unwanted pregnancy, but of an exposition of Malthusian economics. Although the doctrine of over-population appears to have been partially motivated by a genuine concern for the miserable condition of the poor, they had little sympathy for those who 'recklessly' produced large families for which they could not provide.[108]

However, it is clear from the Secularist journals that readers were also familiar with framing the birth control question as one of women's rights. When a sentence of 'guilty' was passed on Besant and Bradlaugh, J. Symes,[109] a regular contributor to the Secularist press, wrote:

> Had those twelve men been replaced by the same number of intelligent matrons the verdict must have been 'Not Guilty'. The question at issue is a woman's question; and the verdict of the jury and the barbarous sentence of the judge are another blow aimed at the 'rights of women'.[110]

Prof. Emile Acollas, author of a manual on French law, also wrote to *The National Reformer* in support of Besant and Bradlaugh but stated that it was unfortunate that the Knowlton Pamphlet viewed the subject 'exclusively from a man's point of view ... woman, to develope [sic] herself morally, intellectually and physically, must have the same rights as man'.[111] Prior the Knowlton trial, in 1869, a woman wrote to *The National Reformer* attacking those who claimed that there was no support for Malthusianism among women. To the contrary, claimed this female correspondent, it was women, over-burdened with large families, who most desired access to preventative checks. Her own experience suggested that many among her sex strongly supported birth control, not because they were concerned with theories of over-population (which she felt to be largely irrelevant to the subject) but because they regarded it a means towards increased personal freedom.[112]

As this woman's letter hinted, the birth control question also suggested the possibility of greater *sexual* freedom for women. During the Knowlton trial, the spectre of unbridled female sexuality was initially invoked by the Prosecution. One of their main arguments was that, by selling the pamphlet at the low price of sixpence, Besant and Bradlaugh had made it too readily available to 'unscrupulous people' including 'young women' who might use it to escape the consequences of their immoral sexual urges.[113] Annie Besant responded with a defence of sexual feeling and the principle of physical pleasure. 'There is nothing wrong in a natural desire rightly and properly gratified,' she asserted, 'and there is no harm in gratifying sexual instinct if it can be exercised in manner without injury to anyone else ...' She went on to argue that '[I]t is only a false and spurious kind of modesty which sees harm in gratification of one of the highest instincts of human nature.'[114]

Others in the Secularist movement made more explicit arguments in favour of women's right to sexual promiscuity and enjoyment free from the fear of pregnancy. As a man, J. Symes was able to draw far more radical conclusions than Besant in his attack on the double sexual standard. He wrote to *The National Reformer* asking, 'In the first place, why should not young girls be allowed to make vice as safe for themselves as the young men do?'[115] Such a statement harked back to an older, minority tradition of supporting birth control on grounds of increased sexual freedom for women. Richard Carlile had also argued that preventative checks should be celebrated for allowing women to initiate sexual liaisons and putting an end to the stigmatisation of women who chose to take lovers.[116] George Drysdale too argued that women should be given access to birth control in order to allow them freely to indulge their sexual passions.[117]

Such positive attitudes to female sexuality were not representative of the entirety of the Freethought movement, and the Knowlton trial also generated far more conservative responses. In his usual misogynist mode, W. S. Ross dismissed arguments that birth control would relieve women from health risks and the economic burden of multiple pregnancies, insisting instead, 'That wives are not always happy is no reason why women should be unmarried harlots.' He then went onto paint a lurid picture of the 'shameless and deflowered harlot ... who constantly carries a syringe in her muff in the name of Mr. Bradlaugh and Freethought.'[118] Francis Newman, however, founded his opposition to the 'Corruption Now Called Neo-Malthusianism' on explicitly feminist grounds. In a pamphlet produced by the Moral Reform Union and annotated by the female doctor and women's rights campaigner Elizabeth Blackwell, Newman argued that birth control was in fact designed to serve the wishes of a 'sensual' husband and was therefore 'very dangerous to his wife.'[119]

Newman's belief that any means of preventing the natural consequences of marital love would in fact compel women to make themselves permanently sexually available to their husbands was shared by many of those active in the women's movement. While the majority of feminists within Secularism supported birth control, the majority of feminists outside organised Freethought opposed it.[120] Birth control was, therefore, an issue on which Freethinking feminists were very much at odds with the rest of the women's movement. The Bradlaugh–Besant trial was totally ignored by the two leading feminist journals of the time, the *Victoria Magazine* and the *Englishwomen's Review*, a bizarre silence given the enormous amount of attention it generated in the rest of the press.[121] Charles Bradlaugh had attempted to call Millicent Garrett Fawcett and her economist husband Henry as witnesses for the defence, in the belief that Henry had previously implied support for the use of preventative checks in his writings on population control. Henry Fawcett was outraged and threatened to send Millicent out of the country in order to prevent her having to attend court.[122] The Fawcetts not only objected to Bradlaugh's assumption that they would defend an obscene book, but also to the practice of birth control itself. Millicent Garrett Fawcett wrote to Bradlaugh stating that 'so far as my knowledge of the [Knowlton] book enables me to speak, I entirely agree with the opinion I have frequently heard Mr. Fawcett express, and this opinion, as I believe you know, is strongly condemnatory of the character of the book'.[123] In May 1887 the National Vigilance Association passed a motion, supported by Elizabeth Blackwell and Laura Chant, which approved the prosecution of 'persons selling indecent publications inciting sexual immoralities' and stated that 'we strongly disapprove of the use of any means ... which in restricting the increase in population, suggests that vice is a necessity ... and ... which tends to relax the incentive for moral restraint'.[124]

However, one should not imagine a polarity between 'pro-pleasure' or 'sensualist' Freethinking feminists and 'anti-sex' or 'anti-sensualist' mainstream (Christian) feminists. As Lucy Bland has shown, attitudes to sexuality during this period were more complex than that.[125] Both Freethinking feminist Neo-Malthusians and feminist opponents of birth control were concerned to increase women's control over their bodies. Freethinking support for birth control was rooted in an older radical tradition of medical self-help: Emma Martin's physiological lectures for ladies, for example, were part of this culture of democratised health care.[126] Yet the desire to acquire a better understanding of one's body in order to promote greater independence and self-control was also central to other feminist approaches to sexual morality during the second half of the nineteenth century.[127] Both the social purity, anti-Malthusian feminist Elizabeth Blackwell and the Secularist Elizabeth Wolstenholme Elmy wrote sex education manuals in the hope that, if women were equipped with knowledge of their reproductive functions they would be less vulnerable to sexual exploitation.[128] The historian Margaret Jackson, in an attempt to set up a dichotomy between social purity feminists and pro-(masculine) sex feminists, classed Elizabeth Wolstenholme Elmy alongside Blackwell as 'militant' feminists who were concerned to replace the male-orientated conception of sex as a primarily physical act with a more woman-centred spiritual vision. She contrasted them to Annie Besant, whose support for free unions and birth control led Jackson to class her as a 'libertarian'.[129] And yet, Besant was an old acquaintance of Wolstenholme Elmy, who was among the first to publicly sign up to Besant and Bradlaugh's defence committee during the Knowlton trial. The boundaries between different feminist positions on birth control, as in the case of attitudes towards free unions, were more blurred than categories such as 'sensualist', 'libertarian' and 'conservative' imply.

THE MALTHUSIAN LEAGUE, 1877–1914

After the Knowlton trial Secularists remained central to pushing the question of birth control in the women's movement, and the Malthusian League, re-established after 1877, committed itself to an explicitly feminist agenda.[130] In 1879 Besant made the basic feminist case for birth control in the pages of the League's journal the *Malthusian*. Husbands complained that their wives 'take no interest in the larger life outside the house' and do not engage with the 'intellectual movement of the age'. Yet, Besant pointed out, a woman forced to bear many children, condemned to the exhausting job of caring for a large family, naturally had no time for discussing 'sociology'. Women needed control over their own bodies not simply to avoid ill health but also to secure an independent existence.

> Woman is not only for man, she also has a right to her own life, and to condemn her to constant childbearing, to consume the prime of her life in continual illness and recovery, is an injustice to herself and a grave injury to society.[131]

Besant and Bradlaugh both stepped back from the Malthusian League in the late 1870s, leaving it largely in the hands of the Freethinking medical couple Alice Vickery and Charles Drysdale (brother of the infamous George).[132] Vickery began lecturing for the League as soon as she finished qualifying as a doctor in 1880 and her main emphasis was on the positive effects of birth control for women, addressing subjects such as 'The Position of Women in Overcrowded Countries' and 'The Position of Women as Affected by Large Families'. Vickery also made various attempts in 1891 and 1904 to form a women's section of the League charged with the task of formulating a 'new morality'. Though no formal women's caucus was ever established, Vickery did host regular 'ladies' meetings at her home which trained other women to lecture and advocate in support of the Neo-Malthusian cause.[133]

Towards the end of the century, support for birth control was slowly beginning to gain ground in the mainstream women's movement. When the Freethinker Florence Fenwick Miller joined Bradlaugh and Besant's defence committee in 1877, she was looked at askance by leaders of the suffrage campaign, endangering her career as lecturer for the cause.[134] By 1896, however, Fenwick Miller was able to place an advertisement for a birth control manual in *The Woman's Signal*, without jeopardising her editorship of this leading feminist periodical.[135] Jane Clapperton and Florence Dixie were among other freethinking feminists publicly advocating Neo-Malthusianism in the 1880s and 1890s.[136] Hypatia Bradlaugh Bonner's *Reformer* also supported birth control, even printing an article in favour of abortion.[137] By the beginning of the twentieth century Neo-Malthusianism also received the support of prominent suffrage activists Edith How-Martyn and Teresa Billington, who, along with Alice Vickery and her daughter-in-law Bessie Drysdale, formed the Women's Freedom League in 1907.

Bessie Drysdale (née Ingman Edwards) was already a freethinking Ethical Society member and supporter of family limitation when she married Alice's son Charles Vickery Drysdale in 1898. Bessie and Charles Vickery quickly assumed a central role in the Malthusian League. Their leadership amplified an already existing current of eugenicist thought, and they argued that physically unfit individuals should be discouraged from reproducing.[138] The new couple combined birth control advocacy with support for a wide range of women's rights: Bessie served time in Holloway Prison for militant suffrage activity in 1907 and Charles Vickery joined the Men's League for Women's Franchise that same year.[139] In 1911 and 1912 he promoted the feminist case for birth control in the pages of *The Freewoman*, calling upon 'feminist leaders' to recognise the centrality of control over maternity to the wider struggle for emancipation. His aim was to both challenge and reassure those in the women's movement who remained hostile to or uncertain of Neo-Malthusian methods: 'in addressing Women's Suffrage meetings, even in the open air,' he insisted, 'I have personally received nothing but the most respectful and interested attention.'[140] Charles Vickery condemned 'the horrible ideas concerning "purity" and "sin" put forward by religion'. These, he argued, 'told chiefly upon women' and often result in the unnatural repression of female sexuality, which was otherwise as powerful as man's.[141]

Secularism, as both intellectual framework and political network, remained important to the birth control movement into the twentieth century. Though the majority of the Malthusian League's propaganda continued to consist of turgid proselytising for Malthusian economics, it did also disseminate some practical advice, first in Besant's *Law of Population* (1878), then in the *Malthusian Handbook* (1893) by Secularist George Standring, and finally in its own pamphlet in 1913.[142] The majority of working-class women were not able to access information on contraception until after the First World War, when Marie Stopes opened the first birth control clinic in Holloway, London in 1921. Historian Miriam Benn has suggested that by this period the Drysdale-Vickery family were becoming outflanked in their own movement by activists such as Stella Browne, who, as a lecturer for the Malthusian League from 1914, eschewed economic lectures in favour of direct and practical advice. Yet Benn also noted the crucial role this Freethinking family played in paving the way for birth control dissemination in the post-war era. Alice Vickery had always advocated some form of district visiting or family visits in which women could be informed about 'hygiene' (the common euphemism for contraception). She had also endorsed the idea of giving practical lectures to single sex audiences as early as 1896, though this was not carried out in any large scale way until 1917 when Vickery provided clinical instruction for about one hundred working-class women in Rotherhithe, London. Along with Charles Vickery and Bessie, Alice also helped to set up and financially support a Women's Welfare Clinic in South London founded only a few months after Stopes' clinic.[143]

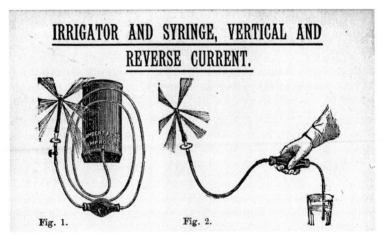

Figure 5 Advertisement for vaginal douche to be used as contraceptive device in 1889 edition of Annie Besant's *Law of Population*.

The intimate relationship between Secularism and Malthusianism has rarely been accounted for, in that many historians have taken it as a given that birth control should have been backed by secular thinkers rather than exploring the 'how' and 'why' of Freethought as a movement disseminating, championing, and agonising over the principles of family limitation.[144] J. A. Bank's work on *Secularism and the Size of Families* is exceptional in providing an in-depth analysis of 'The Religious Roots of Malthusian Controversy', discussing some of the ways in which Freethought lent intellectual foundations to birth control advocacy.[145] Yet Banks conceived of nineteenth-century Secularism as a set of ideas rather than as a political movement, and so failed to identify the links between Freethinkers' Malthusianism and their feminist activities. He concluded that it was not possible to say whether Secularist Malthusians advocated birth control as an aid to female emancipation and incorrectly identified 'pioneer feminists' such as Bessie Raynor Parkes and Barbara Leigh Smith Bodichon as having separate and distinct political goals from the Freethinkers.[146] Foregrounding the role of the Freethought movement in the development of birth control advocacy in fact reveals many hitherto unrecognised women's rights connections and sheds new light on the ambiguous relationship between feminism and family limitation.

Conclusion

Freethought made an important contribution to Victorian thinking on sexuality, especially to the development of feminist attitudes to heterosexual love and marriage. Sexual morality became the focus for Secularists' attempts to establish an ethical framework independent of the Church. Whether they liked it or not, Freethinkers' renunciation of Christianity also entailed a rejection of the very foundations upon which traditional ideas of marriage and sexuality rested. This opened the way to alternative models of sexual relations, resulting in a number of different proposals being put forward within Freethinking circles throughout the century. Some Secularists, such as George Drysdale, favoured an extreme libertarian vision of multiple sexual relationships allowing for the full enjoyment of physical passion. This was justified in explicitly Freethinking terms, as a celebration of the physical and material world over the spiritual, and as the logical conclusion of the Secularist principles of freedom and moral autonomy of the individual. However, this Freethinking vision of sexual freedom was also strongly opposed by others in the movement, who not only feared for the reputation of Secularism but were also concerned to guard against the exploitation of women. Debates and divisions within Freethought need to be understood, therefore, in the context of the movement's longstanding feminist tradition.

Freethought was an important factor in the emergence of sex radicalism at the turn of the twentieth century. Despite ambivalence among the Secularist leadership, the Free Lovers at *The Adult* were right to compare themselves to the 'heretics and freethinkers of old' who sought only the right to question conventional belief systems.[147] The arrest in 1898 of George Bedborough, editor of *The Adult*, proved once and for all that, on questions of free discussion, Free Lovers and Freethinkers were united. Bedborough was charged for selling Havelock Ellis' *Studies in the Psychology of Sex* – a sexology volume that dealt with 'sexual inversion' (homosexuality). Copies of *The Adult* were also seized by police, resulting in ten more obscenity charges. The Secularists immediately rose to the challenge, with G. W. Foote heading up Bedborough's Freedom of the Press Defence Committee, whose members included G. J. Holyoake, and other leading Freethinkers J. M. Robertson, George Standring, Edward Truelove and Charles Watts. Many of these men had themselves faced imprisonment for charges of blasphemy or obscenity. They ultimately proved more stalwart in defence of the sex radicals than Bedborough himself, who made a deal with the police and pleaded guilty to three charges of obscenity.[148] Hypatia Bradlaugh Bonner also opposed the arrest of Bedborough and defended Havelock Ellis' book as 'a scientific work by a writer of such distinction'.[149] Secularists were again at the centre of things when, a decade later, sex radicals at *The Freewoman* mounted a direct challenge to the respectability of the women's movement through an explicit assertion of woman's right to freedom of sexual expression.[150] *The Freewoman* was banned by W. H. Smith newsagents in 1912, but was strongly supported by Freethinkers both as readers and contributors.[151] By the eve of the First World War, as Jacqueline de Vries had noted, the sexual transgression of the 'New Women' and 'Freewomen' was firmly associated in the public mind with religious scepticism and Freethought – an association which can now be understood and traced back to a feminist current which began in the Freethinking movements of the early nineteenth century.[152]

Notes

1 For the influence and importance of *Elements*, see J. M. Benn, *The Predicaments of Love* (London: Pluto Press, 1992); M. Mason, *The Making of Victorian Sexual Attitudes* (Oxford & New York: Oxford University Press, 1994).

2 *The National Reformer* (*NR*), 14 June 1862, pp. 6–7.

3   For a full biography of George Drysdale, see Benn (1992).

4   G. Drysdale, *The Elements of Social Science; or, Physical, Sexual and Natural Religion by a Graduate of Medicine* 7th edn (London: Edward Truelove, 1867) (first published 1854), pp. 1–8, 161.

5   *Ibid.*, pp. 427–31.

6   *Ibid.*, p. 373.

7   *Ibid.*, pp. 368, 78, 353–5, 377.

8   The terms 'birth control' and 'contraception' were unheard of in the nineteenth century, when advocates referred either to 'preventative checks' or, even more obliquely, to 'Malthusianism'. All these terms, however, will be used interchangeably in this chapter for ease of expression.

9   Drysdale (1867), pp. 1, 64, 157–60, 13.

10 *Ibid.*, pp. 355–6, 172.

11 *Ibid.*, pp. 378–9.

12 *Ibid.*, p. 376.

13 *Ibid.*, p. 380.

14 Benn (1992), pp. 10, 14; Mason (1994), p. 204.

15 For a discussion of accusations of sexual depravity levelled at Owenite feminists, see B. Taylor, *Eve and the New Jerusalem. Socialism and Feminism in the Nineteenth Century* (London: Virago, 1983).

16 *Investigator*, August 1854, pp. 77–9.

17 *The Reasoner* (*Reasoner*), 25 March 1855, p. 198.

18 *Ibid.*, 10 September 1854, pp. 161–2.

19 *Ibid.*, 6 May 1855, p. 44.

20 *Ibid.*, 3 June 1855, p. 76.

21 *Ibid.*, 8 July 1855, p. 116.

22 *NR*, 12 May 1860, p. 8.

23 For a fuller account of this split, see Benn (1992), p. 15.

24 *Barker's Review*, 7 September 1861, pp. 3–6.

25 *Barker's Review*, 7 September 1861, p. 16, 28 September 1861, p. 57.

26 For an interesting perspective on the militant moralism of Secularism, see G. Himmelfarb, *Victorian Minds* (London: Weidenfeld & Nicolson, 1968) (first published 1952), pp. 300–13.

27 Mason believes that support within the Secularist movement for *Elements* was about equal to outright hostility to it, with a very large section prevaricating or compromising; Mason (1994), pp. 207–8.

28 *Reasoner*, 5 August 1855, p. 150.

29 *Ibid.*, 29 July 1855, p. 142, 24 February 1856, p. 59.

30 *Barker's Review*, 7 September 1861, pp. 29–30.

31 This is seen as part of a general shift within radicalism away from the utopian visions of the early part of the century in favour of trade unionism and self improvement; J. Belcham, *Popular Radicalism in Nineteenth-Century Britain* (London: Macmillan, 1996). The earlier desire to transform the social roles of men and women, and the ways in which they related to each other, is seen to have disappeared from radical movements in this period; R. Porter & L. Hall (eds.), *The Facts of Life: The Creation of Sexual Knowledge in Britain 1650–1850* (New Haven & London: Yale University Press,

1995); G. Frost, *Living in Sin: Cohabiting as Husband and Wife in Nineteenth-Century England* (Manchester: Manchester University Press, 2008), pp. 195, 197.

32 Mason (1994).

33 Mason has been widely criticised for ignoring the importance of feminist contributions to wider nineteenth-century thinking on sexuality; see M. Vicinus, 'Review of Michael Mason's *The Making of Victorian Sexuality* and *The Making of Victorian Sexual Attitudes*', *Journal of Social History* 29:2 (1995), 470–2; F. Mort & L. Nead, 'Sexuality, Modernity and the Victorians', *Journal of Victorian Culture* 1:1 (Spring 1996), 118–30; J. Bristow, 'Respecting Respectability: "Victorian Sexuality" and the Copulatory Imagination', *History Workshop Journal* 41 (Spring 1996), 286–92.

34 For Law's response to *Elements*, see *NR*, 30 November 1861, p. 8.

35 *NR*, 14 June 1862, pp. 6–7.

36 *Ibid.*, p. 7.

37 P. Annet, *Social Bliss Considered* (1749), quoted in J. Fieser (ed.), *Early Responses to Hume. Moral, Literary and Political Writings* 2 vols (Bristol: Thoemmes, 1999) ii, pp. 13–19. Other works in this tradition of libertine sex reform include Thomas Holcroft, *Anna St. Ives* (1792); W. Godwin, *An Enquiry Concerning Political Justice* (1793); H. Kitchner, *Letter on Marriage* (1812); J. Lawrence, *The Empire of the Nairs* (1811); Dr Thomas Bell's *Kalogynomia* (1821). For a discussion of such work, see M. L. Bush, *What Is Love? Richard Carlile's Philosophy of Sex* (New York & London: Verso, 1998), pp. 32–4; Taylor (2003), pp. 198–202; Frost (2008), pp. 170–80. Iain McCalman has argued that late eighteenth- and early nineteenth-century plebeian infidels encouraged the association between religious and sexual unorthodoxy, and that radical Freethinking circles overlapped with the world of illegal pornography; see I. McCalman, *Radical Underworld. Prophets, Revolutionaries and Pornographers in London, 1815–1840* (Cambridge: Cambridge University Press, 1988).

38 R. Carlile, *Every Woman's Book or What is Love?* (London, 1826, repr. Bush (1998)), pp. 55–80, 88–9.

39 R. Owen, *Lectures on the Marriages of the Priesthood in the Old Immoral World* (Leeds: J. Hobson, 1835); R. Owen, *The Marriage System in the New Moral World* (Leeds: J. Hobson, 1838). For a full account of Owenite critiques of marriage and the family, see Taylor (1983).

40 *New Moral World (NMW)*, 11 July 1840, pp. 19–20. These arguments were made by many others in the movement, including Frances Wright, Frances Morrison and Catherine and Goodwyn Barmby. By the time Martin began her lecturing career they had become a generally, if not universally, accepted part of the Owenite platform; for example, see *NMW*, 12 June 1841, p. 377.

41 *NMW*, 27 October 1838, p. 3.

42 Martin, *Religion Superseded*, pp. 6–7.

43 *NMW*, 9 May 1840, p. 1300.

44 For Christian attacks, see R. Matthews, *Is Marriage Worth Perpetuating? The Ninth of a Series of Lectures against Socialism Delivered in the Mechanics' Institution, Southampton Buildings, Under the Direction of the Committee of the London City Mission* (London: n.p., 1840). For female opposition to Owenite feminism see an account of hostility to Margaret Chappellsmith ('her with the seven husbands'), *NMW*, 26 June 1841, p. 402. See also Taylor (1983), Chapter 6. Working-class women's

concern about attacks on the conventional marriage system had been expressed prior to the emergence of Owenite feminism. When Richard Carlile published *Every Woman's Book* he encountered open hostility from women in some working-class communities; see Bush (1998), p. 122. Secularists faced similar attacks from Christians much later in the century. In 1881, for example, the Bishop of Manchester, Dr Fraser, told an audience of working men that Secularism taught men and women infidelity and encouraged men to abandon their wives when they became sick; *The Freethinker* (*Freethinker*), 23 October 1881, p. 91. Annie Besant's pamphlet, *God's Views on Marriage*, was intended as a reply to such 'slander', and dedicated to Dr Fraser, pointing out that the Bible itself was the purveyor of such 'immoral' views. See also *Freethinker*, 25 December 1881, p. 167.

45 The first organised campaign for marriage reform was sparked off by the publication of Barbara Leigh Smith Bodichon's *A Brief Summary in Plain Language of the Most Important Laws Concerning Women* (1854), which led the Law Amendment Society to introduce a Married Women's Property Bill that proposed to allow wives the same right as single women to make a will and hold property.

46 *NR*, 21 February 1869, p. 125, 25 April 1869, p. 267.

47 A. Besant, *The Political Status of Women* 3rd edn (London: Freethought Publishing Co., 1874[?], repr. J. Saville (ed.), *A Selection of the Social and Political Pamphlets of Annie Besant. With a Preface and Biographical Notes by John Saville*, New York: Augustus M. Kelley, 1970), p. 11; *Secular Review* (*SR*), 27 September 1879, pp. 193-4, 4 October 1879, pp. 212-14, 18 October 1879, pp. 246-7.

48 S. S. Hennell, *Present Religion as Faith Owning Fellowship with Thought*, 3 vols (London: Trubnor & Co., 1865, 1873, 1887) iii (1887), pp. 351-3, 348-9.

49 See P. Levine, '"So Few Prizes and So Many Blanks": Marriage and Feminism in Later Nineteenth-Century England', *Journal of British Studies* 28 (April 1989), 150-74. *The National Reformer* lauded the success of the 1870 Married Women's Property Bill (though it noted that it did not meet all the feminists' demands) and lent its support to Wolstenholme Elmy's continued campaign; *NR*, 28 August 1870, p. 135, 18 August 1874, p. 251, 21 January 1877, p. 39, 18 March 1877, pp. 166-7.

50 L. Bland, *Banishing the Beast. English Feminism and Sexual Morality, 1885-1914* (London: Penguin Books, 1995), pp. 135-9.

51 *NR*, 28 August 1870, p. 135.

52 Hennell, iii (1887), p. 307.

53 *Ibid.*, p. 317.

54 *Reasoner*, 15 July 1855, pp. 121-2.

55 *Ibid.*, 20 May 1855, p. 60.

56 *Ibid.*, 1 July 1855, p. 108.

57 A. Besant, *The Legalisation of Female Slavery In England* (London: Besant & Bradlaugh, 1885), p. 8. First published as a series of articles in *The National Reformer*, 4 June 1876, pp. 352-3; 18 June 1876 pp. 387-8.

58 Besant, *Female Slavery*, p. 8.

59 *Ibid.*, pp. 6, 2.

60 For Besant on Drysdale, see A. Besant, *The Law of Population: Its Consequences, and Its Bearing Upon Human Conduct and Morals* (London: Freethought Publishing Co., 1878[?]).

61 Benn (1992), pp. 147–63.

62 Quoted in Bland (1995), p. 134. Bland found that 'Most feminists disagreed with Besant's "free unions"'; Bland (1995), pp. 153–4.

63 S. S. Holton, 'Free Love and Victorian Feminism: The Divers Matrimonials of Elizabeth Wolstenholme and Ben Elmy', *Victorian Studies* 37:2 (Winter 1994), 199–222, 210, 214, 205. See also S. S. Holton, *Suffrage Days. Stories from the Women's Suffrage Movement* (London & New York: Routledge, 1996). Although she did not explore this further, Holton noted that 'the secularist movement was the main inheritor of the Owenite socialist legacy, a legacy which included a questioning of traditional family forms, and more particularly, women's position in marriage'; Holton (1994), p. 205.

64 B. Caine, *English Feminism 1780–1980* (Oxford: Oxford University Press, 1997), pp. 96–7.

65 *Secular Chronicle (SC)*, 31 March 1878, pp. 145–6.

66 Frost (2008), p. 195.

67 H. Quilter (ed.), *Is Marriage a Failure? The Most Important Letters on the Subject in the Daily Telegraph* (London: Swan Sonnenschein & Co., 1888).

68 M. Caird, 'Marriage', *Westminster Review*, CXXX (1888), 186–201, 190–1.

69 J. Walkowitz, 'Science, Feminism and Romance: The Men and Women's Club 1885–1889', *History Workshop Journal* 21 (Spring 1986), 37–59, 44, 51–2.

70 J. Clapperton, *Scientific Meliorism and the Evolution of Happiness* (London: Kegan Paul & Co., 1885), p. 311.

71 Hennell (1887), p. 346; *The Women's Penny Paper*, 12 October 1889, p. 8.

72 Clapperton (1885), pp. 319–20.

73 A. Humpherys, 'The Journal that Did: Form and Content in *The Adult* (1897–1899)', *Media History* 9:1 (2003), 63–78, 63–5. For Clapperton's ambiguous reply to an invitation to join, see *The Adult (Adult)*, January 1898, pp. 134–5. For Vickery and Drsydale, see January 1898, p. 139.

74 *Adult*, June 1897, September 1897, January 1898.

75 *Ibid.*, October 1897, p. 34.

76 *Adult*, October 1897, pp. 40–41.

77 *Ibid.*, April 1898, p. 88. Northcote viewed Bradlaugh and Besant as champions of this tradition despite their personal ambivalence regarding Free Love; O. Northcote, 'Ruled by the Tomb: A Discussion of Freethought and Free Love' (Chicago: M. Harman, 1898), pp. 8–11.

78 Reported in Northcote (1898), pp. 12–13, and *Adult*, January 1898, p. 156–62.

79 Northcote (1898), p. 12. See also debate in *Free Review*, July 1896, p. 313–18, September 1896, pp. 545–9, October 1896, pp. 191–4. J. M. Robertson edited this Freethought periodical from 1893 to 1895.

80 *Adult*, January 1898, pp. 162–4.

81 For the press, see A. Humpherys, 'The Journals that Did: Writing about Sex in the late 1890s', *19 Interdisciplinary Studies in the Long Nineteenth Century*, 3 (2006) [online edition]. For this radical milieu in general, see S. Rowbotham & J. Weeks, *Socialism and the New Life: The Personal and Sexual Politics of Edward Carpenter and Havelock Ellis* (London: Pluto Press, 1977); S. Rowbotham, *Edward Carpenter: A Life of Liberty and Love* (London & New York: Verso, 2008). For Free Love and anarchism, see J. Greenway, 'Speaking Desire: Anarchism and Free Love as Utopian Performance

in Fin de Siècle Britain', in L. Davis & R. Kinna (eds.), *Anarchism and Utopianism* (Manchester: Manchester University Press, 2009), pp. 153–70.

82 For 'varying and contradictory' attitudes towards free unions within socialist leadership, see K. Hunt, *Equivocal Feminists: The Social Democratic Federation and the Woman Question 1884–1911* (Cambridge: Cambridge University Press, 1996), pp. 81–7. When Edith Lanchester was committed by her family to a lunatic asylum in 1895 for deciding to live in a free union, her release was campaigned for by the Legitimation League but not the SDF nor any prominent feminist organisation; Bland (1995), pp. 159–61.

83 *Adult*, April 1898, p. 62; *Freethinker*, 13 March 1898, pp. 163–4.

84 *The Reformer*, 15 May 1900, pp. 264–74, 15 February 1902, pp. 111–17, 15 December 1902, pp. 758–9. See also 15 December, p. 713, 15 October 1902, pp.628–33.

85 *Adult*, February 1898, p. 3.

86 *Ibid.*, May 1898, pp. 93–5; *Freethinker*, 3 April 1898, p. 218.

87 *Adult*, September 1897, pp. 20–5, October 1897, pp. 40–44.

88 *Ibid.*, October 1897, pp. 34–8. The more radical and potentially promiscuous Free Love could still accommodate a feminist agenda; see *Adult*, September 1897, pp. 30–32, January 1898, pp. 138–40.

89 Charles Watts in *Freethinker*, 13 March 1898, p. 163; *Adult*, April 1898, pp. 61–2. J. M. Robertson likewise reportedly held that under the present economic system which made women so vulnerable, it was not possible to do away with marriage entirely although 'this of course does not preclude the later recognition of the expediency of freedom'; Northcote (1898), p. 12.

90 This was how Foote described the approach of the Legitimation League; *Freethinker* 3 April 1898, p. 220; *Adult*, May 1898, p. 94.

91 'Fortunately, the rank and file of the movement are more logical than their leaders', George Bedborough in *Adult*, April 1898, pp. 88–9.

92 Northcote (1898), p. 20.

93 For the history of the birth control movement in Britain, see P. Fryer, *The Birth Controllers* (London: Secker & Warburg, 1965); A. McLaren, *Birth Control in Nineteenth-Century England* (London: Croom Helm, 1978); H. Cook, *The Longest Revolution: English Women, Sex, and Contraception 1800–1975* (Oxford: Oxford University Press, 2004). Angus McLaren noted the 'often ignored' connection between birth control and Freethought, but implied that it was relatively self-explanatory, referring simply to 'the natural interest freethinkers would have had in contraception' as a means of challenging the 'moral dictates' of the Christian Church. He did not examine further how or why Freethought ideology might have been particularly accommodating to birth control advocacy; McLaren (1978), pp. 56–7.

94 Carlile (1826), p. 102; C. Knowlton, *Fruits of Philosophy. An Essay on the Population Question. A New Edition with Notes* (London: Freethought Publishing Co., 1877) (first published 1832), pp. 5, 41–2.

95 *Reasoner* 4:91 (1848), pp. 177–79. [N.B. Copies of *The Reasoner* held in the Bishopsgate Library for 1847–48 are not individually dated, only volume and number are listed.] Martin was a close friend of birth control advocates Richard Carlile and George Jacob Holyoake and it is likely that, in the Freethought culture of free intellectual exchange between men and women, they would have discussed the issue. She was

also committed to medical self-help, a principle that McLaren sees as central to the early birth control movement. McLaren also noted Martin's lectures and argued that 'the evidence strongly suggests that these contained birth control information'; McLaren (1978), pp. 78, 97.

96 A. Holyoake, *Large or Small Families: On Which Side Lies the Balance of Comfort?* (n.p. London, 1870), p. 1.

97 See, for example, *NR*, 19 July 1862, p. 2, 20 September 1862, pp. 1–2, 1 November 1862, pp. 1–2, 25 October 1862, p. 5, 17 October 1863, p. 7, 21 November 1863, p. 6, 12 December 1863, p. 7.

98 A. Besant & C. Bradlaugh, 'Introduction', in Knowlton (1877), pp. v–viii, vi.

99 For both Watts' and Bradlaugh's views on the matter, see *NR*, 21 January 1877, pp. 34, 42.

100 Besant & Bradlaugh (1877), p. vi.

101 For this argument, see F. H. A. Micklewright, 'The Rise and Decline of English Neo-Malthusianism', *Population Studies* 15:1 (1961), 32–51; Mason (1994), p. 208.

102 K. E. Watts, *Mrs Watts' Reply to Mr. Bradlaugh's Misrepresentations* (London: Co-operative Printing & Stationary Co., 1877[?]), pp. 5–7.

103 G. W. Foote, *Mr Bradlaugh's Trial and the Freethought Party* (London: Charles Watts, 1877[?]), pp. 1, 11, 12.

104 For the various positions of Secularist leaders regarding the Knowlton trial, see *SR*, 16 June 1877, p. 30, 23 June 1877, pp. 41, 47, 30 June 1877, pp. 58, 61, 64, 7 July 1877, pp. 65–6, 14 July 1877, pp. 85–6, 89, 91, 95. See also P. Agate, *Sexual Economy as Taught by Charles Bradlaugh MP. With Addendum by Saladin* (London: W. Stewart & Co., 1886?), p. 5 for a report of Holyoake and Law 'fudging' the issue; *SC*, 22 July 1877, p. 45, 29 July 1877, p. 58 for a report of the meeting in protest at Cleveland Hall.

105 *SC*, 22 July 1877, p. 45, 29 July 1877, p. 58.

106 Foote (1877[?]), pp. 10–11.

107 McLaren (1978), pp. 107–11.

108 See, for example, Besant's revulsion for the working-class practice of 'prolonged nursing' and her belief that if abstinence was the only solution offered to the problem of over-population this would merely result in the 'prudent' avoiding marriage while the inferior classes of society continued to reproduce with abandon; A. Besant, *Law of Population*, pp. 35, 42. For Besant's attempts to combine her support for birth control with her subsequent commitment to socialism, see M. Terrier, 'Annie Besant's Neo-Malthusianism and its Consequences for her Socialism (1877–1891)' (paper presented to the Socialist History Society, Bishopsgate Institute, London, 9 November 2011).

109 Symes was from Newcastle upon Tyne and had been a 'Wesleyan' minister before converting to Secularism, a subject upon he occasionally lectured; see *SR*, 18 March 1877, p. 55.

110 *NR*, 29 July 1877, p. 513.

111 *Ibid.*, 22 April 1877, p. 251.

112 *Ibid.*, 26 September 1869, pp. 196–7.

113 *Ibid.*, 22 April 1877, pp. 241–48.

114 *Ibid.*, 23 June 1877, p. 404.

115 *Ibid.*, 23 September 1877, p. 644.

116 Carlile (1826), pp. 83, 94.

117 Drysdale (1867), p. 376.

118 Agate, *Sexual Economy*, pp. 52, 54.
119 F. W. Newman, *The Corruption Now Called Neo-Malthusianism. Written by Request for the Moral Reform Union. With Notes by Dr. E. Blackwell* (London: The Moral Reform Union, 1889), p. 6.
120 J. A. & O. Banks, *Feminism and Family Planning in Victorian England* (Liverpool: Liverpool University Press, 1964), pp. 9–10.
121 *Ibid.*, p. 92.
122 *Ibid.*, pp. 92–3.
123 R. Strachey, *Millicent Garrett Fawcett* (London: John Murray, 1931), pp. 88–9.
124 Quoted in Bland (1995), p. 195.
125 Bland (1995), p. xix. See also L. Hall, 'Suffrage, Sex and Science', in M. Joannou & J. Purvis (eds.), *The Woman's Suffrage Movement: New Feminist Perspectives* (Manchester: Manchester University Press, 2009), pp. 188–200, 190.
126 McLaren (1978), p. 78.
127 For a culture of radical medical autonomy more generally, see K. Gleadle, 'The Age of Physiological Reformers: Rethinking Gender and Domesticity in the Age of Reform' in A. Burns & J. Innes (eds.), *Rethinking the Age of Reform, 1780-1850* (Cambridge, Cambridge University Press, 2003), pp. 200–19. It is possible that the later mainstream feminist critique of the male medical establishment and hostility to science per se also drew on this tradition. While one might see Freethought, with its celebration of the triumph and dominance of science, as the polar opposite of Frances Power Cobbe's anti-vivisection movement and attacks on 'medical materialism', in fact the two discourses may have shared intellectual origins. Feminist opposition to the male medical establishment during the campaign against the Contagious Diseases Acts echoed Emma Martin's critique of her exclusion as a midwife by male doctors and Harriet Law was also well known for her hostility to medical men.
128 Jackson maintains that Ellis Ethelmer, author of a number of sex education manuals, was the pen name of Elizabeth Wolstenholme Elmy; M. Jackson, *The Real Facts of Life: Feminism and the Politics of Sexuality c. 1850-1940* (London: Taylor & Francis, 1994), p. 81. Bland claims that Ben Elmy was the author, but that Wolstenholme Elmy probably helped to write them; Bland (1995), pp. 140–3. Most recently, Wolstenholme Emly's biographer has argued that Ethelmer was Ben Elmy; M. Wright, 'Elizabeth Wolstenholme Elmy: A Biography' (unpublished doctoral thesis, University of Portsmouth, 2007), p. 18.
129 Jackson (1994), pp. 81–102.
130 Bland (1995), p. 205.
131 *The Malthusian*, April 1879, p. 18; during her trial Besant also discussed the health complications caused by numerous pregnancies; *NR* 23 June 1877, p. 404.
132 R. Ledbetter, *A History of the Malthusian League, 1877-1927* (Columbus: Ohio State University Press, 1976), p. 19. Ledbetter also notes that most initial members of the League were also members of the NSS, p. 25.
133 Benn (1992), pp. 168, 184, 199.
134 R. T. Van Arsdel, *Florence Fenwick Miller. Victorian Feminist, Journalist and Educator* (Aldershot: Ashgate, 2001), pp. 79–80, 92–3. Fenwick Miller began lecturing unofficially for the Central Women's Suffrage Committee in 1875 and continued to lecture on suffrage after 1877, pp. 55, 93.

135 *Ibid.*, p. 190. The advertisement appeared in *The Woman's Signal* on 15 October 1896.

136 Clapperton (1885), pp. 303–4; Benn (1992), p. 184.

137 For Neo-Malthusianism, see *Reformer*, 15 October 1897, p. 232, 15 December 1897, pp. 279–81; for discussion of abortion, see 15 July 1898, pp. 117–18, 15 August 1898, p. 164–5, 15 September, pp. 197–8.

138 Alice Vickery had always felt strongly that women should take responsibility for not passing on hereditary diseases. She and Charles did not believe in restricting marriage laws or in sterilisation, preferring to educate rather than coerce the public, but they did refer to some form of state intervention (the details of which remained vague) to prevent overly large families. Bessie and Charles Vickery had a more dogmatic faith than his parents in the eugenic consequences of limiting families and their views on this subject became increasingly right wing in the twentieth century; Benn (1992), pp. 168–9, 187–8,199–200.

139 Benn (1992), pp. 186, 191.

140 *The Freewoman* (*Freewoman*), 30 November 1911, pp. 35–7.

141 *Freewoman*, 7 December 1911, pp. 51–2, 4 January 1912, pp. 132–5, 11 January 1912, p. 151, 25 January 1912, pp. 194–6.

142 Standring (the publisher of the Malthusian League's literature) wrote the handbook in collaboration with the League's Secretary William Reynolds, though the published pamphlet did not attribute authorship; Benn (1992), pp. 165–6.

143 Benn (1992), pp. 207, 166, 204–5, 213–4.

144 R. A. Soloway, *Birth Control and the Population Question in England, 1877–1930* (University of North Carolina Press: Chapel Hill & London, 1982), esp. Chapter 5. Ledbetter noted the central role played by Secularists but did not explore the implications of their ideology for the development of the birth control movement; pp. 11, 25; Ledbetter (1976).

145 J. A. Banks, *Victorian Values: Secularism and the Size of Families* (London: Routledge & Kegan Paul, 1981), pp. 12–21, 22–30.

146 *Ibid.*, pp. 33, 37.

147 *Adult*, January 1898, p. 173.

148 Humpherys (2003), pp. 68–70; *Adult*, August 1898, p. 191.

149 *Reformer*, 15 June 1898, p. 86.

150 Bland notes that this assertion of women's right to be sexual represented a 'radical development' from earlier feminist discussions of sex and marriage; Bland, 'Freewoman', p. 6.

151 Three out of the eight speakers advertised in the 1912 July–October programme for the Freewoman Discussion Society were directly associated with organised Freethought; *Freewoman* 27 June 1912, p. 115: Dr C. V. Drysdale, Guy Aldred, E. S. P. Haynes. For their contributions, see 14 December 1911, p. 74, 25 January 1912, pp. 186–7, 8 February 1912, pp. 236–8, 25 July 1912, pp. 189–91.

152 J. de Vries, 'More than Paradoxes to Offer. Feminism, History and Religious Cultures', in S. Morgan & J. de Vries (eds), *Women, Gender and Religious Cultures in Britain 1800–1940* (Abingdon: Routledge, 2010), pp. 188–210, 196. Grant Allen's New Woman novel *The Woman Who Did* (1895), for example, became famous for its depiction of free unions, featuring a heroine whose rejection of married life was inseparable from her Freethought.

Conclusion

First wave feminism involved a fierce battle of ideas over religion – a battle which was itself crucial in the creation of modern understandings of religion and secularisation. Freethought was thus a significant current in the women's movement, existing alongside and in competition with the Christian values that dominated it. The Woman Question became a key ground upon which Christians clashed with Secularists over which belief system offered most to women. Such questions were also central *within* the women's movement, as 'religious' feminists of varying perspectives debated their Freethinking sisters.

Infidel Feminism is the first full historical account of these Freethinking feminists, most of whom have received only a passing mention in previous histories of feminism and Freethought. Through their stories it has been possible to trace a distinctive and continuous tradition of Freethinking feminism from the 1830s through to the First World War. Successive generations of women in the Secularist movement identified with the figure of the Freethinking feminist as public intellectual – a role that enabled the few women brave enough to assume it to intervene in male-dominated environments to an unusual degree. The female Freethinker also offered a model of transgressive femininity, the legacy of which can be found in the mass struggles for the suffrage and a growing movement for sexual freedom in the early twentieth century.

Freethinking feminists made an important contribution to the post-1850 women's movement. The early feminist pioneers occupied the same intellectual and social milieu as the leaders of Freethought. And the predominantly Christian tone of the Victorian women's movement did not prevent Freethinkers from making an important impact, as the careers of Elizabeth Wolstenholme Elmy and Annie Besant demonstrate. Yet the anxiety felt by mainstream feminist leaders towards their movement's more radical antecedents, and their concern to avoid being tainted with infidelism, led to a marked downplaying of the role of Freethought in subsequent histories of 'the Cause'.

Uncovering this previously obscured Secularist current has, paradoxically, only been made possible by the 'religious turn' in gender history. Greater attentiveness to the religious identities, motivations and debates that were so important to the Victorian and Edwardian women's movements, has challenged understandings of feminism as a primarily liberal, Enlightened and *secular* rights discourse.[1] But if the secularism of British feminism can no longer be assumed, then the Secularist current which undoubtedly existed within it has to be examined, interrogated and explained. In providing an in-depth account of Freethinking feminism, this book seeks to expand the remit of a historical approach seeking to trace the 'religious roots' of feminism, to incorporate the role of anti-religious or Secularist thought.

A history of female Secularists emphasises the continuities between the feminism associated with the Owenite movement in the first half of the nineteenth century and the organised women's movement post-1850. While the link between class emancipation and women's freedom was largely severed after the collapse of Owenism,[2] many other elements of Owenite feminism persisted as a minority current in the women's movement, kept alive by Freethinkers. The shift from the socially radical and unrespectable Socialist feminism of the Owenite movement to the more sober Christian-influenced feminism of the latter half of the century should not, therefore, be over-emphasised. In fact, many Freethinkers who had been active in or associated with Owenite feminism (such as George Jacob Holyoake and Sophia Dobson Collet) went on to play key roles in the later women's movement. Though the political landscape might have changed considerably, no break in the activities of these Freethinking feminists occurred. They simply struggled on, adjusting their vision to the new conditions. And in many ways, the agenda of the Freethinking feminists changed very little over the course of this period. Harriet Law, for example, was already lecturing on the 'Degraded and Depressed Condition of Women Caused by Religion and Ignorance' in 1861, when the women's movement was only just beginning. It is unlikely that Law would have seen herself as embarking upon a new project; instead she was carrying on the work of Emma Martin, who had passed away only ten years previously.

Identifying these continuities has particularly important implications for a historical understanding of feminist attitudes to sexuality. The Secular movement provided a forum in which the more radical ideas of the Owenite feminists, on the abolition of marriage, free unions and birth control, continued to be discussed. This was the case even during the middle decades of the century when the mainstream of the women's movement refused to countenance the possibility of women expressing their sexuality outside marriage. Freethinking feminism might therefore be viewed as the 'missing link' between radical ideas on love, sex and marriage developed by Owenite feminists in the 1830s and 1840s, and discussions of sexual freedom that began to re-emerge in the women's movement towards the end of the nineteenth century. Given that some of the best-known advocates of Free Love in late-nineteenth and early-twentieth century England were Freethinkers or closely related to the Freethought movement, this study suggests that greater attention needs to be paid to the anti-religious intellectual context in which such arguments were made. In this later period, the religious landscape underwent important transformations. The realm of the 'religious' expanded to include non-Christian forms of theist, pantheist and occult spiritualities. The binary oppositions and outcast status upon which the Secularist movement depended, became more difficult to maintain, and organised Freethought fell into decline.

In the twenty-first century, however, religion, secularism and women's rights have returned to the political agenda in a manner which resonates powerfully with many of the themes of this book.

> The questions of gender and feminism are ... of crucial significance ... On the one hand religious movements are criticised for the notions of gender and sexuality they sanction, while on the other hand widespread participation of women in contemporary religious revivals is noted and even put forward as a characterising feature of these movements.[3]

Here, Sarah Bracke's description of a post-9/11, 'post-secular', contemporary context could equally apply to the world of Harriet Law and Annie Besant. Yet again, women's status, bodies and sexuality are at the centre of debates generated by what is widely considered to be a global 'religious revival'. Battles rage in the Christian churches over extra-marital sex, contraception, abortion, homosexuality, and (in the Church of England) women bishops. Yet it is Islam's attitudes to gender and sexuality that have provoked the most public debate. Western governments, religious leaders and feminist scholars all want to discuss the real or supposed mistreatment of women under religious laws and to ask if secularism offers a better guarantee of women's rights.

In 2001 the Bush administration in the USA referred to the oppression of women under the theocratic Taliban regime as a possible rationale for the invasion of Afghanistan. Since then, the subjection of women under Islam has provided a useful legitimating discourse for further US/UK-led military intervention in the Middle East – sometimes invoked directly, as in Laura Bush's 'radio address' (an official White House address broadcast to the nation soon after the US invasion of Afghanistan)[4], sometimes tangentially in relation to debates over the wearing of the headscarf. Islamic veiling has played a crucial symbolic role also in the redefining of Western European national identities against further immigration and the perceived threat to 'secular' Western values posed by already existing religious (mainly Islamic) minorities. The French government has been most assertive in claiming women's rights as a key signifier of French citizenship as against the religious 'outsider' – leading to the 2004 ban on female students wearing headscarves to school. The 'essential values of the French community' have at times been defined in direct opposition to Islam, when, for example, a French resident of Moroccan birth was denied citizenship in 2008 on the basis that she wore a full burka and therefore failed to comply with the principle of equality between the sexes.[5] In 2011 both France and Belgium became the first European nations to bring into force laws banning the wearing of Islamic face veils in public.

Britain has also witnessed a series of more muted but no less significant flashpoints. In 2006 Jack Straw, Labour MP for Blackburn, provoked outrage from some Muslims when he defended his requiring Muslim women who visited his constituency surgery to remove their face veils.[6] This led to widespread reporting of the case of a teaching assistant, Aishah Azmi, who was dismissed for refusing to remove her burka when her employers complained that it prevented her from fully communicating with her students.[7] These cases renewed the public debate on religion, secularism and women's rights, with commentators focusing upon the position of women in Islam and its teachings on female sexuality.[8] Related issues such as 'forced' marriages, so-called 'honour' killings, and sharia law have also been the subject of intense interest and discussion across the political spectrum.[9]

Many feminists worry that a 'dominant discourse' is beginning to emerge which asserts that:

'our women' (Western, Christian, white or 'whitened' and raised in the tradition of secular Enlightenment) are already liberated and thus do not need any more social incentives or emancipatory policies. 'Their women' (non-Western, non-Christian, mostly not white and not whitened, as well as alien to the Enlightenment tradition), however, are still backwards and need to be targeted for special emancipatory social actions, or even more belligerent forms of enforced 'liberation'.[10]

The situation poses pressing and complex questions for feminists, especially since, as Rosi Braidotti has pointed out, the 'traditionalist opponents' of the 'the West' frequently reiterate this set of binaries so that both sides fail to take into account the work of women's movements in both the Western and non-Western worlds, effectively deleting any feminist political agenda.[11]

Such developments have flummoxed many US and European feminists. How should we respond to right wing governments using, however superficially, women's rights to justify racist and/or aggressively imperialist agendas? Should the state have the power to forcibly liberate women from patriarchal notions of modesty, obedience and sexual purity? Is it permissible for one group of women to declare what constitutes freedom and autonomy for another? How should we understand the turn towards political and social conservatism that features strongly in many aspects of the 'religious revival'? To what extent does the active participation of women in such a revival require us to rethink our understandings of 'agency'?

In the early months of the invasions of Iraq and Afghanistan, some feminists appeared to endorse Western military interventions on the basis that women's rights needed to be defended against religious extremism. In the USA, for example, the liberal feminist organisation the Feminist Majority played a key role in publicising the 'gender apartheid' that took place in Afghanistan under the Taliban.[12] Other feminists argued that any denunciation of the mistreatment of women in Afghanistan needed also to point out the role played by the USA in instigating Taliban rule, urging the need for an anti-racist, anti-imperialist feminist politics.[13] The Revolutionary Association of the Women of Afghanistan, a grass roots feminist organisation from within the country, condemned both religious fundamentalism and US military interventions. They also continue to call for a 'secular' society.[14]

The global imperialist context has also cast a long shadow over the last decade of debate on women's rights *within* Europe. The UK-based Southall Black Sisters,[15] believing the rise of religious fundamentalism poses a threat to women in Britain, has reasserted the idea of secularism and 'secular spaces' as useful in the struggle against female oppression.[16] Elsewhere in Europe, prominent feminists who supported the French and Belgium bans on Islamic dress were strongly criticised by others who stressed that 'any unreflective brand of normative secularism [even in defending women's rights] runs the risk of complicity with anti-Islam racism and xenophobia'.[17]

Much feminist debate has turned on the question of whether secularism is an inherently Eurocentric category. Recent scholarship on the topic is influenced by broader Black feminist and post-colonial critiques which have drawn attention to the problematic race politics of many liberal universalist assumptions embedded within Western feminism.[18] The concept of secularism is increasingly identified with a Western Enlightenment and colonial heritage, and some feminists have begun to ask whether it is still a viable concept at all. Joan Scott's recent book on the French headscarf ban sums up some of the main concerns:

> [Secularism] ... has also been criticised from the left by those who see it as both a way in which states have created acceptable forms of religion (in this sense it is a "regulatory practice") and as a mask for the political domination of 'others', a form of ethnocentrism or crypto-Christianity, the particular product of the history of the European nation-state. Its claim to universalism (a false universalism in the eyes of its critics) has justified the exclusion or marginalisation of those from non-European cultures ... whose systems of belief do not separate public and private in the same way, do not, in other words, conform to those of the dominant group.[19]

Secularism, it is pointed out, is not a neutral category, denoting simply freedom from religious authority, but a historically and geographically specific concept ('the particular product of the history of the European nation-state'), and is therefore imbued with certain Enlightenment or liberal assumptions about what constitutes religion, progress and the individual. It is noted that secularism and religion are 'interdependent and necessarily linked' and that 'the secular' was also intended to imply a distinctive [re-]definition of religion as something that could be relegated to the private realm. Moreover, secularism is fundamentally structured by the religion that it disavows and thus, since it is primarily a product of the Latin Christian West, it is biased in favour of Christianity.[20] Secularity, it has been argued, rests upon a norm of masculine rationality which excludes women and their experiences, while theories of how secularisation occurs are inherently male-centred, whereby 'when men leave religion, religion is said to be dying, regardless of its continuity in women's lives'.[21] In response to Joan Scott's question, 'Is it possible to separate an abstract ideal [secularism] from its concrete history and from the political uses to which it is put?', some feminists, including Scott herself, have given a strong 'No'.[22]

Many of the analyses of secularism put forward in these feminist critiques could apply to the nineteenth- and early twentieth-century Freethought movement. The Secularism promoted by Freethinkers was very clearly the product of the Enlightenment, and was shaped by the British Protestant context in which it operated. At the same time, Secularists made claims for the universalism of their viewpoint, believing that eventually the entire world would break free from the shackles of superstition. Secularists also sought to define religion in a distinctive manner – as superstition, as a form of hysteria, and as a relic of a more primitive age. *Infidel Feminism* has also shown that secularism and religion must be understood in relation to each other – revealing how the Secularism of Freethinking feminists was not only shaped by but also emerged out of their former faith. Moreover, their vision of women's emancipation depended upon a linear conception of progress that invoked ethnocentric binaries such as civilisation vs. superstition and modernity vs. primitivism. The fundamental Freethought principles of intellectual independence, science and reason as against faith, superstition and emotion were constructed as masculine. And this could limit the emancipatory potential of Freethinking feminism, in spite of Secularism's formal commitment to women's rights, by associating femininity with superstition and therefore seeing women as partly implicated in the 'problem' of religion.

This book has insisted on the need to interrogate the category of the 'secular', to uncover the values and assumptions embedded within it. A study of Freethinking feminists shows how debates over women's rights and women's relationship to religion were an important part of the very construction of secularity and the re-definitions of religion that it entailed. It thus provides a crucial historical perspective on twenty-first-century debates, showing how the terms of these contemporary discussions were forged in the nineteenth century when the subject of 'woman' and her rights formed one of the main grounds upon which nineteenth-century religionists and Secularists founded their identities. This book's focus on a very specific historical context, however, also raises some questions regarding the contemporary feminist critique of secularism. The central argument of *Infidel Feminism* is that, although the Freethought movement was by no means unproblematic in its espousal of women's rights, there did exist a small but important cluster of women who laid claim to a language of Secularism. In doing so, they actively disrupted a dominant gender discourse which tended to construct woman as spiritual and man as secular – a binary which we today must be careful not to replicate in critiques of secularism's male-centred logic and 'othering' of female experience.

To focus on the secularism of a historically specific and politically distinctive moment is to reveal that secularism has many histories, many interpretations, and many traditions. Although the possibility of alternative secularisms has been suggested by the contemporary feminist scholars discussed here, it is not a line of thinking that has yet been pursued.[23] The Secularism examined in this book differs in very important ways from the 'dominant' form of secularism that has been subject to recent critiques. Importantly, the Secularism of Freethinking feminists was separate from any form of state power. In fact, Secularists were dissenters from a dominant Christian ideology, which the state broadly endorsed, and were subject to a substantial degree of persecution as a result. Their Secularism, therefore, may have made claims to universalism, but it was in fact an ideology of marginality, minority dissidence and critique of the status quo.

When secularism is positioned in this way, the iconoclastic and radical traditions that it can also embody provide a way of disrupting prevailing assumptions about race and gender that at other times it might be seen as endorsing. Although the Secularists' understanding of progress was imbued with contemporary notions of race and Empire, their opposition to Christianity could at times lead them to condemn not only the imperialism of Christian missions but also the 'imperialist feminism' of those who argued that British women should help to liberate their oppressed Muslim and Hindu sisters. The Secularist rejection of God-given gender roles and Christian-influenced ideas about marriage, birth control and sexual morality, enabled alternative visions of relations between the sexes. Secularism was, in this context, part of a rebel, anti-authoritarian feminist tradition. Conceived differently from formulations which would see secularism as *protecting* women's rights, it shows instead the feminist potential of a secularist emphasis on freedom of thought, and the questioning and challenging of dominant ideologies. Freethinking feminists believed that their Secularism allowed them to argue for a more extensive form of emancipation than that advocated by their Christian sisters, one unrestricted by reference to tradition, cultural norms or religious texts. Such women found secularism a liberating ideology, which allowed them to reject traditional thinking on gender and, most importantly, base their claims to freedom on no authority other than themselves.

Notes

1   The assumed secular identity of European feminism is discussed in R. Braidotti, 'In Spite of the Times: The Postsecular Turn in Feminism', *Theory, Culture and Society* 25:6 (2008), 1–24, 3,7.

2 B. Taylor, *Eve and the New Jerusalem. Socialism and Feminism in the Nineteenth Century* (London: Virago, 1983), p. 263.

3 S. Bracke, 'Conjugating the Modern/Religious, Conceptualising Female Religious Agency: Contours of a 'Post-secular Conjuncture', *Theory, Culture and Society* 25:6 (2008), 51–67, 52.

4 Laura Bush spoke of the 'brutality against women and children by the al-Quaida terrorist network'. She claimed that women especially were 'rejoicing' at the Taliban's retreat in the face of US military forces, and denounced the Taliban's ban on women working or leaving their homes unaccompanied and the 'brutal beatings' they imposed on women for laughing out loud. See L. Bush, 'Radio Address by Mrs Bush, Crawford, Texas' (The White House, 17 November 2001), www.whitehouse.gov/news/releases/2001/11/20011117.html [accessed 23 August 2008]. In March 2005 Laura Bush flew to Afghanistan to address the nation's women and to 'promote' women's education.

5 See M. Kay, 'No French Citizenship for Veiled "Radical" Islamic Wife', *The Independent*, 12 July 2008, www.independent.co.uk/news/world/europe/no-french-citizenship-for-veiled-radical-islamic-wife-865828.html [accessed 18 July 2008].

6 See 'Jack Straw's Veil Comments Spark Anger' (BBC News 5 October 2006), www.news.bbc.co.uk/1/hi/uk_politics/5410472.stm [accessed 18 July 2008]. Straw did not explicitly state that the veil was in contradiction with women's rights but focused on it as an obstacle to integration and 'community relations'. Straw was Home Secretary from 1997 to 2001 and Foreign Secretary until 2005 during the period leading up to and including the invasion of Iraq.

7 See 'School Sacks Woman in Veil Row' (BBC News, 24 November 2006), www.news.bbc.co.uk/1/hi/england/bradford/6179842.stm [accessed 18 July 2008].

8 For commentary discussing the implications of religion for women's rights more generally, see M. Bunting, 'Jack Straw Has Unleashed a Storm of Prejudice and Intensified Division', *The Guardian Online*, 9 October 2006, www.guardian.co.uk/commentisfree/2006/oct/09/comment.politics [accessed 14 August 2008]; P. Toynbee, 'Only a Fully Secular State Can Protect Women's Rights', *The Guardian Online*, 17 October 2006, www.guardian.co.uk/commentisfree/2006/oct/17/comment.politics3 [accessed 14 August 2008].

9 See, for example, J. Revill & A. Asthana, '3,000 Women a Year Forced Into Marriage in the UK, Study Finds', *The Guardian Online*, 8 March 2008, www.guardian.co.uk/politics/2008/mar/08/religion [accessed 14 November 2011]; J. Bingham, 'Honour Killing: Father Convicted of Murder of Tulay Goren', *The Telegraph*, 17 December 2009, www.telegraph.co.uk/news/uknews/crime/6832862/Honour-killing-father-convicted-of-murder-Tulay-Goren.html [accessed 14 November 2011]; 'International Conference on Women's Rights, Sharia Law and Secularism' organised by the International Humanist and Ethical Union (London, 12 March 2011).

10 Braidotti (2008), p. 6. For the argument that gay or 'queer' rights are being appropriated in a similar fashion, see J. Butler, 'Sexual Politics, Torture and Secular Time', *The British Journal of Sociology* 59:1 (March 2008), 1–23; J. Haritaworn, with T. Tauquir, E. Erdem, 'Gay Imperialism: Gender and Sexuality Discourse in the War on Terror', in A. Kuntsman & E. Miyake (eds.), *Out of Place: Interrogating Voices in Queerness/Raciality* (England: Raw Nerve Books Ltd, 2008), pp. 71–95.

11 Braidotti (2008), p. 6.
12 Discussed in Z. Eisenstein, *Against Empire: Feminisms, Racism and the West* (London: Zed, 2004), pp. 165–8.
13 Eisenstein (2004).
14 *Ibid.*, pp. 165–8; A. Brodsky, *With All Our Strength: The Revolutionary Association of the Women of Afghanistan* (New York: Routledge, 2003); 'About Us', Revolutionary Association of the Women of Afghanistan, www.rawa.org/rawa.html.
15 A not for profit feminist organisation designed to meet the needs of Asian and Afro-Caribbean women.
16 R. Gupta, 'Feminism and the Soul of Secularism', 8 March 2011, www.opendemocracy. net/5050/rahila-gupta/feminism-and-soul-of-secularism [accessed 14 November 2011] (Gupta is a member of the SBS management committee but wrote here in a personal capacity); P. Patel & U. Sen, *Cohesion, Faith and Gender: A Report on the Impact of the Cohesion and Faith Based Approach on Black and Minority Ethnic Women in Ealing* (Southall Black Sisters Trust, 2010).
17 Braidotti (2008), p. 4. For example, Elizabeth Badinter supported the 2004 French ban, Ciska DresselHuys and Ayaan Hirsi Ali in the Netherlands publicly opposed Islamic female body covering.
18 See, for example, the seminal article, V. Amos & P. Parmar, 'Challenging Imperial Feminism', *Feminist Review* 17 (July 1984), 3–19. 'Black and postcolonial theories have never been loudly secular ... black feminism and critical theory have been postsecular for a long time', Braidotti (2008), p. 7.
19 J. Scott, *The Politics of the Veil* (Princeton & Oxford: Princeton University Press, 2007), p. 92.
20 Butler (2008); S. Mahmood, 'Is Critique Secular?', (The Immanent Frame: Secularism, Religion and the Public Sphere, The Social Science Research Council, SSRC Blogs, 2008) www.blogs.ssrc.org/tif/2008/03/30/is-critique-secular-2/ [accessed 14 November 2011]; Scott (2007). See also, J. Butler, 'Afterward', in E. Armour & S. M. St. Ville (eds.), *Bodily Citations. Religion and Judith Butler* (New York: Columbia University Press, 2006); S. Mahmood, 'Agency, Performativity and the Feminist Subject', in Armour & St. Ville (2006), pp. 177–221.
21 G. Vincett, S. Sharma, K. Aune, 'Introduction: Women, Religion and Secularisation: One Size Does Not Fit All', in K. Aune, S. Sharma, & G. Vincett (eds.), *Women and Religion in the West: Challenging Secularisation* (Aldershot: Ashgate, 2008), pp. 1–19, 5–6; S. Bracke '"Real" Islam in Kazan: Reconfiguring the Modern, Knowledge and Gender', in Aune et al. (2008), pp. 183–94.
22 Scott (2007), p. 93.
23 Butler (2008), p. 13; Scott (2007), p. 121.

Select bibliography

Periodicals

The Adult
Agnostic Journal
Anti-Infidel
Barker's Review
The Crisis
Freethinker
The Freewoman
Investigator
Isis
Journal of the Vigilance Association for the Defence of Personal Rights
The Malthusian
The Movement
The National Reformer
New Moral World
Oracle of Reason
The Present Day
The Reasoner
The Reformer
Secular Chronicle
Secular Review
The Shield of Faith
The Victoria Magazine
The Women's Penny Paper
The Woman's Signal
Women's Suffrage Journal

Archive collections

Leicester, Leicester Local Archive, Leicester Secular Society
London, Bishopsgate Library, Charles Bradlaugh Archive & George Jacob
Holyoake Archive
London, Wellcome Library, Archives and Manuscripts Collection
London, The Women's Library, Clara Collet Family Papers
Manchester, Co-operative Union Archive, Holyoake Correspondence

Primary sources: published

*Christianity or Secularism: Which is the Better System for Man? Being a verbatim
report of a public debate held in the Olympia Hall, Plymouth, on Monday
and Tuesday evenings, Sept. 24th and 25th, 1888. Between Mrs Annie Besant
(of the National Secular Society) and Mr. William T. Lee (of the Three Town's
Christian Evidence Society; and Missioner at the Exeter Street Hall, Plymouth*
(Plymouth: W.F. Westcott, London: John Kensit, 1888).

'Contagious Diseases', *Transactions of the National Association for the Promotion
of Social Science. Bristol Meeting 1869* Edited by Edwin Pears (London:
Longmans, Green, Reader & Dyer, 1870).

*The Moral Reform Union, Fifth Annual Report. From April 3rd 1886- April 27th
1887* (London: Moral Reform Union, 1887).

Principles and Rules of the Leicester Secular Society (Leicester: Geo Gibbons,
1884).

A Necessarian, *The Contagious Diseases Acts and the Necessarian Philosophy*
(Manchester: Ireland & Co., 1871).

Agate, Peter, *Sexual Economy as Taught by Charles Bradlaugh MP. With
Addendum by Saladin* (London: W. Stewart & Co., 1886[?]).

Allan, James McGrigor, *Woman Suffrage Wrong, in Principle and Practice. An
Essay* (London: Remington & Co., 1890).

Allen, Grant, *The Woman Who Did* (Oxford: Oxford University Press, 1995) (first
published 1895).

Atkinson, Henry George & Harriet Martineau, *Letters on the Laws of Man's
Nature and Development* (London: John Chapman, 1850).

Balfour, Clara L., *The Women of Scripture* (London: Houlston & Stoneman, 1847).

Barker, Joseph, *Seven Lectures on the Supernatural Origin and Divine Authority of
the Bible. Containing his Reply to the Rev. Mr. Sergeant, Delivered in Sheffield,
August 1854* (Stoke-Upon-Trent, London: George Turner, 1854).

Barker, Joseph, *Confessions of Joseph Barker. A Convert from Christianity.
[Reprinted from* The Reasoner, *No.s 646-9]* (London: Holyoake & Co., 1858).

Barker, Joseph, *What Has the Bible Done for Woman?* (London: Barker & Co.,
186?).

Besant, Annie, *The Political Status of Women*, 3rd edn (London: Freethought
Publishing Co., 1874[?], repr. J. Saville (ed.), *A Selection of the Social and*

Political Pamphlets of Annie Besant. With a Preface and Biographical Notes by John Saville, New York: Augustus M. Kelley, 1970).

Besant, Annie, *On the Religious Education of Children* (London: Thomas Scott, 1874).

Besant, Annie, *Is the Bible Indictable? An Enquiry Into Whether the Bible Comes Within the Ruling of the Lord Chief Justice As Obscene Literature* (London: Besant and Bradlaugh, 1877).

Besant, Annie, *The Gospel of Christianity and the Gospel of Freethought* (London: Charles Watts, 1877).

Besant, Annie, *My Path to Atheism* (London: Freethought Publishing Co., 1877).

Besant, Annie, *Christian Progress* (London: Freethought Publishing Co., 1878[?]).

Besant, Annie, *The Fruits of Christianity* (London: Freethought Publishing Co., 1878).

Besant, Annie, *The Law of Population: Its Consequences, and Its Bearing upon Human Conduct and Morals* (London: Freethought Publishing Co., 1878[?]).

Besant, Annie, *Marriage; As it Was, As it is and As it Should Be* (New York: A.K. Butts, 1879).

Besant, Annie, *The Christian Creed; or What it is Blasphemy to Deny* (London: Freethought Publishing Co., 1883).

Besant, Annie, *Autobiographical Sketches* (London: Freethought Publishing Co., 1885).

Besant, Annie, *Is Christianity a Success?* (n.p., 1885[?]).

Besant, Annie, *The Legalisation of Female Slavery In England* (London: Besant & Bradlaugh, 1885).

Besant, Annie, *Woman's Position According to the Bible* (London: Besant & Bradlaugh, 1885).

Besant, Annie, *A World Without God. A Reply to Miss Frances Power Cobbe* (London: Freethought Publishing Co., 1885).

Besant, Annie, *Life, Death and Immortality* (London: Freethought Publishing Co., 1886).

Besant, Annie, *Why I am a Socialist* (London: Besant & Bradlaugh, 1886).

Besant, Annie, *The Socialist Movement* (London: Freethought Publishing Co., 1887, repr. J. Saville (ed.), *A Selection of the Social and Political Pamphlets of Annie Besant. With a Preface and Biographical Notes by John Saville*, New York: Augustus M. Kelley, 1970).

Besant, Annie, *Why I Became a Theosophist* (London: Freethought Publishing Co., 1889).

Besant, Annie, *God's Views on Marriage. As Revealed in the Old Testament* (London: Freethought Publishing Co., 1890).

Besant, Annie, *An Autobiography* (London: T. Fisher Unwin, 1893).

Besant, Annie & Charles Bradlaugh, 'Introduction', in C. Knowlton, *Fruits of Philosophy. An Essay on the Population Question. A New Edition with Notes* (London: Freethought Publishing Co., 1877), v–viii.

Blackwell, Elizabeth, *Christian Duty in Regard to Vice. A Letter Addressed to the Brussels International Congress, Against State Regulation of Vice, with the Hearty Sympathy of Dr. Elizabeth Blackwell* (London: Moral Reform Union, 1892[?]).

Bodichon, Barbara Leigh Smith, *A Brief Summary in Plain Language of the Most Important Laws Concerning Women*, 3rd edn (London: Trubnor & Co., 1869) (first published 1854).

Bonner, Arthur & Charles Bradlaugh Bonner, *Hypatia Bradlaugh Bonner: The Story of Her Life* (London: Watts & Co., 1942).

Bonner, Hypatia Bradlaugh, *Charles Bradlaugh. A Record of his Life and Work by his Daughter Hypatia Bradlaugh Bonner. With an Account of his Parliamentary Struggle, Politics and Teachings by John M. Robertson MP*, 7th edn (London: T. Fisher Unwin, 1908).

Bonner, Hypatia Bradlaugh 'An echo from the past', *Literary Guide* 226 (April 1915), 59–60.

Butler, Josephine (ed.), *Woman's Work and Woman's Culture. A Series of Essays* (London: Macmillan & Co., 1869).

Butler, Josephine, *An Autobiographical Memoir: Edited by George W. and Lucy A. Johnson* 2nd edn (Bristol: J.W. Arrowsmith Ltd, London: Simpkin, Marshall, Hamilton, Kent & Co. Ltd, 1911).

Caird, Mona, *The Morality of Marriage and Other Essays on the Status and Destiny of Woman* (London: George Redway, 1897).

Campbell, Theophila Carlile, *The Battle of the Press, As Told in the Story of the Life of Richard Carlile* (London: A. & H.B. Bonner, 1899).

Carlile, Richard, *Every Woman's Book or What is Love?*, in M. L. Bush, *What Is Love? Richard Carlile's Philosophy of Sex* (New York & London: Verso, 1998), pp.55–80 (first published 1826).

Clapperton, Jane, 'Agnosticism and Women: A Reply', *The Nineteenth Century* 7:39 (May 1880), 840–44.

Clapperton, Jane, *Scientific Meliorism and the Evolution of Happiness* (London: Kegan Paul, Trench & Co., 1885).

Close, Francis, *The Female Chartists' Visit to the Parish Church. A Sermon Addressed to the Female Chartists of Cheltenham. Sunday, August 25th, 1839 On the Occasion of their Attending the Parish Church in a Body* (London: Hamilton, Adams & Co., 1839).

Cobbe, Frances Power, 'Magnanimous Atheism', *The Theological Review* 59 (October 1877), 447–89.

Cobbe, Frances Power, *The Life of Frances Power Cobbe as Told by Herself. With Additions by the Author and Introduction by Blanche Atkinson* (London: Swan Sonnenshein & Co., 1904).

Collet, Sophia Dobson, *George Jacob Holyoake and Modern Atheism. A Biographical and Critical Essay* (London, Trubner & Co., 1855).

Collet, Sophia Dobson, *Phases of Atheism, Described, Examined and Answered* (Holyoake & Co., London, 1860).

Collet, Sophia Dobson, *Indian Theism and its Relation to Christianity* (London: Strahan & Co., 1870).

Collet, Sophia Dobson, *Keshub Chunder Sen's Visit to England* (London: Strahan & Co., 1871).

Collet, Sophia Dobson, *The Life and Letters of Raja Rammohun Roy. Compiled and Edited by the Late Sophia Dobson Collet and Completed by a Friend* (London: Harold Collet, 1900).

Cox, Francis Augustus, *Female Scripture Biography: Including an Essay on What Christianity has Done for Women* (London: Gale & Fenner, 1817).

Davies, Rev. Charles Maurice, *Heterodox London: or, Phases of Freethought in the Metropolis* 2 vols (London: Tinsley Brothers, 1874).

Davies, Rev. Charles Maurice, *Mystic London: or Phases of Occult Life in the Metropolis* (London, 1875 repr. *Labour History Review* 57:3, 1992), pp. 67–71.

Despard, Charlotte, *Theosophy and the Woman's Movement* (London: Theosophical Publishing Society, 1913).

Dixie, Lady Florence, 'Introduction', in J. McCabe, *The Religion of Woman. An Historical Study, with an Introduction by Lady Florence Dixie* (London: Watts & Co., 1905), pp. 5–9.

Drysdale, George, *The Elements of Social Science; or, Physical, Sexual and Natural Religion by a Graduate of Medicine*, 7th edn (London: Edward Truelove, 1867) (first published 1854).

Ellis, Sarah Stickney, *The Women of England, Their Social Duties and Domestic Habits*, 9th edn (London, Fisher, Son & Co., 1850) (first published 1839).

Ethelmer, Ellis, *The Human Flower. A Simple Statement of the Physiology of Birth and the Relations of the Sexes*, 2nd edn (Congleton: Mrs Wolstenholme Elmy, 1894).

Ethelmer, Ellis, 'A Woman Emancipator: A Biographical Sketch', *Westminster Review* 145 (April 1896), 424–8.

Ethelmer, Ellis, *Phases of Love: As It Was; As It Is; As It May Be* (Congleton: Mrs Wolstenholme Elmy, 1897).

Faithfull, Emily, *Three Visits to America* (Edinburgh: D. Douglas, 1884).

Farningham, Marianne, *Women and their Saviour. Thoughts of a Minute for a Month of Mornings* (London: James Clarke & Co., 1904).

Farningham, Marianne, *Women and their Work. Wives and Daughters of the Old Testament* (London: James Clarke & Co., n.d.).

Farningham, Marianne, *A Working Woman's Life. An Autobiography* (London: James Clarke & Co., 1907).

Foote, George W., *Mr Bradlaugh's Trial and the Freethought Party* (London: Charles Watts, 1877[?]).

Hennell, Charles, *An Inquiry Concerning the Origin of Christianity*, 3rd edn (London: Trubner & Co., 1870) (first published 1838).

Hennell, Charles, *Christian Theism*, 3rd edn (London: Trubnor & Co., 1870) (first published 1839).

Hennell, Sara Sophia, *Christianity and Infidelity: An Exposition of the Arguments on Both Sides. Arranged According to a Plan Proposed by George Baillie Esq.* (London: Arthur Hall, Virtue & Co., 1857).

Hennell, Sara Sophia, *Essay on the Sceptical Tendency of Butler's 'Analogy'* (London: John Chapman, 1859).

Hennell, Sara Sophia, *Thoughts in Aid of Faith, Gathered Chiefly from Recent Works in Theology and Philosophy* (London: George Manwaring, 1860).

Hennell, Sara Sophia, *On Need of Dogmas in Religion. A Letter to Thomas Scott* (n.p., 1874).

Hennell, Sara Sophia, *Present Religion as Faith Owning Fellowship with Thought*, 3 vols (London: Trubnor & Co., 1865, 1873, 1887).

Holyoake, George Jacob, *The Trial of George Jacob Holyoake on an Indictment for Blasphemy, Before Mr. Justice Erskin, and a Common Jury at Gloucester – August 15, 1842* (London: Printed for Anti-Persecution Union by Thomas Paterson, 1842).

Holyoake, George Jacob, *The Last Days of Mrs Emma Martin. Advocate of Free Thought* (London: J. Watson, 1851).

Holyoake, George Jacob, *Rudiments of Public Speaking and Debate: or Hints on the Application of Logic* (London: J. Watson, 1852).

Holyoake, George Jacob, *The Last Trial for Atheism in England. A Fragment of Autobiography*, 5th edn (London: N. Trubnor & Co., 1878) (first published 1850).

Holyoake, George Jacob, *Sixty Years of an Agitator's Life*, 2 vols (London: T.F. Unwin, 1892).

Howell, Constance, *A Biography of Jesus Christ. Written for Young Freethinkers* (London: Freethought Publishing Co., 1883).

Howell, Constance, *The After Life of the Apostles. Written for Young Freethinkers* (London: Freethought Publishing Co., 1884).

Howell, Constance, *A More Excellent Way* (London: Swan Sonnenschien, 1888).

James, John Angell, *Female Piety: or the Young Woman's Friend and Guide Through Life to Immortality* (London: Hamilton, Adams & Co., 1852).

James, William, *The Varieties of Religious Experience. A Study in Human Nature Being the Gifford Lectures on Natural Religion at Edinburgh in 1901–1902* (London, New York & Bombay: Longmans, Green, & Co., 1902).

Knowlton, Charles, *Fruits of Philosophy. An Essay on the Population Question. A New Edition with Notes* (London: Freethought Publishing Company, 1877) (first published 1832).

Layard, George Somes, *Mrs Lynn Linton. Her Life, Letters, and Opinions* (London: Methuen & Co., 1901).

Lewis, Sarah, *Woman's Mission*, 7th edn (London: John W. Parker, 1840) (first published 1939).

Linton, Elizabeth Lynn, *My Literary Life. Reminiscences of Dickens, Thackery, George Eliot, etc. With a Prefatory Note by Miss Beatrice Harraden* (London: Hodder & Stoughton, 1899).

Lyttleton, E., 'Women's Suffrage and the Teaching of St. Paul', *Contemporary Review* (May 1896), 680–91.

McCabe, Joseph, *The Religion of Woman. An Historical Study, with an Introduction by Lady Florence Dixie* (London: Watts & Co., 1905).

McCabe, Joseph, *Life and Letters of George Jacob Holyoake* (London[?]: Watts, 1908).

McCabe, Joseph, *A Rationalist Encyclopaedia. A Book of Reference on Religion, Philosophy, Ethics, and Science* (London: Watts & Co., 1948).

Macauley, Eliza, *Autobiographical Memoirs of Miss Macauley* (London: published for the author, 1834).

Macauley, Eliza, *Autobiographical Memoirs of Miss Macauley Written Under the Title of Elizabeth or "A Plain and Simple Tale of Truth"* (London: Charles Fox, 1835).

Martin, Emma, *God's Gifts and Man's Duties. Being the substance of a lecture delivered by Emma Martin at the Hall of Science in Manchester, October 1, 1843, to which is added an address to the Minister, members and congregation of that chapel; and a letter acknowledging the receipt of "The Sinner's Friend" which had been presented to her by that gentleman* (London: J. Watson, 1843).

Martin, Emma, *Baptism, A Pagan Rite. Or a Mythological Essay Proving the Existence of This Ceremony in the Most Remote Ages, with an Exposition of the Materials Used in Its Celebration Being Earth, Water, Fire, Air, Blood, etc. And the Subjects of its Administration in Various Times and Countries, Being Not Only Adults and Infants But Also God's Religious Symbols, Buildings, Bells. By Emma Martin, Formerly a Member of a Baptist Church* (London: n.p., 1844).

Martin, Emma, *The Missionary Jubilee Panic and the Hypocrites Prayer. Addressed to the Supporters of Christian Mission* (London: Hetherington, 1844).

Martin, Emma, *A Few Reasons for Renouncing Christianity and Professing and Disseminating Infidel Opinions* (London: Watson, 1840–50[?]).

Martin, Emma, *Religion Superseded or the Moral Code of Nature Sufficient for the Guidance of Man* (London: n.p.,1840–50[?]).

Martin, Emma, *Second Conversation on the Being of God* (London: the author, 1840–50[?]).

Martin, Emma, *The Bible No Revelation. Or the Inadequacy of Language to Convey A Message from God to Man. To Doctor Conquest. The Reputed Editor of the New Edition of the Bible with Twenty Thousand Emendations, This Second Edition is Most Respectfully Dedicated.* (London: Hetherington, 1850[?]).

Martin, Emma, *A Conversation on the Being of God* (London: n.p.,1840–50[?]).

Martineau, Harriet, *Autobiography* 2 vols, 3rd edn (London: Smith, Elder & Co., 1877: repr. Farnborough: Gregg International Publishers Ltd, 1969).

Matthews, Richard, *Is Marriage Worth Perpetuating? The Ninth of a Series of Lectures against Socialism Delivered in the Mechanics' Institution, Southampton Buildings, Under the Direction of the Committee of the London City Mission,* (London: n.p., 1840).

Miller, Florence Fenwick, *The Lessons of a Life: Harriet Martineau. A Lecture Delivered Before the Sunday Lecture Society, St. George's Hall, Langham Place on Sunday afternoon, 11th March 1877* (London: The Sunday Lecture Society, 1877).

Miller, Florence Fenwick, *Harriet Martineau* (London: John H. Ingram, 1884).

Monod, Adolphe, *The Christian Woman: Her Place and Power* (London: T. Nelson & Sons, 1861[?]).

Neale, Francis, 'Is Woman Indebted to the Bible?', in *British Secular Union Alamanck for 1879* (London: Charles Watts, 1879), pp. 33–35.

Newman, Francis W., *Phases of Faith*, 2nd edn (London: Watts & Co., Rationalist Press Association, 1907) (first published 1850).

Newman, Francis W., *The Corruption Now Called Neo-Malthusianism. Written by Request for the Moral Reform Union. With Notes by Dr. E. Blackwell* (London: The Moral Reform Union, 1889).

Owen, Robert, *Lectures on the Marriages of the Priesthood in the Old Immoral World* (Leeds: J. Hobson, 1835).

Owen, Robert, *The Marriage System in the New Moral World* (Leeds: J. Hobson, 1838).

Pearson, Karl, *The Ethic of Freethought: A Series of Essays and Lectures* (London: T. Fisher Unwin, 1888).

Robertson, J. M., *A History of Freethought in the Nineteenth Century* (London: Watts & Co., 1929).

Saladin [W. S. Ross], *Woman, Her Glory, Her Shame and Her God* 2 vols (London: W. Stewart & Co., 1894[?]).

Sanday, W., *Free-Thinking. A Brief Review of Mrs Besant on the Evidences of Christianity* (London: Rivingtons, 1886).

Stanton, Elizabeth Cady, *The Woman's Bible: The Original Feminist Attack on the Bible* (Glasgow: Polygon Books, 1985) (first published as *The Woman's Bible* 1895).

Strachey, Ray, *The Cause. A Short History of the Women's Movement in Great Britain* (London: G. Bell & Sons Ltd, 1928).

Strachey, Ray, *Millicent Garrett Fawcett* (London: John Murray, 1931).

Watts, J. & Iconoclast (eds.), *Harriet Martineau*, Half Hours with Freethinkers 2:11 (London[?]: n.p., 1864).

Watts, Kate Eunice, *Mrs Watts Reply to Mr. Bradlaugh's Misrepresentations* (London: Co-operative Printing & Stationery Co., 1877[?]).

Wheeler, J. M., *A Biographical Dictionary of Freethinkers of All Ages and Nations* (London: Progressive Publishing Co., 1889).

Wollstonecraft, Mary, *A Vindication of the Rights of Woman* (London: Penguin, 2004) (first published 1792).

Wright, Frances, *Course of Popular Lectures as Delivered by Frances Wright, in New York, Philadelphia, Baltimore, Boston, Cincinnati, St. Louis, Louisville, and other Cities, Towns and Districts of the United States. With Three Addresses on Various Public Occasions and a Reply to the Charges Against the French Reformers of 1789*, 4th edn (New York: published at the Office of the Free Enquirer, Hall of Science, 1831) (first published 1828).

Wright, Frances, *Fanny Wright Unmasked By Her Own Pen. Explanatory Notes. Respecting the Nature and Objects of the Institution of Nashoba and of the Principles Upon Which It Is Founded. Addressed to the friends of human improvement in all countries and of all nations*, 3rd edn (New York: C.N. Baldwin, 1830).

Wright, Frances, *Biography, Notes and Political Letters of Frances Wright D'Arusmont* (Dundee: J. Myles Bookseller, 1844).

Primary: unpublished

Hennell, Sara Sophia, *A Memoir of the Late Charles Hennell* (n.p., for private circulation, 1899).

Holyoake, George Jacob, *On Lecturing: Its Conditions and Character* (printed for private circulation, 1851[?]) [held at Manchester, Co-operative Union Archive, Holyoake Collection].

Holyoake, George Jacob, *My Religious Days* (1901) [held at London, Bishopsgate Library, George Jacob Holyoake Archive].

Miller, Florence Fenwick, 'An Uncommon Girlhood' (unpublished autobiography) [held at London, Wellcome Library, Manuscripts Collection, GC/228].

Secondary sources: published

Amos, Valerie & Pratibha Parmar, 'Challenging Imperial Feminism', *Feminist Review* 17 (July 1984), 3–19.

Anderson, Nancy Fix, *Woman Against Woman in Victorian England. A Life of Eliza Lynn Linton* (Bloomington & Indianapolis: Indiana University Press, 1987).

Anderson, Nancy Fix, 'Bridging Cross-Cultural Feminisms: Annie Besant and Women's Rights in England and India, 1874–1933', *Women's History Review* 3:4 (1994), 563–80.

Anderson, Nancy Fix, 'Linton, Elizabeth Lynn (1822–1898)', *Oxford Dictionary of National Biography* (online edn; Oxford University Press, 2004).

Anderson, Olive, 'Women Preachers in Mid-Victorian Britain: Some Reflections on Feminism, Popular Religion and Social Change', *The Historical Journal* 12:3 (1969), 467–84.

Banks, J. A. & Olive, 'The Bradlaugh-Besant Trial and the English Newspapers', *Population Studies* 8:1 (July 1954), 22–34.

Banks, J. A. & Olive, *Feminism and Family Planning in Victorian England* (Liverpool: Liverpool University Press, 1964).

Banks, Olive, *Faces of Feminism. A Study of Feminism as a Social Movement* (Oxford: Basil Blackwell, 1993) (first published 1981).

Banks, Olive, *Becoming a Feminist: The Social Origins of 'First Wave' Feminism* (Brighton: Wheatsheaf, 1986).

Barbour, John D., *Versions of Deconversion. Autobiography and the Loss of Faith* (Charlottesville & London: University Press of Virginia, 1994).

Bebbington, David, *Evangelicalism in Modern Britain* (London: Unwin Hyman, 1989).

Belchem, John, *Popular Radicalism in Nineteenth-Century Britain* (London & Basingstoke: Macmillan Press, 1996).

Benn, J. Miriam, *The Predicaments of Love* (London: Pluto Press, 1992).

Bevir, Mark, 'Annie Besant's Quest for Truth: Christianity, Secularism and New Age Thought', *Journal of Ecclesiastical History* 50:1 (1999), 62–73.

Bland, Lucy, 'The Married Woman, the "New Woman", and the Feminist: Sexual Politics of the 1890s', in J. Rendall (ed.), *Equal or Different: Women's Politics 1800–1914* (Oxford: Basil Blackwell, 1987), pp. 141–64.

Bland, Lucy, '"Purifying" the Public World: Feminist Vigilantes in Late Victorian England', *Women's History Review* 1:3 (September 1992), 397–412.

Bland, Lucy, *Banishing the Beast. English Feminism and Sexual Morality, 1885–1914* (London: Penguin Books, 1995).

Bland, Lucy, 'Heterosexuality, Feminism and *The Freewoman* Journal in Early-Twentieth-Century England', *Women's History Review* 4:1 (1995), 5–23.

Briggs, J. H. Y., 'She Preachers, Widows and Other Women. The Feminine Dimension in Baptist Life Since 1600', *The Baptist Quarterly* 30:7 (July 1986), 337–52.

Briggs, J. H. Y., *The English Baptists of the 19th Century* (Didcot: The Baptist Historical Society, 1994).

Broughton, T. L., 'Women's Autobiography: The Self at Stake?', in S. Neuman (ed.), *Autobiography and Questions of Gender* (London: Frank Cass, 1991).

Brown, Callum, 'Did Urbanisation Secularise Britain?', *Urban History Yearbook* 1988.

Brown, Callum, *The Death of Christian Britain. Understanding Secularisation, 1800–2000* (London: Routledge, 2001).

Budd, Susan, 'The Humanist Societies: The Consequences of a Diffuse Belief System', in B. R. Wilson (ed.), *Patterns of Sectarianism: Organisation and Ideology in Social and Religious Movements* (London: Heinemann, 1967), pp. 377–405.

Budd, Susan, 'The Loss of Faith: Reasons for Unbelief Among Members of the Secular Movement in England, 1850–1950', *Past and Present* 36 (1967), 106–25.

Budd, Susan, *Varieties of Unbelief: Atheists and Agnostics in English Society 1850–1950* (London: Heinemann, 1977).

Burfield, Diana, 'Theosophy and Feminism: Some Explorations in Nineteenth-Century Biography', in Pat Holden (ed.), *Women's Religious Experience* (London: Croom Helm, 1983), pp. 27–56.

Burton, Antoinette, *Burdens of History. British Feminists, Indian Women, and Imperial Culture, 1865-1915* (Chapel Hill & London: University of North Carolina Press, 1994).

Bush, Michael L., *What Is Love? Richard Carlile's Philosophy of Sex* (New York & London: Verso, 1998).

Bush, Michael L., 'Richard Carlile and the Female Reformers of Manchester: A Study of Gender in the 1820s Viewed Through the Radical Filter of Republicanism, Freethought and a Philosophy of Sexual Satisfaction', *Manchester Region History Review* 16 (2002-3), 2-12.

Butler, Judith, 'Afterward', Ellen Armour & Susan M. St. Ville (eds.), *Bodily Citations. Religion and Judith Butler* (New York: Columbia University Press, 2006).

Butler, Judith, 'Sexual Politics, Torture and Secular Time', *The British Journal of Sociology* 59:1 (March 2008), 1-23.

Caine, Barbara, *Victorian Feminists* (Oxford: Oxford University Press, 1992).

Caine, Barbara, 'Feminist History and Feminist Biography', *Women's History Review* 3:2 (1994), 247-61.

Caine, Barbara, *English Feminism 1780-1980* (Oxford: Oxford University Press, 1997).

Caine, Barbara, 'Feminism, Journalism and Public Debate', in J. Shattock (ed.), *Women and Literature in Britain, 1800-1900* (Cambridge: Cambridge University Press, 2001), pp. 99-118.

Caine, Barbara, 'Review of S. Peacock, *The Theological and Ethical Writings of Frances Power Cobbe, 1822-1904*', *Victorian Studies* 45:4 (2003), 748-9.

Chandrasekhar, S., (ed.), *A Dirty, Filthy Book: the Writings of Charles Knowlton and Annie Besant on Reproductive Physiology and Birth Control, and an Account of the Bradlaugh-Besant Trial* (Berkeley & London: University of California Press, 1981).

Cook, Hera, *The Longest Revolution: English Women, Sex, and Contraception 1800-1975* (Oxford: Oxford University Press, 2004).

Cowie, Grace & Edward Royle, 'Emma Martin (1812-51), Socialist, Free Thinker and Women's Rights Advocate', in J. Bellamy & J. Saville (eds.), *Dictionary of Labour Biography* 12 vols (London & Basingstoke: Macmillan Press, 1972-) vi (1979), pp. 188-91.

Cox, Jeremy, *The English Churches in a Secular Society: Lambeth 1870-1930* (Oxford: Oxford University Press, 1982).

Dagnell, H., *The Taxes on Knowledge. A Brief History 1712-1861* (Middlesex: the author, 1992).

Davidoff Leonora & Catherine Hall, *Family Fortunes. Men and Women of the English Middle Class, 1780-1850* (London: Hutchinson, 1987).

Davie, Grace, 'Sociology of Religion', in R. Segal (ed.), *The Blackwell Companion to the Sociology of Religion* (Oxford: Blackwell Publishing, 2006), pp. 171-91.

Davin, Anna, 'Socialist Infidels and Messengers of Light', in T. Hitchcock & H. Shore (eds.), *The Streets of London from the Great Fire to the Great Stink* (London: Rivers Oram Press, 2003), pp. 165-82.

Dean, Joanna, *Religious Experience and the New Woman: The Life of Lilly Dougall* (Bloomington & Indianapolis: Indiana University Press, 2007).

de Vries, Jacqueline, 'Transforming the Pulpit: Preaching and Prophecy in the British Women's Suffrage Movement', in B. Mayne Kienzle & P. J. Walker (eds.), *Women Preachers and Prophets Through Two Millennia of Christianity* (Los Angeles: University of California Press, 1998), pp. 318–34.

de Vries, Jacqueline, 'Review of S. Peacock, *The Theological and Ethical Writings of Frances Power Cobbe, 1822–1904*', *Albion: A 'Quaterly Concerned with British Studies* 35:4 (Winter, 2003), 692–94.

de Vries, Jacqueline & Sue Morgan, 'Introduction', in Sue Morgan & Jacqueline de Vries (eds), *Women, Gender and Religious Cultures in Britain 1800–1940* (Abingdon: Routledge, 2010), pp. 1–10.

de Vries, Jacqueline, 'More than Paradoxes to Offer. Feminism, History and Religious Cultures', in S. Morgan & J. de Vries (eds), *Women, Gender and Religious Cultures in Britain 1800–1940* (Abingdon: Routledge, 2010), pp. 188–210.

Dixon, Joy, *Divine Feminism: Theosophy and Feminism in England* (Baltimore & London: Johns Hopkins University Press, 2001).

Dixon, Joy, 'Modernity, Heterodoxy and the Transformation of Religious Cultures', in S. Morgan & J. de Vries (eds.), *Women, Gender and Religious Cultures in Britain, 1800–1940* (London & New York: Routledge, 2010), pp. 211–30.

Eckhardt, Celia Morris, *Fanny Wright. Rebel in America* (Cambridge, MA & London: Harvard University Press, 1984).

Eisenstein, Zilla, *Against Empire: Feminisms, Racism and the West* (London: Zed, 2004).

Epstein, James, *Radical Expression: Political Language, Ritual and Symbol in England, 1790–1850* (Oxford: Oxford University Press, 1994).

Eros, John, 'The Rise of Organised Freethought in Mid-Victorian England', *The Sociological Review* 2 (1954), 98–118.

Fraser, Hilary, Stephanie Green & Judith Johnston (eds.), *Gender and the Victorian Periodical* (Cambridge: Cambridge University Press, 2003).

Frawley, Maria H., 'The Editor as Advocate: Emily Faithfull and *The Victoria Magazine*', *Victorian Periodicals Review* 31 (1998), 87–104.

Fryer, Peter, *The Birth Controllers* (London: Secker & Warburg, 1965).

Garnett, Jane, Matthew Grinley, Alana Harris, William Whyte, Sarah Williams (eds.), *Redefining Christian Britain: Post 1945 Perspectives* (London: SCM Press, 2007).

Gaylor, A. L. (ed.), *Women Without Superstition. "No Gods – No Masters". The Collected Writings of Women Freethinkers of the Nineteenth and Twentieth Centuries* (Madison: Freedom from Religion Foundation, 1997).

Gill, Sean, *Women and the Church of England. From the Eighteenth Century to the Present* (London: Society for Promoting Christian Knowledge, 1994).

Gleadle, Kathryn, *The Early Feminists. Radical Unitarians and the Emergence of the Women's Rights Movement, 1831–51* (Basingstoke & London: Macmillan, 1995).

Gleadle, Kathryn, "'Our Several Spheres": Middle-Class Women and the Feminisms of Early Victorian Radical Politics', in K. Gleadle & S. Richardson (eds.), *Women in British Politics 1760–1860. The Power of the Petticoat* (Basingstoke: Macmillan Press, 2000), pp. 134–52.

Gleadle, Kathryn, 'The Age of Physiological Reformers: Rethinking Gender and Domesticity in the Age of Reform', in A. Burns & J. Innes (eds.), *Rethinking the Age of Reform, 1780–1850* (Cambridge, Cambridge University Press, 2003), pp. 200–19.

Gleadle, Kathryn, 'Chappellsmith, Margaret (1806–1883)', *Oxford Dictionary of National Biography* (online edn; Oxford University Press, 2004).

Gleadle, Kathryn, 'Collet, Sophia Dobson (1822–1894)', *Oxford Dictionary of National Biography* (online edn; Oxford University Press, 2004).

Gleadle, Kathryn, 'Revisiting *Family Fortunes*: Reflections on the Twentieth Anniversary of the Publication of L. Davidoff & C. Hall (1987) *Family Fortunes: Men and Women of the English Middle Class, 1780–1850* (London: Hutchinson)', *Women's History Review* 16:5 (November 2007), 773–82.

Gleadle, Kathryn, *Borderline Citizens: Women, Gender and Political Culture in Britain, 1815–1867* (Oxford: Oxford University Press, 2009).

Gouldbourne, Ruth, *Reinventing the Wheel. Women and Ministry in English Baptist Life* (Oxford: Whitley Publications, Regents Park College, 1997–98).

Habgood, John, *Varieties of Unbelief* (London: Darton, Longman & Todd, 2000).

Haight, G. S., *The George Eliot Letters* (London: Oxford University Press, Geoffrey Cumberlege, 1954).

Haight, G. S., *George Eliot's Originals and Contemporaries: Essays in Victorian Literary History and Biography* (Basingstoke: Macmillan, 1992).

Hall, Catherine, 'The Early Formation of Victorian Domestic Ideology', in S. Burman (ed.), *Fit Work for Women* (London: Croom Helm, 1979), pp. 15–32.

Hall, Catherine, *White, Male and Middle Class. Explorations in Feminism and History* (Cambridge: Polity Press, 1992).

Hall, Lesley, 'Suffrage, Sex and Science', in M. Joannou & J. Purvis (eds.), *The Women's Suffrage Movement: New Feminist Perspectives* (Manchester: Manchester University Press, 2009), pp. 188–200.

Harrison, J. F. C., *Robert Owen and the Owenites in Britain and America. The Quest for the New Moral World* (London: Routledge & K. Paul, 1969).

Hartman, Kabi, "'What Made Me a Suffragette": the New Woman and the New (?) Conversion Narrative', *Women's History Review* 12:1 (2003), 35–50.

Heeney, Brian, *The Women's Movement in the Church of England, 1850–1930* (Oxford: Clarendon Press, 1988).

Helmstadter, R. & B. Lightman (eds.), *Victorian Faith in Crisis: Essays on Continuity and Change in Nineteenth-Century Religious Belief* (London & Basingstoke: Macmillan, 1990).

Heineman, H., 'Wright, Frances (1795–1852)', *Oxford Dictionary of National Biography* (online edn; Oxford University Press, 2004).

Hetherington, Naomi, 'Biblical Interpretation and Women's Rights in the Late Nineteenth-Century British Women's Advocacy Press', *Women's History Review* (forthcoming 2013).

Hilary, Frances, '"Dare to be Free!": The Women's Freedom League and its Legacy', in S. S. Holton & J. Purvis (eds.), *Votes for Women* (London: Routledge, 2000), pp. 181–202.

Himmelfarb, Gertrude, *Victorian Minds* (London: Weidenfeld & Nicolson, 1968) (first published 1952).

Hirsh, P., 'Bodichon, Barbara Leigh Smith (1827–1891)', *Oxford Dictionary of National Biography* (online edn; Oxford University Press, 2004).

Holmes, J., 'Women Preachers and the New Orders: Women Preachers in the Protestant Churches', in S. Gilley & B. Stanley (eds.), *World Christianities, c. 1815–1914* (Cambridge: Cambridge University Press, 2005), pp. 84–93.

Holton, Sandra Stanley, *Feminism and Democracy. Women's Suffrage and Reform Politics in Britain 1900–1918* (Cambridge: Cambridge University Press, 1986).

Holton, Sandra Stanley, 'Free Love and Victorian Feminism: The Divers Matrimonials of Elizabeth Wolstenholme and Ben Elmy', *Victorian Studies* 37:2 (Winter 1994), 199–222.

Holton, Sandra Stanley, *Suffrage Days. Stories from the Women's Suffrage Movement* (London & New York: Routledge, 1996).

Holton, Sandra Stanley, 'Feminism, History and Movements of the Soul: Christian Science in the Life of Alice Clark (1874–1934)', *Australian Feminist Studies* 13:28 (October 1998), 281–94.

Holton, Sandra Stanley, 'Now You See It, Now You Don't: The Women's Franchise League and its Place in Contending Narratives of the Women's Suffrage Movement', in M. Joannou & J. Purvis (eds.), *The Women's Suffrage Movement: New Feminist Perspectives* (Manchester: Manchester University Press, 1998), pp. 15–36.

Holton, Sandra Stanley, 'Elmy, Elizabeth Clarke Wolstenholme (1833–1918), *Oxford Dictionary of National Biography* (online edn; Oxford University Press, 2004).

Humpherys, Ann, 'The Journal that Did: Form and Content in The Adult (1897–1899)', *Media History* 9:1 (2003), 63–78.

Humpherys, Ann, 'The Journals that Did: Writing about Sex in late 1890s', *19 Interdisciplinary Studies in the Long Nineteenth Century*, no.3 (2006) [online edition].

Hunter, M. & D. Wooton (eds.), *Atheism From the Reformation to the Enlightenment* (Oxford: Clarendon, 1992).

Jackson, Margaret, *The Real Facts of Life: Feminism and the Politics of Sexuality c. 1850–1940* (London: Taylor & Francis, 1994).

Jay, Elizabeth, *Faith and Doubt in Victorian Britain* (Basingstoke & London: Macmillan Education, 1986).

Jay, Elizabeth, 'Doubt and the Victorian Woman', in D. Jasper & T. Wright (eds.), *The Critical Spirit and the Will to Believe* (Basingstoke: Macmillan, 1989), pp. 88–103.

Jay, Elizabeth, 'Women Writers and Religion', in J. Shattock, *Women and Literature in Britain, 1800–1900* (Cambridge & New York: Cambridge University Press, 2001), pp. 251–74.

Jay, Elizabeth, 'The Return of the Culturally Repressed – Religion and Women', *Nineteenth-Century Studies* 17 (2003), 1–12.

Jay, Elizabeth, 'Hennell, Sara Sophia (1812–1899)', *Oxford Dictionary of National Biography* (online edn; Oxford University Press, 2004).

Jeffreys, Sheila, *The Spinster and Her Enemies: Feminism and Sexuality 1880–1930* (London: Pandora Press, 1985).

Kern, Kathy, *Mrs Stanton's Bible* (Ithica & London: Cornell University Press, 2001).

Kimberling, Clark, '"I am, dear sir, your grateful disciple Margaret Chappellsmith."', *Communal Studies. Journal of Communal Studies Association* 20 (2000), 26–44.

Kirkley, Evelyn A., *Rational Mothers and Infidel Gentlemen: Gender and American Atheism, 1865–1915* (Syracuse New York: Syracuse University Press, 1999).

Klein, Lawrence & La Volpa, Anthony, (eds.), *Enthusiasm and Enlightenment in Europe, 1650–1850* (San Marino, CA: Huntingdon Library, 1999).

Knox, R. A. *Enthusiasm. A Chapter in the History of Religion: With Special Reference to the 17th and 18th Centuries* (London: Collins, 1987) (first published 1950).

Kolmerton, C. A., *The American Life of Ernestine L. Rose* (New York: Syracuse University Press, 1999).

Krueger, Christine, *The Reader's Repentance. Women Preachers, Women Writers and Nineteenth Century Social Discourse* (Chicago: University of Chicago Press, 1992).

Langland, Elizabeth, *Nobody's Angels: Middle Class Women and Domestic Ideology in Victorian Culture* (London: Cornell University Press, 1995).

Larsen, Timothy, *Crisis of Doubt* (Oxford: Oxford University Press, 2006).

Latham, Jackie E. M., 'Emma Martin and Sacred Socialism: the Correspondence of James Pierrepont Greaves', *History Workshop Journal* 38 (1994).

Ledbetter, Rosanna, *A History of the Malthusian League, 1877–1927* (Columbus: Ohio State University, 1976).

Levine, Philippa, '"So Few Prizes and So Many Blanks": Marriage and Feminism in Later Nineteenth-Century England', *Journal of British Studies* 28 (April 1989), 150–74.

Levine, Philippa, *Victorian Feminism, 1850–1900* (London: Hutchinson, 1987).

Levine, Philippa, *Feminist Lives in Victorian England. Private Roles and Public Commitment* (Oxford: Basil Blackwell, 1990).

Levine, Philippa (ed.), *Gender and Empire* (Oxford: Oxford University Press, 2004).

Lloyd, Jennifer M., *Women and the Shaping of British Methodism: Persistent Preachers, 1807–1907* (Manchester: Manchester University Press, 2009).

McCalman, Iain, 'Females, Feminism and Free Love in an Early Nineteenth-Century Radical Movement', *Labour History* 38 (1980), 1–25.

McCalman, Iain, *Radical Underworld. Prophets, Revolutionaries and Pornographers in London, 1815–1840* (Cambridge: Cambridge University Press, 1988).

McCalman, Iain, 'Popular Irreligion in Early Victorian England: Infidel Preachers and Radical Theatricality in 1830s London', in R. W. Davis & R. J. Helmstadter (eds.), *Religion and Irreligion in Victorian Society* (London: Routledge, 1992), pp. 51–67.

McCalman, Iain, 'New Jerusalems: Prophecy, Dissent and Radical Culture in England, 1786–1830', in K. Haakonssen (ed.), *Enlightenment and Religion. Rational Dissent in Eighteenth-Century Britain* (Cambridge: Cambridge University Press, 1996), pp. 312–36.

McCalman, Iain, 'Newgate in Revolution: Radical Enthusiasm and Romantic Counterculture', *Eighteenth-Century Life* 22:1 (1998), 95–110.

McLaren, Angus, 'George Jacob Holyoake and the Secular Society: British Popular Freethought, 1851–1858', *Canadian Journal of History* 7:3 (1972), 235–51.

McLaren, Angus, *Birth Control in Nineteenth-Century England* (London: Croom Helm, 1978).

McLeod, Hugh, *Class and Religion in the Late Victorian City* (London: Croom Helm, 1974).

McLeod, Hugh, *Religion and the People of Western Europe, 1789–1970* (Oxford: Oxford University Press, 1981).

McLeod, Hugh, *Religion and Society in England, 1850–1914* (Basingstoke & London: Macmillan Press, 1996).

McLeod, Hugh, *Secularisation in Western Europe, 1848–1914* (Basingstoke: Macmillan, 2000).

Mack, Phyllis, 'Religion, Feminism and the Problem of Agency: Reflections on Eighteenth-Century Quakerism' in S. Knott & B. Taylor (eds.), *Women, Gender and Enlightenment* (Basingstoke & New York: Palgrave Macmillan, 2005), pp. 434–59.

Mack, Phyllis, *Heart Religion in the British Enlightenment: Gender and Emotion in Early British Methodism* (Cambridge: Cambridge University Press, 2008).

Mahmood, Saba, 'Agency, Performativity and the Feminist Subject', in E. Armour & S. M. St. Ville (eds.), *Bodily Citations. Religion and Judith Butler* (New York: Columbia University Press, 2006), pp. 177–221.

Malmgreen, Gail, *Neither Bread, Nor Roses: Utopian Feminists and the English Working Class, 1800–1850* (Brighton: Noyce, 1978).

Malmgreen, Gail, (ed.), *Religion in the Lives of English Women 1760–1930* (London & Sydney: Croom Helm, 1986).

Mason, Michael, *The Making of Victorian Sexuality* (Oxford & New York: Oxford University Press, 1994).

Mason, Michael, *The Making of Victorian Sexual Attitudes* (Oxford & New York: Oxford University Press, 1994).

Mathers, Helen, 'The Evangelical Spirituality of a Victorian Feminist: Josephine Butler, 1828–1906', *Journal of Ecclesiastical History* 52:2 (April 2001), 282–312.

Mathers, Helen, 'Evangelicalism and Feminism: Josephine Butler, 1828–1906', in S. Morgan (ed.), *Women, Religion and Feminism in Britain, 1750–1900* (Basingstoke: Palgrave Macmillan, 2002), pp. 123–37.

Matthew, H. C. G., 'Law [nee Frost], Harriet Teresa (1831–1897)', *Oxford Dictionary of National Biography* (online edn; Oxford University Press, 2004).

Mattingly, Carol, *Appropriate(ing) Dress: Women's Rhetorical Style in Nineteenth-Century America* (Illinois: Southern Illinois University Press, 2002).

Micklewright, F. H. A., 'The Rise and Decline of English Neo-Malthusianism', *Population Studies* 15:1 (1961), 32–51.

Midgley, Clare, *Women Against Slavery: British Campaigns, 1780–1870* (Oxford: Routledge, 1992).

Midgley, Clare, 'Anti-Slavery and the Roots of "Imperial Feminism"', in C. Midgley (ed.), *Gender and Imperialism* (Manchester: Manchester University Press, 1999), pp. 161–79.

Midgley, Clare, 'From Supporting Missions to Petitioning Parliament: British Women and the Evangelical Campaign against *Sati* in India, 1813–30', in K. Gleadle & S. Richardson (eds.), *Women in British Politics 1760–1860. The Power of the Petticoat* (Basingstoke: Macmillan, 2000), pp. 74–92.

Midgley, Clare, 'Can Women's Be Missionaries? Envisioning Female Agency in the Early Nineteenth-Century British Empire', *Journal of British Studies* 45:2 (2006), 335–58.

Midgley, Clare, *Feminism and Empire. Women Activists in Imperial Britain, 1790–1865* (London & New York: Routledge, 2007).

Midgley, Clare, 'Women, Religion and Reform', in S. Morgan and J. de Vries (eds.), *Women, Gender and Religious Cultures in Britain, 1800–1940* (Abingdon: Routledge, 2010), pp. 138–58.

Melnyk, J. (ed.), *Women's Theology in Nineteenth-Century Britain. Transfiguring the Faith of their Fathers* (New York & London: Garland Publishing, 1998).

Morgan, Sue, *A Passion for Purity: Ellice Hopkins and the Politics of Gender in the Late-Victorian Church* (Bristol: Centre for Comparative Studies in Religion and Gender, University of Bristol, 1999).

Morgan, Sue, 'Introduction: Women, Religion and Feminism: Past, Present and Future Perspectives', in S. Morgan (ed.), *Women, Religion and Feminism in Britain 1750–1900* (Basingstoke: Palgrave Macmillan, 2002), pp. 1–19.

Morgan, Sue & Jacqueline de Vries, 'Introduction', in S. Morgan & J. de Vries (eds.), *Women, Gender and Religious Cultures in Britain 1800–140* (Abingdon: Routledge, 2010), pp. 1–10.

Morris, Jeremy, 'The Strange Death of Christian Britain: Another Look at the Secularisation Debate', *The Historical Journal* 46:4 (December 2003), 963–76.

Mort, Frank, & Lynda Nead, 'Sexuality, Modernity and the Victorians', *Journal of Victorian Culture* 1:1 (Spring 1996), 118–30.

Mullen, Shirley A., *Organised Freethought: the Religion of Unbelief in Victorian England* (New York: Garland, 1987).

Mumm, Susan, '"I Love my Sex": Two Late Victorian Pulpit Women', in J. Bellamy, A. Laurenca & G. Perry (eds.), *Women, Scholarship and Criticism. Gender and Knowledge c.1790–1900* (Manchester: Manchester University Press, 2000), pp. 204–21.

Murphy, H. R., 'The Ethical Revolt Against Christian Orthodoxy in Early Victorian England', *American Historical Review* 60 (1955), 800–17.

Nash, David, *Secularism, Art and Freedom* (Leicester, London & New York: Leicester University Press, 1992).

Nash, David, '"Look in her Face and Lose thy dread of dying": The Ideological Importance of Death to the Secularist Movement in Victorian England', *Journal of Religious History* 19 (1995), 158–80.

Nash, David, 'Unfettered Investigation – the Secularist Press and the Creation of Audience in Victorian England', *Victorian Periodicals Review* 28:2 (Summer 1995), 123–35.

Nash, David, *Blasphemy in Modern Britain, 1789 to the Present* (Aldershot: Ashgate, 1998).

Nash, David, 'Charles Bradlaugh and the Many Chameleon Destinations of Republicanism', in D. Nash & A. Taylor (eds.), *Republicanism in Victorian Society* (Thrupp, Stroud: Sutton Publishing, 2000), pp. 106–24.

Nash, David, '"The Credulity of the Public Seems Infinite": Charles Bradlaugh. Public Biography and the Battle for Narrative Supremacy in *Fin de Siècle* England', *Journal of Victorian Culture* 7:2 (Autumn 2002), 239–62.

Nash, David, 'Taming the God of Battles: Secular and Moral Critiques of the South African War', in G. Cuthbertson, A. Grundlingh & M. Suttie (eds.), *Writing a Wider War: Rethinking Gender, Race and Identity in the South African War 1899–1902* (Athens, Ohio: Ohio University Press, 2002), pp. 266–86.

Nash, David, 'The Blast of Blasphemy: Government, Law and Culture Confront a Chill Wind', in J. Rowbotham & K. Stevenson (eds.), *Behaving Badly: Social Panic and Moral Outrage – Victorian and Modern Parallels* (Aldershot: Ashgate, 2003), pp. 113–26.

Nash, David, 'Reconnecting Religion with Social and Cultural History – Secularisation's Failure as a Master Narrative', *Cultural and Social History* 1:1 (2004), 203–35.

Nash, David, 'Secularism in the City: Geographies of Dissidence and the Importance of Radical Culture in the Metropolis', in M. Cragoe & A. Taylor (eds.), *London Politics 1760–1914* (Basingstoke & New York: Palgrave Macmillan, 2005), pp. 97–120.

Nash, David, *Blasphemy in the Christian World* (Oxford: Oxford University Press, 2007).

Nockles, Peter B., *The Oxford Movement in Context* (Cambridge: Cambridge University Press, 1994).

Onslow, Barbara, *Women of the Press in Nineteenth-Century Britain* (Basingstoke: Macmillan, 2000).

Onslow, Barbara, 'Preaching to the Ladies: Florence Fenwick Miller and her Readers in the *Illustrated London News*', in L. Brake & J. F. Codell (eds.), *Encounters in the Victorian Press: Editors, Authors, Readers* (Basingstoke: Palgrave Macmillan, 2005), pp. 88–102.

Overall, Christine, 'Feminism and Atheism', in M. Martin (ed.), *The Cambridge Companion to Atheism* (Cambridge: Cambridge University Press, 2007).

Owen, Alex, *The Darkened Room. Women, Power and Spiritualism in Late Nineteenth-Century England* (London: Virago Press, 1989).

Owen, Alex, *The Place of Enchantment. British Occultism and the Culture of the Modern* (Chicago & London: University of Chicago Press, 2004).

Parolin, Christina, '"The She-Champion of Impiety": A Case Study of Female Radicalism', in M. Davis & P. Pickering (eds.), *Unrespectable Radicals? Popular Politics in the Age of Reform* (Aldershot: Ashgate, 2008), pp. 185–99.

Paxton, Nancy L., 'Complicity and Resistance in the Writings of Flora Annie Steel and Annie Besant', in N. Chaudhuri & M. Strobel, *Western Women and Imperialism: Complicity and Resistance* (Bloomington & Indianapolis: Indiana University Press, 1992), 158–76.

Peacock, Sandra J., *The Theological and Ethical Writings of Frances Power Cobbe, 1822–1904* (Lampeter: The Edwin Mellen Press, 2002).

Peterson, Linda H., *Traditions of Victorian Women's Autobiography. The Poetics and Politics of Life Writing* (Charlottesville & London: University Press of Virginia, 2000).

Plant, Helen '"Ye Are All One in Christ Jesus": Aspects of Unitarianism and Feminism in Birmingham, c. 1869–1890', *Women's History Review* 9:4 (2000), 721–42.

Rendall, Jane, *The Origins of Modern Feminism. Women in Britain, France and the United States, 1780–1860* (Basingstoke: Macmillan Education, 1985).

Rendall, Jane, '"A Moral Engine": Feminism, Liberalism and the *English Woman's Journal*', in J. Rendall (ed.), *Equal or Different: Women's Politics 1800–1914* (Oxford: Basil Blackwell, 1987), pp. 112–38.

Rendall, Jane, 'The Citizenship of Women and the Reform Act of 1867', in C. Hall, K. McClelland & J. Rendall, *Defining the Victorian Nation. Class, Race, Gender and the British Reform Act* (Cambridge: Cambridge University Press, 2000), pp. 119–78.

Richardson, Angelique, *Love and Eugenics in the Late Nineteenth Century. Rational Reproduction and the New Woman* (Oxford: Oxford University Press, 2003).

Roberts, Caroline, *The Woman and the Hour. Harriet Martineau and Victorian Ideologies* (London: University of Toronto Press, 2002).

Rogers, Helen, 'The Prayer, the Passion and Reason of Eliza Sharples: Freethought, Women's Rights and Republicanism', in E. Yeo (ed.), *Radical Femininity: Women's Self-Representation in the Public Sphere* (Manchester: Manchester University Press, 1998), pp. 52–78.

Rogers, Helen, *Women and the People: Authority, Authorship and the Radical Tradition in Nineteenth-Century England* (Aldershot: Ashgate, 2000).

Rogers, Helen, 'Any Questions? The Gendered Dimensions of the Political Platform', *Nineteenth-Century Prose* 29:1 (Spring 2002), 118–32.

Rogers, Helen, 'In the Name of the Father: Political Biographies by Radical Daughters', in D. Amigoni (ed.), *Life Writing and Victorian Culture* (Aldershot: Ashgate, 2006), 145–64

Rowbotham, Sheila & Jeffrey Weeks, *Socialism and the New Life: The Personal and Sexual Politics of Edward Carpenter and Havelock Ellis* (London: Pluto Press, 1977).

Rowbotham, Sheila, *Edward Carpenter: A Life of Liberty and Love* (London & New York: Verso, 2008).

Royle, Edward, *Victorian Infidels. The Origins of the British Secularist Movement, 1791–1866* (Manchester: Manchester University Press, 1974).

Royle, Edward, 'Law, Harriet Teresa (1831–97), Feminist, Secularist and Radical', in J. Bellamy & J. Saville (eds.), *Dictionary of Labour Biography* 12 vols (London & Basingstoke: Macmillan Press, 1972–) v (1979), pp. 134–6.

Royle, Edward, *Radicals, Secularists and Republicans. Popular Freethought in Britain, 1866–1915* (Manchester: Manchester University Press, 1980).

Royle, Edward, *Religion, Radicalism and Freethought in Victorian and Edwardian Britain: Collection of Periodicals 1834–1916. Contents of the Microfilm Collection with an Introduction by Dr. Edward Royle* (Wakefield: EP Microform, 1981).

Royle, Edward, 'Annie Besant's First Public Lecture', *Labour History Review* 57:3 (1992), 67–9.

Royle, Edward, 'Secularists and Rationalists, 1800–1940', in S. Gilley & W. J. Sheils (eds.), *A History of Religion in Britain: Practice and Belief from Pre-Roman Times to the Present* (Oxford: Blackwell, 1994), pp. 406–22.

Royle, Edward, 'Freethought: The Religion of Irreligion', in D. G. Paz (ed.), *Nineteenth-Century English Religious Traditions. Retrospect and Prospect* (London: Greenwood, 1995), pp. 170–96.

Royle, Edward, *Thomas Paine and Nineteenth Century Freethought: Eric Paine Memorial Lecture* (Nottingham: Thomas Paine Society, 2003).

Royle, Edward, 'Bonner, Hypatia Bradlaugh (1858–1935)', *Oxford Dictionary of National Biography* (online edn; Oxford University Press, 2004).

Royle, Edward, 'Carlile, Elizabeth Sharples (1803–1852)', *Oxford Dictionary of National Biography* (online edn; Oxford University Press, 2004).

Royle, Edward, 'Watts, Charles (1836–1906)', *Oxford Dictionary of National Biography* (online edn; Oxford University Press, 2004).

Saler, Michael, 'Modernity and Enchantment: A Historiographic Review', *The American Historical Review* 3:3 (June 2006), 692–716.

Schroeder, Janice, 'Speaking Volumes: Victorian Feminism and the Appeal of Public Discussion', *Nineteenth-Century Contexts* 25:2 (2003), 97–117.

Scott, Joan, *The Politics of the Veil* (Princeton & Oxford: Princeton University Press, 2007).

Sebastiani, Silvia, '"Race", Women and Progress in the Scottish Enlightenment', in S. Knott & B. Taylor (eds.), *Women, Gender and Enlightenment* (Basingstoke & New York: Palgrave Macmillan, 2005) pp. 75–96.

Sheehan, Jonathan, 'Enlightenment, Religion and the Enigma of Secularisation: A Review Essay', *The American Historical Review* 108:4 (October 2003), 1061–80.

Sheehan, Jonathan, *The Enlightenment Bible: Translation, Scholarship, Culture* (Princeton: Princeton University Press, 2005).

Shipley, Stan, *Club Life and Socialism in Mid-Victorian London* History Workshop Pamphlets No. 5 (1971).

Smith, F. B., 'The Atheist Mission, 1840–1900', in R. Robson (ed.) *Ideas and Institutions of Victorian Britain: Essays in Honour of George Kitson Clark* (London: G. Bell & Son, 1967), pp. 205–35.

Soloway, Richard Allen, *Birth Control and the Population Question in England, 1877–1930* (London: University of North Carolina Press, 1982).

Soloway, Richard Allen, 'Feminism, Fertility, and Eugenics in Victorian and Edwardian England', in S. Drescher et al. (ed.), *Political Symbolism in Modern Europe* (New Brunswick & London: Transaction Books, 1982), pp. 121–45.

Spender, Dale, 'Introduction', in E. Cady Stanton, *The Woman's Bible: The Original Feminist Attack on the Bible* (Glasgow: Polygon Books, 1985) (first published as *The Woman's Bible* 1895), i–v.

Stone, James, *Emily Faithfull: Victorian Champion of Women's Rights* (Toronto: P.D. Meany, 1994).

Styler, Rebecca, 'A Scripture of their Own: Nineteenth-Century Bible Biography and Feminist Bible Criticism', *Christianity and Literature* 57:1 (Autumn 2007), 65–85.

Suhl, Y., *Ernestine L. Rose: Women's Rights Pioneer*, 2nd edn (New York: Biblio Press, 1990).

Summers, Anne, *Female Lives, Moral States: Women, Religion and Public Life in Britain 1800–1930* (Newbury: Threshold Press, 2000).

Summers, Anne, 'Which Women? What Europe? Josephine Butler and the International Abolitionist Federation', *History Workshop Journal* 62:1 (2006), 214–31.

Summers, Anne, 'Introduction: the International Abolitionist Federation', *Women's History Review* 17:2 (April 2008), 149–52.

Taylor, Anne, *Annie Besant: A Biography* (Oxford: Oxford University Press, 1992).

Taylor, Barbara, 'The Woman-Power. Religious Heresy and Feminism in Early English Socialism', in S. Lipshitz (ed.) *Tearing the Veil. Essays on Femininity* (London: Routledge & Kegan Paul, 1978), pp. 117–44.

Taylor, Barbara, *Eve and the New Jerusalem. Socialism and Feminism in the Nineteenth Century* (London: Virago, 1983).

Taylor, Barbara, *Mary Wollstonecraft and the Feminist Imagination* (Cambridge: Cambridge University Press, 2003).

Taylor, Barbara, 'Macauley, Elizabeth Wright (1785?–1837)', *Oxford Dictionary of National Biography* (online edn; Oxford University Press, 2004).

Taylor, Barbara, 'Martin, Emma (1811/12–1851)', *Oxford Dictionary of National Biography* (online edn; Oxford University Press, 2004).

Taylor, Barbara, 'Feminism and Enlightened Discourses: Introduction', in S. Knott & B. Taylor (eds.), *Women, Gender and Enlightenment* (Basingstoke, New York: Palgrave Macmillan, 2005), pp. 410–34.

Taylor, Charles, *Sources of the Self. The Making of the Modern Identity* (Cambridge: Cambridge University Press, 1989).

Taylor, Charles, *A Secular Age* (Cambridge, MA & London: The Belknap Press of Harvard University Press, 2007).

Thompson, Dorothy, 'Women and Nineteenth-Century Radical Politics: A Lost Dimension', in J. Mitchell & A. Oakley (eds.), *The Rights and Wrongs of Women* (Harmondsworth: Penguin, 1976), pp. 112–38.

Tribe, David, *100 Years of Freethought* (London: Elek, 1967).

Turner, Frank M., *Between Science and Religion: the Reaction to Scientific Naturalism in Late Victorian England* (London & New Haven: Yale University Press, 1974).

Van Arsdel, Rosemary T., *Florence Fenwick Miller. Victorian Feminist, Journalist and Educator* (Aldershot: Ashgate, 2001).

Vincett, Giselle, Sonya Sharma & Kristen Aune, 'Introduction: Women, Religion and Secularisation: One Size Does Not Fit All', in K. Aune, S. Sharma, and G. Vincett (eds.), *Women and Religion in the West: Challenging Secularisation* (Aldershot: Ashgate, 2008), pp. 1–19.

Walkowitz, Judith, *Prostitution and Victorian Society. Women, Class and the State* (Cambridge: Cambridge University Press, 1980).

Wallis, Robert & Steven Bruce, 'Secularisation: The Orthodox Model', in S. Bruce (ed.), *Religion and Modernisation. Sociologists and Historians Debate the Secularisation Thesis* (Oxford: Clarendon, 1992), pp. 8–30.

Watts, Ruth, *Gender, Power and the Unitarians in England 1760–1860* (Harlow: Addison Wesley Longman Ltd, 1998).

Webb, R. K., 'Martineau, Harriet (1802–1876)', *Oxford Dictionary of National Biography* (online edn; Oxford University Press, 2004).

Wiener, Joel H., *The War of the Unstamped. The Movement to Repeal the British Newspaper Tax, 1830–1836* (Ithaca & London: Cornell University Press, 1969).

Wiener, Joel H., *Radicalism and Freethought in Nineteenth-Century Britain: The Life of Richard Carlile* (Westport, Connecticut: Greenwood Press, 1983).

Williams, Sarah, 'The Language of Belief: An Alternative Agenda for the Study of Victorian Working-Class Religion', *Journal of Victorian Culture* 1:2 (Autumn 1996), 303–17.

Williams, Sarah, 'Victorian Religion: A Matter of Class or Culture?' *Nineteenth Century Studies* 17 (2003), 13–17.

Williamson, Lori, *Power and Protest. Frances Power Cobbe and Victorian Society* (London: Rivers Oram Press, 2005).

Wilson, Linda, *Constrained By Zeal. Female Spirituality Amongst Nonconformists, 1825–1875* (Carlile: Paternoster Biblical and Theological Monographs, 2000).

Wootton, David, 'New Histories of Atheism', in M. Hunter & D. Wooton (eds.), *Atheism From the Reformation to the Enlightenment* (Oxford: Clarendon, 1992), pp. 13–53.

Wright, Maureen, *Elizabeth Wolstenholme Elmy and the Victorian Feminist Movement: The Biography of An Insurgent Woman* (Manchester: Manchester University Press, 2011).

Wright, Maureen, 'The Women's Emancipation Union and Radical-Feminist Politics in Britain, 1891–99', *Gender and History* 22:2 (August 2010), 382–406.

Yeo, Eileen Janes (ed.), *Radical Femininity. Women's Self-Representation in the Radical Public Sphere* (Manchester: Manchester University Press, 1998).

Secondary: unpublished

Martin, Janette, 'Popular Political Oratory and Itinerant Lecturing in Yorkshire and the North East in the Age of Chartism, c. 1837–1860' (unpublished doctoral thesis, University of York, 2010).

Morgan, Simon, 'Middle-Class Women, Civic Virtue and Identity: Leeds and the West Riding of Yorkshire, c.1830–c.1860' (unpublished doctoral thesis, University of York, 2000).

Nash, David, 'The Leicester Secular Society: Unbelief, Freethought and Freedom in a Nineteenth-Century City' (unpublished doctoral thesis, University of York, 1990).

Rogers, Helen, 'Poetesses and Politicians: Gender, Knowledge and Power in Radical Culture, 1830–1870' (unpublished doctoral thesis, University of York, 1994).

Rogers, Helen, '"Facing Her Public": The Actress, Eliza Macauley (1785–1837)' (unpublished manuscript).

Van Reyk, William, 'Christian Ideals of Manliness During the Period of the Evangelical Revival, c.1730–1840' (unpublished doctoral thesis, University of Oxford, 2007).

Williams, Sarah, 'Religious Belief and Popular Culture: A Study of the South London Borough of Southwark c.1880–1939' (unpublished doctoral thesis, University of Oxford, 1993).

Wright, Maureen, 'Elizabeth Wolstenholme Elmy: A Biography' (unpublished doctoral thesis, University of Portsmouth, 2007).

Internet sources

www.news.bbc.co.uk
www.guardian.co.uk
www.independent.co.uk
www.ssrc.org/blogs/immanent_frame [The Immanent Frame: Secularism, Religion and the Public Sphere, The Social Science Research Council, SSRC Blogs, 2008]
www.whitehouse.gov

Index

Adult, The 166, 195–8, 208
Anti-Persecution Union 8, 47

Barker, Joseph 133, 138–40, 180, 184–5
Becker, Lydia 143–5, 170, 192
Besant, Annie
  biography 52–3, 192, 217, 219
  birth control 9, 53, 198–206
  Bradlaugh, relationship with 53, 55
  Christianity
    former Anglican faith 52, 76–7,
      79, 117
    view of 79
  Contagious Diseases Acts 162–4,
    165
  counter-conversion 74, 79, 83–4, 87
    feminism and 89, 90–2
  Elements of Social Science 192
  feminism
    Christianity and women 136,
      137, 140–1
    marriage 189, 191–2
    sexual difference 131–2
    suffrage 168
  journalism 114, 116
  National Secular Society 42
  public speaking 106, 107–8, 110,
    111
  Scripture 117, 136
  Socialism 53–4
  Theosophy 20, 54, 93–4

Bible *see* Scripture
birth control 159, 164, 179, 198–208
  Knowlton trial 53–4, 59, 61, 63,
    159, 179, 198–204
  Malthusian League 63, 159, 185,
    199, 201, 204–8
  Secularist movement and 198–202,
    204–6
  women's movement and 179,
    202–4, 205, 218–19
  see also Elements of Social Science
Bland, Lucy 203
Blatch, Harriet Stanton 63
Bodichon, Barbara Leigh Smith 141,
  156–8, 169, 207
Bonner, Hypatia Bradlaugh
  biography 58–9
  birth control 205
  Freethought Federation 59
  Legitimation League 196, 208
  marriage 196–7
  National Secular Society 42
  public speaking 111, 113, 119
  Reformer 59
  Suffrage 170
Bracke, Sarah 219
Bradlaugh, Alice 42, 58–9
Bradlaugh, Charles 46
  birth control 185, 198–205
  counter-conversion 84
  Elements of Social Science 184

Bradlaugh, Charles (*continued*)
National Secular Society 9–11
parliamentary oath 9
Braidotti, Rosi 221
British Secular Union 10, 42, 52
Brown, Callum 23
Budd, Susan 11, 84
Butler, Josephine 154, 158, 160–1,
163, 165

Caine, Barbara 192
Caird, Mona 64, 138, 194–5
Carlile, Richard 4, 6, 46, 103, 179, 187,
198, 202
Central Secular Society 5–6, 8
Chappellsmith, Margaret 8, 47, 76,
105, 187–8
Chartism 102–3
Christianity
Anglo-Catholicism 16, 18, 92
Broad Churchmen 16, 18
decline 15
dissenting churches 18
'enthusiasm' 19, 89–90
evangelicalism 3, 15–16
feminism
influence on *see* woman's
mission; women's movement
opposition to 142, 143
Secularist movement
influence on *see* Secularist
movement
opposition to 116
'serious Christianity' 15
teaching on women 3, 18, 110, 137,
139, 146
see also St Paul
twenty-first century 219
Unitarianism 18
women's religiosity 18–19, 102,
133–5
see also Scripture; theology
Clapperton, Jane 64, 112, 121, 135,
195

Cobbe, Frances Power 58, 61, 76–7,
79, 86, 89, 114, 132, 169–70
Collet, Sophia Dobson
biography 57, 157, 218
Christianity
former Unitarian faith 57
return to 58
view of 87
Elements of Social Science 185
feminism 58, 136–7, 140, 165, 166,
194
Freethought 58, 116, 120
Secularist movement, view of 108,
115, 118
writing 114–15, 118
Contagious Diseases Acts
campaign against 154, 160–6, 171,
191–2, 194
see also social purity

Darwin, Charles 12–13
Davidoff, Leonore 17
de Vries, Jacqueline 208
divorce *see* marriage
Dixie, Lady Florence 63, 140, 205
domestic ideology 16–17, 102, 133
Drysdale, Bessie 63, 170, 205
Drysdale, George *see* Elements of
Social Science

Elements of Social Science 178–87,
192, 199
Eliot, George 48, 57, 114, 131–2
Elmy, Elizabeth Wolstenholme
biography 62–3, 217
birth control 204
Contagious Diseases Acts 154,
157–9, 160–3, 165
marriage 192
Secularist movement 107–8
sex education 165, 203
suffrage 167, 170, 171
English Woman's Journal, The 114,
141, 156–7, 159

Enlightenment
  feminism 155–6
    see also Wollstonecraft
  freethought 4, 12, 84, 156
  secularism 220, 222–3
  esoteric religion 20, 92–3, 219

Faithfull, Emily 141–3, 144
Female Medical Society 159
feminism see women's movement
Feminist Majority 221
Foote, G. W. 10, 59, 166, 196, 200, 208
free inquiry 103–4, 117–18, 119, 122
  see also Secularist movement: ideology, public life
Free Love
  'enlightened libertinage', tradition of 4, 187
  fin de siècle 2, 179, 194–8, 219
  Owenite movement and 179, 187, 218
  Secularist movement and 171–2, 178, 184–6, 190–1, 196–8, 208, 218–19
  see also Elements of Social Science; marriage
Freethought Federation 59
Freethought League 42, 52
Freethought movement see Secularist movement
Freewoman, The 21, 64, 111, 122, 139, 147, 205, 208

Hall, Catherine 17
Hennell, Sara
  biography 55, 157
  Christianity
    former Unitarian faith 56, 76
    view of 75, 87, 120
  counter-conversion 81–2, 87
  feminism 132, 138, 165, 166, 189–90, 195

Freethought 56–7, 116, 120
  writing 114–17
Hinduism 139–40, 224
Holyoake, George Jacob
  birth control 198, 200
  Elements of Social Science 183–4
  free discussion 104
  Free Love 184, 190
  free press, campaign for 103
  marriage 190
  public speaking 108
  rivalry with Bradlaugh 9–10
  Secularism, definition of 184
  women's movement 101, 157, 159, 165, 218
Holyoake Smith, Caroline 63
Howell, Constance 91

Infidelism 1, 8
  see also Secularist movement
Islam 139–40, 219–22, 224

James, William 75
journalism see press

Knowlton trial see birth control

Law, Florence 51
Law, Harriet
  atheism 50, 56
  biography 49, 219
  birth control 200
  British Secular Union 52
  Christianity
    former Baptist faith 49, 76
    view of 14, 50
  counter-conversion
    feminism and 89, 91
  Elements of Social Science 180, 186–7, 194
  feminism 138, 158, 192–3
    Christianity and women 136, 145–6
  marriage 188–9

Law, Harriet (*continued*)
  feminism (*continued*)
    sexual difference 131
    suffrage 168–9, 170, 171
  Freethought League 52
  National Secular Society 42, 52
  public speaking 49, 106–7, 108,
    109–10
  Scripture 1, 23, 110, 117, 136, 141,
    145–6
  Secular Chronicle 5, 49–50, 52, 119,
    131
  Socialism 50–1
Law, Harriet Teresa 51–2, 60, 79, 89,
  193
Legitimation League 64, 166, 195–6
  see also The Adult
Lynn Linton, Eliza 62, 77

Macauley, Eliza 46, 131
Malthusian League *see* birth control
marriage
  freethinking critique 179, 187
  Owenite critique 179, 187–8
  Secularist movement, view of
    188–98
  women's movement, view of 188,
    189, 192, 194
Marsden, Dora 111–12
Martin, Emma 47–8
  birth control 198, 203
  Christianity
    former Baptist faith 76, 78–9
    view of 75
  counter-conversion 73, 78, 80–1
  feminism and 89, 90, 91
  marriage 187–8, 191
  materialism 13
  public speaking 7, 105–6
  Owenite leadership, conflict with
    7–8
Martineau, Harriet 60, 76, 79–80, 82,
  87, 89, 114, 132, 160
Mason, Michael 185

Men and Women's Club 195
Miller, Florence Fenwick 60–1, 63,
  110, 111, 114–15, 121, 159, 205

Nash, David 12, 41
National Secular Society 9, 10–11, 42
National Society for Women's
  Suffrage 167–8
National Union of Women's Suffrage
  Societies 170
neo-Malthusianism *see* birth control
Newman, Francis 57, 115, 138, 160,
  163, 184, 190–1, 194, 202

Owenite movement
  feminism 2, 4–5, 45–8, 102, 130,
    155–6, 166, 179, 187–8, 218
  freethought 6–8

Parkes, Bessie Raynor 141, 156–8, 207
Pearson, Karl 112, 195
post-secular 219
preaching *see* public speaking
press 103, 114–15
public speaking 102, 104, 105–14
  see also free inquiry; Secularist
    movement: public culture
public sphere 102–3, 119
  see also public speaking; Secularist
    movement: public culture,
    women's participation

Reasoner, The 114–15, 118, 145,
  157–8, 184–5, 190
respectability 2, 4–5, 41, 55, 77–8,
  108–9, 185, 196, 200
Revolutionary Association of the
  Women of Afghanistan 221
Ross, W. S. 132–3, 134–5, 140, 202
Royle, Edward 5, 11, 22, 160

St Paul 110–11, 137, 142
Scripture 12, 16–17, 49, 50, 58, 82,
  84–6, 109, 112, 116–17

and women 141–7
see also Christianity: teaching on
    women; St Paul; Secularist
    movement: teaching on
    women; theology; women's
    movement: religious debate
Scott, Joan 222
secularism
    concept 2, 23–5, 223–4
    secularisation thesis 22–5, 222
    women and 219–24
Secularist Movement
    Christianity
        relationship with 21–2, 26, 76,
        85–8, 156
        view of 14–15, 20, 23, 75, 78–9
    Contagious Diseases Acts 160–6
    see also social purity
    Elements of Social Science 180–7
    Enlightenment, influence of 4, 12,
    84
    feminism 129–53
        marriage 187–98
        sexual difference 129–36
        suffrage 166–72
        women's inequality, religious
        causes 136–41, 144–7
    see also birth control; Free Love;
        women's movement
    history of 5–15
    ideology 12–14, 101–4
    see also free inquiry
    imperialism and anti-imperialism
        139–41
    membership
        class make-up 11–12, 46–7
        male to female ratio 5, 41
        size 10–11
    public culture 103–5, 109, 111,
        112–13, 119, 217
    see also public speaking; free
        inquiry
    women's participation 42–4, 48–64,
        101, 104–5, 114, 118, 119, 217

women's religiosity, view of 19,
    88–9, 129, 133–6
    see also Christianity: enthusiasm,
        women's religiosity
sex see Elements of Social Science;
    Free Love
Sharpe, Maria 195
Sharples, Eliza
    biography 45–6
    Christianity
        former Methodist faith 76–8
        counter-conversion 80
        feminism and 89–90
    social purity 164–6, 171
Southall Black Sisters 221
Stanton, Elizabeth Cady 63, 146

Taylor, Barbara 4
Taylor, Charles 24–5, 75, 86
theology 115–17
    see also Christianity: teaching on
        women; St Paul; Scripture
Theosophy see esoteric religion

Unitarianism 3

Vickery, Alice 63, 159, 170, 192, 195,
    204–6
Victoria Discussion Society 141–2,
    144
Victoria Magazine 114, 203

Watts, Charles 54, 197, 199, 208
Watts, Kate 54–5, 134, 189, 200
Wollstonecraft, Mary 4, 27, 130–1,
    155, 192–3
woman's mission 17
Women's Emancipation Union 63,
    170
Women's Franchise League 63, 170
Women's Freedom League 63, 205
Women's Penny Paper, The 114, 146
Women's Social and Political Union
    63, 113–14, 170

women's movement
  Christian feminism 142–4, 145–6, 158
  Christianity, influence of 3, 79, 92, 155
  conversion 92
  esoteric religion 92–4, 146
  'imperial feminism' 130, 139–40, 220–1, 223, 224
  religious debate 21, 111–12, 130, 142, 146–7, 217

Scripture 141–4
Secularist movement, relationship with 92, 154–5, 158–60, 171, 191–2
suffrage 92, 113–14, 119, 155, 166–72, 205
see also birth control; Contagious Diseases Acts; Free Love; marriage; social purity
Wright, Frances, 45, 57, 104, 105